lonely planet

# Crete

**Paul Hellander**
**Jeanne Oliver**

LONELY PLANET PUBLICATIONS
Melbourne • Oakland • London • Paris

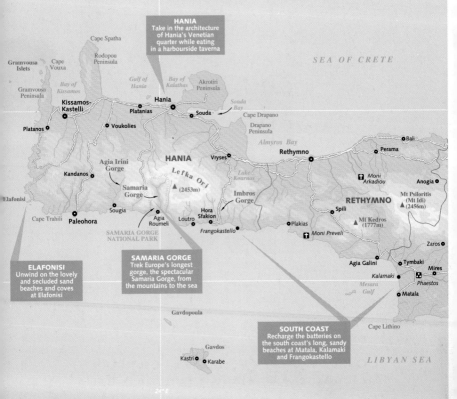

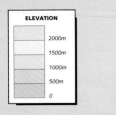

**ELEVATION**

2000m
1500m
1000m
500m
0

0   10   20km
0   5   10mi

**HANIA**
Take in the architecture
of Hania's Venetian
quarter while eating
in a harbourside taverna

SEA OF CRETE

Gramvousa
Islets

Cape Spatha

Cape
Vouxa

Rodopou
Peninsula

Gramvousa
Peninsula

Bay of
Kissamos

Gulf of
Hania

Bay of
Kalathas

Akrotiri
Peninsula

Kissamos-
Kastelli

Platanias

Hania

Souda

Souda
Bay

Cape Drapano

Platanos

Voukolies

Drapano
Peninsula

Almyros Bay

Bali

Agia Irini
Gorge

HANIA

Vryses

Rethymno

Perama

Lefka Ori

Lake
Kournas

Moni
Arkadiou

Anogia

Kandanos

Samaria
Gorge

(2453m)

Imbros
Gorge

RETHYMNO

Mt Psiloritis
(Mt Idi)
(2456m)

Elafonisi

Sougia

Agia
Roumeli

Loutro

Hora
Sfakion

Spili

Mt Kedros
(1777m)

Cape Trahili

Paleohora

Frangokastello

Plakias

Moni Preveli

Zaros

SAMARIA GORGE
NATIONAL PARK

Agia Galini

Tymbaki

Mires

**ELAFONISI**
Unwind on the lovely
and secluded sand
beaches and coves
at Elafonisi

**SAMARIA GORGE**
Trek Europe's longest
gorge, the spectacular
Samaria Gorge, from
the mountains to the sea

Kalamaki

Phaestos

Mesara
Gulf

Matala

Gavdopoula

Cape Lithino

**SOUTH COAST**
Recharge the batteries on
the south coast's long, sandy
beaches at Matala, Kalamaki
and Frangokastello

Gavdos

Kastri

Karabe

LIBYAN SEA

24°E

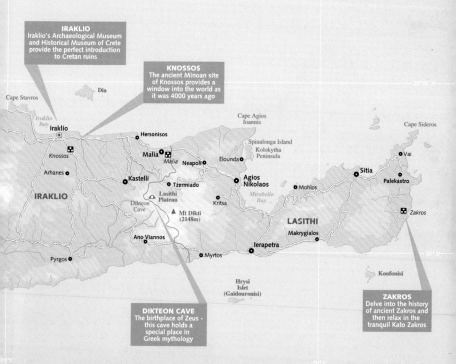

**IRAKLIO**
Iraklio's Archaeological Museum and Historical Museum of Crete provide the perfect introduction to Cretan ruins

**KNOSSOS**
The ancient Minoan site of Knossos provides a window into the world as it was 4000 years ago

**DIKTEON CAVE**
The birthplace of Zeus – this cave holds a special place in Greek mythology

**ZAKROS**
Delve into the history of ancient Zakros and then relax in the tranquil Kato Zakros

Crete
**2nd edition** – February 2002
**First published** – April 2000

**Published by**
**Lonely Planet Publications Pty Ltd** ABN 36 005 607 983
90 Maribyrnong St, Footscray, Victoria 3011, Australia

**Lonely Planet offices**
**Australia** Locked Bag 1, Footscray, Victoria 3011
**USA** 150 Linden St, Oakland, CA 94607
**UK** 10a Spring Place, London NW5 3BH
**France** 1 rue du Dahomey, 75011 Paris

**Photographs**
Many of the images in this guide are available for licensing from
Lonely Planet Images.
email: lpi@lonelyplanet.com.au
Web site: www.lonelyplanetimages.com

**Front cover photograph**
Fresco on a wall at the Palace of Knossos, Iraklio Province, Crete (Neil
Setchfield)

ISBN 1 74059 049 X

Printed by SNP SPrint (M) Sdn Bhd
Printed in Malaysia

**Although the authors
and Lonely Planet try
to make the informa-
tion as accurate as
possible, we accept
no responsibility for
any loss, injury or
inconvenience sus-
tained by anyone
using this book.**

# Contents – Text

# Contents – Maps

# CRETE MAP INDEX

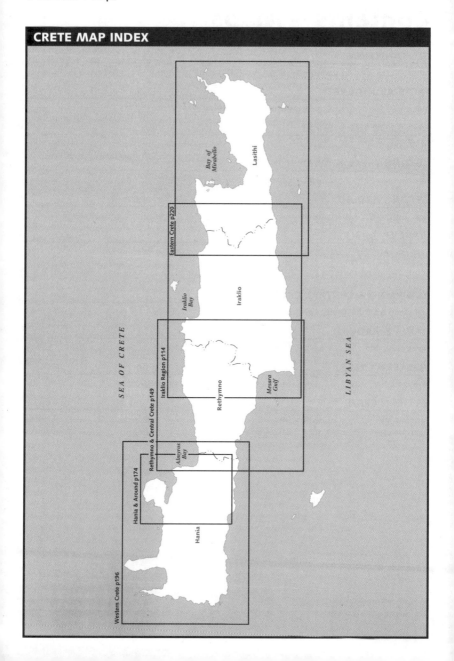

SEA OF CRETE

LIBYAN SEA

Bay of Mirabello

Lasithi

Eastern Crete p220

Iraklio Bay

Iraklio

Iraklio Region p114

Rethymno & Central Crete p149

Rethymno

Mesara Gulf

Hania & Around p174

Almyros Bay

Western Crete p196

Hania

# The Authors

### Paul Hellander

Paul has never stopped travelling since he first looked at a map in his native England. He graduated from Birmingham University with a degree in Greek before heading for Australia. He taught Modern Greek and trained interpreters and translators for many years before donning the hat of travel writer and photographer. Paul has contributed to a variety of LP titles including guides to Greece, Greek Islands, Rhodes & the Dodecanese, Cyprus, France, Israel & the Palestinian Territories, Singapore, Eastern Europe, Central America and South America. His photos have graced a number of LP travel guides. When not travelling, he lives in Adelaide, South Australia where he studies the history of political intelligence, listens to BBC World Service, cooks Thai food and grows hot chillies. He was last seen heading to seek out new destinations in the Dodecanese Islands and Cyprus. Paul updated this edition of *Crete*.

### Jeanne Oliver

Born in New Jersey, Jeanne spent her childhood mulling over the New York Times travel section and plotting her future voyages. After a BA in English at the State University of New York at Stony Brook and a stint at the Village Voice newspaper, Jeanne got a law degree. After working as a prosecutor in the Manhattan District Attorney's office, Jeanne started her own legal practice. It was interrupted by ever-more-frequent trips to far-flung destinations and eventually she set off on a round-the-world trip that landed her in Paris. A job in the tourist business led to freelance writing assignments for magazines and guidebooks. She joined Lonely Planet in 1996 and has written 1st editions of Lonely Planet's Croatia, Crete, Crete Condensed and Normandy as well as updating chapters on Crete, Croatia and Slovenia in Greece, Mediterranean Europe, Central Europe and Eastern Europe. She currently lives in the south of France.

## FROM THE AUTHOR

Paul Hellander Crete in the heat of summer was a whirl of sun, sand and dust, of people and music, fine food and fiery raki taken in the company of a bunch of indomitable and spirited Cretans who made my time on the *megalonisos* unforgettable. Nonetheless, updating this guide to Crete involved the input of many people and I would like to thank some of them who helped to make my work possible: Angeliki Kanelli (Athens), Nikos Perakis (Kato Zakros), Vasilis Skoulas (Anogia), Tony Fennymore (Hania), Vangelis Skoulakis (Kissamos) and Mihalis Manousakis (Hania). Professional thanks also to Paul Tuffin, Margaret O'Hea (University of Adelaide), Geoff Harvey, DriveAway Holidays (Sydney), Peugeot-Sodexa (Paris), Minoan Lines (Iraklio) and finally the adept editors and designers at LP who put this book together. Stella Hellander – wife, companion and photographer – this time, this one is just for you! Byron & Marcus, thanks for your time and the fun we had in Greece.

# This Book

This is the 2nd edition of LP's *Crete* guide. The 1st edition was written by Jeanne Oliver. This 2nd edition was updated by Paul Hellander.

## FROM THE PUBLISHER

The 2nd edition of Crete was produced in Lonely Planet's Melbourne office. Production was coordinated by Helen Yeates (editorial) and Joelene Kowalski (mapping and design). Will Gourlay and Nina Rousseau assisted with editing and proofing. Darren O'Connell, Justin Flynn and Agustín Poó y Balbontin assisted with layout. Special thanks to Paul Hellander for his help with the Greek script.

Matt King coordinated the illustrations, and new illustrations were drawn by Martin Harris. Emma Koch prepared the language section and the cover was designed by Jenny Jones. Photographs were supplied by Barbara Dombrowski at Lonely Planet Images.

# Thanks

Many thanks to the following travellers who used the last edition and wrote to us with helpful hints, useful advice and interesting anecdotes:

Yvonne Adams, Costa Androulakis, James Annesley, Penny Anson, Catherine Barron, Joanna Beals, Joran Boch, Florian Bode, Mike Bowler, Abra Brayman, Tania Cortazzo, Tom Crossley, Aart & D de Jong, Gwyneth De Lacey, Terje Dokland, John Dynan, Alex Engelsman, Derek Excell, Debroah Filcoff, Lara Fontijn, Carin Forssell, Argo Georgandis, Georg Gruber, Dr PC Hedger, Marilyn Hughes, Joanne Hutchinson, Christian Ilcus, GM King, DE Knox, Stephen Lamb, Geraldine Moran, Guy Neuman, Lan Anh Nguyen, Asher Rodwell, Mette Nygerd, Andrew Oliphant, Niko Plaitakis, Beth Powell, Philip Roberts, Bjorn Sandstrom, Mark & Stephanie Shattuck, Robert Thijssen, James Travers-Murison, Lene Troelso, Marja van den Tweel, Maurice Vandererckhove, Julie Walker, Karen Walsh, Joanne Woo.

# Foreword

## ABOUT LONELY PLANET GUIDEBOOKS

The story begins with a classic travel adventure: Tony and Maureen Wheeler's 1972 journey across Europe and Asia to Australia. Useful information about the overland trail did not exist at that time, so Tony and Maureen published the first Lonely Planet guidebook to meet a growing need.

From a kitchen table, then from a tiny office in Melbourne (Australia), Lonely Planet has become the largest independent travel publisher in the world, an international company with offices in Melbourne, Oakland (USA), London (UK) and Paris (France).

Today Lonely Planet guidebooks cover the globe. There is an ever-growing list of books and there's information in a variety of forms and media. Some things haven't changed. The main aim is still to help make it possible for adventurous travellers to get out there – to explore and better understand the world.

At Lonely Planet we believe travellers can make a positive contribution to the countries they visit – if they respect their host communities and spend their money wisely. Since 1986 a percentage of the income from each book has been donated to aid projects and human rights campaigns.

**Updates** Lonely Planet thoroughly updates each guidebook as often as possible. This usually means there are around two years between editions, although for more unusual or more stable destinations the gap can be longer. Check the imprint page (following the colour map at the beginning of the book) for publication dates.

Between editions up-to-date information is available in two free newsletters – the paper *Planet Talk* and email *Comet* (to subscribe, contact any Lonely Planet office) – and on our Web site at www.lonelyplanet.com. The *Upgrades* section of the Web site covers a number of important and volatile destinations and is regularly updated by Lonely Planet authors. *Scoop* covers news and current affairs relevant to travellers. And, lastly, the *Thorn Tree* bulletin board and *Postcards* section of the site carry unverified, but fascinating, reports from travellers.

**Correspondence** The process of creating new editions begins with the letters, postcards and emails received from travellers. This correspondence often includes suggestions, criticisms and comments about the current editions. Interesting excerpts are immediately passed on via newsletters and the Web site, and everything goes to our authors to be verified when they're researching on the road. We're keen to get more feedback from organisations or individuals who represent communities visited by travellers.

Lonely Planet gathers information for everyone who's curious about the planet – and especially for those who explore it first-hand. Through guidebooks, phrasebooks, activity guides, maps, literature, newsletters, image library, TV series and Web site we act as an information exchange for a worldwide community of travellers.

**Research** Authors aim to gather sufficient practical information to enable travellers to make informed choices and to make the mechanics of a journey run smoothly. They also research historical and cultural background to help enrich the travel experience and allow travellers to understand and respond appropriately to cultural and environmental issues.

Authors don't stay in every hotel because that would mean spending a couple of months in each medium-sized city and, no, they don't eat at every restaurant because that would mean stretching belts beyond capacity. They do visit hotels and restaurants to check standards and prices, but feedback based on readers' direct experiences can be very helpful.

Many of our authors work undercover, others aren't so secretive. None of them accept freebies in exchange for positive write-ups. And none of our guidebooks contain any advertising.

**Production** Authors submit their manuscripts and maps to offices in Australia, USA, UK or France. Editors and cartographers – all experienced travellers themselves – then begin the process of assembling the pieces. When the book finally hits the shops, some things are already out of date, we start getting feedback from readers and the process begins again …

## WARNING & REQUEST

Things change – prices go up, schedules change, good places go bad and bad places go bankrupt – nothing stays the same. So, if you find things better or worse, recently opened or long since closed, please tell us and help make the next edition even more accurate and useful. We genuinely value all the feedback we receive. A well-travelled team reads and acknowledges every letter, postcard and email and ensures that every morsel of information finds its way to the appropriate authors, editors and cartographers for verification.

Everyone who writes to us will find their name listed in the next edition of the appropriate guidebook. They will also receive the latest issue of *Planet Talk*, our quarterly printed newsletter, or *Comet*, our monthly email newsletter. Subscriptions to both newsletters are free. The very best contributions will be rewarded with a free guidebook.

We may edit, reproduce and incorporate your comments in all Lonely Planet products, such as guidebooks, Web sites and digital products, so let us know if you don't want your comments reproduced or your name acknowledged.

Send all correspondence to the Lonely Planet office closest to you:

**Australia:** Locked Bag 1, Footscray, Victoria 3011
**USA:** 150 Linden St, Oakland, CA 94607
**UK:** 10a Spring Place, London NW5 3BH

Or email us at: talk2us@lonelyplanet.com.au

**For news, views and updates see our Web site: www.lonelyplanet.com**

## HOW TO USE A LONELY PLANET GUIDEBOOK

The best way to use a Lonely Planet guidebook is any way you choose. At Lonely Planet we believe the most memorable travel experiences are often those that are unexpected, and the finest discoveries are those you make yourself. Guidebooks are not intended to be used as if they provide a detailed set of infallible instructions!

**Contents** All Lonely Planet guidebooks follow roughly the same format. The Facts about the Destination chapters or sections give background information ranging from history to weather. Facts for the Visitor gives practical information on issues like visas and health. Getting There & Away gives a brief starting point for researching travel to and from the destination. Getting Around gives an overview of the transport options when you arrive.

The peculiar demands of each destination determine how subsequent chapters are broken up, but some things remain constant. We always start with background, then proceed to sights, places to stay, places to eat, entertainment, getting there and away, and getting around information – in that order.

**Heading Hierarchy** Lonely Planet headings are used in a strict hierarchical structure that can be visualised as a set of Russian dolls. Each heading (and its following text) is encompassed by any preceding heading that is higher on the hierarchical ladder.

**Entry Points** We do not assume guidebooks will be read from beginning to end, but that people will dip into them. The traditional entry points are the list of contents and the index. In addition, however, some books have a complete list of maps and an index map illustrating map coverage.

There may also be a colour map that shows highlights. These highlights are dealt with in greater detail in the Facts for the Visitor chapter, along with planning questions and suggested itineraries. Each chapter covering a geographical region usually begins with a locator map and another list of highlights. Once you find something of interest in a list of highlights, turn to the index.

**Maps** Maps play a crucial role in Lonely Planet guidebooks and include a huge amount of information. A legend is printed on the back page. We seek to have complete consistency between maps and text, and to have every important place in the text captured on a map. Map key numbers usually start in the top left corner.

Although inclusion in a guidebook usually implies a recommendation we cannot list every good place. Exclusion does not necessarily imply criticism. In fact there are a number of reasons why we might exclude a place – sometimes it is simply inappropriate to encourage an influx of travellers.

# Introduction

Cretans say that visitors to their island cry twice – first when they come and then when they leave. Overdevelopment along the northern coast can make a poor first impression but it doesn't take long to fall under the spell of Greece's largest and most southerly island. The sun-drenched south coast is a paradise of long sandy beaches and isolated coves. Major urban centres such as Iraklio, Rethymno, and Hania are within easy reach of crowded beaches, but tranquillity is not hard to find. In the east, Vai Beach contains Europe's only palm forest; Elafonisi Islet in the west is nearly undeveloped, Frangokastello Beach in the south sees few visitors. In the island's rugged interior, the salty air and barren coastal cliffs give way to bracing mountain breezes and steep gorges blanketed with flowers and aromatic herbs.

The famous Samaria Gorge is Europe's longest, and an enduring attraction for hikers. However, there are many kilometres of remote mountain trails used only by goats, shepherds and donkeys.

Crete's stunning natural beauty is equalled only by the richness of a culture that spans millennia. For the ancient Greeks, Crete was the foundation of their elaborate mythology. Legend holds that the God Zeus was born and raised within the island's caves. Myths of the Minotaur, Daedalus and the Labyrinth emerged from Crete, perhaps inspired by the glorious Minoan civilisation that once ruled the Aegean. Knossos is the best known archaeological site but a profusion of evocative ruins scattered throughout the island conjure up this mysterious civilisation that vanished over 3000 years ago.

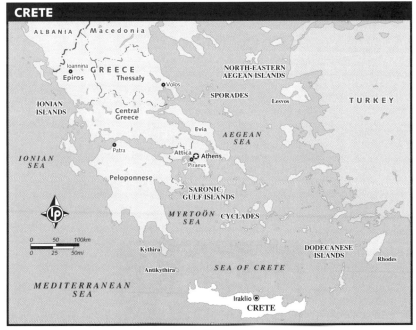

Yet the past and present coexist easily in Crete. Only kilometres away from ancient temples and palaces, coastal cities entertain several million tourists each year with luxurious resorts and sizzling nightlife.

Stroll through the old towns of Hania and Rethymno where 17th-century Venetian mansions have been turned into elegant hotels and restaurants. Drive into the country and you'll share the road with tractors, BMWs, pick-up trucks and mules. In the urban centres, stylish Cretans run shops and businesses while, in the interior, the back-breaking work of shepherding, olive growing, and farming continues as it has for centuries.

Cretans have a unique ability to reconcile tradition with modernity. Their ferocious struggles for independence from foreign occupiers – Romans, Venetians, Turks and Germans – have left them with a profound attachment to the songs, dances and cuisine that have forged their identity.

As a practical people, Cretans have no trouble serving up international dance music in the discos and international food in the tourist restaurants, but their own tastes lie elsewhere. At traditional feasts and weddings, Cretans still sing *mandinades*, their age-old songs of love and betrayal, and stamp their feet to a vigorous, leaping folk dance accompanied by a lyre.

Crete is unique in the sheer variety of experiences packed into a relatively small space. Laze on the beach, hike through a gorge, poke around an archaeological site, take a harbourside walk at sunset or spend an evening listening to Cretan songs in a taverna. Maybe you won't cry when you leave; you'll be too busy planning your next trip back.

Happy is the man who before dying has the good fortune to travel the Aegean Seas. Nowhere else can one pass so easily from reality to the dream.

**Nikos Kazantzakis**

# Facts about Crete

## HISTORY

From ancient Minoan palaces and Roman cities to spectacular Byzantine churches and Venetian fortresses, the legacy of Crete's long and colourful history is evident everywhere.

## Stone Age

Although the island may have been inhabited since the Palaeolithic period, the oldest evidence of human habitation was found at Knossos, and dates to what is known as the pre-pottery period (6100–5700 BC).

Little is known about these early inhabitants of Crete except that they survived by hunting and fishing and engaged in ancestor worship. Evidence is also sketchy about the people who inhabited Crete during the Neolithic period (5700–2800 BC). The earliest Neolithic people lived in caves or rough stone, mud or wood houses and worshipped female fertility goddesses. They were hunter-gatherers who also farmed, raised livestock and made primitive pottery.

In the late Neolithic period, trade routes developed between Crete and the Cyclades, Egypt and the Near East.

## The Minoans

More than any other civilisation in Crete it was the Minoans that left the longest-lasting mark on the character of the island. Arriving in around 3000 BC immigrants from the North African or Levantine mainland brought with them the skills necessary for making bronze. It was this technological quantum leap that enabled the nascent Minoan civilisation to flourish almost uninterrupted for over one and a half millennia. The palaces, jewellery, art and everyday artefacts that we see in Crete and in the island's museums today all reflect the glory and brilliance of perhaps the most peaceful era in the recorded history of Crete. For the full lowdown on Minoan Crete, see 'The Minoans' special section in this chapter.

## Chronology of Major Events

| | |
|---|---|
| **6000 BC** | **Neolithic age** |
| | Migration from the coast of Asia Minor and settlement of Crete by cave-dwellers |
| **3000 BC** | **Pre-palatial period** |
| | Another migration from the coast of Asia Minor and development of crafts and jewellery |
| **2000 BC** | **Proto-palatial period** |
| | First palaces built in Knossos, Phaestos, Malia and Zakros |
| **1700 BC** | **Neo-palatial period** |
| | Old Minoan palaces destroyed in earthquake; new palaces built |
| **1450 BC** | Minoan palaces destroyed |
| **1100 BC** | **Post-palatial period** |
| | Dorian colonists replace Mycenaeans as Crete's new masters |
| **67 BC** | **Roman Rule** |
| | Romans conquer Crete making Gortyn new capital |
| **AD 395** | Roman Empire splits with Crete ruled by Byzantium (Eastern Roman Empire) |
| **1204** | **Byzantine Empire** |
| | Byzantine prince Alexios sells Crete to Venice |
| **1363** | **Venetian Empire** |
| | St Titus revolution challenges Venetian rule |
| **1669** | Iraklio falls to the Turks leaving Crete under Ottoman rule |
| **1821** | **Ottoman Empire** |
| | Greek War of Independence spreads to Crete |
| **1830** | Crete given to Egypt |
| **1866** | Explosion at Arkadiou Monastery |
| **1898** | **Independence** |
| | Turkish rule ends; Crete ruled by Prince George of Greece |
| **1913** | Greece and Crete officially united |
| **1941** | Battle of Crete results in German occupation |
| **1945** | Liberation |

## Mycenaean Civilisation

The Mycenaean civilisation (1900–1100 BC), which reached its peak between 1500 and 1200 BC, was the first great civilisation on the Greek mainland. Named after the ancient city of Mycenae, it is also known as the Achaean civilisation after the Indo-European branch of migrants who had settled on mainland Greece and absorbed many aspects of Minoan culture.

Unlike Minoan society, where the lack of city walls seems to indicate relative peace under some form of central authority, Mycenaean civilisation was characterised by independent city-states such as Corinth, Pylos, Tiryns and, the most powerful of them all, Mycenae. These were ruled by kings who inhabited palaces enclosed within massive walls on easily defensible hilltops.

The Mycenaeans' most impressive legacy is magnificent gold jewellery and ornaments, the best of which can be seen in the National Archaeological Museum in Athens. The Mycenaeans wrote in Linear B (see 'The Minoans' special section in this chapter for further information). Clay tablets inscribed with the script have been found at the palace of Knossos providing strong evidence of Mycenaean occupation of the island. Their colonisation of Crete lasted from 1400–1100. Although Knossos probably retained its position as capital of the island, its rulers were now subject to the mainland Mycenaeans. The Minoan Cretans either left the island or hid in the interior while the Mycenaeans founded new cities such as Lappa (Argyroupolis), Kydonia (Hania), and Polyrrinia.

The economy of the island stayed more or less the same, still based upon the export of local products, but the fine arts fell into decline. Only the manufacture of weapons flourished, reflecting the new militaristic spirit that the Mycenaeans brought to Crete. The Mycenaeans also replaced worship of the Mother Goddess with new Greek gods such as Zeus, Hera and Athena.

Mycenaean influence stretched far and wide, but eventually weakened by internal strife, they were no match for the warlike Dorians who overran their cities.

## Dorian Crete

The origins of the Dorian civilisation remain uncertain. They are generally thought to have come from Epiros or northern Macedonia, but some historians argue that although they arrived from there, they had been driven out of Doris, in central Greece, by the Mycenaeans.

The Dorians settled first in the Peloponnese, but soon fanned out over much of the mainland, razing the city-states and enslaving the inhabitants. Despite fierce resistance, they conquered Crete around 1100 BC causing many of the inhabitants to flee to Asia Minor. Others, known as Eteo-Cretans or true Cretans retreated to the hills and thus preserved their culture.

The Dorians brought a traumatic break with the past; the next 400 years are often referred to as Greece's 'dark age'. It would be unfair to dismiss the Dorians completely; they brought iron with them and developed a new style of pottery, decorated with striking geometrical designs. They worshipped male gods instead of fertility goddesses and adopted the Mycenaean gods of Poseidon, Zeus and Apollo, paving the way for the later Greek religious pantheon.

The Dorians reorganised the political system of Crete and divided the society into three classes: free citizens who owned property and enjoyed political liberty; which included land-holding peasants, merchants and seamen; and slaves. The monarchical system of government was replaced by a rudimentary democracy. Ruling committees were elected by free citizens and set policy. They were guided by a Council of Elders and answered to an Assembly of free citizens.

By about 800 BC, local agriculture and animal husbandry had become productive enough to trigger a resumption of maritime trading. New Greek colonies were established throughout the Mediterranean basin and this colonial expansion favoured Crete, which took a prominent trade role.

The people of the various city-states were unified by the development of a Greek alphabet, the verses of Homer and the establishment of the Olympic Games. The establishment of central sanctuaries such as

Delphi, gave Cretans, for the first time, a sense of national identity as Greeks.

Most city-states were built to a similar plan, with a fortified acropolis at the highest point. Outside the acropolis was the agora (market), a bustling commercial quarter, and beyond it the residential areas. Rethymno, Polyrrinia, Kydonia (Hania), Falasarna, Gortyn, Phaestos and Lato were built according to this new defensive style.

The 6th-century-BC Laws of Gortyn, found at the end of the 19th century AD at the Gortyn archaeological site, opens a window onto the societal structure of Dorian Crete. Inscribed on 12 large stone tablets, the laws covered civil and criminal matters with clear distinctions drawn among the classes of free citizens and between citizens and slaves.

## The Classical Age

As the rest of Greece entered its golden age from the 6th to 4th centuries BC, Crete remained a backwater. Suffering from the constant warfare between large commercial centres and smaller traditional communities, the island became increasingly impoverished and isolated from mainland Greece. Although Crete did not participate in the Persian wars or the Peloponnesian War, their economic circumstances forced many Cretans to sign up as mercenaries in foreign armies or turn to piracy.

At the same time, Crete's role as the birthplace of Greek culture drew the attention of philosophers such as Plato and Aristotle who wrote extensively about Crete's political institutions.

The century preceding the Roman conquest of Crete was marked by continued turmoil on the island as Knossos, Gortyn, Lyttos and Kydonia (Hania) vied for supremacy. Egypt, Rhodes and the powerful city-state of Sparta involved themselves in Cretan squabbles and piracy flourished. Meanwhile Rome was emerging as a great power.

## Roman Rule

While Alexander the Great was forging his vast empire in the East, the Romans had been expanding theirs to the west and now also began making inroads into Greece. They had various interests in Crete which included reducing piracy and exerting control over important sea routes. A Roman presence in Crete dated back to the 3rd century BC but it wasn't until the second Mithridatic War, from 74 to 64 BC, that they found a pretext for intervention. Using piracy as an excuse Marcus Antonius, father of Mark Antony, undertook a naval campaign against Crete which failed. The Cretans tried to negotiate and send envoys to Rome but they were rebuffed. Expecting a Roman invasion, the island united and assembled an army of 26,000 men. The Roman campaign began in 69 BC under the Roman consul Metellus near Kydonia, then spread throughout the island. Although the Cretans fought valiantly the Romans succeeded in subjugating the island two years later.

For the next 300 years Greece, as the Roman province of Achaea, experienced an unprecedented period of peace, the Pax Romana. The Romans had always venerated Greek art, literature and philosophy, and aristocratic Romans sent their offspring to the many schools in Athens. Indeed, the Romans adopted most aspects of Hellenistic culture, spreading its unifying traditions throughout their empire.

Although Crete lost power and influence under the Romans it did usher in a new era of peace, bringing to an end Crete's internal wars. Crete did not mount a major challenge to Roman rule although they became embroiled in the later rivalry between Antony and Octavian. When Antony ruled he punished the cities that supported Octavian and when Octavian triumphed he punished the cities that supported Antony.

In the early years of Roman rule, parts of Crete were given as favours to various Roman allies. In 27 BC Crete was united with Libya to form the Roman province of Cyrene. Gortyn became the capital and most powerful city of Crete. The Romans built an amphitheatre, temples and public baths and the population increased. Knossos appeared to fall into disuse but Kydonia (Hania) in the west became an important centre. Roman towns were linked by a network of roads, bridges and aqueducts, parts of which can still be seen. Under the Romans, the Cretans continued to worship Zeus in the Dikteon and Ideon Caves and also incorporated Roman and Egyptian deities into their religious rituals.

## Christianity & the Byzantine Empire

Christianity arrived early in Crete with St Paul's visit in AD 63. He left it to his disciple, Titus, to convert the island. Little is known about the early years of Christianity in Crete but by the 3rd century persecution of Christians began in earnest. The first Christian martyrs in Crete were the so-called Ten Saints (Agii Deka) killed in the village of the same name in AD 250.

Nonetheless, Christianity began to emerge as the country's new religion. The definitive boost to the spread of Christianity in this part of the world came with the conversion of the Roman emperors and the rise of the Byzantine Empire, which blended Hellenistic culture with Christianity.

In 324 Emperor Constantine I (also known as Constantine the Great), a Christian convert, transferred the capital of the empire from Rome to Byzantium, a city on the western shore of the Bosphorus, which was renamed Constantinople (now İstanbul). This was as much due to insecurity in Italy itself as to the growing importance of the wealthy eastern regions of the empire. By the end of the 4th century, the Roman Empire was formally divided into a western and eastern section; Crete, along with the rest of Greece, found itself in the eastern half. While Rome went into terminal decline, the eastern capital grew in wealth and strength, long outliving its western counterpart (the Byzantine Empire lasted until the capture of Constantinople by the Turks in 1453).

Crete was a self-governing province in the Byzantine Empire with Gortyn as its administrative and religious centre. Piracy decreased and trade flourished leaving the island wealthy enough to build many churches. Crete's attachment to the worship of icons provoked a revolt in 727 when Emperor Leo III banned their worship as part of the iconoclastic movement. The uprising was smashed and the Byzantine emperors unleashed a fierce wave of retribution.

In the early 7th century Crete was attacked by Slavs but the more serious threat was posed by the Arabs in the mid-7th century. Naval attacks by the Arabs were unremitting and they finally conquered Crete around 824. The Arabs established a fortress called Chandax in what is now Iraklio. Its main function was to store the treasure they amassed by piracy. Crete was an ideal base for Arab ships to launch attacks as the island's criminal reputation grew its economy dwindled and its cultural life ground to a halt.

The Byzantines were in no position to help Crete despite its strategic importance. The island was far away from Constantinople and the Byzantines had enough problems defending territories closer to home. Not until the Byzantine general Nikiforas Fokas attacked Chandax in a bitter siege in 960 did the Arabs finally yield.

The Byzantines lost no time in fortifying the Cretan coast and consolidating their power. Chandax emerged as the island's new capital and the seat of the Cretan archdiocese while Gortyn faded away. The Byzantines established 12 aristocratic families on the island who eventually became powerful voices of rebellion against later Venetian rule. By the late 11th century a powerful land-holding class had emerged on Crete.

## The Crusades

It is one of the ironies of history that the demise of the Byzantine Empire was accelerated not by invasions of infidels from the east, nor barbarians from the north, but by fellow Christians from the west – the Frankish crusaders.

The stated mission of the crusades was to liberate the Holy Land from the Muslims, but in reality they were driven as much by greed as by religious fervour. Constantinople was sacked in 1204 in the 4th Crusade and the crusaders installed

[Continued on page 27]

**Title Page:** A Minoan urn, one of the many remarkable exhibits on show at the Iraklio Archaeological Museum (photo by Neil Setchfield)

**Top left:** This Bull's Head stone rhyton is an example of Minoan pottery which often took the shape of animal's heads.

**Top right:** The faience figurine of the snake goddess, which was found at Knossos, is a fine example of Minoan sculpture.

**Bottom:** The hieroglyphic inscription on the famous *Phaestos Disc*, found just north of the palace at Phaestos, has yet to be deciphered.

# The Minoans

## MINOAN ART & Early Periods

Little is known about the Neolithic cave dwellers of Crete but it appears that they made crude and undecorated pottery. Since the potter's wheel had not yet been invented, the pots were simply baked in a fire resulting in uneven colouring. The first figurines depicted human forms and were usually carved from stone. A male marble figurine found at Knossos is a good example of this early style that seems related to similar figurines in the Cyclades. Pottery technique advanced in the early Minoan years. Spirals and curvilinear motifs in white were painted on dark vases and several distinct styles emerged. Pyrgos pottery was characterised by black, grey or brown colours and, later on, Vasiliki pottery, made near Ierapetra, displayed polychrome surfaces. Gold, silver and bronze jewellery and daggers were finely crafted and foreshadowed the later achievements of Minoan art.

## Protopalatial Period

The founding of the first Minoan palaces on Crete in 2000 BC coincided with the production of the so-called Kamares pottery in the workshops of Knossos and Phaestos. Named after the cave at Kamares where the pottery was first found, this elegant, beautifully crafted pottery flourished during the entire Middle Minoan period. Cups, spouted jars and pithoi (large Minoan storage jars) could now be produced quickly with the invention of the potter's wheel. The use of the wheel also gave a new crispness to the designs. The stylised motifs were derived from plant and marine life and were balanced with curvilinear abstract patterns. The finely worked designs were usually painted in white, red, orange and yellow on black or grey backgrounds. The most striking pottery was the 'eggshell' vases characterised by extremely thin walls.

Other crafts also reached a high degree of artistry during this period. Using semi-precious stones and clay, artisans made miniature masterpieces out of carved sealstones which sometimes contained hieroglyphic letters. The exquisite bee pendant found at Malia displays extraordinary delicacy and imagination in jewellery making.

## Neopalatial Period

From 1700 to 1450 BC Minoan civilisation reached its 'golden age'. Although fresco painting probably existed before 1700 BC, all remnants were destroyed in the cataclysm that destroyed Minoan palaces around that time. The palace at Knossos yielded the richest trove of frescoes from the Neopalatial period. Although only fragments survive, they were very carefully restored and the technique of using plant and mineral dyes has kept the colours relatively fresh. The subjects reflect the

## Minoan Trade

As the population of Crete increased and vibrant commercial centres emerged in the eastern part of the island, the Minoans became well placed to trade with their neighbours in the eastern Mediterranean. Prevailing winds from the north meant that trade followed a general circular route, from the Nile delta, up the coast of today's Levant, across to Cyprus and along the southern coast of Asia Minor to Greece and beyond. Crete initially exported its natural products such as olive oil and livestock and imported silver from the Cyclades, gold from the North Aegean, and ivory and tin from the Near East. Minoan pottery from the Neopalatial period, textiles and agricultural produce subsequently found ready markets throughout the Cyclades as well as in Egypt, Syria and possibly Sicily. Kamares pottery in particular was exported to Cyprus, Egypt and the Levant.

full variety of Minoan experience and influenced wall paintings on the Greek mainland. Landscapes rich with animals and birds; marine life teeming with fish and octopuses; banquets; games and rituals are rendered with vivid naturalism. Griffins are repeatedly represented indicating that they may have had a protective function. Minoan fresco painters borrowed heavily from certain Egyptian conventions – men's skin was bronze and women's was white, for example – but the figures are far less rigid than most Egyptian wall paintings.

Pottery also flourished in the Neopalatial era. In the early years there was the marine style and a floral style that reflected the same themes

LEE FOSTER

as the era's frescoes. Octopuses, dolphins and fish appeared on some pottery while others showed flowers, leaves and branches along with religious symbols. In contrast to earlier pottery the decoration was often in dark colours such as brown and rust painted on light backgrounds. After 1500 BC, vases spouted three handles and were frequently shaped as animal heads. The stone rhyton in the shape of a bull's head is a particularly fine example from this period.

The art of sealstone carving also advanced in the palace workshops. Knossos, Zakros and Agia Triada were the most productive. Naturalistic subjects such as goats, lions and griffins were rendered in minute detail on hard stones, usually in an almond shape. Minoan sculptors also created fine idols in faience (quartz paste with a glazed surface), gold, ivory, bronze and stone. The serpent goddess in faience is one of the most outstanding surviving examples.

### Post Palatial Period

The second cataclysm of 1750 BC that destroyed Minoan palaces saw the decline of Minoan culture. The lively marine pottery of previous centuries degenerated into dull rigidity. Whether because of less trade with Egypt or the loss of the palace workshops, frescoes became uninspired. The production of jewellery and sealstones was replaced by the production of weaponry reflecting the influence of the warlike Mycenaeans.

## MINOAN HISTORY

*Above Right:* Dolphin mural in the Palace of Knossos (c.1700BC) on Crete. The palace is the largest (over 22,000 square metres) and the most spectacular of the Minoan palatial area.

The Bronze Age began around 3300 BC when Indo-European migrants introduced the processing of bronze (an alloy of copper and tin) into the Mediterranean basin. This significant event gave rise to three major civilisations within the territory of present day Greece: the Cycladic, Minoan and the Mycenaean. The Minoan civilisation (named after King Minos) was the first advanced civilisation to emerge in Europe, drawing its inspiration from two great Middle Eastern civilisations: the

## Minoan Archaeological Sites on Crete

We have already seen that Homer referred to 'ninety cities' in Minoan Crete. This is a sizeable number of settlements even by today's standards. This means that there is a wealth of Minoan settlements – both large and small – scattered across the island. The majority of Homer's 'ninety cities' are yet undiscovered or have disappeared completely, but there are enough to keep even the amateur archaeologist occupied for a month or more. Following are some of the sites that we have looked at in this book.

**Agia Triada** A small Minoan site at the western edge of the Mesara Plain in south-central Crete. Principally a royal summer residence, Agia Triada nonetheless yielded a number of impressive finds that are representative of Minoan art.

**Anemospilia** Discovered in 1979, the Anemospilia (Wind Cave) sanctuary is a late Minoan site and significant because it demonstrated that human sacrifice may well have played a part in Minoan society.

**Gournia** An important late Minoan site dating from 1550 to 1450 BC, the thriving community of Gournia consisted of a town and a small palace. Ruled by an overlord rather than a king, the Gournia site is less showy than Knossos or Phaestos.

**Kamares Cave** It was in the Kamares Cave on the southern slopes of Mt Psiloritis that fine examples of Kamares pottery were first found. Characterised by crisp designs and produced on pottery wheels, the pottery flourished throughout the whole of the Protopalatial period.

**Kamilari** The site of a well-preserved Minoan tomb dating from 1900 BC. The tomb has two metre high stone walls. It is 3km from the village of Kamilari on the western edge of the Mesara Plain in south-central Crete.

**Knossos** The most significant Minoan site in Crete. Knossos had been inhabited since Neolithic times, but remained undiscovered from the time of its second destruction in 1450 BC until the beginning of the 20th century.

**Kommos** The small site of Kommos is believed to have been the port for the major city of Phaestos 12km to the east. It contains a wealth of Minoan structures and the layout of the ancient town can still be seen.

**Malia** The palace at Malia was one of the four major palace sites in Crete. Built in 1900 BC and rebuilt in 1700 BC after destruction by an earthquake, what we see today is the remains of the second structure. Malia is one of the better-preserved Minoan sites.

**Mohlos** The site at Mohlos is one of the less-known Minoan sites and dates back to the Protopalatial period. Primarily a site for professional archaeologists rather than casual visitors, Mohlos is still being excavated.

**Phaestos** The second most important Minoan site in Crete, Phaestos dates back to at least 4000 BC though the first palace was built in about 2000 BC. The impressive citadel was the administrative centre of the Minoan Mesara Plain. Unlike Knossos, it yielded few frescoes and has not been partially restored.

**Zakros** The last of the Minoan places to be discovered, Zakros in far eastern Crete was uncovered as late as 1962. The site was unique in that it had hitherto been unplundered and revealed a vast trove of Minoan treasures.

**MINOAN & BRONZE AGE SITES**

SEA OF CRETE

Dia

Malia

Mohlos Island

Knossos

Kamares Cave

Anemospilia

Agia Triada   Kamilari

Gournia

Zakros

Kommos   Phaestos

Koufonisi

Gavdos

Hrysi Islet

LIBYAN SEA

Mesopotamian and Egyptian. Archaeologists divide the Minoan civilisation into three phases: Protopalatial (3400-2100 BC), Neopalatial (2100-1580 BC) and Postpalatial (1580-1200 BC). It was the Minoans who assumed the starring role in prehistoric Crete.

Many aspects of Neolithic life endured during the Early period, but the advent of bronze, which was imported from Cyprus, allowed the Minoans to build better boats and thus expand their trade opportunities. Pottery and goldsmithing became more sophisticated, foreshadowing the subsequent great achievements of Minoan art. The island prospered from trade and the groundwork was laid for the development of the two main periods of Minoan history.

## Protopalatial Period

The Minoan civilisation reached its peak during the Protopalatial period, also called the Old Palace or Middle period. Around 2000 BC the large palace complexes of Knossos, Phaestos, Malia, and Zakros were built, marking a sharp break with Neolithic village life. Crete is believed to have been governed by local rulers with power and wealth

**Right:** Exploring the Palace of Knossos – Knossos, Iraklio Province

## Minos: Man or Myth?

Whether King Minos existed can only ever be the subject of wishful conjecture. Homer, at least, was convinced of his existence and wrote *'Out on the dark blue sea there lies a rich and lovely land called Crete that is densely populated and boasts ninety cities...One of the ninety cities is called Knosos and there for nine years, King Minos ruled and enjoyed the friendship of the mighty Zeus.'* (Odyssey XIX, 172-179). Either way, legend has it that Minos was the legendary ruler of Crete. He was the son of Zeus and Europa and attained the Cretan throne with the help of Poseidon.

With Knossos as his base he gained control over the whole Aegean basin, colonising many of the islands and ridding the seas of pirates. He married Pasiphae, the daughter of Helios who bore him a number of children including Ariadne, Androgeos and Phaedra. Pasiphae also bore him the infamous half bull-half human Minotaur.

How long King Minos actually reigned however, is open to debate. The Homeric word *enneaoros* used to describe Minos in the original Greek of the *Odyssey* could mean 'for nine years', or 'from the age of nine years'. Was Minos able to create an empire in nine short years, or was he a long-reigning monarch who started his kingly career long before he became a teenager? Controversy aside, it is believed that he did eventually come to a sticky end in Sicily when he was killed by the daughters of King Kokalios who poured boiling water over him as he was taking a bath.

Although presented as a tyrannical ruler through post-Homeric mythology, Minos is generally thought of in a benevolent light and as a just and powerful ruler. Scholars now assume that the name Minos is used to mean a royal or dynastic title for the priestly rulers of Bronze Age, or Minoan, Crete.

concentrated at Knossos. Society was organised on hierarchical lines and contained a large population of slaves.

The architectural advances were accompanied by great strides in pottery making. Kamares vases, named after the Kamares Cave where they were first produced, manifested highly advanced artisanship. The vases were used for barter as well as home and ceremonial use.

The first Cretan script also emerged during this period. At first highly pictorial, the writing gradually transformed from the representations of natural objects to more abstract figures that resembled Egyptian hieroglyphics.

## Neopalatial Period

The Middle period came to an end with the sudden destruction of the Minoan palaces of Knossos, Phaestos, Malia and Zakros in 1700 BC. Although there is some disagreement, most archaeologists believe that the destruction was caused by the eruption of a volcano on nearby Santorini which caused a massive earthquake. The Minoans rebuilt the palaces to a more complex design with multiple storeys, sumptuous royal apartments, reception halls, storerooms, workshops, living quarters for staff and an advanced drainage system. The complex design of the palaces later gave rise to the myth of the Cretan Labyrinth.

## The Minoan Language

To this day no-one knows what language was spoken in the court of King Minos. Frustratingly for historians and linguists, the only written records to have come from the Minoan golden age are clay slabs inscribed with what historical linguists have called Linear A. The language hidden by these elusive scripts can only be guessed at. It is believed to be of either Anatolian or Semitic origin, though even this remains pure conjecture.

What is somewhat more encouraging is the finding and later decipherment of scripts on clay tablets which came to be called Linear B. These tablets are more or less definitively connected to Mycenaean culture which dominated Crete after the destruction of the palaces. Historical linguists assumed that this script was a sequential development of Linear A.

MARTIN HARRIS

Linear B was written on clay tablets that lay undisturbed for centuries until they were unearthed at Knossos in Crete. Further clay tablets were unearthed later on the mainland at Mycenae, Tiryns and Pylos in the Peloponnese and at Thebes in Boeotia. The clay tablets consisted of about 90 different signs dating from the 14th to 13th century BC. Little of the social and political life of these times can be deduced from the tablets, though there is enough to give a glimpse of a complex and well-organised commercial structure.

The methodical decipherment of the Linear B script by English architect and part-time linguist Michael Ventris was the first tangible evidence that the Greek language had a recorded history longer than any scholar had previously believed. The decipherment demonstrated that the language disguised by these mysterious scribblings was an archaic form of Greek 500 years older than the Ionic Greek used by Homer, thus giving the modern-day Greek language the second-longest recorded written history, after Chinese.

THE MINOANS

## Sir Arthur Evans & Knossos

Sir Arthur John Evans (1851–1941) was the curator of the Ashmolean Museum in Oxford from 1884 to 1908 and became an extraordinary professor of prehistoric archaeology in 1909. His interest in ancient coins and the writing on stone seals from Crete brought him to the island for the first time in 1894. As an avid amateur journalist and adventurer he had a hunch that the mainland Mycenaean civilisation derived originally from Crete. In 1899 he bought a parcel of land near Iraklio and spent a year digging. He discovered the ruins of a lost palace that covered an area of 5½ acres (2.2 hectares). Evans named the palace civilisation Minoan after the legendary King Minos.

MARTIN HARRIS

Evans was so enthralled by his discovery that he spent 35 years and £250,000 of his own money excavating and reconstructing sections of the palace. Some archaeologists have disparaged Evans' reconstruction, believing he sacrificed accuracy to his overly vivid imagination. Unlike other archaeological sites in Crete however, substantial reconstruction helps the visitor to visualise what the palace might have looked like at the peak of its glory. Evans maintained that he was obliged to rebuild columns and supports in reinforced concrete or the palace would have collapsed, but many archaeologists feel that the integrity of the site was irretrievably damaged. Most nonspecialists maintain that Sir Arthur did a thorough job and that Knossos is a knockout. Without these reconstructions it would be impossible to visualise what a Minoan palace looked like.

Over the next 25 years, Evans continued digging and unearthed the remains of a Neolithic civilisation beneath the remains of the Bronze Age Minoan palace. He also discovered some 3000 clay tablets containing Linear A and Linear B script and wrote his own definitive description of his work at Knossos in a four-volumed opus called *The Palace of Minos*. Evans received many honours for his work and was knighted in 1911.

The excavation of Knossos begun by Sir Arthur Evans in 1900 uncovered many remnants of Minoan Neopalatial society. Brightly coloured frescoes (now on view in the Archaeological Museum of Iraklio) depict white-skinned women with elaborately coiffured glossy black locks. Proud, graceful and uninhibited, these women had hourglass figures and were dressed in stylish gowns that revealed perfectly shaped breasts. The bronze-skinned men were tall, with tiny waists,

## Murder in the Temple

Human sacrifice is not commonly associated with the peace-loving Minoans but the evidence found at the site of Anemospilia near the village of Arhanes, 18km south of Iraklio, irrefutably suggests otherwise. A simple three-room temple was excavated in the 1980s. To the immense surprise of the scientists they found a young man placed on an altar and trussed, with a huge sacrificial bronze dagger incised with the shape of a boar-like beast amid the bones. The remains of two other skeletons nearby which were probably those of a priestess and an assistant, seemed to indicate that the boy's death was part of a sacrificial rite. The sacrifice was probably made just as the 1700 BC earthquake began, in a desperate attempt to appease the gods. See the February 1981 *National Geographic* article for the full story.

narrow hips, broad shoulders and muscular thighs and biceps; the children were slim and lithe.

The Minoans knew how to enjoy themselves. They played board games, boxed and wrestled, played leap-frog over bulls and over one another, and performed bold acrobatic feats. The Minoan dancing portrayed in the frescoes was famous throughout ancient Greece.

Minoans had good reason to be happy. Their state had become a powerful thalassocracy or sea-based power. Trade with the eastern Mediterranean continued to boom and was helped by Minoan colonies in the Aegean and in Asia Minor. According to ancient Greek historians, King Minos was the head of this powerful naval empire and promoted the expansion of Minoan interests.

The Minoans were not given to building colossal temples or religious statuary. Historians have concluded that their spiritual life was organised around the worship of a Mother Goddess – often represented with snakes or lions, the Mother Goddess was the deity-in-chief and the male gods were clearly subordinate. The double-axe symbol that appears in frescoes and on the palace walls of Knossos was a sacred symbol for the Minoans. Called 'labrys', it was the origin of the word labyrinth, which later Greeks associated with Knossos. Other religious symbols that frequently appear in Minoan art include the mythical griffin bird, and figures with a human body and an animal head. It is also assumed that the Minoans worshipped the dead and believed in some form of afterlife.

Whether or not related to the worship of a Mother Goddess, women apparently enjoyed a high degree of freedom and autonomy in Minoan society. Although the evidence for a matriarchal society is scanty, Minoan art shows women participating in games, hunting, and all public and religious festivals. It was not until the later invasions by the Dorians that women were condemned to a subordinate role.

## Postpalatial Period

Minoan culture came to an abrupt halt around 1450 BC in a mystery that has not yet been fully unravelled. In a great cataclysm around

1450 BC the palaces (except Knossos) and numerous smaller settlements were smashed to bits and burned. A cataclysmic volcano that erupted on nearby Santorini in or around 1550 BC may have caused damage on Crete from the resulting tidal waves and ash fallout, but it is no longer believed by archaeologists to be the reason for the ultimate destruction of the Neopalatial Period. This was most likely caused by a second, powerful earthquake a century later. Other archaeologists believe that the damage was caused by the invading Mycenaeans eager to grab the Minoans' maritime commerce. Whether the Mycenaeans caused the catastrophe or merely profited from it, it is clear that their presence on the island closely coincided with the destruction of the palaces and Minoan civilisation that had existed for over one and a half millennia.

NEIL SETCHFIELD

**Left:** Excavations at the ancient Minoan site of Malia, Iraklio Province

*[Continued from page 16]*

Baldwin of Flanders as head of the short-lived Latin Empire of Constantinople. Meanwhile, to secure the throne, the Byzantine Prince Alexios promised Crete to Boniface of Montferrat. After the sacking of Constantinople, Boniface sold Crete to Venice.

## Venetian Rule

Despite Crete's importance to Venetian control of the Mediterranean, Venice was slow to assert mastery over the island. Their rivals for naval supremacy, the Genoese, moved in on the island but after a series of campaigns the Venetians finally prevailed in 1217. Genoa made periodic and futile efforts to recapture the island which remained under Venetian rule until 1669.

In order to solidify its authority, Venice rapidly colonised Crete with noble and military families, many of whom settled in Iraklio (Candia). During the first century of Venetian rule about 10,000 settlers came to Crete. In order to induce Venetians to settle on Crete the authorities seized the island's best and most fertile land and gave it to the newcomers. The former Cretan owners now worked as serfs for their new Venetian masters. Not only were the major landholders Venetian but political control was also firmly in Venetian hands.

Cretan peasants were ruthlessly exploited under Venetian rule and oppressive taxation added to the peasants' woes. Religious life also suffered under the Venetians. Although not particularly religious themselves, the Venetians viewed the church as a symbol of national identity for the Cretans. The Orthodox Church was dismantled and replaced with the Catholic Church, but despite the relentless persecution, Orthodox monasteries remained hotbeds of resistance and kept the spirit of national unity alive.

Cretans rebelled regularly against Venetian rule and the frequent rebellions followed a predictable pattern of Cretan uprising followed by brutal Venetian reprisals. Eventually the rebellions forced concessions from Venice. By the 15th century the Cretan and Venetian communities reached an uneasy compromise that allowed Cretan cultural and economic life to flourish.

## The Ottoman Empire

Venice was soon facing a much greater threat from the east. The Muslim Ottomans – the followers of Osman, who ruled from 1289 to 1326 had established themselves as the dominant Turkish power. They rapidly expanded the areas under their control and by the mid-15th century were harassing the Byzantine Empire on all sides. Western Europe was too embroiled in the Hundred Years' War to come to the rescue, and in 1453 Constantinople fell to the Turks under Mohammed II.

The fall of Constantinople left Crete as the last remaining bastion of Hellenism. Byzantine scholars and intellectuals fled the dying empire and settled in Crete, establishing schools, libraries and printing presses. The cross-pollination between Byzantine traditions and the flourishing Italian Renaissance that was imported into Crete sparked a major cultural revival. Poetry and drama flourished and a 'Cretan School' of icon painting developed in the 16th and 17th centuries that combined Byzantine and Venetian elements. In the midst of this artistic ferment, the painter Dominikos Theotokopoulos was born in Iraklio in 1541. He studied in Italy under Titian and later moved to Spain where he became known as El Greco.

With the fall of Cyprus to the Turks in 1570 it seemed that Crete would be next on the Ottoman agenda but the Turkish defeats at the Battle of Lepanto in 1571 crimped Ottoman plans for further western expansion. By the early 17th century the Ottomans were on the move again while Venice was under severe economic pressure from the rise of Spanish, English and Dutch shipping. As a resource-rich and strategically well-located island, Crete was obviously attractive to the Ottomans. The island's defences had previously been strengthened against piracy but Venice was slow to rearrange its defences in the face of the looming Ottoman threat.

The Turks were looking for a pretext to invade the island and in 1644 they found one when pirates attacked a Turkish ship off the Cretan coast. The Turks amassed a huge force that landed in Hania in the early summer of 1645. Although the fortress was bravely defended it fell within two months and the Turks established their first foothold on the island. Rethymno was the next town to suffer siege, bombardment and defeat. With the western part of the island secured the Turks turned their attention to Iraklio (Candia).

The siege began in May 1648 but the massive walls of the city kept the enemy at bay for 21 years. Both sides threw everything they had into the struggle, but Candia fell in 1669 leaving the entire island except for Spinalonga and Souda (which fell in 1715) in Turkish hands.

Life was not easy under the Ottomans although they did allow the Orthodox Church to re-establish itself on the island. Nevertheless, there were tremendous political and economic advantages to embracing Islam. Mass conversions were common; sometimes entire villages changed their faith.

Economically, the Cretans were no better off under Ottoman rule than they were under the Venetians. The Ottomans devised highly imaginative taxes to wring every last drop of wealth out of the island and in the early years of Ottoman rule the economy degenerated to a subsistence level. Trade activity picked up around the beginning of the 18th century and living standards improved thereafter. Crete exported grain and the abundance of olive oil launched a soap industry.

Rebellion was brewing however. Many Cretans fled to the mountains and harassed the Turks with sporadic attacks and raids. In 1770 a more serious challenge to Turkish rule arose. The Turks never succeeded in fully subjugating the mountainous Sfakian region and, under their leader Daskalogiannis, 2000 Sfakians mounted an assault upon the Turks in western Crete. Although Daskalogiannis had received assurances of support from Russia, the aid never materialised and the rebellion was viciously suppressed. Daskalogiannis was skinned alive in the central square of Iraklio. See the boxed text 'The Spirits of Frangokastello' in the Western Crete chapter.

## The War of Independence

Sfakia was once again the nucleus of rebellion when the Greek War of Independence spread to Crete in 1821. With bitter memories of the 1770 fiasco, the Sfakian rebels fired the first shots in the struggle that soon spread throughout the island. Unfortunately the revolutionaries were hampered by poor organisation and constant infighting. The Turks swiftly retaliated and launched a wave of massacres primarily directed at the clergy.

Bogged down fighting rebels in the Peloponnese and mainland Greece, the Turks were forced to turn to Mehmet Ali of Egypt for help in dealing with the Cretans. Chronically short of arms and undisciplined, the Cretans fought furiously but were outnumbered by the Turkish-Egyptian forces.

With the rest of Greece torn by war, Crete was left on its own; the revolutionary movement flickered out in 1824. Fighting continued for a few more years provoking fearsome massacres of Cretan civilians but it was only a matter of time until the Turks prevailed. When a Greek state was finally established in 1830, Crete was not part of it and instead was given to Egypt.

Egyptian rule initially brought improvements. A general amnesty was issued that asked Cretans to lay down their arms. Muslims and Christians were to be treated equally, schools were organised and the authorities began rebuilding the island's infrastructure. Nevertheless, taxes remained high and soon new protests were under way. Meanwhile Mehmet Ali was defeated by the Turks in Syria and the Great Powers decided to give Crete back to the Ottomans in 1840.

Upon the restoration of Ottoman rule, Crete won important new privileges in the writ of Hatti Humayun allowing more religious freedom and the right to own property. A further decree granted Cretans more civil rights but the Sultan's repeated violations of these new laws sparked yet another uprising and a demand for *enosis*, or union with free Greece. Although Russia was partial to the Cretan position, Great Britain and France wished to maintain the status quo and refused any military or economic help. Rallying around the slogan 'Union Or Death', fighting broke out in western Crete. Once again the Turks joined forces with the Egyptians and attacked the civilian population in their mountain villages. About 900 rebels and their families took refuge in Moni Arkadiou. When 2000 Turkish soldiers staged an attack on the building, rather than surrender, the Cretans set light to a store of gun powder. The explosion killed almost everyone, Turks included.

With the heroic stand at Moni Arkadiou, the Cretan cause gained worldwide attention. Although demonstrations erupted throughout Europe in support of the rebels, Great Britain and France maintained a pro-Turkish stance. The Great Powers forbade Greece from aiding the Cretan rebels and the revolution petered out.

The 1877 Russo-Turkish War prompted another uprising in Crete. Sensing that Turkey might be defeated the Greek government decided to support Crete. Although the rebels seized major north-coast cities, the Berlin conference of 1878 resolving the Russo-Turkish War firmly rejected Cretan union with Greece. Turkey made new concessions in the Haleppa Charter of 1878 turning Crete into a semi-autonomous province, sanctioning Greek as the official language and granting a general amnesty.

In 1889, fierce political infighting within the Cretan parliament inflamed passions and prompted a new rebellion against Turkish rule, prompting Turkey to revoke the Haleppa Charter and return to the iron-fisted policies of the past. A new figure of resistance emerged from Sfakia. Manousos Koundouros headed a secret fraternity with the goal of securing autonomy for the island believing that it would eventually lead to unification with Greece. The rebels laid siege to the Turkish garrison at Vamos which led to violent reprisals by the Turks and an eventual intervention by the Great Powers. The Turks were forced to agree to a new constitution for Crete.

When violence erupted again in 1896, the Greek government sent a small force to the island and declared unification between Crete and Greece. The Great Powers rejected the idea and blockaded the coast, refusing to allow either the Turks or the Greeks to reinforce their position. Greece became embroiled in a war with Turkey and recalled its forces. The Great Powers appointed Prince George, son of King George of Greece, as High Commissioner of Crete.

In 1898, a detachment of British soldiers was implementing the transfer of power in Iraklio when an enraged mob of Turks stormed through the city slaughtering hundreds of Christian civilians and 17 British soldiers as well as the British Consul to the island. The British swiftly rounded up 17 Turkish troublemakers, hanged them and sent a squadron of ships steaming into the Iraklio Harbour. The Turks were ordered out of all their island fortresses, ending Ottoman rule over Crete forever.

## Independence

Crete was placed under international administration, but union with its cultural brethren in Greece remained an unquenchable desire. A new movement coalesced around Eleftherios Venizelos. Born near Hania, this charismatic figure was Prince George's Minister of Justice and a member of the Cretan Assembly. In the face of Prince George's stubborn refusal to consider unification, Venizelos convened a revolutionary assembly in Theriso in 1905 which raised the Greek flag and declared unity with Greece.

Venizelos then set up a rival government to administer the island. The rebellion spread, forcing the Great Powers to concede that Prince George had lost all support. They mediated a solution, allowing King George of Greece to appoint a new governor of Crete, which brought the island another step closer to union.

Although a new governor was appointed, the populace continued to agitate for unification. In 1908 the Cretan assembly issued a proclamation declaring unity with Greece but the Greek government refused to allow Cretan deputies to sit in the Greek Parliament. Even though Eleftherios Venizelos had become Prime Minister, Greece remained fearful of antagonising Turkey and the Great Powers who were adamantly opposed to the plan. Not until Greece, Serbia and Bulgaria declared war on the Ottoman Empire over Macedonia in the first Balkan War (1912) were Cretans finally allowed into the Greek Parliament. The 1913 Treaty of Bucharest ended the war and formally recognised Crete as part of the Greek state.

## WWI & Smyrna

King Constantine, who was married to the sister of the German emperor, understandably insisted that Greece remain neutral when WWI broke out in August 1914. As the war dragged on, the Allies (Britain, France and Russia) put increasing pressure on Greece to join forces with them against Germany and Turkey. They made promises which they couldn't hope to fulfil, including land in Asia Minor. Venizelos favoured the Allied cause, placing him at loggerheads with the king. Tensions between the two came to a head in 1916, and Venizelos set up a rebel government, first in Crete and then in Thessaloniki, while the pressure from the Allies eventually persuaded Constantine to leave Greece in June 1917. He was replaced by his more amenable second son, Alexander.

Greek troops served with distinction on the Allied side, but when the war ended in 1918 the promised land in Asia Minor was not forthcoming. Venizelos took matters into his own hands and, with Allied acquiescence, landed troops in Smyrna (present-day İzmir) in May 1919 under the guise of protecting the half a million Greeks living in that city. With a firm foothold in Asia Minor, Venizelos now planned to push home his advantage against a war-depleted Ottoman Empire. He ordered his troops to attack in October 1920. By September 1921, the Greeks had advanced as far as Ankara.

The Turkish forces were commanded by Mustafa Kemal (later to become Atatürk). Kemal first halted the Greek advance outside Ankara in September 1921 and then routed them with a massive offensive the following spring. The Greeks were driven out of Smyrna and many of the Greek inhabitants were massacred.

The outcome of the failed Greek invasion and the revolution in Turkey was the Treaty of Lausanne of July 1923. This gave eastern Thrace and the islands of Imvros and Tenedos to Turkey, while the Italians kept the Dodecanese.

The treaty also called for a population exchange between Greece and Turkey to prevent any future disputes. Almost 1.5 million Greeks left Turkey and almost 400,000 Turks left Greece. On Crete, the entire Turkish population of about 30,000 people was ordered off the island, abandoning their homes to the incoming Greek refugees.

## The Republic of 1924–35

The arrival of the refugees coincided with, and compounded, a period of political instability unprecedented even by Greek standards. In October 1920, King Alexander had died, resulting in the restoration of his father, King Constantine. Constantine identified himself too closely with the war against Turkey, and abdicated after the fall of Smyrna. He was replaced by his first son, George II, but George was no match for the group of army officers who seized power after the war. A republic was proclaimed in March 1924 amid a series of coups and counter-coups.

A measure of stability was attained with Venizelos' return to power in 1928. He pursued a policy of economic and educational reforms, but progress was inhibited by the Great Depression. His anti-royalist Liberal Party began to face a growing challenge from the monarchist Popular Party, culminating in defeat at the polls in March 1933. The new government was preparing for the restoration of the monarchy when Venizelos and his supporters staged an unsuccessful coup in March 1935.

Venizelos was exiled to Paris, where he died a year later. In November 1935, King George II was restored to the throne by a rigged plebiscite, and he installed the right-wing General Ioannis Metaxas as prime minister. Nine months later, Metaxas assumed dictatorial powers with the king's consent under the pretext of preventing a communist-inspired republican coup.

## WWII

Metaxas' grandiose vision was to create a Third Greek Civilisation based on its glorious ancient and Byzantine past, but what he actually created was more like a Greek version of the Third Reich. He exiled or imprisoned opponents, banned trade unions and the KKE (Kommounistiko Komma Ellados), the Greek Communist Party, imposed press censorship, and created a secret police force and a fascist-style youth movement.

Metaxas is best known, however, for his reply of *ohi* (no) to Mussolini's request to allow the Italian forces to traverse Greece at the beginning of WWII, thus maintaining Greece's policy of strict neutrality. The Italians invaded Greece, but were driven back into Albania.

A prerequisite of Hitler's plan to invade the Soviet Union was a secure southern flank in the Balkans. The British, realising this, asked Metaxas if they could land troops in Greece. He gave the same reply he had given the Italians, but died suddenly in January 1941. The king replaced him with the more timid Alexandros Koryzis, who agreed to British forces landing in Greece and then committed suicide when German troops marched through Yugoslavia and invaded Greece on 6 April 1941. The country was rapidly overrun and on 23 April the leader of the Greek government, Emmanouil Tsouderos, set up a government in exile in his native Crete.

## Battle of Crete

With all available Greek and Cretan troops fighting the Italians in Albania, Greece asked Britain to defend Crete. Churchill was more than willing to oblige as he was determined to block Germany's advance through south-eastern Europe. British, Australian and New Zealand troops poured on to the last remaining part of free Greece.

The Allies were in a poor position to defend the island, since commitments in the Middle East were already draining military resources. The island's defences had been seriously neglected, particularly its defence against an air assault. There were few fighter planes and military preparation was hampered by six changes of command on the island in the first six months of 1941. The terrain was also a problem. The only viable ports were on Crete's exposed northern coast; inadequate roads precluded the use of the more protected ports on the southern coast to resupply the army.

Meanwhile Hitler was determined to seize the island and use it as an air base to attack British forces in the eastern Mediterranean. In a stunning disregard for Crete's rebellious history, Hitler actually believed that German forces would be welcomed by the native population. They were not.

After a week-long aerial bombardment, an airborne invasion began on 20 May. Aiming to capture the airport at Maleme 17km west of Hania, thousands of parachutists floated down over Hania, Rethymno and Iraklio.

Old men, women and children grabbed rifles, old shotguns, sickles and whatever else they could find to defend their homeland. German casualties were appalling but they managed to capture the Maleme airfield. Although the Allies probably could have recaptured the airfield before the Germans had time to secure it, confusion and a lack of wireless sets prevented the Allies from redeploying their troops around the vital air base. Although the fighting continued until 30 May, once Maleme was in German hands at the end of the first day, the battle was effectively lost.

With Hania, Rethymno, and Iraklio under German control Allied soldiers were forced to retreat to the southern port of Hora Sfakion. About 12,000 men made their way over the eastern flank of the Lefka Ori (White Mountains) under attack by German soldiers all the way.

About three quarters of them were evacuated by ship from Hora Sfakion. Meanwhile King George and Emmanouil Tsouderos walked through the Samaria Gorge to Agia Roumeli and were then evacuated to Egypt.

## The Cretan Resistance

Most of the Allied soldiers that were not evacuated were hidden by the Cretans and helped to escape. During the German occupation Allied undercover agents supplied from North Africa coordinated the guerilla warfare waged by the Cretan fighters, known as *andartes*. Allied soldiers and Cretans alike were under constant threat from the Nazis while they lived in caves, sheltered in monasteries, trekked across peaks or unloaded cargo on the southern coast. One of the most daring feats of the resistance movement was the kidnapping of General Kreipe in 1944. The German commander was snatched outside Iraklio and spirited down to the south coast and away to Egypt.

German reprisals against the civilian population were fierce, especially after the kidnapping of General Kreipe. Cities were bombed and villages were annihilated with the men, women and children lined up and shot. When the Germans finally surrendered in 1945 they insisted on surrendering to the British fearing that the Cretans would inflict upon them some of the same punishment they had suffered for four years.

## Postwar Crete

With the defeat of the Germans, the Allies turned their attention to the political complexion of postwar Greece. Throughout the occupation of mainland Greece, the resistance was dominated by the Greek Communists. Winston Churchill wanted the king back and was afraid of a communist takeover, especially after the two leading resistance organisations formed a coalition and declared a provisional government in the summer of 1944.

An election held in March 1946, and boycotted by the Communists, was won by the royalists with British backing. A rigged plebiscite put George II back on the throne and civil war broke out, lasting until 1949.

On Crete the situation was different. The close cooperation between the Cretans and British soldiers left the islanders with strong pro-British sentiments that left little room for communist infiltration.

The British also made sure that the scarce supplies and equipment available went to noncommunist resistance organisations. The result was that Crete was largely spared the bloodshed and bitterness that left Greece a political and economic basket case in the 1950s.

A national election was held in 1950. The system of proportional representation resulted in a series of unworkable coalitions. The electoral system was changed to majority voting in 1952, which excluded the communists from future governments. The following election was a victory for the newly formed right-wing Ellinikos Synagermos (Greek Rally) party led by General Papagos, who had been a field marshal during the civil war.

## The Colonel's Coup

Greece joined NATO in 1951, and in 1953 the US was granted the right to operate sovereign bases. Intent on maintaining a right-wing government, the US gave generous aid and even more generous military support. Despite improved living standards during the 1950s, Greece remained a poor country.

A succession of right-wing governments was supplanted by the centrist EK or Enosi Kendrou (Centre Union) party led by Georgos Papandreou in 1964. His government was short-lived; a group of army colonels led by Georgos Papadopoulos and Stylianos Pattakos staged a coup d'etat on 21 April 1967 and established a military junta with Papadopoulos as prime minister.

The colonels imposed martial law, abolished all political parties, banned trade unions, imposed censorship, and imprisoned, tortured and exiled thousands of Greeks who opposed them. Cretan resentment towards the colonels intensified when the colonels muscled through major tourist development projects on the island that were rife with favouritism. Suspicions that the coup had been aided by the CIA remain conjecture, but criticism of the coup, and the ensuing regime, was certainly not forthcoming from the CIA or the US government. The perception of US involvement in the coup has left a residue of ill feeling that has not entirely dissipated.

## After the Colonels

In July and August 1974 Turkish forces invaded Cyprus following a botched Junta-sponsored coup attempt to depose Archbishop Makarios, the president of Cyprus. Discredited by the Turkish invasion of Cyprus, the junta was dismantled within the same month. An election was arranged for November 1974, and the ban on communist parties was lifted. Andreas Papandreou (son of Georgos) formed PASOK (the Panhellenic Socialist Union), and a national plebiscite voted 69% against restoration of the monarchy with Cretans even more overwhelmingly in favour of a republican system.

Karamanlis' right-wing New Democracy (ND) party won the 1974 elections, but his personal popularity, which was never very high in Crete, began to decline. One of his biggest achievements before accepting the largely ceremonial post of president was to engineer Greece's entry into the European Economic Community (now the European Union) and on 1 January 1981 Greece became the 10th member of the EEC.

## The Socialist 1980s

Andreas Papandreou's PASOK party won the election of October 1981 with 48% of the vote, giving Greece its first socialist government. PASOK promised removal of US bases and withdrawal from NATO.

Their international stance was and is particularly popular in Crete where the US naval base at Souda Bay is a regular target for protests. Crete's history of foreign occupation has given islanders a strong antipathy to the presence of foreign troops in any way, shape, manner or form.

After seven years in government, these promises were unfulfilled (although the US military presence was reduced), unemployment was high and reforms in education and welfare had been limited. Women's issues had fared better, though: the dowry system was abolished, abortion legalised, and civil marriage and divorce were implemented.

### Facts & Figures

- Crete has a population of 550,000
- Over two million tourists visit Crete each year
- 80% of tourists to the island are on package tours
- The annual turnover from the tourist sector is about US$1.4 billion
- There are 25 million olive trees
- A one-bedroom house in Hania's Old Town costs about €67,505
- 3500 square kilometres of land is devoted to agriculture

The crunch came in 1988 when Papandreou's love affair with flight attendant Dimitra Liani (whom he subsequently married) hit the headlines, and PASOK became embroiled in a financial scandal involving the Bank of Crete.

In July 1989 an unlikely coalition of conservatives and communists took over to implement a *katharsis* (campaign of purification) to investigate the scandal. In September it ruled that Papandreou and four former ministers should be tried for embezzlement, telephone tapping and illegal grain sales. The trial of Papandreou ended in January 1992 with his acquittal on all counts.

## The 1990s

An election in 1990 brought the ND back to power with a majority of only two seats, and with Konstandinos Mitsotakis, a Cretan, as prime minister. Intent on redressing the country's economic problems – high inflation and high government spending – the government imposed austerity measures, including a wage freeze for civil servants and steep increases in public-utility costs and basic services. It also announced a privatisation program aimed at 780 state-controlled enterprises; OTE (the telecommunications company), electricity and Olympic Airways were first on the list. The government also cracked down on widespread tax evasion. None of Mitsotakis' reforms were popular in Crete although the prime minister himself retained strong personal popularity.

By late 1992 corruption allegations were being made against the government and it was claimed that Mitsotakis had a large, secret collection of Minoan art, and in mid-1993 there were allegations of government telephone tapping. Former Mitsotakis supporters began to cut their losses: in June 1993 Antonis Samaras, the ND's former foreign minister, founded the Political Spring party and called upon ND members to join him. So many of them joined that the ND lost its parliamentary majority and hence its capacity to govern.

An early election was held in October, in which Andreas Papandreou's PASOK party won with 47% of the vote against 39% for ND and 5% for Political Spring. Through the majority voting system, this translated into a handsome parliamentary majority for PASOK.

In light of 74-year-old Papandreou's ailing health brought about by a chronic heart condition, the focus of political interest now shifted to speculation on the succession. Papandreou was rarely sighted outside his villa, where he lived surrounded by his ministerial coterie of family and friends. He was finally forced to step down as PASOK leader in early 1996 after another bout of ill-health, and his death on 26 June marked the end of an era in Greek politics.

## Politics Today

Papandreou's departure produced a dramatic change of direction for PASOK, with the party abandoning his left-leaning politics and electing economic reformer Costas Simitis as prime minister. The new leader had been an outspoken critic of Papandreou and had been sacked as industry minister four times before his death. He surprised many by calling a snap poll in September 1996, and campaigned hard in support of his 'Mr Clean' image. He was rewarded with almost 42% of the vote, which translated into a comfortable parliamentary majority.

Simitis belongs to much the same school of politics as Britain's Tony Blair. Since he took power, PASOK policy has shifted right to the extent that it now agrees with the opposition New Democracy on all major policy issues, including further integration with Europe and monetary union. Securing the 2004 Olympic Games was an enormous coup for Simitis bringing a flood of money into Greece for improvements to the infrastructure, yet his austerity packages designed to whip Greece into fiscal shape in order to become a full member of the European Monetary Union have caused discontent in some quarters.

Although anti-Turkish sentiment still runs strong, the earthquakes that slammed Turkey and Athens in 1999 prompted an exchange of relief workers that may herald a thaw in relations between the two countries. Relations with the United States have grown increasingly testy since the 1999 NATO bombardment of Kosovo which was wildly unpopular in Greece. Elections held in April 2000 saw Simitis returned to power with PASOK gaining 43.8% of the votes over ND's 42.7%. The next elections are due in April 2004, just before the Athens Olympics. Whoever wins those elections will take the credit – or rap – for the outcome of the games. It promises to be an interesting merry-go-round.

## GEOGRAPHY

Crete is the largest island in the Greek archipelago with an area of 8335 kilometres. It includes Gavdos Island, the most southerly point in Europe, just 300km from Africa. Crete is 250km long, about 60km at its widest point and 12km at its narrowest. Three major mountain groups – the Lefka Ori (White Mountains) in the west, Mt Psiloritis (also known as Mt Idi) in the centre and the Lasithi Mountains in the east – define the rugged interior. The Lefka Ori are known for their spectacular gorges, such as Samaria, as well as the snow that lingers on the mountains well into spring. The Omalos Plateau is in the Lefka Ori at an altitude of 1000m. Mt Psiloritis contains hundreds of caves, including the Ideon Andron Cave where Zeus allegedly grew up, and the Rouva Forest on the southern slopes. The highest mountain peak in Crete is Psiloritis itself at 2447m.

The Lasithi Mountains harbour the famous Lasithi Plateau and Mt Dikti (2148m) whose southern slopes preserve an example of the magnificent forests that once blanketed the island.

Western Crete is the most mountainous and greenest part of the island while eastern Crete tends to be barren and rocky. Most of the interior is mountainous and marked by olive trees, scrub and wild herbs. High upland plateaus are either cultivated like the Lasithi Plateau or used for pasturing goats like the Omalos Plateau. The largest cultivable area in the south is the fertile Mesara Plain which is about 40km long and up to 20km wide. Steep mountains in the south and gently sloping mountains in the north border the 1046km coastline. There is only one lake on the island, Lake Kournas, outside of Hania.

## CLIMATE

Crete has a Mediterranean climate, with hot, dry summers and mild winters. With 300 days of sunshine every year, it's the sunniest island in the Mediterranean after Cyprus. Crete also stays warm the longest of all the Greek islands – you can swim off its southern coast from mid-April to November.

There's no rain at all in July and August and the sea temperature hovers at a comfortable 25°C. During these months, the mercury can soar to 40°C in the shade just about anywhere on the coast although the highlands are much cooler. July and August are also the months of the *meltemi*, a strong northerly wind that sweeps the eastern coast of mainland Greece through the Aegean Islands, the Cyclades and Crete. The wind is caused by air pressure differences between North Africa and the Balkans. The wind is a mixed blessing: it reduces humidity, but plays havoc with ferry schedules and sends everything flying – from beach umbrellas to washing hanging out to dry. Between May and August you may encounter the sirocco wind which blows up from Africa bringing dust and sand. The air becomes stifling but fortunately the wind only lasts from 24 to 72 hours.

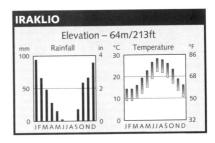

The island begins to cool down in September and there is occasional rain. December, January and February are the rainiest months especially in the interior mountains, and there is snow on the peaks of the Lefka Ori. The clouds begin to lift in March when the temperature is mild enough to make outdoor activities, such as hiking through the hills, a pleasure.

## ECOLOGY & ENVIRONMENT

Crete has not achieved a very high level of environmental awareness and environmental regulation is practically nonexistent.

Despite severe water shortages in many parts of the island, you will still see storekeepers wash the footpaths with water. There are no recycling programs even though the huge influx of summer visitors entails tons of rubbish. Most tourist areas are kept relatively rubbish-free but in the interior you will often be treated to the pungent odour of garbage decomposing in a dump.

Crete's air and water outside the major cities is clean but the flora and fauna are under pressure from deforestation. Olive cultivation, firewood gathering, shipbuilding, uncontrolled livestock breeding and arson over the centuries have laid waste to the forests that had carpeted the island at one time. There is no tree replanting program, possibly because the 90,000 goats living on the island would chew through the saplings. The use of pesticides and herbicides in farming has eliminated many bird and plant species and hunting has decimated the animal population.

It is along Crete's shoreline that environmental damage is most acute. Marine life has suffered from the local habit of fishing with dynamite and overdevelopment of the northern coast is chasing away migratory birds. Worldwide concern has been roused for the plight of the loggerhead sea turtles, that nest on the same sandy beaches that tourists prize. *Caretta Caretta* is the Latin name for the turtle that has been nesting on Crete since the days of the dinosaurs. The beaches of Rethymno, Hania and the Mesara Gulf in the south can host from 500 to 800 nests each summer. Sadly, the ribbon of taverns and hotels on the beachfront has seriously disturbed the nesting habits of this ancient species. Because these bulky creatures are so vulnerable on land, the females are frightened by objects on the beach at night and can refuse to lay eggs. When the hatchlings emerge at night they find the sea by the reflection of moon and starlight but are easily disoriented by tavern lights.

As tourism on Crete has ballooned over the last two decades, the island has had to cope with increasing demands for electricity. Although the power supply had long been reliant on fossil fuels, Greenpeace launched a major campaign in 1996 and persuaded the Greek government to help build the world's largest solar power plant on Crete. When completed in 2003, the plant will provide 50MW of solar power, which is enough power for almost 100,000 people. In order to encourage the installation of solar materials the government has offered subsidies and tax deductions to businesses and households. It is expected that the cost of electricity will be low enough to make the Crete installation a prototype for other solar power projects in the Mediterranean. Huge wind generators scattered around Crete also inject much needed power into the island's electricity grid.

## FLORA & FAUNA
### Flora

One of the major attractions of a visit to Crete is the opportunity to enjoy the amazing variety of plants and wildflowers growing on the island. It has been estimated that there are about 2000 species of plants on the island and about 160 species of those are found only on Crete.

### Loggerhead Turtles

The Sea Turtle Protection Society of Greece has the following advice for visitors:

• Leave the beaches clear at night during the May to October nesting season

• Remove umbrellas and lounge chairs at night

• Don't touch baby turtles on the way to the sea; they must orient themselves and the walk strengthens them

• Urge hotel and tavern owners to cooperate with the society and shade their lights when necessary

• Dispose of rubbish properly; plastic bags, mistaken by the turtles as jellyfish, are lethal

KATE NOLAN

As a rule, a visit in March or April is the surest way to see the island in full flower but mountain plants and flowers often bloom later and late rains can also extend the growing season.

What you see depends upon when you come and where you are. Along the coast you'll come across sea daffodils that flower in August and September, and knapsweeds on the west coast that flower in April and May. The purple or violet petals of stocks provide pretty splashes of colour on sandy beaches from April to May. In eastern Crete, especially around Sitia, watch for crimson poppies on the borders of the beach in April and May. At the edge of sandy beaches that are not yet lined with a strip of hotels you'll find delicate pink bindweeds and jujube trees that flower from May to June and bear fruit in September and October. In the same habitat is the tamarisk tree that flowers in the spring.

Further away from the beach in the lowlands are junipers and holm oak trees as well as poppies and purple lupins that flower in the spring. If you come in the summer, you won't be deprived of colour since milky white and magenta oleanders bloom from June through August.

On the hillsides look for cistus and brooms in the early summer and in the fields fabulous yellow chrysanthemums flower from March to May.

Orchid buffs will find a lot to appreciate on Crete. Many varieties of orchids and ophrys bloom in the spring on the lower slopes of the mountains turning the hills and meadows bright with pink, purple and violet flowers. Dense-flowering orchids, pink-flowered butterfly orchids and Cretan cyclamens are found on the Lasithi Plateau. Purple and crimson anemones are found in the same habitat in early spring followed by yellow buttercups and crowfoots in late spring.

## Fauna

Bird life is varied on Crete and includes both resident and migratory species. Along the coast you'll find birds of passage such as egrets and herons during the spring and autumn migrations. Various species of gulls nest on coastal cliffs and offshore islets. Rare hawks migrate up from Africa during the summer to nest on the offshore islets. Woodpigeons still nest in cliffs along the sea but have been hunted to near extinction.

The mountains host a wealth of interesting birds. Look for blue rock thrushes, buzzards and huge vultures such as the griffin vulture. In the Samaria Gorge you may spot the rare *lammergeier*, or bearded vulture, now threatened with extinction. Other birds in the mountains include Alpine swifts, stonechats, blackbirds and Sardinian warblers. The fields around Malia host tawny and red-throated pipits, stone-curlews, fan-tailed warblers and short-toed larks. On the hillsides below the Moni Preveli you may find ruppell's and subalpine warblers. The Akrotiri Peninsula is a good place to look for birds. Migrating species such as waders, egrets and gulls are found on Souda Bay. Around the Agia Triada and Gouvernetou monasteries you'll find collared and pied flycatchers, wrynecks, tawny pipits, black-eared wheatears, blue rock thrushes, stonechats, chukars and northern wheatears.

Mammal life on Crete is divided between livestock and endangered species. Sheep, goats, and cows are treated with the respect appropriate to any money-making endeavour but all other mammals have been hunted ferociously. Crete's most famous animal is the *kri-kri*, or wild goat, only a few of which survive in and around the

## The Herbs of Crete

The pungent smell of wild mountain herbs is one that visitors to the island will never forget in the height of summer. Crete has one of the richest varieties of indigenous herbs in the world and Cretans have not been lax in collecting them for uses ranging from flavouring their scrumptious dishes to curing toothache. Among the more common and widely used herbs to be found in Crete are the following: Dittany *(diktamo)* used primarily for making herbal tea, is a herb with a long history. The ancients believed it would help heal wounds, or that it would ease the pains of women in labour. The goddess Aphrodite was convinced it was an aphrodisiac. Oregano *(rigani)* grows in profusion all over the island and is one of the better-known herbs. It can be made into a tea and drunk to combat diarrhoea, but it is more commonly dried and used to flavour meat dishes, or sprinkled on *dakos* the Cretan rusk topped with olive oil, chopped tomatoes and cottage cheese. Sage *(faskomilo)* is a herb with a strong aroma and is used primarily as a medicine in cases of colds or stomach problems. Its oil it particularly good for the relief of toothache. Rosemary *(dendrolivano)* is easily spotted by its long thin aromatic leaves and is used in flavouring dishes of fish, snails or lamb. It is also used medicinally as an antiseptic, for headache relief and even for hair loss.

Samaria Gorge. Apparently the animal was more prevalent in Minoan times and was often depicted in Minoan art.

One of the more intriguing rare animals on Crete is the *fourokattos* (wild cat). Shepherds have been telling tales for centuries about the mysterious wild cat but scientists assumed that the cat existed in legend only. The first indication that the cat may have been real occurred in 1905 when a British scientist bought two pelts at a market in Hania. Proof of the cat's existence occurred in 1996 when Italian scientists studying Cretan fauna found the 5.5kg cat in a trap one morning. It remains unclear whether the cat was indigenous to the island or whether it was a domesticated animal that ran wild. No further cats have been found.

Other mammals found on Crete include the indigenous Cretan spiny mouse and a large population of bats.

## National Parks

The only national park in Crete is the Samaria Gorge, the largest and most impressive gorge in Europe. It is 18km long and has a visitors centre. The Samaria Gorge is an important sanctuary for birds and animals; no-one lives in the gorge.

## GOVERNMENT & POLITICS

Greece is a parliamentary republic with a president as head of state. It is divided into regions and island groups. The regions of the mainland are the Peloponnese, Central Greece, Epiros, Thessaly, Macedonia and Thrace.

The island groups are the Cyclades, Dodecanese, North-Eastern Aegean, Sporades and Saronic Gulf, all in the Aegean Sea, and the Ionian Islands, which are in the Ionian Sea. The large islands of Evia and Crete do not belong to any group. For administrative purposes these regions and groups are divided into 51 prefectures or nomes (*nomi* in Greek). Crete contains four of these: Lasithi, Iraklio, Rethymno and Hania. The island's capital and Greece's fifth-largest city is Iraklio. As the island's capital until 1971, Hania considers itself the historical heart of the island while Rethymno claims to be its

cultural centre. Rivalries between the prefectures are strong as each competes for investment, tourism and, more recently, distribution of the island's water supply.

Centuries of battling foreign occupiers have left the island with a stubbornly independent streak that sometimes leads to clashes with Athens. A NATO base on the Akrotiri Peninsula is a sore point with the local population who would like to see it removed despite foreign policy commitments by the national government. National laws that conflict with local customs are simply disregarded. Guns are strictly regulated in Greece but nearly every household in Crete has at least one illegal firearm and many harbour small arsenals.

Politically, the island is more moderate. The dominant ideology is left-of-centre with the socialist PASOK party repeatedly outdrawing the conservative New Democracy party in local and national elections. Extremists on either the right or left have little support.

## ECONOMY

Greece is an agricultural country, but the importance of agriculture to the economy has declined rapidly since WWII. Some 50% of the workforce is now employed in services (contributing 59.2% of GDP), 19.8% in agriculture (contributing 15%), and 21% in industry and construction (contributing 26%). Tourism is by far the biggest industry; shipping comes next. The eight million tourists who visit Greece each year contribute around US$3 billion to the economy.

Although Greece has the second-lowest income per capita of all the EU countries (after Portugal), its economic future looks brighter now than it has for some time. The economy suffered badly from the fighting in the Balkans in the early 1990s, which cut Greece's major overland trade route to the rest of Europe. Peace in the Balkans has done much to restore business confidence. The austerity measures imposed by successive governments also appear to have had the desired effect, with inflation cut to a healthier (2.6%) for the first time in 22 years, and unemployment officially running at 9.9%. Greece joined the European Monetary Union in January 2002 and now has the euro as its national currency.

Agriculture and tourism are the twin engines of the Cretan economy leaving the island with an unemployment rate of only 5.5% – more than half the national rate. Olives, olive oil, sultanas, wine, vegetables and fruit are produced in quantity for export. Although fewer people are working in agriculture than in the postwar period, improvements in roads and better techniques are allowing the output to remain the same and in some cases, to increase. Tourism has expanded to the point where it constitutes two-thirds of the Gross Regional Product of Crete and provides employment to 40% of the island's workforce. The labour-intensive tourism sector draws seasonal workers from mainland Greece, the EU and Eastern Europe to work in hotels, restaurants, shops and bars.

## POPULATION & PEOPLE

Crete is Greece's most populous island with 537,000 people. The populations of the island's major cities are: Iraklio (115,000), Hania (50,000), Rethymno (23,500), Agios Nikolaos (8000). After the exodus of the Turkish population in 1923 Crete became ethnically homogenous, consisting solely of Greek Orthodox residents. Modern Cretans are a mixture of all the races and ethnic groups that occupied them over the centuries.

## EDUCATION

Education in Greece is free at all levels of the state system from kindergarten to tertiary. Primary schooling begins at the age of six, but most children attend a state-run kindergarten from the age of five. Private kindergartens are popular with those who can afford them.

Primary school classes tend to be larger than those in most European countries – usually 30 to 35 children. Primary school hours are short (8am to 1pm), but children get a lot of homework.

At 12, children enter the *gymnasio*, and at 15 they may leave school, or enter the *lykio*,

from where they take university entrance examinations. Although there is a high percentage of literacy, many parents and pupils are dissatisfied with the education system, especially beyond primary level. The private sector therefore flourishes, and even relatively poor parents struggle to send their children to one of the country's 5000 *frontistiria* (intensive coaching colleges) to prepare them for the very competitive university entrance exams. Grievances reached a peak in 1991, when lykio students staged a series of sit-ins in schools throughout the country, and organised protest marches. In 1992, gymnasio pupils followed suit, and the government responded by calling for stricter discipline and a more demanding curriculum. After more sit-ins the government changed its plans and by 2000 had instigated reforms including a more suitable, primarily school-based assessment system for progress to tertiary education.

## ARTS
### Minoan Art

See 'The Minoans' special section in this chapter for a detailed look at the history of Minoan art in Crete.

### Dorian & Roman Periods

There was a brief artistic renaissance on Crete that lasted from the 8th to the 7th centuries BC. A new movement in sculpture emerged called the Daedalic movement after a sculptor called Daedalos. Although the existence of this sculptor is uncertain, it is clear that a group of sculptors called the Daedalids perfected a new technique of making sculptures in hammered bronze. They worked in a style that combined Eastern and Greek aesthetics and their influence spread to mainland Greece. Cretan culture went into decline at the end of the 7th century BC. There was a brief revival under the Romans, mainly notable for the richly decorated mosaic floors and marble sculpture such as the colossal statue of Apollo.

### Byzantine & Venetian Periods

Although Byzantine icons and frescoes were created from the earliest years of

Byzantine rule much was destroyed in popular rebellions in the 13th and 14th centuries. In the 11th century, emigres from Constantinople brought portable icons to Crete but the only surviving example from this period is the icon of the virgin at Mesopantitissa, now in Venice. From the 13th to the early 16th centuries, churches around Crete were decorated with frescoes – many of which can still be seen. Byzantine art flowered under the Paleologan emperors who ruled from 1258 to 1453, and its influence spread to Crete. The great icon painter of the 14th century was Ioannis Pagomenos who worked in western Crete.

With the fall of Constantinople in 1453 many Byzantine artists fled to Crete. At the same time, the Italian Renaissance was in full bloom and many Cretan artists studied in Italy. The result was the 'Cretan school' of icon painting that combined technical brilliance and dramatic richness. In Hania alone there were over 200 painters working from the mid-16th to mid-17th centuries who were equally at ease in Venetian and Byzantine styles. The Cretan Theophanes Sterlitzas painted monasteries throughout Greece that spread the techniques of the Cretan school.

Too few examples of the Cretan school are on display in Crete but visitors to Iraklio are fortunate to have the church and museum of Agia Ekaterini. Six portable icons from the great Michael Damaskinos, the finest exponent of the Cretan school, form the centrepiece of the collection. Damaskinos' long sojourn in Venice introduced him to new techniques of rendering perspective, which he brought to the Byzantine style of icon painting.

## Cretan Dance

In addition to its own traditional music and dances, Crete incorporates music and dance from all over Greece. The folk dances of today derive from the ritual dances performed in ancient Greek temples. One of

## El Greco

One of the geniuses of the Renaissance, El Greco (meaning 'The Greek' in Spanish; his real name was Dominikos Theotokopoulos) was born and educated on Crete but had to travel to Spain to earn recognition.

El Greco was born in the Cretan capital of Candia (present-day Iraklio) in 1541 during a time of great artistic activity in the city following the arrival of large numbers of painters fleeing Ottoman-held Constantinople. These painters had a formative influence upon the young El Greco, giving him the early grounding in the traditions of late Byzantine fresco painting that was to give such a powerful spiritual element to his later paintings.

Because Candia was a Venetian city it was a logical step for El Greco to head to Venice to further his studies, and he set off when he was in his early 20s to join the studio of Titian. It was not, however, until he moved to Spain in 1577 that he really came into his own as a painter. His highly emotional style struck a chord with the Spanish, and the city of Toledo was to become his home until his death in 1614. To view the most famous of his works, like his masterpiece *The Burial of Count Orgaz* (1586), you will have to travel to Toledo. The only El Greco work on display in Crete is *View of Mt Sinai and the Monastery of St Catherine* (1570), painted during his time in Venice. It hangs in Iraklio's Historical Museum of Crete.

A white marble bust of the painter stands in the city's Plateia El Greco, and there are streets named after him throughout the island.

MARTIN HARRIS

MARTIN HARRIS

The mandolin is often used to accompany *mandinades*, traditional Cretan songs often with improvised lyrics.

these dances, the *syrtos*, is depicted on ancient Greek vases, and there are references to dances in Homer's works. Homer commented on the ability of Cretan dancers, which were often depicted in Minoan frescoes.

Many Greek folk dances, including the syrtos, are performed in a circular formation. In ancient times, dancers formed a circle to seal themselves off from evil influences.

Dancing has always been a large part of Cretan celebrations. In addition to Greek dances Cretans dance the *pendozalis*, a circle dance involving male dancers leaping to a fast beat. Other Cretan dances include the *kastrinos* and *maleviziotikos*, also fast dances, and the *sousta* dance for couples.

## Cretan Music

Singing and the playing of musical instruments have also been an integral part of life in Greece since ancient times. Cycladic figurines holding musical instruments resembling harps and flutes date back to 2000 BC. Musical instruments of ancient Greece included the *lyra* (lyre), lute, *piktis* (pipes), *kroupeza* (a percussion instrument), *kithara* (a stringed instrument), *aulos* (a wind instrument), *barbitos* (similar to a violin cello) and the *magadio* (similar to a harp). In Crete, music is woven into the fabric of everyday life and accompanies weddings, births, deaths, holidays, harvesting and simply relaxing. The main instruments are the lyra, similar to a violin, the eight-stringed *laouto* (lute), which is played like a guitar and the *mandolino* (mandolin). One of Crete's favourite forms of musical expression is

*mandinades*, improvised couplets of 30 syllables that express the age-old concerns of love, death and the vagaries of fate. Probably originating as love songs in 15th-century Venice, thousands of mandinades helped forge a sense of national identity during the centuries of occupation. Since the verses are improvised, 'rhymers' at Cretan festivals tailor the songs to the people present and try to outdo each other in skill.

Another popular form is *rizitika* which are centuries-old songs from the Lefka Ori that derived from the songs of the border guards of the Byzantine Empire.

There are two kinds of rizitika – *tis tavlas* (table) songs that accompany feasts and *tis stratas* (round) songs which accompany travellers. Many of the rizitika songs deal with historical or heroic themes. One of the most popular is the song of Daskalogiannis, the Sfakian hero who led the rebellion against the Turks in 1770. The song has 1034 verses and is still sung throughout Sfakia.

The *bouzouki*, heard everywhere in Greece, is a mandolin-like instrument with a long neck. While it is heard on radio in Crete and used in live performances by visiting mainland artists, the bouzouki plays very much second fiddle to traditional Cretan musical instruments and is rarely played in public in Crete.

Crete has produced a rich tapestry of musicians, including a swathe of artists from the village of Anogia (see the boxed text 'Anogia's Musical Heritage' in the Rethymno & Central Crete chapter) as well as the contemporary composer Giannis Markopoulos from Ierapetra. He wrote the internationally known *Who Pays the Ferryman* composition. Markopoulos has also promoted many singers and lyra players such as the widely respected Haralambos Garganourakis who has sung and played on several of Markopoulos' albums.

Some of the better albums featuring Cretan musicians or composers are the following.

***Rizitika (1970) by Giannis Markopoulos, sung by Nikos Xylouris.*** A classic must-have album featuring 11 traditional rizitika (brigand) songs.

***Oropedio (1976) by composer Giannis Markopoulos and a group of singers including Haralambos Garganourakis*** is perhaps Markopoulos' most seminally rich, yet least known work. The album title 'Plateau' is inspired by the many plateaues of Crete, while its arresting harmonic content deals with human strife in the face of increasing urbanisation and alienation. Oropedio features the excellent vocal talents of five of Greece's best singers.

***Nikos Xylouris (1982)*** The homonymous album is probably the best overall introduction to the music and voice of one of Crete's lost and now much-lamented musical sons.

***Concert and Rhapsody for Lyra and Orchestra (1988) by Giannis Markopoulos and Haralambos Garganourakis.*** An unusual melange of classical motifs and traditional Cretan lyre, this musical journey is worth obtaining especially as it includes a seven-part work entitled Music for Dominikos Theotokopoulos (El Greco).

***Tou Livykou to Pelagos (1996) by Kostas Avyssinos.*** Along with fellow band member Dimitris Apostolakis from Cretan band Haïnides, Kostas Avyssinos sings a collection of delicate and mainly original Crete and Asia Minor-inspired ballads. All songs are woven together by the svelte violin and rhythmic percussion of Kurdish musician Senih Undeger.

***To Megalo Taxidi (1997) by Haïnides.*** 'The Long Voyage' is an eclectic collection of original compositions and traditional arrangements by this excellent Cretan sextet. The band lays down a rich sound tapestry from their range of musical instruments as well as engaging vocal harmonies.

***Tesseris Dromi gia ton Erotokrito (2000) by composer Loudovikos ton Anogion and performed by Nikos Xylouris' brother Psarandonis and others.*** This richly produced, but complex compilation is four interpretations of segments of the Cretan epic poem Erotokritos.

***Ta Agria Poulia (2001) by singer and lyra player Vasilis Skoulas.*** This is a new album from one of Anogia's most prolific producers of traditional Cretan music. It is as good an introduction as any to the inimitable style and voice of Vasilis Skoulas.

## Literature

Crete has a rich literary tradition that sprang from the Cretan love of songs, verses and word play. In the late 16th or early 17th centuries, Crete had a tremendous literary flowering under Venetian rule. The era's greatest masterpiece was undoubtedly the epic poem *Erotokritos* written by Vitsentzos Kornaros of Sitia. More than 10,000 lines long, this poem of courtly love is full of nostalgia for the dying Venetian regime that was threatened by the rise in Turkish power. The poem was recited for centuries by illiterate peasants and professional singers alike, embodying the dreams of freedom that enabled Cretans to endure their many privations. Many of the verses were incorporated into Crete's beloved mandinades. It is available in translation from The Hellenic Bookservice (☎ 020 7267 9499, fax 7267 9498, e hellenicbooks@btinternet.com) at 91 Fortress Road, Kentish Town, London, NW5 1AG.

Greece's best-known writer since Homer is Nikos Kazantzakis, born in Iraklio in 1883 amid the last spasms of Crete's struggle for independence from the Turks. Kazantzakis had a chequered and at times troubled literary career, clashing frequently with the Orthodox Church for his professed atheism. See the boxed text 'Nikos Kazantzakis – Crete's Prodigal Son' in the Iraklio chapter for more detail.

Iraklio may have Kazantzakis but Rethymno has Pandelis Prevelakis. Born in Rethymno in 1900, Prevelakis also studied in Athens and at the Sorbonne. Primarily known as a poet, Prevelakis also wrote plays and novels. His best-known work is *The Tale of a Town* about Rethymno.

## Film

Cretans are avid cinema-goers, although most of the films are North American or

British. The Greek film industry is in the doldrums, largely due to inadequate government funding. The problem is compounded by the type of films the Greeks produce which have a reputation for being slow moving, loaded with symbolism and generally too avant-garde to have mass appeal, despite being well-made with some outstanding cinematography.

Greece's most acclaimed film director is Theodoros Angelopoulos, whose films include *The Beekeeper*, *Alexander the Great*, *Travelling Players*, *Landscapes in the Mist* and *The Hesitant Step of the Stork*. All have received awards at national and international festivals.

## SOCIETY & CONDUCT
### Traditional Culture
Proud, patriotic, hospitable and religious, today's Cretan's strong connection to their ancestors is apparent as soon as you leave the major tourist centres. Mountain villages are repositories of traditional culture and you'll find that most older women and many men are still clad in black garb. During weddings and festivals even young men don black boots, shirt and baggy pants, tucking a pistol into their belt to be fired into the air as the evening wears on.

One of the more remarkable features of Cretan life is the ability of the islanders to maintain many aspects of their traditional culture in the face of a seasonal invasion of foreign tourists. Cretans have learned to co-exist partly by operating in a different time-space continuum than their guests.

From April to around October, the islanders live in the hurly-burly of the coastal resorts running shops, pensions or tavernas and then return to their traditional life in the hills for the autumn olive and grape harvest. Tourists eat early in the evening in restaurants along a harbour or beach while Cretans drive out to a village taverna for a dinner that begins around 11pm. Dance clubs play Western music until around 3am when the Greek crowd arrives and the music switches to Cretan or Greek music.

Men and women also occupy different spheres. When not tending livestock or olive trees, Cretan men can usually be found in a *kafeneio* playing cards and drinking coffee or *raki*. Although exceptions are made for foreign women, kafeneia are off-limits to Cretan women who are usually occupied with housework and child rearing. In their off-hours, women busy themselves with sewing, crocheting or embroidery, often in a circle of other women. Old attitudes towards the 'proper role' for women are changing, however, as more women enter the workforce.

Young Cretan women have discarded shapeless dresses in favour of skin-tight slacks and are more likely to be found in a disco than behind a loom. Friction has developed between the older generation and a younger generation more attuned to European influences. Fortunately the employment opportunities brought by the tourist business has discouraged young people from leaving the island, thus allowing them to retain at least a nominal contact with their parent's culture.

### Dos & Don'ts
If you go into a kafeneio, taverna or shop, it is customary to greet the waiters or assistants with '*kalimera*' (good day) or '*kalispera*' (good evening). Personal questions are not considered rude, so prepare to be inundated with queries about your age, salary, marital status etc, and to be given sympathy if you are over 25 and not married!

Cretans have a well-justified reputation for hospitality. The tradition was to treat strangers as honoured guests and invite them for coffee, a meal or to spend the night. Obviously Cretans are no longer offering free food and lodging to several million tourists a year but if you wander off the beaten track into mountain villages you may be invited to someone's home.

If you're served a glass of water, coffee and some preserves it is the custom to first drink the water then eat the preserves and then drink the coffee.

When visiting someone, it is bad manners to refuse the coffee or raki they'll offer you. You may feel uneasy, especially if your host is poor, but don't offend them by offering money. Give a gift, perhaps to a child in the family, instead.

If you go out for a meal with Cretans, the bill is not shared but rather paid by the host. When drinking wine, only half fill the glass and don't let it become empty (a no-no).

Cretans have a long tradition of welcoming foreigners which has made them tolerant of different customs. Although Greek women are unlikely to go topless, in most places topless sunbathing is allowed. The few south coast beaches where it is frowned upon post signs to that effect.

## Treatment of Animals

The Cretan attitude to animals depends on whether the animal is a cat or not. It's definitely cool to be a cat. Even the mangiest-looking stray can be assured of a warm welcome and a choice tidbit on approaching the restaurant table of a Greek. Most other domestic animals are greeted with a certain indifference or put to work. Most shepherds have dogs for guarding the flock and these dogs are generally well looked after since they play a valuable role in the shepherd's job of guarding his sheep or goats.

The main threat to animal welfare is hunting. Cretan hunters are notorious for blasting anything that moves, and millions of animals are killed during the long 'open' season, from 20 August to 10 March, which encompasses the bird migratory period.

## RELIGION

About 98% of Greeks belong to the Greek Orthodox Church. Most of the remainder are either Roman Catholic, Jewish or Muslim.

The Greek Orthodox Church is closely related to the Russian Orthodox Church and together with it forms the third-largest branch of Christianity. Orthodox, meaning 'right belief', was founded in the 4th century by Constantine the Great, who was converted to Christianity by a vision of the Cross.

By the 8th century, there were a number of differences of opinion between the pope in Rome and the patriarch of Constantinople, as well as increasing rivalry between the two.

By the 11th century these differences had become irreconcilable, and in 1054 the pope and the patriarch excommunicated one another. Ever since, the two have gone their own ways as the (Greek/Russian) Orthodox Church and the Roman Catholic Church.

During Ottoman times membership of the Orthodox Church was one of the most important criteria in defining a Greek, regardless of where he or she lived. The church was the principal upholder of Greek culture and traditions.

Religion is still integral to life in Greece, and the Greek year is centred on the festivals of the church calendar. Most Greeks, when they have a problem, will go into a church and light a candle to the saint they feel is most likely to help them. On the islands you will see hundreds of tiny churches dotted around the countryside. Most have been built by individual families in the name of their family's selected patron saint as thanksgiving for God's protection.

The Orthodox religion held Cretan culture together during the many dark centuries of repression despite numerous, largely futile efforts by the Venetians and Turks to turn the Cretans toward Catholicism and Islam.

Cretans still celebrate Greek Orthodox holidays with enthusiasm, though it's interesting to note that the Orthodox Church of Crete is independent from the Greek Orthodox Church and answers directly to the Patriarch of Constantinople.

If you wish to look around a church, you should dress appropriately. Women should wear skirts that reach below the knees, men should wear long trousers and arms should be covered. Regrettably, many churches are kept locked nowadays, but it's usually easy enough to locate the caretakers, who will be happy to open them for you.

The influence of the church on the affairs of state was fully demonstrated in September 2001 when a major row erupted over plans to introduce a new EU-compliant identity card which made no mention of the religion of the card holder. How this politically and religiously charged initiative will pan out is anyone's guess.

## LANGUAGE

Greek is the official language in Crete. English is spoken only in areas catering to large numbers of tourists, so away from major towns you'll need at least some Greek. See the Language chapter at the back of this book for a brief guide to Greek and a list of useful words and phrases.

## Transliteration & Variant Spellings: An Explanation

The issue of correctly transliterating Greek into the Latin alphabet is a vexed one, fraught with inconsistencies and pitfalls. The Greeks themselves are not very consistent when it comes to providing transliterated names on their signs, though things are gradually improving. The town of Iraklio, for example, has been variously represented by the following transliterations: Iraklion, Heraklion and Heracleion; and when appearing as a street name (eg, Iraklio Street) it becomes Irakliou!

This is compounded by the linguistic minefield of diglossy, or the two forms of the Greek language. The purist form is called Katharevousa and the popular form is Dimotiki (Demotic). The Katharevousa form was never more than an artificiality and Dimotiki has always been spoken as the mainstream language, but this linguistic schizophrenia means there are often two Greek words for each English word. Thus, the word for 'baker' in everyday language is *fournos*, but the shop sign will more often than not say *artopoieion*. The baker's product will be known in the street as *psomi*, but in church as *artos*.

As if all that wasn't enough, there is also the issue of anglicised vs hellenised forms of place names: Athina vs Athens, Pireas vs Piraeus, Festos vs Phaestos, Knosos vs Cnossus – the list goes on and on! Cross cultural differences are responsible for such alternative variants as Corfu/Kerkyra, Zante/Zakynthos, and Santorini/Thira. In this guide we have usually provided modern Greek equivalents for town names, with one exception, Athens. For ancient sites, settlements or people from antiquity, we have attempted to stick to the more familiar classical names; so we have Homer instead of Omiros, Pasiphae instead of Pasifaï.

Problems in transliteration have particular implications for vowels, especially given that Greek has six ways of rendering the vowel sound *ee*, two ways of rendering the *o* sound and two ways of rendering the *e* sound. In most instances in this book, *y* has been used for the *ee* sound when a Greek *upsilon* (υ, Υ) has been used, and *i* for Greek *ita* (η, Η) and *iota* (ι, Ι). In the case of the Greek vowel combinations that make the *ee* sound, that is οι, ει and υι, an *i* has been used. For the two Greek *e* sounds, αι and ε, an *e* has been employed.

As far as the transliteration of consonants is concerned, the Greek letter gamma (γ, Γ) appears as *g* rather than *y* throughout this book. This means that *agios* (Greek for male saint) is used rather than *ayios*, and *agia* (female saint) rather than *ayia*. The letter *delta* (δ, Δ) appears as *d* rather than *dh* throughout this book, so *domatia* (rooms), rather than *dhomatia*, is used. The letter *fi* (φ, Φ) can be transliterated as either *f* or *ph*. Here, a general rule of thumb is that classical names are spelt with a *ph* and modern names with an *f*. So Phaestos is used rather than Festos, and Folegandros is used rather than Pholegandros. The Greek *chi* (Χ, χ) has usually been represented as *h* in order to approximate the Greek pronunciation as closely as possible. Thus, we have 'Haralambos' instead of 'Charalambos' and 'Polytehniou' instead of 'Polytechniou'. Bear in mind that the *h* is to be pronounced as an aspirated *h*, much like the *ch* in loch. The letter *kapa* (κ, Κ) has been used to represent that sound, except where well known names from antiquity have adopted by convention the letter *c*, eg Polycrates, Acropolis.

Wherever reference to a street name is made, we have omitted the Greek word '*odos*', but words for avenue *(leoforos)* and square *(plateia)* have been included.

For a more detailed guide to the Greek language, check out Lonely Planet's comprehensive Greek *phrasebook*.

# Facts for the Visitor

## PLANNING
### When to Go

The best times to visit Crete are in late spring/early summer and in autumn. Winter is pretty much a dead loss. Most of the tourist infrastructure goes into hibernation from November until the beginning of April – hotels and restaurants are closed and bus and ferry services are either drastically reduced or cancelled.

The cobwebs are dusted off in time for Easter, when the first tourists start to arrive. Conditions are perfect between Easter and mid-June, when the weather is pleasantly warm in most places, but not too hot; beaches and ancient sites are relatively uncrowded; public transport operates on close to full schedules; and accommodation is cheaper and easy to find.

Mid-June until the end of August is the high season. It's party time on the island and everything is in full swing. It's also very hot – in July and August the mercury can soar to 40°C (100°F) in the shade, the beaches are crowded, the ancient sites are swarming with tour groups, and in many places accommodation is booked solid.

The season starts to wind down in September, and conditions are ideal once more until the end of October.

## Maps

Mapping is an important feature of this guide. Unless you are going to trek or drive, you probably won't need additional maps.

Most tourist offices hand out free maps, but they are often out of date and not particularly accurate. The same applies to the cheap (€1.20 to €1.50) 'tourist maps'.

The best maps are published by the Greek company Road Editions (☎ 21 0364 0723, e road@enet.gr, w www.road.gr). Crete is covered by the company's 1:250,000 maroon-covered *Crete* map (€5.40). Even the smallest roads and villages are clearly marked, and the distance indicators are spot-on – important when negotiating your way around the

---

## The Best & Worst

### The Best

It's tough trying to pick just 10 of the best things about Crete. These are the personal favourites of the author:

- Cretan hospitality
- Easter festivities
- Eating fresh seafood by the sea
- Exploring the island on foot
- Good raki
- Late night dinners at village tavernas
- Listening to *mandinades* at midnight on the slopes of Mt Psiloritis
- Swimming at uncrowded beaches in southern Crete
- Watching the moon rise from the sea at Kato Zakros
- Wedding feasts that include an entire village

### The Worst

The author would be very happy not to experience the following again:

- Bad raki
- Bland, over-priced food
- Lager louts on the loose in Malia and Hersonisos
- Manic smokers in restaurants and bars
- Nonexistent road signposting
- Over-development along Crete's north-central coast
- Picture menus at tourist restaurants
- Restaurant touts accosting passers-by
- The attitude to rubbish
- Tourists in hire cars on winding mountain roads

backblocks. A new, two sheet improved 1:100,000 map of Crete, with contour intervals depicted every 20m will be published by Road Editions in May 2002.

A newcomer to the map scene is Emvelia Editions (☎ 21 0771 7616, e info@emvelia.gr). Its blue and yellow 1:185,000 map of *Crete* (€5.90) is a little clearer to read. The map contains good maps of the major towns in Crete, as well as the five major archaeological sites on the island. Both this and the Road Editions map are widely available in Crete.

The German-published Harms Verlag 1:100,000 *Kreta Touristikkarte* come in two versions: the East (Der Osten) and the West (Der Westen) and cost a steep €10 each. These are probably the best maps for hikers and trekkers and depict the E4 Trekking Route very clearly. The maps are available in Crete, or you can contact Harms Verlag (☎ 07275 8201, fax 8594, e Kartographie Harms@t-online.de, w www.kartographie harms.de) in Germany.

Finally the plasticised and hard-wearing B&B 1:200,00 *Crete* map (€5.60) is handy for drivers who need a quick reference. There is a useful inset of the Samaria Gorge walking map. Contact Berndtson & Berndtson (☎ 08141 32 410, e vertrieb@berndt son.de, w www.mapway.com) in Germany.

## What to Bring

Sturdy shoes are essential for clambering around ancient sites and wandering through historic towns and villages, which tend to have lots of steps and cobbled streets.

A day-pack is useful for the beach, and for sightseeing or trekking. A compass is essential if you are going to trek in remote areas, as is a whistle, which you can use should you become lost or disorientated. A torch (flashlight) is not only needed if you intend to explore caves, but comes in handy during occasional power cuts. If you like to fill a washbasin or bathtub (a rarity in Crete), bring a universal plug as Greek bathrooms rarely have plugs.

Many camping grounds in Crete have covered areas where tourists without tents can sleep in summer, so you can get by with a lightweight sleeping bag and foam bedroll.

You will need only light clothing – preferably cotton – during the summer months. During spring and autumn you'll need a light sweater or jacket in the evening.

In summer, a broad-rimmed sunhat and sunglasses are essential (see the Health section later in this chapter). Sunscreens are expensive in Crete, as are moisturising and cleansing lotions.

If you read a lot, it's a good idea to bring along a few disposable paperbacks to read and swap.

## TOURIST OFFICES

Tourist information is handled by the Greek National Tourist Organisation, known by the initials GNTO abroad and EOT (Ellinikos Organismos Tourismou) in Greece.

### Local Tourist Offices

The address of the EOT's head office (☎ 21 0331 0561, fax 21 0325 2895, e info@gnto .gr) is Amerikis 2, Athens 105 64. There are about 25 EOT offices throughout Crete. Most EOT staff speak English, but they vary in their enthusiasm and helpfulness.

Some offices, like that in Agios Nikolaos, have loads of useful local information, but others have nothing more than glossy brochures and a few maps. Some have absolutely nothing to offer.

In addition to EOT offices, there are also municipal tourist offices. They are often more helpful.

### Tourist Offices Abroad

GNTO offices abroad include:

**Australia**
  (☎ 02 9241 1663) 51 Pitt St, Sydney NSW 2000
**Austria**
  (☎ 01 512 5317) Opernring 8, Vienna A-10105
**Belgium**
  (☎ 02 647 5770) 172 Ave Louise Louizalaan, B-1050 Brussels
**Canada**
  (☎ 416-968 2220) 1300 Bay St, Toronto, Ontario M5R 3K8
**Denmark**
  (☎ 38 32 53 32) Vester Farimagsgade 1, DK-1606 Copenhagen

**France**
 (☎ 01 42 60 65 75) 3 Ave de l'Opéra, Paris
 F-75001
**Germany**
 *Berlin*: (☎ 030 217 6262) Wittenbergplatz 3A,
 D-10789 Berlin 30
 *Frankfurt*: (☎ 069 237 735) Neue Mainzer-
 strasse 22, D-60311 Frankfurt
 *Hamburg*: (☎ 040 454 498) Abteistrasse 33,
 D-20149 Hamburg 13
 *Munich*: (☎ 089 222 035/036) Pacellistrasse 5,
 D-80333 Munich 2
**Israel**
 (☎ 03 517 0501) 5 Shalom Aleichem St, Tel
 Aviv IL- 61262
**Italy**
 *Milan*: (☎ 02 860 470) Piazza Diaz 1, I-20123
 *Rome*: (☎ 06 474 4249) Via L Bissolati 78-80,
 Rome I-00187
**Japan**
 (☎ 03 350 55 911) Fukuda Building West, 5F
 2-11-3 Akasaka, Minato-Ku, Tokyo 107
**Netherlands**
 (☎ 020 625 4212/3/4) Leidsestraat 13,
 Amsterdam NS 1017
**Norway**
 (☎ 22 42 65 01) Ovre Slottsgate 15B, N-0157
 Oslo 1
**Sweden**
 (☎ 08 679 6480) Birger Jarlsgatan 30, Box
 5298 S, S-10246 Stockholm
**Switzerland**
 (☎ 01 221 01 05) Löwenstrasse 25, CH 8001
 Zurich
**UK**
 (☎ 020 7499 4976) 4 Conduit St, London
 W1R ODJ
**USA**
 *Chicago*: (☎ 312-782 1084) Suite 600, 168
 North Michigan Ave, Chicago, Illinois 60601
 *Los Angeles*: (☎ 213-626 6696) Suite 2198, 611
 West 6th St, Los Angeles, California 92668
 *New York*: (☎ 212-421 5777) Olympic Tower,
 645 5th Ave, New York, NY 10022

## Tourist Police

The tourist police work in cooperation with
the regular Cretan police and EOT. Each
tourist police office has at least one member
of staff who speaks English. Hotels, restaurants, travel agencies, tourist shops, tourist
guides, waiters, taxi drivers and bus drivers
all come under the jurisdiction of the tourist
police. If you think that you have been ripped
off by any of these, report it to the tourist

police and they will investigate. If you need
to report a theft or loss of a passport, the
tourist police will act as interpreters between you and the regular police. The
tourist police also fulfil the same functions
as the EOT and municipal tourist offices,
dispensing maps and brochures, and giving
information on transport.

## VISAS & DOCUMENTS
### Passport

To enter Greece you need a valid passport
or, for EU nationals, travel documents (ID
cards). You must produce your passport or
EU travel documents when you register in a
hotel or pension in Crete. You will find that
many accommodation proprietors will want
to keep your passport during your stay. This
is not a compulsory requirement; they need
it only long enough to take down the details.

### Visas

The list of countries whose nationals can stay
in Greece for up to three months without a
visa include Australia, Canada, all EU countries, Iceland, Israel, Japan, New Zealand,
Norway, Switzerland and the USA. Other
countries included are Cyprus, Malta, the
European principalities of Monaco and San
Marino, and most South American countries.
The list changes, so contact Greek embassies
for the full list. Those not on the list can expect to pay about $20 for a three month visa.

**Turkish-Occupied North Cyprus** Greece
may be reluctant to grant entry to people
whose passport indicates that they have visited Turkish-occupied North Cyprus since
November 1983. This can be overcome if,
upon entering North Cyprus, you ask the
immigration officials to stamp a piece of
paper (loose-leaf visa) rather than your passport. If you enter North Cyprus from the
Greek Republic of Cyprus (only possible for
a day visit), an entry stamp is not put into
your passport.

**Visa Extensions** If you want to stay in
Greece for longer than three months, apply at

*[Continued on page 56]*

Head to the Hills

**Title page:** Samaria Gorge, Hania Province (photo by Neil Setchfield)

**Top:** View over the hills on the drive to Imbros Gorge

**Bottom:** Hikers in Samaria Gorge

# Head to the Hills

## INTRODUCTION

Crete is more than beaches and archaeological sites, yet few visitors to the island are aware of it. The rugged terrain, soaring mountains, dramatic gorges and cobalt blue seas offer visitors the chance to get back to nature and enjoy an active and challenging holiday.

Crete is a land for all seasons: whether it be skiing on the slopes of the Lefka Ori in December, hiking their high peaks in spring or cycling the Lasithi Plateau in summer, there is an activity for every traveller. This special section will give you an overview of some of the options that will help you to head to the hills and make the most of it.

## CYCLING & MOUNTAIN BIKING

Cycling has caught on in a big way in Crete over the past few years. At face value, the mountains and high passes seem enough to deter all but the most determined cyclist. While it is possible to cycle from one end of Crete to the other and barely raise a sweat, north-south routes and southern coast cycling will test the will and stamina of most cyclists.

Many do it the easy way. Tour companies now transport you and your machine to the top of the mountains and you cycle down. Plateau tours – such as those that can be spotted daily around the Lasithi Plateau – are big business. Group tours of villages in eastern Crete are also very popular with one company offering at least seven customised rides of varying difficulty for groups of 12 to 15 riders. In Hania one company offers extreme biking or even all-inclusive eight-day tours for racing cyclists. Independent cyclists coming to Crete with their own bikes are advised to bring sturdy touring bikes with multiple gears, while riders on a short fly-in, fly-out visit can hire mountain bikes for around €9 and €15 per day.

See the Eastern Crete and Hania & Around chapters for contact details of specialist operators running cycling tours and bicycle rentals.

## HIKING & TREKKING

Crete offers an enormous variety of options for keen hikers and trekkers. The problem is, that the excellent hiking opportunities are poorly documented – there are few detailed English language guides in publication – and the trails themselves are generally inadequately marked. The exception to this is the E4 trail which runs the length of Crete. Add to that the generally rugged and arid nature of Crete's terrain and you'll soon see why hiking and trekking here can be a blessing and a bane. Nonetheless, the island's generally untrodden interior is probably its attraction and while the majority of visitors may opt for a guided trek, experienced walkers will find plenty to challenge and stimulate.

## The E4 Route

The trans-European E4 walking trail starts in Portugal and ends in Crete. In Crete the trail picks up at the port of Kissamos-Kastelli in the west and ends, after 320km on the pebbly shore of Kato Zakros in eastern Crete. Enthusiasts planning to tackle the Cretan leg can do it in a minimum of three weeks allowing for 15km per day, or more comfortably in four weeks allowing for stops and/or shorter hiking legs. You can, of course, tackle only sections of it, if your time is limited. However, you will need to make important decisions early on as the trail splits up into two distinct sections through Western Crete – the coastal route and the more obviously fitting alpine route. The trail is marked throughout its length with black and yellow posts and signs.

From Kissamos-Kastelli the route first takes a long dip south, following the west coast via Elafonisi to Paleohora. From Paleohora there is a pleasant hike to Sougia. See the boxed text 'Paleohora-Sougia Coastal Walk' in the Western Crete chapter. The first decision must be made at Sougia. Here the E4 alpine route shoots north and upwards and heads across the high alpine tracts of the barren Lefka Ori, while the E4 coastal route hugs the rugged coastline as far as Kato Rodakino, between Frangokastello and Plakias. The alpine route is for serious trekkers and will involve overnighting in one of three refuges along the way. The E4 coastal route, while not a picnic stroll, is easier, but can be quite rough in parts, particularly between Sougia and Hora Sfakion.

Neither trail actually incorporates the Samaria Gorge as part of its route, but you can easily include it. At Sougia take the first leg of the E4 alpine route as far as Omalos and hike south down the Samaria Gorge to the coast (and the E4 coastal route) at Agia Roumeli. Alpine trekkers can, of course, head north up the gorge from Agia Roumeli and pick up the E4 alpine route at Omalos. The E4 alpine route from Omalos is perhaps the toughest section of the trail and should not be attempted in the heat and aridity of July and August. It is high and exposed and there is no water other than the odd snow bank that may have lingered from winter.

From Argyroupolis, near where the two trails cross each other, the E4 alpine route now runs south of the E4 coastal route which itself loops northwards along the escarpment of the Psiloritis massif. The E4 alpine route runs through the Amari Valley for some way, via Spili and Fourfouras before veering west and up to the summit of Mt Psiloritis (2456m). Both trails meet once more at the Nida Plateau on the eastern side of Crete's highest mountain. See the boxed text 'Hiking on Mt Psiloritis' in the Rethymno & Central Crete chapter.

Heading eastward the now unified trail meanders through the more populated Iraklio prefecture via the villages of Profitis Ilias, Arhanes and Kastelli before climbing once more to the Lasithi Plateau.

From Lasithi the route becomes alpine with a crossing of the Mt Dikti (2148m) range to the south, then turning eastwards for the remote passage down to the narrow 'neck' of Crete between Ierapetra and the Gulf of Mirabello. Mountains take over as the trail threads it way between Mt Thriptis (1476m) to the south and Mt Orno (1238m) to the

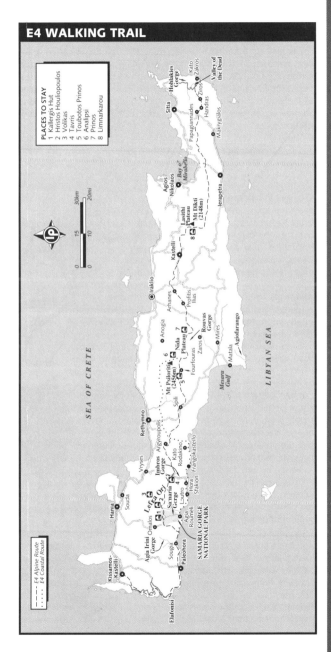

# E4 WALKING TRAIL

PLACES TO STAY
1 Kallergis Hut
2 Hristos Houliopoulos
3 Volikas
4 Tavris
5 Toubotos Prinos
6 Analipsi
7 Prinos
8 Limmarkarou

E4 Alpine Route
E4 Coastal Route

north. Settlements are fewer this end of the island so each day's trekking leg should be planned carefully.

The final leg from Papagiannades and through the villages of Handras and Ziros is less taxing and the last village, Zakros marks the start of the hike through the Valley of the Dead to the sea at Kato Zakros. This is the final leg on the long walk from Portugal (if you have come all the way!). The E4 is no more at the end of the Valley of the Dead. See the boxed text 'Walking the Valley of the Dead' in the Eastern Crete chapter.

The best overall map for anyone planning to walk the E4 is the 1:100,000 Kreta Touristikkarte published by Harms Verlag. See Maps in the Facts About Crete chapter.

## Gorge Walking

Over the aeons, the mountainous terrain of Crete has created a disproportionate number of gorges that rent its often scarred but sometimes lush and verdant landscape. Hikers looking for an invigorating day out often seek these gorges and walk their length. Along the way they enjoy the aroma of wild herbs and flowers, shaded picnic spots, stream wading (in spring and autumn) and the sheer sense of adventure that can be wedged in between days otherwise spent on a beach.

Gorge walking will involve a bit of planning if you have your own transport. You will either have to walk back the same way to pick it up, or arrange for someone to pick you up at the other end of the gorge. Bus riders can normally get to within striking distance of a gorge entrance and can often plan to arrive at an accommodation stop. Most gorge walks are doable by anyone with a reasonable level of fitness, while one or two are possible for a select few only: the Ha Gorge near Mt Thriptis in eastern Crete has apparently been traversed by only 10 persons!

Apart from the famous Samaria Gorge (described in detail in the Western Crete chapter) there are a number of others worth considering. Here is a select list of some of the more accessible ones.

**Agia Irini Gorge** is a full day walk best tackled from the village of Agia Irini north of Sougia. This is a challenging hike with dramatic landscape varying from alpine to coastal. It ends at Sougia.

**Agiofarango** is a popular hike in south-central Crete running from Moni Odigitrias, 24km

MARTIN HARRIS

south-west of Mires. It ends at Agios Nikolaos beach, or hikers can pick up the asphalt again at Kali Limenes to the east.

**Hohlakies Gorge** is not as well known as its near neighbour at Zakros, this short, 3km walk runs from Hohlakies village to the coast. Hikers can walk a further 7km northwards to Palekastro.

**Imbros Gorge** is perhaps the second most popular gorge walk after Samaria. It runs from the village of Imbros 8km to Komitades, near Hora Sfakion. See the description in the Hania & Around chapter.

**Rouvas Gorge** is a short link hike that runs from the village of Zaros on the southern slopes of Psiloritis to meet up with the alpine route of the E4 trail. A convenient way to get to and from the trans-Crete trek.

**The Valley of the Dead** is a three hour hike in far eastern Crete. The valley is the last section of the E4 trekking route and runs from Zakros to the Palace of Kato Zakros. See the description in the Eastern Crete chapter.

## MOUNTAIN CLIMBING

While Crete doesn't offer the kind of stunning alpine terrain to be found in Austria or Switzerland, the island does have a large number of mountains and two mountaineering clubs cater to local and visiting climbers. There are 12 documented climbing sites in Crete that can be virtually assessed at **w** www.climbincrete.com/english/diadromes.htm.

The mountaineering and skiing club of Iraklio (see Places to Stay) was established in 1940 and is a member of the association of Greek Mountaineering Clubs. The club has approximately 200 active members whose activities include mountain climbing, cross country walking and skiing. It is open every day from 8.30pm to 10.30pm. Almost every weekend, the club organises excursions to various locations in Crete and visitors are welcome to participate.

The Mountaineering Club of Hania (see Places to Stay in this special section) was established in 1930 and is also a member of the association of Greek Mountaineering Clubs. The club actively maintains the E4 trail and organises climbing, skiing, canoeing and speleology trips. Contact both clubs before planning a mountaineering trip to Crete.

## SOLO OR PACKAGED?

Whether you DIY or join a group is a matter of personal taste. Ultimately, the main deciding factor is cost. A group tour will generally cost more than if you plan your trip yourself. For cyclists a group tour is usually a better option. Tour companies provide the latest bikes, helmets, support vehicles and can arrange accommodation. Factor that against the cost of freighting your own bike in and working it out yourself. Tour groups are generally more fun since you share the experience with other riders, but you must follow the group's pace rather than set your own.

Hiking and trekking are somewhat different, but the companionship and security afforded by group hikes or climbs should be compared to the higher chances of getting lost in remote areas for independent trekkers. In short, a tour is a better option for travellers with limited time and budget, while a DIY adventure is better suited for travellers with time and experience on their hands.

## PLACES TO STAY

Many accommodation options have been proposed throughout this guide, but our suggestions are not comprehensive, nor do they cover every possible destination. Travellers with bicycles or motorised transport will be spoiled for choice as you will be able to plan your overnight stops to suit your own flexibility. If you are on an organised tour, accommodation may well be part of the deal. Problem solved.

Hikers tackling the E4 trail will need to do some pre-planning. While there is nearly always some accommodation within the range of a six to seven hours daily hike, some of it will need to be arranged beforehand – most particularly the mountain refuge huts on the alpine legs of the E4.

The Mountaineering Club (EOS) of Hania (☎ 2821 074 560, Stratigou Tzanakaki 90, Hania), in Iraklio (EOS; ☎ 281 022 7609, e myrto@her.forthnet.gr, Dikeosynis 53, Iraklio), and in Rethymno (EOS; ☎ 2831 057 766, Dimokratias 12, Rethymno) maintains the following huts:

| name | location | altitude (m) | capacity (beds) | EOS |
| --- | --- | --- | --- | --- |
| Analipsi | Nida Plateau | 1420 | 20 | Rethymno |
| Hristos Houliopoulos | Svourihtis peak, Central Lefka Ori | 1970 | 25 | Hania |
| Kallergis Hut | Near the Samaria Gorge | 1680 | 50 | Hania |
| Prinos | Asites, East Psiloritis | 1100 | 45 | Iraklio |
| Limnarkarou | Lasithi Plateau | 1350 | 15 | Hania |
| Tavris | Plateau of Askyfou | 1200 | 42 | Hania |
| Toubotos Prinos | Mt Psiloritis | 1500 | 28 | Rethymno |
| Volikas | Volikas Keramion | 1400 | 40 | Hania |

You will need to contact the clubs beforehand to organise bookings and key collection. See also w www.multimedia-sa.gr/outdoor/k00eng .htm for a more detailed description of all the huts.

## INTERNET RESOURCES

Outdoor tour operators are slowly making a show of strength on Crete. A few of them have already clocked up a large stock of experience and run very solid operations. Searching the Internet will dredge up a number of leads; meantime the following will give interested travellers enough grist to the mill for an unforgettable experience.

w www.classicadventures.com/crete.htm
   Hiking tour with Classic Adventures
w www.classicadventures.com/crete_bike.htm
   Cycling tour with Classic Adventures
w www.climbincrete.com/indexenglish.shtml
   Excellent information on climbing and mountaineering in Crete including a report on the Ha Gorge
w www.cycling.gr
   Trekking Plan tours

- **w** www.forthnet.gr/internetcity/diexodos
  Diexodos hiking and cycling tours
- **w** www.happywalker.nl
  The Happy Walker of Rethymno
- **w** www.hellasbike.com/SportNet/clients/Michael/Wandern/en/index.htm
  Hiking and biking with Hellas Bike Tours
- **w** www.interkriti.org/orivatikos/hania1.htm
  Mountaineering Club of Hania
- **w** www.interkriti.org/orivatikos/orivat.html
  Mountaineering/Skiing Club of Iraklio
- **w** www.multimedia-sa.gr/outdoor
  Information on rock climbing, hiking, parapente and mountaineering
- **w** www.trekking.gr
  Trekking Hellas tours

*[Continued from page 48]*

a consulate abroad or at least 20 days in advance to the Aliens Bureau (☎ 21 0770 5711), Leoforos Alexandras 173, Athens. Take your passport and four passport photographs along. You may be asked for proof that you can support yourself financially, so keep all your bank exchange slips. These slips are not always automatically given – you may have to ask for them. The Aliens Bureau is open 8am to 1pm weekdays. In Crete apply to the main prefecture in Iraklio. You will be given a permit which will authorise you to stay in Greece for a period of up to six months. Most travellers get around this by visiting Bulgaria or Turkey briefly and then re-entering Greece.

## Travel Insurance

A travel insurance policy to cover theft, loss and medical problems is a good idea. The policies handled by STA Travel and other student travel organisations are usually good value. There is a wide variety of policies available; check the small print. Some policies specifically exclude 'dangerous activities' which can include scuba diving, motorcycling, even trekking. A locally acquired motorcycle licence is not valid under some policies. You may prefer a policy that pays doctors or hospitals direct rather than you having to pay on the spot and claim later. If you have to claim later make sure you keep all documentation. Some policies ask you to call back (reverse charges) to a centre in your home country where an immediate assessment of your problem is made. Check that the policy covers ambulances or an emergency flight home.

## Driving Licence & Permits

Crete recognises all national driving licences, provided the licence has been held for at least one year. It also recognises an International Driving Permit, which should be obtained before you leave home. If you plan to rent a motorcycle in Crete it is a good idea to have a separate motorcycle licence, as a growing number of rental agencies are now asking for them.

## Hostel Cards

A Hostelling International (HI) card is of no use in Crete.

## Student & Youth Cards

The most widely recognised (and thus the most useful) form of student ID is the International Student Identity Card (ISIC). Holders qualify for half-price admission to some museums and ancient sites. There are no travel agencies authorised to issue ISICs in Crete, so it would be wise to arrange for one before leaving home.

## Copies

All important documents (passport data page and visa page, credit cards, travel insurance policy, air/bus/train tickets, driving

---

### Student Cards

An ISIC (International Student Identity Card) is a plastic ID-style card displaying your photograph. These cards are widely available from budget travel agencies (take along proof that you are a student). In Athens you can get one from the International Student & Youth Travel Service (ISYTS; ☎ 21 0323 3767), 2nd floor, Nikis 11, Athens.

Some travel agencies in Greece offer discounts on organised tours to students. However, there are no student discounts for travel within Greece (although Olympic Airways gives a 25% discount on domestic flights that are part of an international flight). Turkish Airlines (THY) gives 55% student discounts on its international flights. THY has flights from Athens to İstanbul and İzmir. Most ferries to Cyprus, Israel and Egypt from Piraeus give a 20% student discount and a few of the services between Greek and Italian ports do so also. If you are under 26 years but not a student, the Federation of International Youth Travel Organisation (FIYTO) card gives similar discounts. Many budget travel agencies issue FIYTO cards including London Explorers Club (☎ 020 7792 3770), 33 Princes Square, Bayswater, London W2 and SRS Studenten Reise Service (☎ 030 2 83 30 93), Marienstrasse 23, Berlin.

licence etc) should be photocopied before you leave home. Leave one copy with someone at home and keep another with you, separate from the originals.

It is also a good idea to store details of your vital travel documents in Lonely Planet's free online Travel Vault (**W** www .ekno.lonelyplanet.com) in case you lose the photocopies or can't be bothered with them. Your password-protected Travel Vault is accessible online from anywhere in the world.

## EMBASSIES & CONSULATES
### Greek Embassies & Consulates
The following is a selection of Greek diplomatic missions abroad:

**Australia** (☎ 02 6273 3011) 9 Turrana St, Yarralumla, Canberra ACT 2600
**Bulgaria** (☎ 02 946 1027) San Stefano 33, Sofia 1504
**Canada** (☎ 613-238 6271) 76-80 Maclaren St, Ottawa, Ontario K2P OK6
**Cyprus** (☎ 02 441 880) Byron Boulevard 8–10, Lefkosia
**Denmark** (☎ 33 11 45 33) Borgergade 16, DK-1300 Copenhagen K
**France** (☎ 01 47 23 72 28) 17 Rue Auguste Vacquerie, F-75116 Paris
**Germany** (☎ 0228 83 010) An Der Marienkapelleb 10, D-53179 Bonn
**Ireland** (☎ 21 676 7254) 1 Upper Pembroke St, Dublin 2
**Israel** (☎ 03 605 5461) 47 Bodenheimer St, Tel Aviv 62008
**Italy** (☎ 06 854 9630) Via S Mercadante 36, Rome I-00198
**Japan** (☎ 03 340 0871/0872) 3-16-30 Nishi Azabu, Minato-ku, Tokyo 106
**Netherlands** (☎ 070 363 87 00) Koning-innegracht 37, NL-2514 AD, Den Hague
**New Zealand** (☎ 04 473 7775) 5–7 Willeston St, Wellington
**Norway** (☎ 22 44 2728) Nobels Gate 45, N-0244 Oslo 2
**South Africa** (☎ 12 437 351/352) 995 Pretorius Street, Arcadia, Pretoria 0083
**Spain** (☎ 91 564 4653) Avenida Doctor Arce 24, Madrid E-28002
**Sweden** (☎ 08 663 7577) Riddargatan 60, S-11457 Stockholm
**Switzerland** (☎ 031 951 08 14) Postfach, CH-3000 Berne 6, Kirchenfeld
**Turkey** (☎ 312 436 8860) Ziya-ul-Rahman Caddesi 9-11, Gaziosmanpaşa 06700, Ankara

**UK** (☎ 020 7229 3850) 1A Holland Park, London W11 3TP
**USA** (☎ 202-939 5818) 2221 Massachusetts Ave NW, Washington DC 20008

### Embassies & Consulates in Crete
The UK embassy in Iraklio is the only foreign embassy in Crete. The rest are in Athens and its suburbs.

They include:

**Australia** (☎ 21 0645 0404), Dimitriou Soutsou 37, GR-115 21
**Bulgaria** (☎ 21 0647 8105) Stratigou Kalari 33A, Psyhiko, GR-154 52
**Canada** (☎ 21 0727 3400) Gennadiou 4, GR-115 21
**Cyprus** (☎ 21 0723 7883) Irodotou 16, GR-106 75
**France** (☎ 21 0339 1000) Leoforos Vasilissis Sofias 7, GR-106 71
**Germany** (☎ 21 0728 5111) Dimitriou 3 & Karaoli, Kolonaki, GR-106 75
**Ireland** (☎ 21 0723 2771) Leoforos Vasileos Konstantinou 7, GR-106 74
**Israel** (☎ 21 0671 9530) Marathonodromou 1, Psyhiko, GR-154 52
**Italy** (☎ 21 0361 7260) Sekeri 2, GR-106 74
**Japan** (☎ 21 775 8101) Athens Tower, Leoforos Mesogion 2-4, GR-115 27
**Netherlands** (☎ 21 0723 9701) Vasileos Konstantinou 5-7, GR-106 74
**New Zealand (Consulate)** (☎ 21 0771 0112) Xenias 24, GR-115 28
**South Africa** (☎ 21 0680 6645) Kifisias 60, Marousi, GR-151 25
**Turkey** (☎ 21 0724 5915) Vasileos Georgiou 8, GR-106 74
**UK** (☎ 21 0723 6211) Ploutarhou 1, GR-106 75; (☎ 281 022 4012) Papalexandrou 16, Iraklio, Crete
**USA** (☎ 21 0721 2951) Leoforos Vasilissis Sofias 91, GR-115 21

Generally speaking, your own country's embassy won't be much help in emergencies if the trouble you're in is remotely your own fault. Remember that you are bound by Greek laws. Your embassy will not be sympathetic if you end up in jail after committing a crime locally, even if such actions are legal in your own country.

In genuine emergencies you might get some assistance, but only if other channels have been exhausted. For example, if you need to get home urgently, a free ticket home is exceedingly unlikely – the embassy would expect you to have insurance. If you have all your money and documents stolen, it might assist with getting a new passport, but a loan for onward travel is out of the question.

## CUSTOMS

There are no longer duty-free restrictions within the European Union (EU). This does not mean, however, that customs checks have been dispensed with – random searches are still made for drugs. Upon entering the country from outside the EU, customs inspection is usually cursory for foreign tourists. There may be spot checks, but you probably won't have to open your bags. You may bring the following into Crete duty-free: 200 cigarettes or 50 cigars; 1L of spirits or 2L of wine; 50g of perfume; 250ml of eau de Cologne; one camera (still or video) and film; a pair of binoculars; a portable musical instrument; a radio or tape recorder; a typewriter; sports equipment; and dogs and cats (with a veterinary certificate).

Importation of works of art and antiquities is free, but they must be declared on entry, so that they can be re-exported. Import regulations for medicines are strict; if you are taking medication, make sure you get a statement from your doctor before you leave home. It is illegal, for instance, to take codeine into Crete without an accompanying doctor's certificate.

An unlimited amount of foreign currency and travellers cheques may be brought into Crete. If, however, you intend to leave the country with foreign banknotes in excess of $1000, you must declare the sum upon entry.

It is strictly forbidden to export antiquities (anything over 100 years old) without an export permit. This crime is second only to drug smuggling in the penalties imposed. It is an offence to remove even the smallest article from an archaeological site.

The place to apply for an export permit is the Antique Dealers & Private Collections Section, Archaeological Service, Polygnotou 13, Athens.

Cars can be brought into Greece for six months without a carnet (a customs licence); only a green card (international third party insurance) is required. Cars entering from EU Italy will be subject to no customs formalities whatsoever.

## MONEY
### Currency

The unit of currency in Crete is the euro (€). Coins come in denominations of one, two, five, 10, 20, and 50 cents. Banknotes come in €5, €10, €20, €50, €100 and €500.

### Exchange Rates

| country | unit | | euro |
|---|---|---|---|
| Australia | A$1 | = | €0.57 |
| Canada | C$1 | = | €0.71 |
| Cyprus | CY£ | = | €1.82 |
| Japan | ¥100 | = | €0.91 |
| New Zealand | NZ$1 | = | €0.47 |
| Norway | NK1 | = | €0.13 |
| South Africa | SAR1 | = | €0.12 |
| Switzerland | SFr1 | = | €0.68 |
| Turkey | TL1,000,000 | = | €0.71 |
| United Kingdom | UK£1 | = | €1.60 |
| United States | US$1 | = | €1.12 |

### Exchanging Money

Banks will exchange all major currencies in either cash, travellers cheques or Eurocheques. The best-known travellers cheques in Crete are Thomas Cook and American Express. A passport is required to change travellers cheques, but not cash.

Commission charged on the exchange of banknotes and travellers cheques varies not only from bank to bank but from branch to branch. It's less for cash than for travellers cheques. For travellers cheques the commission is €1 for up to €60; €1.30 for amounts between €60 and €100; and a flat rate of 1.5% on amounts over €100.

Post offices can exchange banknotes – but not travellers cheques – and charge less commission than banks. Many travel agencies and hotels will also change money and travellers cheques at bank rates, but their commission charges are higher.

If there is a chance that you may apply for a visa extension, make sure you receive, and keep hold of, a bank exchange slip after each transaction.

**Cash** Nothing beats cash for convenience – or for risk. If you lose it, it's gone for good and very few travel insurers will come to your rescue. Those that will, normally limit the amount to about $300. It's best to carry no more cash than you need for the next few days, which means working out your likely needs when you change travellers cheques or withdraw cash from an ATM (automatic teller machine).

It's also a good idea to set aside a small amount of cash, say $50, as an emergency stash.

**Travellers Cheques** The main reason to carry travellers cheques rather than cash is the protection they offer against theft. They are, however, losing popularity as more and more travellers opt to put their money in a bank at home and withdraw it at ATMs as they go along.

American Express, Visa and Thomas Cook cheques are all widely accepted and have efficient replacement policies. Maintaining a record of the cheque numbers and recording when you use them is vital when it comes to replacing lost cheques. Keep this record separate from the cheques themselves. US dollars is a good currency to use.

**ATMs** ATMs are to be found in almost every town large enough to support a bank – and certainly in all the tourist areas. If you've got MasterCard or Visa/Access, there are plenty of places to withdraw money.

Cirrus, Plus and Maestro users can make withdrawals in all major towns and tourist areas.

AFEMs (Automatic Foreign Exchange Machines) are common in major tourist areas. They take all the major European currencies, Australian and US dollars and Japanese yen, and are useful in an emergency.

**Credit Cards** The great advantage of credit cards is that they allow you to pay for major items without carrying around great wads of cash. Credit cards are now an accepted part of the commercial scene just about everywhere in Crete. They can be used to pay for a wide range of goods and services such as upmarket meals and accommodation, car hire and souvenir shopping.

If you are not familiar with the card options, ask your bank to explain the workings and relative merits of the various schemes: cash cards, charge cards and credit cards. Ask whether the card can be replaced in Crete if it is lost or stolen.

The main credit cards are MasterCard, Visa (Access in the UK) and Eurocard, all of which are widely accepted in Crete. They can also be used as cash cards to draw euros from ATMs of affiliated Greek banks in the same way as at home. Daily withdrawal limits are set by the issuing bank. Cash advances are given in local currency only. Credit cards can be used to pay for accommodation in all the classier hotels. Some C-class hotels will accept credit cards, but D- and E-class hotels rarely do. Most upmarket shops and restaurants accept credit cards but the village tavernas do not.

The main charge cards are American Express and Diner's Club card, which are widely accepted in tourist areas but unheard of elsewhere.

**International Transfers** If you run out of money, or need more for whatever reason, you can instruct your bank back home to send you a draft. Specify the city and the bank as well as the branch that you want the money sent to. If you have the choice, select a large bank and ask for the international division. Money sent by electronic transfer should reach you within 24 hours.

### Security

The safest way of carrying cash and valuables (passport, travellers cheques, credit cards etc) is a favourite topic of travel conversation. The simple answer is that there is no foolproof method. The general principle is to keep things out of sight. The front pouch belt, for example, presents an obvious target for a would-be thief – only marginally less inviting than a fat wallet bulging from your back pocket.

**Phone numbers listed incorporate changes due in Oct 2002; see p61**

The best place is under your clothes in contact with your skin where, hopefully, you will be aware of an alien hand before it's too late. Most people opt for a money belt, while others prefer a leather pouch hung around the neck. Whichever method you choose, put your valuables in a plastic bag first – otherwise they will get soaked in sweat as you wander around in the heat.

## Costs

Crete is cheap by northern European standards, but it is no longer dirt-cheap, especially in the high season (July and August). A rock-bottom daily budget would be €25.

This would mean hitching, staying in youth hostels or camping, staying away from bars, and only occasionally eating in restaurants or taking ferries. Allow at least €40 per day in the summer for a simple room, meals in local tavernas, drinks at night and some sightseeing. Outside of the high season you could get by on about 25% less. If you really want a holiday – comfortable rooms and restaurants all the way – you will need closer to €60 per day. These budgets are for individuals. Couples sharing a double room can get by on less.

## Tipping & Bargaining

In restaurants the service charge is included in the bill but it is the custom to leave a small tip. The practice is often just to round off the bill. Likewise for taxis – a small amount is appreciated.

Bargaining is not as widespread in Crete as it is further east. Prices in most shops are clearly marked and non-negotiable. The same applies to restaurants and public transport. However, it is always worth bargaining over the price of hotel rooms or *domatia* (the Greek equivalent of the British bed and breakfast, minus the breakfast), especially if you are intending to stay a few days. You may get short shrift in peak season, but prices can drop dramatically in the off season. Souvenir shops and market stalls are other places where your negotiating skills will come in handy. If you feel uncomfortable about haggling, walking away can be just as effective – you can always go back.

## POST & COMMUNICATIONS

Post offices *(tahydromia)* are easily identifiable by means of the yellow signs outside. Regular post boxes are also yellow. The red boxes are for express mail only.

## Postal Rates

The postal rate for postcards and airmail letters to destinations within the EU is €0.50 for up to 20g and €0.80 for up to 50g. To other destinations the rate is €0.60 for up to 20g and €0.90 for up to 150g. Post within Europe takes four to five days and to the USA, Australia and New Zealand, five to eight days. Some tourist shops also sell stamps, but with a 10% surcharge.

Express mail costs an extra €1.20 and should ensure delivery in three days within the EU – use the special red post boxes. Valuables should be sent registered post, which costs an extra €1.

## Sending Mail

It is usually advisable not to wrap a parcel before you post it. The post office may (but not always) wish to inspect the contents. In Iraklio, take your parcel to the central post office on Plateia Daskalogianni, and elsewhere to the parcel counter of a regular post office.

## Receiving Mail

You can receive mail poste restante (general delivery) at any main post office. The service is free, but you are required to show your passport. Ask senders to write your family name in capital letters on the envelope and underline it, and to mark the envelope 'poste restante'. It is a good idea to ask the post office clerk to check under your first name as well if letters you are expecting cannot be located.

After one month, uncollected mail is returned to the sender. If you are about to leave a town and expected mail hasn't arrived, ask at the post office to have it forwarded to your next destination, c/o poste restante.

Parcels are not delivered in Crete, they must be collected from the post office.

## Warning: Phone Number Changes

Greece is implementing a new national numbering plan to alleviate a shortage of numbers in the telephone system and to allow users to better understand call charges. As a result dialling numbers in Greece could be a little problematic during 2002.

The new plan means that all numbers now have 10 digits. The key features of the scheme are:

The area code now has to be dialled for every number, even when calling from within the same geographical area. So, for instance, to call an Athens number from within Athens, you need to include the area code 01.

Also, all numbers now have a 0 added at the start of the local number (which follows the area code). For example, if you want to dial the old Athens number 01-123 4567 it now becomes 01 0123 4567.

To further complicate things, from **20 October 2002**, the area code's leading 0 will be replaced with a 2 for fixed phones and with a 6 for mobile phones. So the Athens number 01 0123 4567 will change to 21 0123 4567. The numbers listed in this book incorporate this change, so **if you dial any number in this book before 20 October 2002 remember to dial 0 instead of the first digit.**

The old numbers will work until 20 January 2002; from then until 20 October 2002 callers to old numbers will get a recorded message.

## Telephone

The Greek telephone service is maintained by the public corporation known as Organismos Tilepikinonion Elladas, which is always referred to by the acronym OTE (pronounced o-tay). The system is modern and efficient. Public telephones all take phonecards, which cost €3 for 100 units, €5.30 for 200 units, €12.30 for 500 units, and €24 for 1000 units. The 100-unit cards are widely available at *periptera*, corner shops and tourist shops; the others can be bought at OTE offices.

The phones are easy to operate and can be used for local, long distance and international calls. The 'i' at the top left of the push-button dialling panel brings up the operating instructions in English. Don't remove your card before you are told to do so or you will wipe out the remaining credit. Local calls cost one unit per minute.

It is possible to use various national card schemes, such as Telstra Australia's Telecard, to make international calls. You will still need a phonecard to dial the scheme's access number, which will cost you one unit, and the time you spend on the phone is charged at local call rates.

Villages and remote islands without OTE offices almost always have at least one metered phone for international and long distance calls – usually in a shop, *kafeneio* (cafe) or taverna.

Reverse charge (collect) calls can be made from an OTE office. If you are using a private phone to make a reverse charge call, dial the operator (domestic ☎ 151, international ☎ 161).

To call overseas direct from Crete, dial the Greek overseas access code (☎ 00), followed by the country code for the country you are calling, then the local area code (dropping the leading zero if there is one) and then the number. The following table lists some country codes and per-minute charges:

| country | code | cost per minute |
|---|---|---|
| Australia | ☎ 61 | €0.70 |
| France | ☎ 33 | €0.53 |
| Germany | ☎ 49 | €0.53 |
| Ireland | ☎ 353 | €0.53 |
| Italy | ☎ 39 | €0.53 |
| Japan | ☎ 81 | €0.70 |
| Netherlands | ☎ 31 | €0.53 |
| New Zealand | ☎ 64 | €0.70 |
| Turkey | ☎ 90 | €0.53 |
| UK | ☎ 44 | €0.53 |
| USA & Canada | ☎ 1 | €0.70 |

Off-peak rates are 25% cheaper. They are available to Africa, Europe, the Middle East and India between 10pm and 6am; to the Americas between 11pm and 8am; and to Asia and Oceania between 8pm and 5am.

## Mobile Phones/Cellphones

If you have a compatible GSM mobile/ cellphone from a country with an overseas global roaming arrangement with Greece, you will be able to use your phone in Crete. You must inform your mobile/cellphone service provider before you depart in order to have global roaming activated.

Greece has three mobile/cellphone service providers – Panafon, CosmOTE and Telestet. Of the three CosmOTE tends to have the best coverage in more remote areas like some of the remoter villages, so you could try re-tuning your phone to CosmOTE if you find mobile coverage is patchy. All three companies offer pay-as-you-talk services so you can buy a rechargeable SIM card and have your own Greek mobile number: a good idea if you plan to spend time in Greece. The Panafon system is called *à la Carte*, the Telestet system *B-free* and CosmOTE's *COSMO KARTA*. These pay-as-you-talk services now automatically revert to global roaming when you leave Greece and can be used to send and receive short email messages.

### Useful Phone Numbers

| Directory inquiries | ☎ 131 |
| International dialling instructions in English, French and German | ☎ 169 |
| International access code to call Greece | ☎ 30 |
| International access code from within Greece | ☎ 00 |
| International Operator | ☎ 161 |

**Toll-free 24-hour emergency numbers:**

| Ambulance | ☎ 100 |
| Fire Brigade | ☎ 199 |
| Forestry Fire Service | ☎ 191 |
| Police | ☎ 100 |
| Roadside Assistance (ELPA) | ☎ 104 |
| Tourist Police | ☎ 171 |

USA and Canadian mobile phone users will not be able to use their mobile phones in Greece, unless they are dual system equipped.

## Fax & Telegraph

Most post offices have fax machines; telegrams can be sent from any OTE office.

## Email & Internet Access

Crete has a reasonable number of Internet cafes and each major town will have several places to surf and check your mail. Smaller towns and villages may have just the one place. Access costs vary little and range from €2.40 to €3.50 per hour. Travellers with their own PCs or modem equipped personal organisers may be able to arrange Internet roaming with their local ISP as there are reliable dialup numbers in Crete.

There has also been a huge increase in the number of hotels and businesses using email, and these addresses have been listed where available. Some hotels catering for travellers offer Internet access.

## INTERNET RESOURCES

The Lonely Planet Web site (W www.lonely planet.com) has information on Crete, as well as travel news, updates to our guidebooks and links to other travel resources. You may also find these sites useful:

**Explore Crete** Good general travel site for Crete
  W www.explorecrete.com
**GNTO** GNTO's page for Crete
  W www.areianet.gr/infoxenios/english/crete/
**goCrete.com** Internet guide to Crete
  W www.gocrete.com
**GTP schedule** Greek ferry schedules
  W www.gtpnet.gr
**InfoCrete** A site with about 100 Crete tourist site Web links
  W www.infocrete.com
**Interkriti** Links to hotels, apartments, shops and restaurants as well as an active bulletin board
  W www.interkriti.gr
**KTEL** Maps and schedules of buses around the island
  W www.ktel.org
**OTE** Online telephone directory for Crete with white pages in Greek and yellow pages in English
  W www.ote.gr

Stigmes Magazine of Crete
**W** www.forthnet.gr/stigmes/destcret.htm

## BOOKS

Most books are published in different editions by different publishers in different countries. As a result, a book might be a hardcover rarity in one country while it's readily available in paperback in another. Fortunately, bookshops and libraries search by title or author, so your local bookshop or library is best placed to advise you on the availability of the following titles.

### Lonely Planet

The 5th edition of Lonely Planet's guide to *Greece* has comprehensive coverage of mainland Greece as well as the islands (including Crete), while the Lonely Planet guides to *Mediterranean Europe* and *Western Europe* also include coverage of Crete, as does *Europe on a Shoestring*. If you are heading for the Dodecanese Islands from Agios Nikolaos or Sitia in eastern Crete, Lonely Planet's *Rhodes & the Dodecanese Islands* is the ideal follow-on companion. Lonely Planet's *Athens* guide will give you the full low-down to the nation's capital. The handy *Greek Phrasebook* will help enrich your visit.

Katherine Kizilos vividly evokes Greece's landscapes, people and politics in her book *The Olive Grove: Travels in Greece*. She explores the islands and borderlands of her father's homeland, and life in her family's village in the Peloponnese Mountains. The book is part of Lonely Planet's Journeys travel literature series.

These titles are available at major English-language bookshops in Iraklio, Hania and Rethymno. See the Bookshops entries in these sections for more details.

### Guidebooks

For archaeology buffs, the *Crete Blue Guide* is hard to beat. It goes into tremendous detail about all the major sites, and many of the lesser known ones.

### Travel

*Still Life in Crete* by Anthony Cox is a humorous and off-beat look at migration from Kent to Crete by an early-retired British couple. It is big on food and wine and tongue-in-cheek observations of life away from the grey skies of England.

*Crete* by John Freely is a slightly dated (1990) but still quite readable travelogue about Crete based on the writer's time spent as a resident of Hania. The book covers Cretan history as well as tips on where to go and what to see.

*Winds of Crete* by David MacNeill Doren is widely available on Crete. It's an amusing account of island life as experienced by an American and his Swedish wife.

*The Colossus of Maroussi* by Henry Miller is now regarded as a classic. Miller relates his travels in Crete at the outbreak of WWII with feverish enthusiasm.

*Across Crete* by Richard Pokocke, Robert Pashley, Captain Spratt and Edward Lear and edited by Johan de Bakker is the first of a three-part series that takes the traveller from Hania to Iraklio as seen through the eyes of the 18th- and 19th-century British travellers.

### People & Society

*The Chania Town News* by Douglas Bullis, published in 2001 is, by one account, 'the best book about modern Crete and by another', 'a brilliant you-are-there travelogue'. The Town News is a witty, wacky look at Crete by an ebullient American writer.

*The Greeks* by James Pettifer is a worthwhile read for a remarkably accurate look at Greek contemporary life from a historical, societal, environmental and ethnographical perspective.

*Culture Shock! Greece* another title in this ever-expanding series, is good for intending long-term visitors to Greece, or for persons planning to settle in the country. It is a rather dry guide to customs and etiquette and seen through occasionally tinted, British-made spectacles, but worth a browse.

Patricia Storeace's *Dinner with Persephone* is as much a travelogue as it is a series of sociological observations seen through the eyes of an American woman living in Greece. Every woman traveller to Greece should read this book.

**Phone numbers listed incorporate changes due in Oct 2002; see p61**

## History & Mythology

*Knossos: Searching for the Legendary Palace of King Minos* by Alexandre Farnaux is an English translation of an eminently readable archaeological account of the search for the mythical palace.

*Minoan & Mycenaean Art* by Reynold Higgins is a thorough pictorial catalogue of the finest examples of early Greek art from Crete, Mycenae and the Cyclades.

*Minotaur: Sir Arthur Evans and the Archaeology of the Minoan Myth* by Joseph Alexander McGillivray is a fascinating portrait of the British archaeologist who revealed the Palace of Knossos to the world.

*Linear B and Related Scrips* by John Chadwick is a riveting insight into the process of decipherment of the Linear B scripts that extended Greek linguistic history further than had been imagined possible.

*Post Minoan Crete* by W J Cavanagh. What happened after the collapse of the Cretan palaces in 1450 BC? Did Crete become a backwater or just devolve into a different civilisation? This study looks at a hitherto little known period of Cretan history.

*Herakleion Museum – Illustrated Guide* by JA Sakelarakis and *Knossos – A Complete Guide to the Palace of King Minos* by Anna Mihaelidou are two glossy guides to Crete's best-known archaeological attractions.

Mythology was an intrinsic part of life in ancient Crete, and some knowledge of it will enhance your visit. *The Greek Myths* by Robert Graves is regarded as the definitive book on the subject. Maureen O'Sullivan's *An Iconoclast's Guide to the Greek Gods* presents entertaining and accessible versions of the myths.

Mary Renault's novels provide an excellent feel for ancient Crete. *The King Must Die* and *The Bull from the Sea* are vivid tales of Minoan times.

*History of Crete* by Theoharis E Detorakis is an extraordinarily complete guide to Cretan history from the Minoan times up to, but not including, the Battle of Crete.

George Psychoundakis' *The Cretan Runner* is an exciting and personal account of the Cretan resistance. The author was a runner delivering messages to the Allies.

*The Road to Prevelly* by Geoffrey Edwards, published in 1989, is an autobiographical account of Edwards' experiences during the Battle of Crete in 1941. Under German attack, he was rescued and sheltered by the monks of the Preveli Monastery and eventually repatriated to Australia.

*Crete: The Battle and the Resistance* by Antony Beevor is a short and readable analysis of the Allied defeat.

## Poetry & Theatre

Cretan literature flourished in the 16th and 17th centuries, a time when Crete enjoyed an enlightened renaissance and rich literary output. Among the many works that appeared between 1570 and 1669 were two worth mentioning here, both available in translation.

*Erotokritos* by Vitsentzos Kornaros is the archetypal, classic Cretan epic love story. Experts prefer to call it a narrative poem or a verse romance. Either way, *Erotokritos* is a love story about the hero Erotokritos and his love, Princess Aretousa. Set in ancient Athens but written in the Middle Ages (1650) it is the story of a princess and the commoner who seeks her hand but who is not considered quite suitable. The epic poem tells the story of the lovers' eventual triumph against adversity. David Holton's commentary *Erotokritos* is the best academic study of the epic.

The *Sacrifice of Abraham* most probably written by Vitsentzos Kornaros in his youth (1635) is the theatrical adaptation of the well-known biblical episode. The play was a popular piece of literature at the time as the succession of editions proves.

*Literature and Society in Renaissance Crete* by David Holton is a comprehensive study of the literature of the Cretan Renaissance in its historical, social and cultural context, with chapters on the poetic and dramatic genres contributed by leading experts in the field.

## Novels

The most well-known and widely-read Greek author is the Cretan Nikos Kazantzakis, whose novels are full of drama and larger-than-life characters. His most famous works are *The Last Temptation*, *Zorba the Greek*, *Christ Recrucified* and *Freedom or Death*. The first two have been made into films. *Zorba the Greek* takes place on Crete and provides a fascinating glimpse of the harsher side of Cretan culture. Zorba is one of the world's greatest literary characters but women need to be prepared for a mega-dose of misogyny.

## Botanical Field Guides

*The Flowers of Greece & the Aegean* by William Taylor and Anthony Huxley is the most comprehensive field guide to flowers in Greece and Crete.

## Cookbooks

*Cretan Cooking* by Maria and Nikos Psilakis is a well-compiled and, for once, well-translated version of their widely popular guide to Cretan cooking. It contains 265 mouth-watering recipes and a series of fascinating asides on the history of the dishes and background to the Cretan dietary phenomenon so strongly supported and promoted by health officials the world over. It is available in most tourist bookshops in Crete.

## Children's Books

The Greek publisher Malliaris-Paedia produces a good series of books on Greek myths, retold in English for young readers by Aristides Kesopoulos. The titles are *The Gods of Olympus and the Lesser Gods*, *The Labours of Hercules*, *Theseus and the Voyage of the Argonauts*, *The Trojan War and the Wanderings of Odysseus* and *Heroes and Mythical Creatures*.

*The Moon Over Crete* by Jyotsna Sreenivasen and Sim Gellman is a modern day story based in Crete written for young girls but with a mature message.

## Bookshops

There are several English-language bookshops in Iraklio, as well as shops selling books in French, German and Italian. There are also good foreign-language bookshops in Hania, Rethymno and Agios Nikolaos (see those sections for details).

All other major towns and tourist resorts have bookshops that sell some foreign-language books. Imported books are expensive – normally two to three times the recommended retail price in the UK and the USA. Many hotels have second-hand books to read or swap.

Abroad, the best bookshop for new and second-hand books about Crete, written in English and Greek, is the Hellenic Book Service (☎ 020 7267 9499, fax 020 7267 9498), 91 Fortess Rd, Kentish Town, London NW5 1AG. It stocks almost all of the books recommended here.

## FILMS

The most famous movie filmed on Crete was undoubtedly *Zorba the Greek* which was shot in Stavros on the Akrotiri Peninsula as well as other locations. In 1956, the American director Jules Dassin *(Never On Sunday)* chose Kritsa as the backdrop for *He Who Must Die*, the film version of Katzantzakis' novel *Christ Recrucified* starring Dassin's wife, Melina Mercouri. The film lovingly captured the worn faces of the villagers, many of whom acted in the film.

## NEWSPAPERS & MAGAZINES

Greeks are great newspaper readers. There are 15 daily newspapers, of which the most widely read are *Ta Nea*, *Kathimerini* and *Eleftheros Typos*.

The main English-language newspapers are the daily (except Monday) *Athens News* (€0.90) which carries Greek and international news, and the weekly *Hellenic Times* (€0.90), with predominantly Greek news. The English and German newspaper, *Cretasummer*, is published monthly during the summer in Rethymno and contains Greek news, Cretan features and many ads. The monthly magazine, *Kreta*, is on sale in a variety of languages and contains useful information amidst the ads. In addition to these, the Athens edition of the *International Herald Tribune* (€1.20) includes an eight page English-language section of the Greek daily *Kathimerini*. All are widely available in Iraklio and at major resorts. You'll find the electronic edition of the

*Athens News* at W athensnews.dolnet.gr on the Internet. The site's archives date back to 1995.

Foreign newspapers are also widely available. You'll find all the British and other major European dailies at all tourist centres, as well as international magazines such as *Time*, *Newsweek* and the *Economist*.

## RADIO & TV

Crete has two state-owned radio channels, ET 1 and ET 2. ET 1 runs three programs; two are devoted to popular music and news, while the third plays mostly classical music. It has a news update in English at 7.30am Monday to Saturday, and at 9pm Monday to Friday. It can be heard on 91.6 MHz and 105.8 MHz on the FM band, and 729 KHz on the AM band. ET 2 broadcasts mainly popular music.

Commercial radio stations tend to confine their broadcasts to major urban areas. The mountains that dominate most of the Cretan landscape mean that FM station receptivity changes very rapidly as you move from one valley to another.

Very few AM band radio stations can now be picked up in Crete.

The best shortwave frequencies for picking up the BBC World Service are:

| GMT | frequency |
| --- | --- |
| 3am to 7.30am | 9.41 MHz (31m band) |
| | 6.18 MHz (49m band) |
| | 15.07 MHz (19m band) |
| 7.30am to 6pm | 12.09 MHz (25m band) |
| | 15.07 MHz (19m band) |
| 6.30pm to 11.15pm | 12.09 MHz (25m band) |
| | 9.41 MHz (31m band) |
| | 6.18 MHz (49m band) |

As far as Greek TV is concerned, it's a case of quantity rather than quality. There are nine TV channels and various pay TV channels. All the channels show English and US films and soapies with Greek subtitles. A bit of channel-swapping will normally turn up something in English. Local Cretan channels include Creta Channel, Kastro TV, Kidon TV, CreteTV, Crete 1, and Sitia TV. Most of the better quality hotels and a growing number of domatia or studios include a TV as part of the room package deal and some have satellite TV on tap. Similarly, many traveller bars and hostels now have satellite TV where you can pick up CNN, BBC and all your favourite sport or music channels.

## VIDEO SYSTEMS

If you want to record or buy video tapes to play back home, you won't get a picture unless the image registration systems are the same. Crete uses PAL, which is incompatible with the North American and Japanese NTSC system. Australia and most of Europe use PAL.

## PHOTOGRAPHY & VIDEO
### Film & Equipment

Major brands of film are widely available. In Iraklio, expect to pay about €4.40 for a 36 exposure roll of Kodak Gold ASA 100; less for other brands. You'll find all the gear you need in the photography shops of Iraklio and other major towns and tourist areas.

Because of the brilliant sunlight in summer, you'll get better results using a polarising lens filter.

As elsewhere in the world, developing film is a competitive business. Most places charge around €0.25 per print, plus a €1.20 service charge.

### Restrictions

Never photograph a military installation or anything else that has a sign forbidding photography. Flash photography is not allowed inside churches, and it's considered taboo to photograph the main altar.

Cretans usually love having their photos taken, but always ask permission first. The same goes for video cameras.

## TIME

Crete is two hours ahead of GMT/UTC and three hours ahead on daylight-saving time, which begins on the last Sunday in March when clocks are put forward one hour. Daylight-saving ends on the last Sunday in September. So, when it is noon in Crete it is 10am in London, 11am in Rome, 2am in San Francisco, 5am in New York and

Toronto, 8pm in Sydney and 10pm in Auckland.

## ELECTRICITY
Electricity is 220V, 50 cycles. Plugs are the standard continental type with two round pins. All hotel rooms have power points and most camping grounds have supply points.

## WEIGHTS & MEASURES
Crete uses the metric system. Liquids – especially barrel wine – are sold by weight rather than volume: 959g of wine, for example, is equivalent to 1000mL.

Remember that, like other continental Europeans, Greeks indicate decimals with commas and thousands with points.

## LAUNDRY
Large towns and some islands have laundrettes. They charge from €6 to €7.50 to wash and dry a load whether you do it yourself or have it service-washed. Hostels and room owners will usually provide you with a washtub.

## TOILETS
Most places in Crete have Western-style toilets, especially hotels and restaurants that cater for tourists. You'll occasionally come across Asian-style squat toilets in older houses, *kafeneia* and public toilets.

Public toilets are rare, except at airports and bus and train stations. Cafes are the best option if you get caught short, but you'll be expected to buy something for the privilege.

One peculiarity of the Cretan plumbing system is that it can't handle toilet paper, apparently the pipes are too narrow. Whatever the reason, anything larger than a postage stamp seems to cause a problem. Flushing away tampons and sanitary napkins is guaranteed to block the system. Toilet paper etc should be placed in the small bin provided in every toilet.

## HEALTH
Travel health depends on your pre-departure preparations, your day-to-day health care while travelling and how you handle any medical problem or emergency that does

develop. While the list of potential dangers can seem frightening, few travellers experience more than upset stomachs.

## Pre-departure Planning
**Health Insurance** See Travel Insurance under Visas & Documents earlier in this chapter for information.

**Warning** Codeine, which is commonly found in headache preparations, is banned in Crete; check labels carefully, or risk prosecution.

There are strict regulations applying to the importation of medicines into Crete, so obtain a certificate from your doctor which outlines any medication you may have to carry into the country with you.

**Health Preparations** Make sure you're healthy before you start travelling. If you are embarking on a long trip make sure your teeth are OK.

If you wear glasses take a spare pair and your prescription.

If you require a particular medication take an adequate supply with you, as it may not be available in Crete. Take the prescription or, better still, part of the packaging showing the generic rather than the brand name you use at home (which may not be locally available), as it will make getting replacements easier.

## Basic Rules
Care in what you eat and drink is the most important health rule. Stomach upsets are the most likely travel health problem (between 30% and 50% of travellers in a two week stay experience this) but the majority of these upsets will be relatively minor. Don't become paranoid; trying the local food is part of the experience of travel, after all.

**Food & Water** Tap water is safe to drink in Crete, but mineral water is widely available if you prefer it. You might experience mild intestinal problems if you're not used to copious amounts of olive oil; however, you'll get used to it and current research says it's good for you.

**Phone numbers listed incorporate changes due in Oct 2002; see p61**

## Medical Kit Check List

Following is a list of items you should consider
including in your medical kit – consult your
pharmacist for brands available in your country.

☐ **Aspirin or paracetamol (acetaminophen
  in the USA)** – for pain or fever
☐ **Antihistamine** – for allergies, eg, hay
  fever; to ease the itch from insect bites or
  stings; and to prevent motion sickness
☐ **Cold and flu tablets, throat lozenges
  and nasal decongestant**
☐ **Multivitamins** – consider for long trips,
  when dietary vitamin intake may be inadequate
☐ **Antibiotics** – consider including these if
  you're travelling well off the beaten
  track; see your doctor, as they must be
  prescribed, and carry the prescription
  with you
☐ **Loperamide or diphenoxylate** –'blockers'
  for diarrhoea
☐ **Prochlorperazine or metaclopramide** –
  for nausea and vomiting
☐ **Rehydration mixture** – to prevent dehydration, which may occur, for example,
  during bouts of diarrhoea; particularly
  important when travelling with children
☐ **Insect repellent, sunscreen, lip balm and
  eye drops**
☐ **Calamine lotion, sting relief spray or
  aloe vera** – to ease irritation from sunburn and insect bites or stings
☐ **Antifungal cream or powder** – for fungal
  skin infections and thrush
☐ **Antiseptic (such as povidone-iodine)** –
  for cuts and grazes
☐ **Bandages, Band-Aids (plasters) and
  other wound dressings**
☐ **Water purification tablets or iodine**
☐ **Scissors, tweezers and a thermometer** –
  note that mercury thermometers are
  prohibited by airlines

MICK WELDON

It pays to be sun smart

If you don't vary your diet, are travelling
hard and fast and missing meals, or simply
lose your appetite, you can soon start to
lose weight and place your health at risk.
Fruit and vegetables are good sources of vi-
tamins and Crete produces a greater variety
of these than almost any other European
country. Eat plenty of grains (including rice)
and bread. If your diet isn't well-balanced or
if your food intake is insufficient, it's a good
idea to take vitamin and iron pills.

In hot weather make sure you drink
enough – don't rely on feeling thirsty to indicate when you should drink. Not needing
to urinate or very dark yellow urine is a
danger sign.

Always carry a water bottle with you on
long trips. Excessive sweating can lead to
loss of salt and therefore muscle cramping.
Salt tablets are not a good idea as a preventative, but in places where salt is not used
much, adding salt to food can help.

### Environmental Hazards

**Sunburn** By far the biggest health risk in
Crete comes from the intensity of the sun.
You can get sunburnt surprisingly quickly,
even through cloud. Using a sunscreen and
taking extra care to cover the areas which
don't normally see sun helps, as does zinc
cream or some other barrier cream for your
nose and lips. Calamine lotion is good for
mild sunburn. Cretans claim that yogurt ap-
plied to sunburn is soothing. Protect your
eyes with good quality sunglasses.

**Prickly Heat** Prickly heat is an itchy rash
caused by excessive perspiration trapped
under the skin. Keeping cool but bathing
often, using a mild talcum powder or even
resorting to air-conditioning may help until
you acclimatise.

## Everyday Health

Normal body temperature is up to 37°C (98.6°F); more than 2°C (4°F) higher indicates a high fever. The normal adult pulse rate is 60 to 100 per minute (children 80 to 100, babies 100 to 140). As a general rule the pulse increases about 20 beats per minute for each 1°C (2°F) rise in fever.

Respiration (breathing) rate is also an indicator of illness. Count the number of breaths per minute: Between 12 and 20 is normal for adults and older children (up to 30 for younger children, 40 for babies). People with a high fever or serious respiratory illness breathe more quickly than normal. More than 40 shallow breaths a minute may indicate pneumonia.

**Heat Exhaustion** Dehydration or salt deficiency can cause heat exhaustion. Take time to acclimatise to high temperatures, and drink sufficient liquids. Wear loose clothing and a broad-brimmed hat. Do not do anything too physically demanding.

Salt deficiency is characterised by fatigue, lethargy, headaches, giddiness and muscle cramps and in this case salt tablets may help. Vomiting or diarrhoea can deplete your liquid and salt levels.

**Heat Stroke** This serious, sometimes fatal, condition can occur if the body's heat-regulating mechanism breaks down and the body temperature rises to dangerous levels. Long, continuous periods of exposure to high temperatures can leave you vulnerable to heat stroke. You should avoid excessive alcohol consumption or strenuous activity when you first arrive in a hot climate.

The symptoms are feeling unwell, not sweating very much or at all and a high body temperature (39°C to 41°C or 102°F to 106°F). Where sweating has ceased, the skin becomes flushed and red. Severe, throbbing headaches and lack of coordination will also occur, and the sufferer may be confused or aggressive. Eventually the victim will become delirious or convulsive. Hospitalisation is essential, but in the interim get victims out of the sun, remove their clothing, cover them with a wet sheet or towel and then fan continually. Give fluids if they are conscious.

**Fungal Infections** Fungal infections, which occur with greater frequency in hot weather, are most likely to occur on the scalp, between the toes or fingers, in the groin and on the body. You get ringworm (which is a fungal infection, not a worm) from infected animals or by walking on damp areas like shower floors.

To prevent fungal infections wear loose, comfortable clothes, avoid artificial fibres, wash frequently and dry carefully. If you do get an infection, wash the infected area daily with a disinfectant or medicated soap and water, and rinse and dry well. Apply an antifungal cream or powder like the widely available Tinaderm. Try to expose the infected area to air or sunlight as much as possible and wash all towels and underwear in hot water as well as changing them often.

**Motion Sickness** Sea sickness can be a problem. The Aegean is unpredictable and gets very rough when the *meltemi* wind blows. If you are prone to motion sickness, eat lightly before and during a trip and try to find a place that minimises disturbance – near the wings on aircraft, close to midships on boats, near the centre on buses. Fresh air usually helps; reading and cigarette smoke don't. Commercial motion-sickness preparations, which can cause drowsiness, have to be taken before the trip commences; when you're feeling sick it's too late. Ginger (available in capsule form) and peppermint (including mint-flavoured sweets) are natural preventatives.

### Infectious Diseases

**Diarrhoea** Simple things like a change of water, food or climate can all cause a mild bout of diarrhoea, but a few rushed toilet trips with no other symptoms is not indicative of a major problem.

Dehydration is the main danger with any diarrhoea, particularly in children or the elderly as dehydration can occur quite quickly.

Under all circumstances *fluid replacement* (at least equal to the volume being lost) is the most important thing to remember. Weak black tea with a little sugar, soda water, or soft drinks allowed to go flat and diluted 50% with clean water are all good.

**Hepatitis** Hepatitis is a general term for inflammation of the liver. It is a common disease worldwide. The symptoms are fever, chills, headache, fatigue, feelings of weakness and aches and pains, followed by loss of appetite, nausea, vomiting, abdominal pain, dark urine, light-coloured faeces, jaundiced (yellow) skin and the whites of the eyes may turn yellow.

**Hepatitis A** is transmitted by contaminated food and drinking water. The disease poses a real threat to the Western traveller. You should seek medical advice, but there is not much you can do apart from resting, drinking lots of fluids, eating lightly and avoiding fatty foods. People who have had hepatitis should avoid alcohol for some time after the illness, as the liver needs time to recover.

**Hepatitis E** is transmitted in the same way, and can be very serious in pregnant women.

There are almost 300 million chronic carriers of **Hepatitis B** in the world. It is spread through contact with infected blood, blood products or body fluids; for example, through sexual contact, unsterilised needles and blood transfusions, or contact with blood via small breaks in the skin. Other risky situations include having a shave, tattoo, or having your body pierced with contaminated equipment. The symptoms of type B may be more severe and may lead to long-term problems. **Hepatitis D** is spread in the same way, but the risk is mainly in shared needles.

**Hepatitis C** can lead to chronic liver disease. The virus is spread by contact with blood and blood products – usually via contaminated transfusions or shared needles – or bodily fluids.

**Tetanus** This potentially fatal disease is found worldwide. It is difficult to treat but is preventable with immunisation.

**Rabies** Rabies is a fatal viral infection caused by a bite or scratch by an infected animal. It's rare, but it is found in Crete. Dogs are noted carriers, as are cats. Any bite, scratch or even lick from a warm-blooded, furry animal should be cleaned immediately and thoroughly. Scrub with soap and running water, and then clean with an alcohol or iodine solution. If there is any possibility that the animal is infected medical help should be sought immediately to prevent the onset of symptoms and death. Even if the animal is not rabid, all bites should be treated seriously as they can become infected or can result in tetanus. A rabies vaccination is now available and should be considered if you are in a high risk category – eg, if you intend to explore caves (bat bites can be dangerous), work with animals, or travel so far off the beaten track that medical help is more than two days away.

**Sexually Transmitted Diseases** Sexual contact with an infected sexual partner spreads these diseases. While abstinence is the only 100% preventative, using condoms is also effective. Gonorrhoea, herpes and syphilis are among these diseases; sores, blisters or rashes around the genitals, discharges or pain when urinating are common symptoms. In some STDs, such as wart virus or chlamydia, symptoms may be less marked or not observed at all in women. Syphilis symptoms eventually disappear completely but the disease continues and can cause severe problems in later years. The treatment of gonorrhoea and syphilis is with antibiotics.

There are numerous other sexually transmitted diseases, for most of which effective treatment is available. But there is no cure for herpes and currently no cure for AIDS.

**HIV/AIDS** Infection with the human immunodeficiency virus (HIV) may lead to acquired immune deficiency syndrome (AIDS), which is a fatal disease. Any exposure to blood, blood products or body fluids may put the individual at risk. The disease is often transmitted through sexual contact or dirty needles – vaccinations, acupuncture, tattooing and body piercing can be potentially as dangerous as intravenous drug use.

If you do need an injection, ask to see the syringe unwrapped in front of you, or take a needle and syringe pack with you.

Fear of HIV infection should never preclude treatment for serious medical conditions.

## Insect-Borne Diseases

**Typhus** Tick typhus is a problem from April to September in rural areas, particularly areas where animals congregate. Typhus begins with a fever, chills, headache and muscle pain, followed a few days later by a body rash. There is often a large painful sore at the site of the bite and nearby lymph nodes are swollen and painful. There is no vaccine available. The best protection is to check your skin carefully after walking in danger areas such as long grass and scrub. A strong insect repellent can help, and walkers in tick areas should consider having their boots and trousers impregnated with benzyl benzoate and dibutylphthalate. (See the Cuts, Bites & Stings section following for information about ticks.)

**Lyme Disease** Lyme disease is a tick-transmitted infection which may be acquired throughout Europe. The illness usually begins with a spreading rash at the site of the bite and is accompanied by fever, headache, extreme fatigue, aching joints and muscles and mild neck stiffness. If untreated, these symptoms usually resolve over several weeks but over subsequent weeks or months disorders of the nervous system, heart and joints may develop. The response to treatment is best early in the illness. The longer the delay, the longer the recovery period.

## Cuts, Bites & Stings

Skin punctures can easily become infected in hot climates and may be difficult to heal. Treat any cut with an antiseptic such as povidone-iodine. Where possible avoid bandages and Band-Aids, which can keep wounds wet.

Although there are a lot of bees and wasps in Crete, their stings are usually painful rather than dangerous. Calamine lotion or sting relief spray will give relief and ice packs will reduce the pain and swelling.

**Snakes** Always wear boots, socks and long trousers when walking through undergrowth where snakes may be present. Don't put your hands into holes and crevices, and be careful when collecting firewood.

Snake bites do not cause instantaneous death and antivenenes are usually available. Keep the victim calm and still, wrap the bitten limb tightly, as you would for a sprained ankle, and attach a splint to immobilise it. Then seek medical help, if possible with the dead snake for identification. Don't attempt to catch the snake if there is even a remote possibility of being bitten again. Tourniquets and sucking out the poison are now comprehensively discredited.

**Jelly Fish, Sea Urchins & Weever Fish** Watch out for sea urchins around rocky beaches; if you get some of their needles embedded in your skin, olive oil will help to loosen them. If they are not removed they will become infected. Be wary also of jelly fish, particularly during the months of September and October. Although they are not lethal in Crete, their stings can be painful. Dousing in vinegar will deactivate any stingers which have not 'fired'. Calamine lotion, antihistamines and analgesics may reduce the reaction and relieve the pain.

Much more painful than either of these, but thankfully much rarer, is an encounter with the weever fish. It buries itself in the sand of the tidal zone with only its spines protruding, and injects a painful and powerful toxin if trodden on. Soaking your foot in very hot water (which breaks down the poison) should solve the problem. In the worst instance, it can cause permanent local paralysis.

**Bedbugs & Lice** Bedbugs live in various places, but particularly in dirty mattresses and bedding. Spots of blood on bedclothes or on the wall around the bed can be read as a suggestion to find another hotel. Bedbugs leave itchy bites in neat rows. Calamine lotion or sting relief spray may help.

All lice cause itching and discomfort. They make themselves at home in your hair, your clothing or in your pubic hair. You catch lice through direct contact with infected people or by sharing combs, clothing and the like. Powder or shampoo treatment will kill the lice and infected clothing should then be washed in very hot water.

**Leeches & Ticks** Leeches may be present in damp areas; they attach themselves to your skin to suck your blood. Trekkers often get them on their legs or in their boots. Salt or a lighted cigarette end will make them fall off. Do not pull them off, as the bite is then more likely to become infected. An insect repellent may keep them away. You should always check your body if you have been walking through a potentially tick-infested area as ticks can cause skin infections and other more serious diseases.

**Sheepdogs** These dogs are trained to guard sheep, and are often underfed and sometimes ill-treated by their owners. They are almost always 'all bark and no bite', but if you are going to trek into remote areas, you should consider having rabies injections (see Rabies earlier in the chapter). You are most likely to encounter these dogs in the mountainous regions of Crete. Wandering through a flock of sheep (over which one of these dogs is watching) is asking for trouble.

## Women's Health
Antibiotic use, synthetic underwear, sweating and contraceptive pills can lead to fungal vaginal infections, especially when travelling in hot climates. Fungal infections are characterised by a rash, itch and discharge and can be treated with a vinegar or lemon-juice douche, or with yogurt. Nystatin, miconazole or clotrimazole pessaries or vaginal cream are the usual treatment. Maintaining good personal hygiene and wearing loose-fitting clothes and cotton underwear may help prevent these infections.

Sexually transmitted diseases are a major cause of vaginal problems. Symptoms include a smelly discharge, painful intercourse and sometimes a burning sensation when urinating. Medical attention should be sought and sexual partners must also be treated. For more details see the section on Sexually Transmitted Diseases earlier. Besides abstinence, the best thing is to practise safe sex using condoms.

## Hospital Treatment
Citizens of EU countries are covered for free treatment in public hospitals within Crete on presentation of an E111 form. Inquire at your national health service or travel agent in advance. Emergency treatment is free to all nationalities in public hospitals. In an emergency, dial ☎ 166. Pharmacies can dispense medicines which are available only on prescription in most European countries, so you can consult a pharmacist for minor ailments.

All this sounds fine, but although medical training is of a high standard in Greece, the health service is badly underfunded and one of the worst in Europe.

Hospitals are overcrowded, hygiene is not always what it should be and relatives are expected to bring in food for the patient – which could be a problem for a tourist. Conditions and treatment are better in private hospitals, which are expensive. All this means that a good health insurance policy is essential.

## WOMEN TRAVELLERS
Many women travel alone in Crete. The crime rate remains relatively low, and solo travel is probably safer than in most European countries. This does not mean that you should be lulled into complacency; bag snatching and rapes do occur, although violent offences are rare.

The biggest annoyance to foreign women travelling alone are the guys the Greeks have nicknamed *kamaki*. The word means 'fishing trident' and refers to the kamaki's favourite pastime, 'fishing' for foreign women. You'll find them everywhere there are lots of tourists; young (for the most part), smooth-talking guys who aren't in the least bashful about sidling up to foreign women in the street. They can be very persistent, but they are a hassle rather than a threat.

The majority of Greek men treat foreign women with respect, and are genuinely helpful.

## GAY & LESBIAN TRAVELLERS
In a country where the church still plays a prominent role in shaping society's views on issues such as sexuality, it should come as no surprise that homosexuality is generally frowned upon. While there is no legislation against homosexual activity, it pays to be discreet and to avoid public displays of togetherness.

Although other islands have a thriving gay scene, Crete does not. Since homosexuality is generally frowned upon and Crete has never been marketed as a gay destination to package tourists there is no overtly gay nightlife.

There are a number of venues in Iraklio that are gay-friendly although not exclusively gay. Relaxed Paleohora is gay-friendly and most nude beaches are welcoming to gays.

**Information** The *Spartacus International Gay Guide*, published by Bruno Gmunder (Berlin), is widely regarded as the leading authority on the gay travel scene. The 1998/99 edition has a wealth of information on gay venues around the Greek Islands.

There's also stacks of information on the Internet. *Roz Mov* at **W** www.geocities.com /WestHollywood/2225/index.html, is a good place to start. It has pages on travel info, gay health, the gay press, organisations, events and legal issues – and links to lots more sites.

Gayscape has a useful site with lots of links at **W** www.gayscape.com.

**Organisations** The main gay rights organisation in Greece is the Elladas Omofylofilon Kommunitas (☎ 21 0341 0755, fax 21 0883 6942, **e** eok@nyx.gr), upstairs at Apostolou Pavlou 31 in the Athens suburb of Thisio.

## DISABLED TRAVELLERS
If mobility is a problem, visiting Crete presents some serious challenges. The hard fact is that most hotels, ferries, museums and ancient sites are not wheelchair accessible.

If you are determined, then take heart in the knowledge that disabled people do go to Crete for holidays. But the trip needs careful planning, so get as much information as you can before you go. The British-based Royal Association for Disability and Rehabilitation (RADAR) publishes a useful guide called *Holidays & Travel Abroad: A Guide for Disabled People*, which gives a good overview of facilities available to disabled travellers in Europe. Contact RADAR (☎ 020-7250 3222, fax 020-7250 0212, **e** radar@radar.org.uk), at 12 City Forum, 250 City Road, London EC1V 8AF.

## SENIOR TRAVELLERS
Card-carrying EU pensioners can claim a range of benefits such as reduced admission charges at museums and ancient sites and discounts on trains.

## TRAVEL WITH CHILDREN
Crete is a safe and relatively easy place to travel with children. It's especially easy if you're staying by the beach or at a resort hotel. If you're travelling around, the main problem is a shortage of decent playgrounds and recreational facilities.

Don't be afraid to take children to ancient sites. Many parents are surprised by how much their children enjoy them. Young imaginations go into overdrive when let loose somewhere like the 'labyrinth' at Knossos.

Hotels and restaurants are usually very accommodating when it comes to meeting the needs of children, although highchairs are a rarity outside resorts. The service in restaurants is normally very quick, which is great when you've got hungry children on your hands.

Fresh milk is readily available in large towns and tourist areas, but harder to find in small villages. Supermarkets are the best place to look. Formula is available everywhere, as is condensed and heat-treated milk.

Mobility is an issue for parents with very small children. Strollers (pushchairs) aren't much use in Crete unless you're going to spend all your time in one of the few flat spots. They are hopeless on rough stone paths and up steps, and a curse when getting on/off buses and ferries. Backpacks or front pouches are best.

Children under four travel for free on ferries and buses. They pay half fare up to the age of 10 (ferries) and 12 (buses). Full fare applies otherwise. On domestic flights, you'll pay 10% of the fare to have a child under two sitting on your knee. Kids aged two to 12 pay half fare.

## USEFUL ORGANISATIONS

ELPA (☎ 21 0779 1615), the Greek automobile club, has its headquarters on the ground floor of Athens Tower, Mesogion 2–4, Athens 115 27. ELPA offers reciprocal services to members of national automobile associations on production of a valid membership card. If your vehicle breaks down, dial ☎ 104.

## DANGERS & ANNOYANCES
### Theft

Crime, especially theft, is low in Crete, but unfortunately it is on the increase. Keep track of your valuables on public transport and in markets. Do not leave luggage unattended in cars. The vast majority of thefts from tourists are still committed by other tourists; the biggest danger of theft is probably in dormitory rooms in hostels and at camping grounds. So make sure you do not leave valuables unattended in such places. If you are staying in a hotel room, and the windows and door do not lock securely, ask for your valuables to be locked in the hotel safe – hotel proprietors are happy to do this.

## LEGAL MATTERS
### Consumer Advice

The Tourist Assistance Programme exists to help people who are having trouble with any tourism-related service. Free legal advice is available in English, French and German from 1 July to 30 September. The main office (☎ 281 024 0666) in Crete is in Iraklio at Milatou 1 and Agiou Titou. It's open 10am to 2pm Monday to Friday.

## Drugs

Greek drug laws are the strictest in Europe. Greek courts make no distinction between possession and pushing. Possession of even a small amount of marijuana is likely to land you in jail.

## BUSINESS HOURS

Banks are open 8am to 2pm Monday to Thursday, and 8am to 1.30pm Friday. Some banks in large towns and cities open between 3.30pm and 6.30pm in the afternoon and on Saturday morning.

Post offices are open 7.30am to 2pm Monday to Friday. In the major cities they stay open until 8pm, and open from 7.30am to 2pm on Saturday.

The opening hours of OTE offices vary according to the size of the town. In smaller towns they are usually open 7.30am to 3pm daily; from 6am until 11pm in larger towns; and 24 hours in major cities like Athens and Thessaloniki.

In summer, shops are open 8am to 1.30pm and 5.30pm to 8.30pm Tuesday, Thursday and Friday, and 8am to 2.30pm Monday, Wednesday and Saturday. They open 30 minutes later in winter. These times are not always strictly adhered to. Many shops in tourist resorts are open seven days a week. *Periptera* (street kiosks) are open from early morning until late at night. They sell everything from bus tickets and cigarettes to hard-core pornography.

Opening times of museums and archaeological sites vary, but most are closed on Monday.

## PUBLIC HOLIDAYS

All banks and shops and most museums and ancient sites close public holidays. Greek national public holidays observed in Crete are:

**New Year's Day** 1 January
**Epiphany** 6 January
**First Sunday in Lent** February
**Greek Independence Day** 25 March
**Good Friday** March/April
**(Orthodox) Easter Sunday** March/April
**Spring Festival/Labour Day** 1 May
**Feast of the Assumption** 15 August

Ohi Day 28 October
Christmas Day 25 December
St Stephen's Day 26 December

## SPECIAL EVENTS

The Greek year is a succession of festivals and events, some of which are religious, some cultural, others an excuse for a good knees-up, and some a combination of all three. The following is by no means an exhaustive list, but it covers the most important events, both national and regional. If you're in the right place at the right time, you'll certainly be invited to join the revelry.

### January

**Feast of Agios Vasilios (St Basil)** The year kicks off with this festival on 1 January. A church ceremony is followed by the exchanging of gifts, singing, dancing and feasting; the New Year pie *(vasilopitta)* is sliced and the person who gets the slice containing a coin will supposedly have a lucky year.

**Epiphany (the Blessing of the Waters)** On 6 January, Christ's baptism by St John is celebrated throughout Greece. Seas, lakes and rivers are blessed and crosses immersed in them.

### February-March

**Shrove Monday (Clean Monday)** On the Monday before Ash Wednesday (the first day of Lent), people take to the hills throughout Greece to have picnics and fly kites.

### March

**Independence Day** The anniversary of the hoisting of the Greek flag by Bishop Germanos at Moni Agias Lavras is celebrated on 25 March with parades and dancing. Germanos' act of revolt marked the start of the War of Independence. Independence Day coincides with the Feast of the Annunciation, so it is also a religious festival.

### March-April

**Easter** is taken much more seriously than any other religious holiday. On Palm Sunday (the Sunday before Orthodox Easter), worshippers return from church services with a cross woven of palm and myrtle. If you are in Crete at Easter you should endeavour to attend this ceremony, which ends with fireworks and a candle-lit procession through the streets.

**Feast of Agios Georgos (St George)** The feast day of St George, Crete's patron saint and patron

## Easter in Crete

Easter in Crete and throughout Greece is the most important religious festival of the year. The ceremonies take place throughout Holy Week culminating in the resurrection of Christ on the eve of Easter Sunday.

The Monday evening service is the 'Bridegroom Service' because the priest carries an icon of Christ, 'the bridegroom' through the church. Tuesday is dedicated to Mary Magdalene and Wednesday is the 'Day of Atonement'. On Thursday worshippers mourn for Christ in the evening service and on Good Friday, the symbolic body of Christ is carried through the streets in a funeral procession.

The climax of the week is the Saturday evening service. At midnight all lights in the churches are extinguished until the priest appears with a lighted candle and the cry *Hristos Anesti!* 'Christ has arisen'.

He lights each worshipper's candle and people make their way home, trying to keep the candle lit. Fireworks and gunshots herald the start of feasting that lasts through Easter Sunday.

The ceremony of the lighting of candles is the most significant moment in the Orthodox year, for it symbolises the Resurrection. Its poignancy and beauty are spellbinding.

The Lenten fast ends immediately after church with the ritual eating of *mayiritsa* (tripe soup) at home. Cretans also celebrate with the cracking of red-dyed Easter eggs and the following afternoon with an outdoor feast of spit roast lamb followed by dancing and merrymaking.

saint of shepherds, takes place on 23 April or the Tuesday following Easter (whichever comes first). The most elaborate celebration is in Asi Gonias where thousands of goats and sheep are gathered at the town church for shearing, milking and blessing. Fresh milk accompanies the ensuing feast.

### May

**May Day** On the first day of May there is a mass exodus from towns to the country. During picnics, wildflowers are gathered and made into wreaths to decorate houses.

**Battle of Crete** During the last week of May, the town of Hania commemorates the Battle of Crete in athletic competitions, folk dancing and ceremonial events.

## June

**Navy Week** is celebrated in even-numbered years during the last week in June and commemorates Crete's relationship with the sea. In Crete's harbour cities there are music and dancing events on land and swimming and sailing competitions on the water.

**Feast of St John the Baptist** This feast day on 24 June is widely celebrated. Wreaths made on May Day are kept until this day, when they are burned on bonfires.

## July

**Feast of Agia Marina (St Marina)** This feast day is celebrated on 17 July in many parts of Crete, and is a particularly important event in Agia Marina outside of Hania.

**Feast of Profitis Ilias** This feast day is celebrated on 20 July at hill-top churches and monasteries dedicated to the prophet, especially in the Cyclades.

**Wine Festival** The Wine Festival of Rethymno is held in the municipal park with wine tastings and local cuisine

**Yakinthia Festival** The mountain village of Anogia stages an annual cultural and musical extravaganza lasting one week. There are poetry recitals, talks, exhibitions and outdoor concerts featuring Cretan music. The festival takes place in the last week of July.

## August

**Assumption Day** Greeks celebrate Assumption Day (15 August) with family reunions. The whole population is on the move either side of the day, so it's a good time to avoid public transport. The island of Tinos gets particularly busy because of its miracle-working icon of Panagia Evangelistria. It becomes a place of pilgrimage for thousands, who come to be blessed, healed or baptised, or just for the excitement of being there. Many are unable to find hotels and sleep out on the streets.

**Paleohora Music Festival** is devoted to music. The first 10 days of August are filled with song contests and concerts staged every night.

**Cultural Festival** In Ano Viannos, there's a three-day Cultural Festival at the beginning of August with concerts, plays and art exhibits.

**Wine Festival** In the town of Arhanes, 15 August is the conclusion of a five-day Wine Festival celebrating their excellent local wine.

**Sultana Festival** Sitia celebrates their superior sultana raisins with wine, music and dancing in a Sultana Festival held the last week of the month.

**Potato Festival** Lasithi produces superior potatoes, a product which is celebrated in the Potato Festival held for three days at the end of August in Tzermiado.

**Traditional Cretan wedding** In late August Kritsa stages a traditional Cretan wedding replete with songs, dancing and traditional food for an admission of about €8.80.

## September

**Genisis tis Panagias** (the Virgin's Birthday) This day is celebrated on 8 September throughout Greece with various religious services and feasting.

## October

**Chestnut Festival** The village of Elos stages a chestnut festival on the third Sunday of the month when everyone is offered roasted chestnuts, chestnut sweets and *tsikoudia*.

**Ohi (No) Day** Metaxas' refusal to allow Mussolini's troops free passage through Crete during WWII is commemorated on 28 October with a number of remembrance services, military parades, folk dancing and feasting.

## November

One of the most important local holidays celebrated in Crete is the anniversary of the explosion at Moni Arkadiou. From 7–9 November, this tragic event is commemorated at Moni Arkadiou.

## December

**Christmas Day** Although not as important as Easter, Christmas is still celebrated with religious services and feasting. Nowadays much Western influence is apparent, including Christmas trees, decorations and presents.

# Summer Festivals & Performances

There are cultural festivals throughout Crete in summer. The most important are the annual Renaissance Festival in Rethymno that features dance, drama and films as well as art exhibitions; the Kyrvia Festival in Ierapetra includes various musical, theatrical and artistic presentations.

Sitia's Kornaria Festival presents music, theatre, art exhibits and a beach volleyball competition; Iraklio's Summer Arts Festival attracts inter- national artists as well as local singers and dancers to perform in the Kazantzakis Open Air Theatre, and the Lato Festival in Agios Nikolaos features traditional and modern works performed by local and international orchestras and dance troupes.

## ACTIVITIES

Crete's adventurous terrain lends itself to a host of activities for the more active traveller. For the full low-down see the 'Head to the Hills' special section in this chapter.

## Cycling

Crete's mountainous terrain isn't ideal for easy cycling, but the escarpment villages and valleys of the north coast and the Mesara Plain of the south do allow for some relatively flat cycling experiences. One of the more popular cycling activities is cycling *down* from one of Crete's many plateaus. This will more conveniently involve participation in a group tour, as the bikes need to be transported up to the plateau by vehicle first. Cycling tours are usually graded in difficulty from 1 (easy) to 3 (hard) so you can select your level before attempting the tour. You can also rent bikes ranging in price from €8.50 to €15 per day. One company even organises an eight-day program for racing cyclists covering a total of 650km.

Outfits such as Trekking Plan (☎/fax 2821 060 861, e sales@cycling.gr, w www .cycling.gr) at Agia Marina, 9km west of Hania or Diexodos Adventure Unlimited (☎/fax 2841 028 098, e diexodos@acci.gr, w www.forthnet.gr/internetcity/diexodos) at Havania just north of Agios Nikolaos rents bikes and offers organised tours.

## Mountain Biking

Equipped with a serious mountain bike and enough strength in your legs you can tackle a whole range of terrain throughout what is in essence a mountain biker's paradise. There are no dedicated mountain bike guides to Crete available yet, so you are probably better off joining a guided tour.

Both of the companies listed in the Cycling section offer alternative mountain biking tours while Trekking Plan offers a level 3 extreme biker experience for the seriously fit and committed.

## Snorkelling & Diving

The warm, clear waters of Crete make snorkelling and diving a pleasure. Some of the more interesting snorkelling is around the sunken city of Olous in Elounda, while for clearer waters head for the generally less-populated southern coast.

There are a number of diving centres that allow you to get acquainted with diving, become a certified diver or explore the underwater wonders if you're already certified. Under Greek law, you must dive as part of a licensed diving operation and you are forbidden to disturb any antiquities you may come across. In Hania, you have a choice of Blue Adventures Diving (☎ 2821 40 608), Daskalogianni 69, or Creta's Diving Centre (☎ 2821 093 616), Papanikoli 6, Nea Hora. In Bali, there's Hippocampos (☎ 2834 094 193) near the port. In Agios Nikolaos, there's a diving centre affiliated with the aquarium and a diving centre on the beach of the Coral Hotel (☎ 2841 082 546). In Rethymno, there's the Paradise Dive Centre (☎ 2831 053 258), El Venizelou 76. It's wise to call at least a day in advance.

## Trekking & Mountain Climbing

Crete is a veritable paradise for trekkers – at the right time of the year. Trekking is no fun at all in June, July and August, when the temperatures are constantly up around 40°C. Spring (April–May) is the perfect time.

There are dozens of interesting hikes throughout Crete that will take you through remote villages, across plains and into gorges. Some of the most popular treks, such as the Samaria Gorge, are detailed in this book.

There are a number of private companies in Crete running organised treks, including Trekking Plan and Diexodos Adventure Unlimited (see Cycling), while Athens-based Trekking Hellas (☎ 21 0323 4548,

fax 21 0325 1474, e trekking@compulink
.gr, W www.trekking.gr), at Filellinon 7 is
one of the biggest mainland operators.

You can also try The Happy Walker
(☎/fax 2831 052 920, e info@happy
walker.nl, W www.happywalker.nl) at To-
bazi 56 in Rethymno. They organise less
strenuous hikes.

## Water Sports

Parasailing, water-skiing, jet skiing, pedal-
boating, canoeing and windsurfing are
available on most of the major beaches. On
the north coast, you'll find a water sports
centre attached to most luxury hotels and
you don't need to stay there to avail yourself of the facilities. Outside Iraklio, try the
water sports centre at the Grecotel Agapi
Beach (☎ 281 025 0502) in Ammoudara.

Outside Hania in nearby Platanias,
there's Argyris Sea Sports (☎ 2821 093 493
449). If you're staying in Agios Nikolaos,
head out to the beach resort of Elounda,
12km north of town. There's a water sports
centre at the Elounda Bay Hotel (☎ 2841
041 502) and the neighbouring Elounda
Beach Hotel (☎ 2841 041 412). In Bali,
there's the Water Sports Lefteris (☎ 2834
094 102) and in Vaï, there's Vaï Watersports (☎ 2843 061 070).

The best windsurfing is at Kouremenos
beach, the town beach of Palekastro, east of
Sitia. Call the Kouremenos Watersports
Centre (☎ 69-3751 7444). Windsurfing is
also good in Paleohora. Try Westwind
(☎ 69-4681 9777) near the Pal Beach
Hotel. Almyrida near Hania is also a popular spot. There's a water sports centre
(☎ 2825 032 062) there where you can
windsurf or rent a kayak or a catamaran.

## Yachting

Yachties can get the lowdown on sailing
around Crete and Greece at W www.sailing
.gr where you'll find a huge list of links to
Greek and English language sailing-related
sites. Agios Nikolaos has its own site at
W www.forthnet.gr/internetcity/yachting
/marina. Here you'll find details of the
Agios Nikolaos marina as well as local information for waterborne visitors.

## WORK
### Permits

EU nationals don't need a work permit, but
they need a residency permit if they intend
to stay longer than three months. Nationals
of other countries are supposed to have a
work permit.

### Bar & Hostel Work

The best bar and hotel jobs can pay quite
well, so well that they are usually taken by
young Greeks from the mainland. Language
training has improved dramatically in recent years eliminating the need for multilingual foreign workers. Resorts such as
Hersonisos and Malia that cater to British
travellers are the best bet for Brits looking
for bar work.

### Courier

As a package tour destination par excel-
lence Crete provides terrific opportunities
for those interested in working as a courier
for a package tour company. Package tour
companies based in Britain begin looking
for personnel around February to fill the
summer season needs.

You need to have a good presentation
and outgoing personality and, usually, some
college education. The pay is poor but you
can make tips and some companies allow
couriers to earn a percentage of the excursions they sell.

### Summer Harvest

Seasonal harvest work seems to be monopo-
lised by migrant workers from Albania, and
is no longer a viable option for travellers.

### Volunteer Work

The Sea Turtle Protection Society of Crete
(☎/fax 21 0523 1342, e stps@compulink
.gr), at Solomou 57, Athens GR-104 32,
uses volunteers for its monitoring programs
on Crete.

### Other Work

There are often jobs advertised in the classi-
fieds of the English-language newspapers, or
you can place an advertisement yourself. EU
nationals can also make use of the OAED

(Organismos Apasholiseos Ergatikou Dynamikou), the Greek National Employment Service, in their search for a job.

## ACCOMMODATION

There is a range of accommodation available in Crete to suit every taste and pocket. All places to stay are subject to strict price controls set by the tourist police. By law, a notice must be displayed in every room, which states the category of the room and the price charged in each season.

Accommodation owners may add a 10% surcharge for a stay of less than three nights, but this is not mandatory. A mandatory charge of 20% is levied if an extra bed is put into a room.

During July and August, accommodation owners will charge the maximum price, but in spring and autumn, prices will drop by up to 20%, and perhaps by even more in winter. These are the times to bring your bargaining skills into action.

Rip-offs rarely occur, but if you suspect you have been exploited by an accommodation owner, report it to either the tourist police or regular police and they will act swiftly.

### Camping

There are only about a dozen or so camping grounds in Crete. Most are privately run and very few are open outside the high season (April–October). The Panhellenic Camping Association (☎/fax 21 0362 1560), at Solonos 102, Athens GR-106 80, publishes an annual booklet listing all the camp sites and their facilities.

Camping fees are highest from 15 June to the end of August. Most camping grounds charge from €3.50 to €4.50 per adult and €1.80 to €2.40 for children aged four to 12. There's no charge for children aged under four. Tent sites cost from €2.70 per night for small tents, and from €3.50 per night for large tents. Caravan sites start at around €7.40.

Between May and mid-September it is warm enough to sleep out under the stars, although you will still need a lightweight sleeping bag to counter the pre-dawn chill.

It's a good idea to have a foam pad to lie on and a waterproof cover to protect your sleeping bag.

Freelance (wild) camping is illegal, but the law is not always strictly enforced. It's wise to ask around before camping wild.

### Hostels

There are hostels in Iraklio, Rethymno, Sitia and Plakias that are run by the Greek Youth Hostel Organisation (☎ 21 0751 9530, fax 21 0751 0616, e y-hostels@otenet.gr), at Damareos 75, GR-116 33 in Athens.

Hostel rates vary from €7 to €10 and you don't have to be a member to stay in any of them.

### Domatia

Domatia are the Greek equivalent of the British bed and breakfast, minus the breakfast. Once upon a time domatia comprised little more than spare rooms in the family home which could be rented out to travellers in summer; nowadays, many are purpose-built appendages to the family house. Some come complete with fully-equipped kitchens.

Standards of cleanliness are generally high. The decor runs the gamut from cool grey marble floors, coordinated pine furniture, pretty lace curtains and tasteful pictures on the walls, to so much kitsch you are almost afraid to move in case you break an ornament.

Domatia remain a popular option for budget travellers. They are classified A, B or C. Expect to pay from €15 to €27 for a single, and €17 to €44 for a double, depending on the class, whether bathrooms are shared or private, the season and how long you plan to stay.

Many domatia are open only between April and October.

### Studios & Apartments

There is a growing trend in Crete to build self-catering studios or apartments for visitors. Studios are usually two-person affairs, while an apartment can take anywhere from two to five persons. These are excellent options for families and groups of friends.

**Phone numbers listed incorporate changes due in Oct 2002; see p61**

Facilities usually include a kitchenette, fridge and TV and many include air-conditioning, heating for winter, a separate lounge area and separate bedrooms. Costs for a studio in high season range from €27 to €44 while an apartment for four people in high season will cost between €65 and €88.

## Hotels

Hotels in Crete are divided into six categories: deluxe, A, B, C, D and E. Hotels are categorised according to the size of the room, whether or not they have a bar, and the ratio of bathrooms to beds, rather than standards of cleanliness, comfort of the beds and friendliness of staff – all elements which may be of greater relevance to guests.

As one would expect, deluxe, A- and B-class hotels have many amenities, private bathrooms and constant hot water.

They usually, but not always, have air-conditioning. Even in expensive hotels the air-conditioning may only function part of the day. Often it is turned off at night. C-class hotels have a snack bar, rooms have private bathrooms, but hot water may only be available at certain times of the day. D-class hotels may or may not have snack bars, most rooms will share bathrooms, but there may be some with private bathrooms, and they may have solar heated water, which means hot water is not guaranteed. E-class hotels do not have a snack bar, bathrooms are shared and you may have to pay extra for hot water – if it exists at all.

Prices are controlled by the tourist police and the maximum rate that can be charged for a room must be displayed on a board behind the door of each room. The classification is not often much of a guide to price. Rates in D- and E-class hotels are generally comparable with domatia. You can pay anywhere from €30 to €60 for a C-class single in high season and €45 to €75 for a double. Prices in B-class range from €45 to €75 for singles, and from €75 to €105 for doubles. A-class prices are not much higher.

## Traditional Settlements

Traditional settlements are old buildings of architectural merit that have been renovated and converted into tourist accommodation. The best in Crete are at Milia and Vamos. They're not cheap but traditional features such as fireplaces and stone kitchens provide an unusual and appealing lodging experience. A traditional house for four persons in Vamos will cost around €100, while a small stone cottage for two in Milia will cost around €47.

## Mountain Refuges

Mountain refuges are not plentiful on Crete but there are some lodges scattered in the Lefka Ori, Mt Psiloritis and Kallergi. A bunk bed will cost between €4-6.

## FOOD

Cretan food shares much of its inheritance with the cuisine of the mainland and the Mediterranean basin. It is a solid, balanced and healthy cuisine rather than 'haute' in the French sense and bases its range on the wide variety of natural products that occur and are grown in abundance on the island. Studies by the World Health Organization in 1987 show that the Cretan diet is one of the world's healthiest and that the incidence of heart-related diseases were considerably lower in Crete than in many other places in the world.

This is due to a greater reliance on pulses, fresh vegetables and fruit than on meats and processed foodstuffs. Olive oil, produced in vast quantities in Crete is among the world's best and consumed as an integral part of meals in Crete. Meat while now consumed in greater quantity than before, still constitutes only a small part of the traditional Cretan family meal, while the consumption of fish and seafood play an important part in the diet.

Restaurant food on the whole in Crete is uniformly mediocre, particularly where tourists congregate and where palates are more delicate. When you see Cretans eating out in a restaurant you can usually be certain that the food served is of a higher quality. As a general rule of thumb, the further away you move from the northern coast (where most tourists are) the better the food becomes.

Ready-prepared food *(mayirefta)* is commonly served at temperatures much lower than what you might be used to. This is both considered healthier by Cretans and more practical from the restaurant owner's point of view, as it is hard to keep all food piping hot. Food cooked to order *(tis oras)* such as grills and special dishes will always be served hot. Mezedes will be either hot or cold depending on what is on offer.

Cretans eat out regularly, regardless of socioeconomic status. Enjoying life is paramount to Greeks and a large part of this enjoyment comes from eating and drinking with friends. Cretans consider it good form to order plenty of dishes and have food left over at the end of the meal. Ordering a Greek salad, or a tzatziki as a meal – a common practice among the young and hungry – is considered poor form and is often quietly sneered at by the restaurant staff.

By law, every eating establishment must display a written menu including prices. Restaurant staff will automatically put bread on your table and meals usually cost between €0.30 and €0.60, depending on the restaurant's category.

## Where to Eat

**Tavernas** Traditionally, the taverna is a basic eating place with a rough-and-ready ambience, although some are more upmarket, particularly in Iraklio, Hania and Rethymno as well as in major resorts. All tavernas have a menu, often displayed in the window or on the door, but it's usually not a reliable guide as to what's actually available on the day. You'll be told about the daily specials – or ushered into the kitchen to peer into the pots and point to what you want. This is not merely a privilege for tourists; Cretans also do it because they want to see the taverna's version of the dishes on offer. Some tavernas don't open until 9pm or 10pm, and then stay open until the early hours. Some are closed on Sunday.

**Psistarias** These places specialise in spit roasts and charcoal-grilled food – usually lamb, pork or chicken. You can often order takeaway or dine in.

**Restaurants** A restaurant *(estiatorio)* is normally more sophisticated than a taverna or psistaria with damask tablecloths, smartly attired waiters and printed menus at each table with an English translation. Ready-made food is usually displayed in a *bain-marie* and there may also be a charcoal grill.

**Ouzeri** An *ouzeri* serves ouzo or, in the case of Crete, raki. Greeks believe it is essential to eat when drinking alcohol so, in traditional establishments, your drink will come with a small plate of titbits or *mezedes* (appetisers) – perhaps olives, a slice of feta and some pickled octopus. Ouzeris are becoming trendy and many now offer menus with appetisers and main courses.

**International Food** Cretans like their own food so much that they rarely move outside of its all-encompassing ambit. As a result, most international food outlets cater primarily to foreigners longing for a stir-fry, a curry or a taco. That said, younger, urbane and widely-travelled Cretans have developed a penchant for Mexican, Indian, Indonesian or Chinese cuisines and can be spotted patronising these eateries more and more. On the whole, the Chinese food you will eat in Agios Nikolaos will be no better than what you eat in Bristol or Boston and will invariably be more expensive.

**Galaktopoleia** A *galaktopoleio* (literally 'milk shop') sells dairy produce including milk, butter, yogurt, rice pudding, cornflour pudding, custard, eggs and bread. It may also sell home-made ice cream. Most have seating and serve coffee and tea. They are inexpensive for breakfast and usually open from very early in the morning until evening.

**Zaharoplasteia** A *zaharoplasteio* (patisserie) sells cakes (traditional and Western), chocolates, biscuits, sweets, coffee, soft drinks and, possibly, bottled alcoholic drinks. They usually have some seating.

**Kafeneia** Kafeneia are often regarded by foreigners as the last bastion of male chauvinism in Europe. With bare light bulbs, nicotine-stained walls, smoke-laden air, rickety wooden tables and raffia chairs, they are frequented by middle-aged and elderly Cretan men in cloth caps who while away their time fiddling with worry beads, playing cards or backgammon, or engaging in heated political discussions.

It was once unheard of for women to enter a kafeneia but in large cities this situation is changing.

In rural areas, Cretan women are rarely seen inside kafeneia. When a female traveller enters one, she is invariably treated courteously and with friendship if she manages a few Greek words of greeting. If you feel inhibited about going into a kafeneio, opt for outside seating.

Kafeneia originally only served Greek coffee but now, most also serve soft drinks, Nescafé and beer. They are generally fairly cheap, with Greek coffee costing about €0.60 and Nescafé with milk €1.20. Most kafeneia are open all day every day, but some close during siesta time (roughly from 3pm to 5pm).

## Meals

**Breakfast** Most Cretans have Greek coffee and perhaps a cake or pastry for breakfast. Budget hotels offering breakfast generally provide it continental-style (rolls or bread with jam, and tea or coffee), while more upmarket hotels serve breakfast buffets (Western and continental-style). Otherwise, restaurants and galaktopoleia serve bread with butter, jam or honey; eggs; and the budget travellers' favourite, yogurt *(yiaourti)* with honey. In tourist areas, many menus offer an 'English' breakfast – which means bacon and eggs.

**Lunch** This meal is eaten late – between 1pm and 3pm – and may be either a snack or a complete meal.

The main meal in a Cretan's day can be lunch or dinner – or both. Cretans enjoy eating and it is quite common for them to have two large meals a day.

**Dinner** Cretans also eat dinner late. Many people don't start to think about food until after 9pm, which is why some restaurants don't bother to open their doors until after 8pm. In tourist areas dinner is often served earlier. A full dinner in Crete begins with appetisers and/or soup, followed by a main course of either ready-made food, grilled meat or fish.

Only very posh restaurants or those pandering to tourists include Western-style desserts on the menu. Dessert as such is commonly fresh fruit of the season.

Cretans usually eat cakes separately in a galaktopoleio or zaharoplasteio.

## Cretan Specialities

Greek and Cretan dishes often overlap but there are a few Cretan specialties worth searching out. Cretan food is based upon the vegetables, grain and livestock produced on the island. Barley *dakos* is a round rusk that is softened in water and soaked in oil and tomato. Crete also produces wonderful cheeses including sweet *myzithra*, and the yellow, sheep's milk cheese, *graviera*. Cretans are also fond of rabbit which is made into *stifado*, or stew. Snails are gathered on hillsides after rainfall and prepared in dozens of interesting ways. Try *hohlii boubouristi*, snails simmered in vinegar or snails with barley. For centuries Cretans have been gathering wild greens from the hills and making them into *horta*, a delicious, tart vegetable side dish.

**Snacks** Favourite Greek snacks include pretzel rings sold by street vendors, *tyropitta* (cheese pie), *bougatsa* (custard-filled pastry) or *spanakopitta* (spinach pie). Street vendors sell various nuts and dried seeds such as pumpkin for €0.65 to €1.20 a bag.

**Mezedes** In a simple taverna, possibly only three or four mezedes (appetisers) will be offered – perhaps *taramasalata* (fish-roe dip), *tzatziki* (yogurt, cucumber and garlic dip), olives and feta. Ouzeris and restaurants usually offer wider selections.

Mezedes include *ohtapodi* (octopus), *garides* (shrimps), *kalamaria* (squid), *dolmades* (stuffed vine leaves), *melitzanosalata* (aubergine or eggplant dip) and

## Another helping of horta?

An influential study concluded in 1960, after 15 years of research, found that Cretan men had the lowest rate of heart disease and cancer of all seven countries studied (Finland, USA, Netherlands, Italy, Yugoslavia, Japan and Crete). The extraordinary longevity of Cretan men is a puzzle. Doctors noted that the traditional Cretan diet was high in fruits, vegetables, beans, whole grains and olive oil – the so-called 'Mediterranean diet'. Another important factor may be the wild greens that Cretans were accustomed to gathering in the hills. Used in pies, salads, or *horta*, the greens may have protective properties that are not yet fully understood. Unfortunately the Cretan beans and greens diet is changing as the island has prospered and urbanised. As Cretans have included more meat and cheese in their diets and no longer work (out) in the fields, heart disease and cancer rates are rising. Cretans have not completely abandoned their old ways however. Anyone who wants to clean up their coronaries will find plenty of healthy choices on Cretan menus.

*mavromatika* (black-eyed beans). Hot mezedes include *keftedes* (meatballs), *fasolia* (white haricot beans), *gigantes* (lima beans), *loukanika* (little sausages), tyropitta, spanakopitta, *bourekaki* (tiny meat pie), *kolokythakia* (deep-fried zucchini), *melitzana* (deep-fried aubergine) and *saganaki* (fried cheese).

It is quite acceptable to make a full meal of these instead of a main course. Three plates of mezedes are about equivalent in price and quantity to one main course. You can also order a *pikilia* (mixed plate).

**Soups** Soup is not normally eaten as a starter, but can be an economical meal in itself with bread and a salad. *Psarosoupa* is a filling fish soup with vegetables, while *kakavia* (Greek bouillabaisse) is laden with seafood and is more expensive. *Fasolada* (bean soup) is also a meal in itself. *Avgolemono soupa* (egg and lemon soup) is usually prepared from a chicken stock. If you're into offal, don't miss the traditional Easter soup, *mayiritsa*, at this festive time.

**Salads** The ubiquitous (and no longer inexpensive) Greek or village salad, *horiatiki salata*, is a side dish for Greeks, but many budget-conscious tourists make it a main dish. It consists of peppers, onions, olives, tomatoes and feta cheese, sprinkled with oregano and dressed with olive oil and lemon juice. A tomato salad often comes with onions, cucumber and olives, and, with bread, makes a satisfying lunch. In spring, try *radikia salata* (dandelion salad).

**Main Dishes** The most common main courses are *mousakas* (layers of eggplant or zucchini, minced meat and potatoes topped with cheese sauce and baked), *pastitsio* (baked cheese-topped macaroni with or without minced meat), dolmades, and *yemista* (stuffed tomatoes or green peppers). Other main courses include *giouvetsi* (casserole of lamb or veal and pasta), *stifado* (meat stewed with onions), *soutzoukakia* (spicy meatballs in tomato sauce) and *salingaria* (snails in oil with herbs). *Melitzanes papoutsakia* are baked eggplant stuffed with meat and tomatoes and topped with cheese, which looks, as its Greek name suggests, like a little shoe. Spicy *loukanika* (sausages) are a good budget choice and comes with potatoes or rice. *Arni fricassée me maroulia* (lamb fricassee, cooked with lettuce) is usually filling enough for two to share.

Fish is usually sold by weight in restaurants, but is not as cheap nor as widely available as it used to be. Calamari (squid), deep-fried in batter, remains a tasty option for the budget traveller at €3.50 to €4.70 for a generous serve. Other reasonably priced fish (about €3.50 a portion) are *marides* (whitebait), sometimes cloaked in onion, pepper and tomato sauce, and *gopes*, which are similar to sardines. More expensive are *ohtapodi* (octopus), *bakaliaros* (cod), *xifias* (swordfish) and *glossa* (sole). Ascending the price scale further are *synagrida* (snapper) and *barbounia* (red mullet). *Astakos* (lobster) and *karavida* (crayfish) are top of the range at about €29.50 per kg.

Fish is mostly grilled or fried. More imaginative fish dishes include shrimp casserole and mussel or octopus *saganaki* (fried with tomato and cheese).

**Desserts** Greek cakes and puddings include *baklava*, *loukoumades* (puffs or fritters with honey or syrup), *kataïfi* (chopped nuts inside shredded wheat pastry or filo soaked in honey), *rizogalo* (rice pudding), *loukoumi* (Turkish delight), *halva* (made from semolina or sesame seeds) and *pagoto* (ice cream). Tavernas and restaurants usually only have a few of these on the menu. The best places to go for these delights are *galaktopoleia* or *zaharoplasteia*.

### Fruit

Crete grows many varieties of beautiful fruit. Most visitors will be familiar with *syka* (figs), *rodakina* (peaches), *stafylia* (grapes), *karpouzi* (watermelon), *mila* (apples), *portokalia* (oranges) and *kerasia* (cherries).

Many will not, however, have encountered the *frangosyko* (prickly pear). Also known as the Barbary fig, it is the fruit of the opuntia cactus, recognisable by the thick green spiny pads that form its trunk. The fruit are borne around the edge of the pads in late summer and autumn and vary in colour from pale orange to deep red. They are delicious but need to be approached with extreme caution because of the thousands of tiny prickles (invisible to the naked eye) that cover their skin. Never pick one up with your bare hands. They must be peeled before you can eat them. The simplest way to do this is to trim the ends off with a knife and then slit the skin from end to end.

Another fruit that will be new to many people is the *mousmoulo* (loquat). These small orange fruit are among the first of summer, reaching the market in mid-May. The flesh is juicy and pleasantly acidic.

### Fast Food

**Fast Food Outlets** All the major international fast food outlets have found a foothold in Greece as well as a veritable plethora of one-owner copycat stores peddling much the same food but at cheaper prices. Expect to see plenty of Pizza Hats, or Kretan Fried Chicken scattered in among the real items.

It's hard, though, to beat eat-on-the-street Greek offerings. Foremost among them are the *gyros* and the souvlaki. The gyros is a giant skewer laden with slabs of seasoned meat which grills slowly as it rotates and the meat is trimmed steadily from the outside; souvlaki are small individual kebab sticks. Both are served wrapped in pitta bread, with salad and lashings of tzatziki.

### Vegetarian Food

Crete has few vegetarian restaurants per se, and unfortunately, many vegetable soups and stews are based on meat stocks. Fried vegetables are a safe bet as olive oil is always used – never lard. The Cretans do wonderful things with artichokes *(anginares)*. They can be served stuffed, as a salad, as a mezes (particularly with *raki*) or used as the basis of a vegetarian stew. Vegetarians who eat eggs can rest assured that an economical omelette can be whipped up anywhere. Salads are cheap, fresh, substantial and nourishing. Other options are yogurt, rice pudding, cheese and spinach pies, and nuts.

Lent, incidentally, is a good time for vegetarians because the meat is missing from many dishes.

### Self-Catering

Eating out in Crete is as much an entertainment as a gastronomic experience, so to self-cater is to sacrifice a lot. But if you are on a low budget you will need to make the sacrifice – for breakfast and lunch at any rate.

All towns and villages of any size have supermarkets, fruit and vegetable stalls and bakeries.

Only in isolated villages and on remote islands is food choice limited. There may only be one all-purpose shop – a *pantopoleio* which will stock meat, vegetables, fruit, bread and tinned foods.

**Markets** Most larger towns have huge indoor *agora* (food markets) which feature a large variety of fruit and vegetable stalls, butchers, dairies and delicatessens, all under one roof. They are lively places that are worth visiting for the atmosphere as much as for the shopping. The markets at Hania are a good example.

Smaller towns have a weekly *laïki agora* (street market) with a variety of stalls selling local produce.

## DRINKS
## Nonalcoholic Drinks
**Coffee & Tea** Greek coffee is the national drink. It is a legacy of Ottoman rule and, until the Turkish invasion of Cyprus in 1974, the Greeks called it Turkish coffee. It is served with the grounds, without milk, in a small cup. Connoisseurs claim there are at least 30 variations of Greek coffee, but most people know only three – *glykos* (sweet), *metrios* (medium) and *sketos* (without sugar).

The next most popular coffee is instant, called Nescafé (which it usually is). Ask for Nescafé *me ghala* (pronounced 'me-**ga**-la') if you want it with milk. In summer, Cretans drink Nescafé chilled, with or without milk and sugar – this version is called *frappé*. Espresso and filtered coffee, once sold only in trendy cafes, are now also widely available.

Tea is not the beverage of choice in Crete but it is available, usually in bags. Herbal tea is becoming popular, especially *diktamo* or dittany tea.

**Fruit Juice & Soft Drinks** Packaged fruit juices are available everywhere. Fresh orange juice is also widely available, but doesn't come cheap.

The products of all the major soft drink multinationals are available everywhere in cans and bottles, along with local brands.

**Milk** Fresh milk can be hard to find in remote areas. Elsewhere, you'll have no problem. A litre costs about €1. UHT milk is available almost everywhere, as is condensed milk.

**Water** Tap water is safe to drink in Crete, although sometimes it doesn't taste too good. Many tourists prefer to drink bottled spring water, sold widely in 500mL and 1.5L plastic bottles. If you're happy with tap water, fill a container with it before embarking on ferries or you'll wind up paying through the nose for bottled water. Sparkling mineral water is rare.

## Alcoholic Drinks
**Beer** Beer lovers will find the market dominated by the major northern European breweries. The most popular beers are Amstel and Heineken, both brewed locally under licence. Other beers brewed locally are Henninger, Kaiser, Kronenbourg and Tuborg.

The only local beer is Mythos, launched in 1997 and widely available. It has proved popular with drinkers who find the northern European beers a bit sweet.

Imported lagers, stouts and beers are found in tourist spots such as music bars and discos. You might even spot Newcastle Brown, Carlsberg, Castlemaine XXXX and Guinness.

Supermarkets are the cheapest place to buy beer, and bottles are cheaper than cans. A 500mL bottle of Amstel or Mythos costs about €0.90 (including €0.10 deposit on the bottle), while a 500mL can costs about €0.80. Amstel also produces a low-alcohol beer and a bock, which is dark, sweet and strong.

**Wine** According to mythology, the Greeks invented or discovered wine and have produced it in Crete on a large scale for more than 3000 years.

The modern wine industry, though, is still very much in its infancy. Until the 1950s, most Greek wines were sold in bulk and were seldom distributed any farther afield than the nearest town. It wasn't until industrialisation (and the resulting rapid urban growth) that there was much call for bottled wine. Quality control was unheard of up until 1969, when appellation laws were introduced as a precursor to applying for membership of the then European Community. Wines have improved significantly since then.

Cretan wine may not make connoisseurs tremble with delight but it can be pleasant and even distinguished. The quality is uneven but the best brands tend to come from Peza, Dafnes, Sitia and Arhanes. There's also the popular Vin de Crete which is a mediocre blend of local wines. The best wines are labelled with the region of origin clearly stated. The most popular wine grapes are Villana and Thrapsathiri. The oldest grape variety is Liatiko which has been used to make red wine for the last 4000 years.

House wines served up in restaurants are usually very presentable and are a much cheaper option than bottled wine. You can usually ask for and get red *(kokkino)*, rose *(roze)* or white *(lefko)*. It is served in half-kilo or one kilo carafes and costs around €3 for a kilo – about one litre.

**Spirits** Raki is the most popular aperitif in Crete. Distilled from grape stems, it is similar to the Middle Eastern *arak*, Italian *grappa*, Irish *pocheen* or Turkish *raki*. Cretans make a big thing about the quality of their raki and go to great lengths to make sure they drink only the best – or what they believe to be the best. Not widely available commercially – and no Cretan would drink commercially produced raki anyway – raki is normally served in kafeneia, ouzeris or *tsipouradika*, or more often than not, in private homes. Good raki has a smooth mellow taste with no noticeable afterburn. As long as you eat while you consume raki, don't mix it with other alcoholic drinks and accompany it with the odd glass or two of water, you can drink considerable amounts without serious after effects or hangovers. Raki is usually served in mini-carafes costing around €3.

While commonly available in Crete, ouzo has a much more limited following and is usually only drunk by mainlanders or foreigners. Clear and colourless, ouzo turns white when water is added. A 700mL bottle of a popular brand like Ouzo 12, Olympic or Sans Rival costs about €4 in supermarkets. In an ouzeri, a glass costs from €0.75 to €1.50. It will be served neat, with a separate glass of water to be used for dilution.

## ENTERTAINMENT
### Discos & Music Bars
Discos can be found in big cities and resort areas, though not in the numbers of a decade ago. Most young Greeks prefer to head for the music bars that have proliferated to fill the void. These bars normally specialise in a particular style of music – Greek, modern rock, 1960s rock, techno and, very occasionally, jazz.

### Rock
Western rock music continues to grow in popularity, but live music remains a rarity. Concerts by Greek performers regularly come to Crete and some of the best names can be heard during the summer months. Look for posters advertising upcoming events, many of which are held in sports stadiums or other outdoor venues.

### Traditional Music & Dancing
Cretans are proud of their rich tradition of folk songs and dances. In village tavernas late at night someone is bound to produce a lyra and inspire a group sing along. Weddings are great opportunities to catch a glimpse of authentic local culture. Cretan music is often played in restaurants and clubs during the tourist season although it's usually altered to appeal to tourists.

### Cinemas
Greeks are keen movie-goers and almost every town of consequence has a cinema. English-language films are shown in English with Greek subtitles. Admission ranges from €3 in small-town movie houses to €5.50 at plush big-city cinemas.

### Theatre
The highlight of the Cretan dramatic year is the staging of ancient Greek dramas during Iraklio's Summer Festival. See Iraklio's Entertainment section for more details.

### Ballet, Classical Music & Opera
High-brow European culture has never caught on in Crete, perhaps because local music and dancing are so complex and interesting. Very few international troupes

come to Crete but if they do it would be during the Iraklio Summer Festival.

## SPECTATOR SPORTS

Cretan men are football (soccer) and basketball mad, both as spectators and participants. If you happen to be eating in a taverna on a night when a big match is being televised, expect indifferent service.

## SHOPPING

Crete has a long tradition of artisanship that has metamorphosed into a giant industry. Blue ceramics, clay pottery, handmade leather goods, woven rugs, icons, embroidered linen and finely wrought gold jewellery fill shops in all the tourist centres. In addition to crafted objects there's also wild herbs, olive oil, Cretan wine, jellies, cheeses, olives and other edibles.

Most of the products displayed in the ubiquitous souvenir stores are mass-produced. Although they can still be good value, it's worthwhile to seek out special shops that offer authentic Cretan items. Of all the large towns, you'll find the best selection of crafts in Hania.

Maybe it's the beauty of the city's architecture that has inspired artisans, but you'll find the island's most artful leather, jewellery and rugs in the streets behind the harbour.

Rethymno and Agios Nikolaos have a few good craft places but you have to plough through miles of souvenir shops. As the island's capital and richest city, Iraklio has more high-end stores for clothing, appliances and records but fewer souvenir and crafts shops.

Several villages in the interior are known for their crafts. You can get theoretically good buys on linen in Anogia and Kritsa while spending a pleasant afternoon tooling around the countryside. Take note however, many of the items on sale are these days mass-produced in Hong Kong or Indonesia. Check carefully about the origin of the item before buying. Weaving shops in Hania or lace ateliers in Gavalohori near Hania can usually be relied upon to provide the genuine article. See those chapters for details.

## Antiques

It is illegal to buy, sell, possess or export any antiquity in Crete (see Customs earlier in this chapter). However, there are antiques and 'antiques'; a lot of items only a century or two old are regarded as junk, rather than part of the national heritage. These items include handmade furniture and odds and ends from rural areas, ecclesiastical ornaments from churches and items brought back from far-flung lands.

## Ceramics

You will see ceramic objects of every shape and size – functional and ornamental – for sale throughout Crete.

The shiny dark blue glaze of Cretan ceramics is easily distinguishable from the lighter matt finish of other Greek ceramics.

The glaze should be hard enough not to scratch under the blade of a knife; a glazed bottom is the best sign of machine-made pottery.

There are a lot of places selling plaster copies of statues, busts, grave stelae and so on.

## Jewellery

You'll find more idiosyncratic pieces in silver than gold. Look for replicas of Minoan objects such as the Phaestos disk, which are well crafted and available only in Crete.

## Knives

The Cretans are rightly proud of their distinctive, hand-crafted knives with ramshorn handles and heat-forged razor sharp blades. You will see them on sale in many tourist centres. However, few of them these days are made the old fashioned way and while they may look good, they don't always cut the mustard. See the Hania & Around chapter for tips on where to find the genuine item and watch them being made – the old fashioned way.

## Leather Work

The leather is hard rather than supple but reasonably priced nonetheless; durable bags, wallets, shoes and boots are best bought on 'Leather Lane' in Hania.

Phone numbers listed incorporate changes due in Oct 2002; see p61

## Weaving

You will see many woven rugs and wall hangings for sale all over Crete. While these may look good and even be of a reasonable quality, much of the product on sale is machine made in Crete or worse still, in Asia. For really genuine articles that you can see being woven, look no further than Hania's Old Town. See that chapter for details.

## Wicker Chairs

There was a time when all Cretan tavernas had these wonderfully whacky wicker chairs that were incredibly uncomfortable to sit on for long periods, were usually too small for big bottoms and generally expensive to maintain. Sadly, plastic fantastic is now taking over the taverna seating scene and handmade, wicker chairs are seen and sat on less and less. One place in Kissamos-Kastelli is still churning them out by hand and can be bought relatively inexpensively. Shipping them home to your own suburban patio is the hard bit. See the Western Crete chapter for where to find and buy them.

# Getting There & Away

For most visitors, getting to Crete means getting first to mainland Greece, usually Athens. However, it is also possible to fly directly to Crete.

## AIR

Most travellers arrive in Crete by air, the cheapest and quickest way to get there. There's no shortage of direct charter flights between the UK, Europe and Iraklio, but very few direct scheduled flights; most flights to the island change at Athens or Thessaloniki. Direct international connections are usually via a charter airline during the busy summer months.

## Airports

If you are flying to Crete on a scheduled flight, chances are you'll arrive in Athens (or possibly Thessaloniki) and then take a domestic flight to your final destination.

Athens' Eleftherios Venizelos airport (☎ 21 0369 8300, fax 21 0369 8302, e info @aia.gr, w www.aia.gr), 27km east of Athens near the village of Spata, handles most of Greece's international connections. The modern and well-run airport opened in 2001 and most domestic flights within Greece involve a stop in Athens. It is a massive improvement on the old airports at Alimos, on Athens' western foreshore. The airport sports all the facilities that can be expected of Europe's newest international airport, with banks, shops, restaurants and tourist information. The airport can be reached by the E96 bus from either Piraeus, or the E95 from central Athens (€2.90). The travelling time is anywhere between one hour and two hours depending on traffic. Always allow plenty of time to get there.

Crete's main airport is Iraklio's Nikos Kazantzakis International Airport, the point-of-entry for most travellers arriving on the island. Built many years ago when tourism was just taking off in Crete, it is adequate, though can be strained at times with the massive influx of arrivals during the summer months. Its advantage is the proximity to Iraklio and its central location.

Hania's airport is smaller and somewhat more isolated, at 14km from Hania's town centre. It is however convenient for travellers heading to the west of Crete. By arriving in Hania, travellers avoid an extra one-hour bus ride west from Iraklio.

Sitia's minuscule domestic airport sees only two flights a week via an Olympic Airways Dornier turboprop. Still, this vital link is useful for getting quickly to the quieter, less touristy spots in eastern Crete.

## Airlines

The vast majority of domestic flights are handled by the country's much-maligned national carrier, Olympic Airways, together with its offshoot, Olympic Aviation.

Olympic Airways (☎ 0801 44 444, w www .olympic-airways.gr) has offices wherever there are flights, as well as in other major towns. The head office in Athens is at Leoforos Syngrou 96, but its most accessible ticket office is at Filellinon 15, just off Syntagma Square. Tickets can be purchased at the airport, from Olympic Airways offices or any travel agent.

Olympic offers a 25% student discount on domestic flights, but only if the flight is part of an international journey.

Olympic lost its monopoly on domestic and international routes in 1993. It took a while for any serious opposition to emerge, but there are now three established competitors on the scene.

Aegean Airlines (☎ 0801 20 000 or ☎ 21 0998 8300, w www.aegeanair.com) is the main challenger to Olympic Airways' hitherto monopoly. It flies between Athens, Hania and Iraklio. Aircraft are modern and well-appointed and the service is excellent, by most customer accounts. Its partner airline Cronus Airlines (☎ 081 20 000 or ☎ 21 0994 4444, w www.cronus.gr) handles international connections to and from Athens, but has no direct flights from Crete. Their

## Air Travel Glossary

**Alliances** Many of the world's leading airlines are now intimately involved with each other, sharing everything from reservations systems and check-in to aircraft and frequent-flyer schemes. Opponents say that alliances restrict competition. Whatever the arguments, there is no doubt that big alliances are the way of the future.

**Courier Fares** Businesses often need to send urgent documents or freight securely and quickly. Courier companies hire people to accompany the package through customs and, in return, offer a discount ticket which is sometimes a bargain. However, you may have to surrender your baggage allowance and take only carry-on luggage.

**Fares** Airlines traditionally offer 1st class (coded F), business class (coded J) and economy class (coded Y) tickets. These days there are so many promotional and discounted fares available that few passengers pay full fare.

**Lost Tickets** If you lose your airline ticket, an airline will usually treat it like a travellers cheque and, after inquiries, issue you with another one. Legally, however, an airline is entitled to treat it like cash and if you lose it then it's gone forever. Take very good care of your tickets.

**Onward Tickets** An entry requirement for many countries is that you have a ticket out of the country. If you're unsure of your next move, the easiest solution is to buy the cheapest onward ticket to a neighbouring country or a ticket from a reliable airline which can later be refunded if you do not use it.

**Open-Jaw Tickets** These are return tickets where you fly out to one place but return from another. If available, this can save you backtracking to your arrival point.

**Overbooking** Since every flight has some passengers who fail to show up, airlines often book more passengers than they have seats. Usually excess passengers make up for the no-shows, but occasionally somebody gets 'bumped' onto the next available flight. Guess who it is most likely to be? The passengers who check in late. If you do get 'bumped', you are normally offered some form of compensation.

**Reconfirmation** Some airlines require you to reconfirm your flight at least 72 hours prior to departure. Check your travel documents to see if this is the case.

**Restrictions** Discounted tickets often have various restrictions on them – such as needing to be paid for in advance and incurring a penalty to be altered or cancelled. Others are restrictions on the minimum and maximum period you must be away.

**Round-the-World Tickets** RTW tickets give you a limited period (usually a year) in which to circumnavigate the globe. You can go anywhere the carrying airlines go, as long as you don't backtrack. The number of stopovers or total number of separate flights is decided before you set off and they usually cost a bit more than a basic return flight.

**Ticketless Travel** Airlines are gradually waking up to the realisation that paper tickets are unnecessary encumbrances. On simple one-way or return trips, reservations details can be held on computer and the passenger merely shows ID to claim their seat.

**Transferred Tickets** Airline tickets cannot be transferred from one person to another. Travellers sometimes try to sell the return half of their ticket, but officials can ask you to prove that you are the person named on the ticket. On an international flight, tickets are compared with passports.

joint ticket office is at Othonos 10 on Syntagma Square.

New in 2001, Axon Airlines (☎ 21 0372 6000) has moved into the domestic market and offers daily flights from Athens to both Iraklio and Hania. Like Aegean Airlines, Axon Airlines utilises modern, new generation aircraft and offers excellent customer-oriented service. Its Athens ticket office is at Filellinon 14.

Forward planning on all airlines is advisable as domestic flights to Crete can be packed in the high season. See individual destination chapters for the specific details of flights to and from the various destination options.

This information in this book is for flights from mid-June to late-September. Outside these months, the number of flights to the islands drops considerably. Prices quoted herein are generally for one-way standard fares, though discount price ranges (where applicable) are also given.

## Buying Tickets

If you are flying to Crete from outside Europe, the plane ticket will probably be the most expensive item in your travel budget, and buying it can be an intimidating business. There will be a multitude of airlines and travel agents hoping to separate you from your money, so take time to research the options. Start early – some of the cheapest tickets must be bought months in advance, and popular flights tend to sell out early. Surf the Internet for good ticket buys. A good place to start is **W** www.travelocity.com or **W** www.itn.net.

## Charter Flights

Charter flight tickets are for seats left vacant on flights that have been block-booked by package companies. Tickets are cheap but conditions may apply on charter flights to Greece. This may involve being issued with 'compulsory' accommodation vouchers, though in practice this requirement may well be conveniently overlooked nowadays. This is particularly so with the advent of cheap scheduled services with operators such as Easyjet, or rock bottom discounts

on night flights with mainline operators such as British Airways.

Charter flight tickets are valid for up to four weeks, and usually have a minimum-stay requirement of at least three days. Sometimes it's worth buying a charter return even if you think you want to stay for longer than four weeks. The tickets can be so cheap that you can afford to throw away the return portion.

The travel section of major newspapers is the place to look for cheap charter deals. More information on charter flights is given later in this chapter under specific point-of-origin headings.

## Courier Flights

Another budget option (sometimes even cheaper than a charter flight) is a courier flight. This deal entails accompanying freight or a parcel that will be collected at the destination. The drawbacks are that your time away may be limited to one or two weeks, your luggage is usually restricted to hand luggage (the parcel or freight you carry comes out of your luggage allowance). You may also have to be a resident of the country that operates the courier service and apply for an interview before you'll be taken on board. However, courier flights to Greece are fairly thin on the ground and you will inevitably have to purchase an add-on ticket to get to Crete.

The International Association of Air Travel Couriers in the US (☎ 561-582 8320, fax 582 1581, **W** www.courier.org) has flights from six US cities to a range of European capitals – but not Athens.

For courier flights originating in Canada, contact FB On Board Courier Services in Montreal (☎ 514-631 2677). They can send you to London for C$575 return.

## Travel Agents

Many of the larger travel agents use the travel pages of national newspapers and magazines to promote their special deals. Before you make a decision, there are a number of questions you need to ask about the ticket. Find out the airline, the route, the duration of the journey, the stopovers allowed, any restrictions on the ticket and – above all – the price. Ask whether the fare quoted includes all taxes and other possible inclusions.

You may discover when you start ringing around that those impossibly cheap flights, charter or otherwise, are not available, but the agency just happens to know of another one that 'costs a bit more'. Or the agent may claim to have the last two seats available to Greece for the whole of July, which they will hold for a maximum of two hours only. Don't panic – keep ringing around.

The fares quoted in this book are intended as a guide only. They are approximate and are based on the rates advertised by travel agents at the time of writing.

### Travel Insurance

The kind of cover you get depends on your insurance and type of ticket, so ask both your insurer and your ticket-issuing agency to explain where you stand. Ticket loss is usually covered.

### Travellers with Special Needs

If you've broken your leg, require a special diet, are travelling in a wheelchair, are taking a baby or have some other special need, let the airline staff know as soon as possible – preferably when booking your ticket. Check that your request has been registered when you reconfirm your booking (at least 72 hours before departure) and again when you check in at the airport.

### Departure Tax

There is an airport tax of €20.50 on all international departures from Greece. This is paid when you buy a ticket, not at the airport.

The airport tax for domestic flights is €10, paid as part of the ticket. All prices quoted in this book include this tax.

### Domestic Baggage Allowance

The free-baggage allowance on domestic flights is 15kg. This does not apply when the domestic flight is part of an international journey, however The international free-baggage allowance of 20kg is then extended to the domestic sector. This allowance applies to all tickets for domestic travel sold and issued outside Greece.

### Mainland Greece

The following table will give you an idea of the high season frequency and approximate range of direct flight costs between the mainland and Crete. 'Daily' flights mean anywhere from one to seven flights daily.

| origin | destination | days | one way (€) |
|---|---|---|---|
| Athens | Hania | daily | 53-76 |
| Athens | Iraklio | daily | 70-80 |
| Athens | Sitia | Fri, Sun | 75 |
| Thessaloniki | Hania | daily | 103 |
| Thessaloniki | Iraklio | daily | 90-97 |
| Rhodes | Iraklio | daily | 75 |
| Santorini | Iraklio | Sat, Thu | 56 |

### The USA

The North Atlantic is the world's busiest long-haul air corridor, and the flight options to Europe – including Greece – are bewildering.

Microsoft's popular Web site (W www .expedia.msn.com) gives a broad overview of the possibilities. Other sites worth checking out are the ITN (W www.itn.net) and Travelocity (W www.travelocity.com) sites.

The *New York Times, LA Times, Chicago Tribune, San Francisco Chronicle* and *San Francisco Examiner* all publish weekly travel sections in which you'll find any number of advertisements for travel agents. Council Travel (W www.counciltravel.com) and STA Travel (W www.sta-travel.com) have offices in major cities nationwide.

New York has the highest number of direct flights to Athens, with more or less immediate connections to Crete. Olympic Airways has at least one flight a day and Delta Airlines has three a week. Apex fares range from US$960 to US$1600, depending on the season and how long you want to stay away.

Boston is the only other east coast city with flights to Athens (via Manchester) – twice weekly with Olympic Airways. Fares are the same as for flights from New York.

There are no direct flights to Athens from the west coast. There are, however, connecting flights to Athens from many US cities, either linking with Olympic Airways in New York or flying with one of the European national airlines to their home country, and then on to Athens. These connections usually involve a stopover of three or four hours.

One-way fares can work out very cheap on a stand-by basis. Airhitch (☎ 212-864 2000, W www.airhitch.org) specialises in this. It can get you to Europe one way for US$165 from the east coast and US$245 from the west coast, plus tax.

## Canada

Olympic Airways has four flights weekly from Toronto to Athens via Montreal. There are no direct flights from Vancouver, but there are connecting flights via Toronto, Amsterdam, Frankfurt and London on Canadian Airlines, KLM, Lufthansa and British Airways.

Travel CUTS (☎ 1-888-838 CUTS) has offices in all major cities and is a good place to ask about cheap deals. You should be able to get to Athens from Toronto and Montreal for about C$1150 or from Vancouver for C$1500. The *Toronto Globe & Mail*, the *Toronto Star*, the *Montreal Gazette* and the *Vancouver Sun* all carry advertisements for cheap tickets.

## Australia

Olympic Airways has two flights a week from Sydney and Melbourne to Iraklio or Hania, via Athens. Return fares are normally priced from about A$1549 in the low season to A$2199 in the high season.

Thai International and Singapore Airlines also have convenient connections to Athens, as well as a reputation for good service. However you will need to arrange an add-on leg (AU$110 one way) to Iraklio or Hania with one of the three domestic carriers.

STA Travel and Flight Centre International are two of Australia's major dealers in cheap fares. The Sunday tabloid newspapers and the travel sections of the *Sydney Morning Herald* and Melbourne's *Age* are a good place to look for cheap flights.

AXIS Travel Centre (☎ 08 8331 3222, fax 08 8364 2922, e axistravel@msn.com .au) in Adelaide offer special deals to Athens with Gulf Air and Egypt Air starting at A$1499 return in low season. These fares may include free hotel accommodation if no immediate connection to Athens is available.

## New Zealand

There are no direct flights from New Zealand to Athens. There are connecting flights via Sydney, Melbourne, Bangkok and Singapore on Olympic Airways, United Airlines, Qantas Airways, Thai Airways and Singapore Airlines.

## The UK

British Airways (☎ 0845 773 3377, W www .britishairways.com), Olympic Airways (☎ 0870 606 0460, W www.olympic-air ways.gr) and Virgin Atlantic (☎ 01293 747 747, W www.virginatlantic.com), operate daily flights between London and Athens. Pricing is very competitive, with all three offering return tickets for around UK£200 in the high season, plus tax. These prices are for midweek departures; you will pay about UK£40 more for weekend departures.

There are connecting flights to Athens from Edinburgh, Glasgow and Manchester.

Cronus Airlines (☎ 020 7580 3500, W www.cronus.gr) flies the London-Athens route five times a week for £210, and offers connections to Thessaloniki on the same fare. Olympic Airways has five direct London-Thessaloniki flights a week. Most scheduled flights from London leave from Heathrow.

The cheapest scheduled flights are with no-frills specialist EasyJet (☎ 0870 6 000 000, W www.easyjet.com), which has two Luton-Athens flights daily. One-way fares range from a ridiculously cheap UK£17 to UK£177 depending on the date of travel. You can calculate your own fare by visiting their Web site.

There are numerous charter flights between the UK and Crete. Typical UK-Crete charter fares are UK£79/129 one way/return in the low season and UK£99/189 in the high season. These prices are for advance bookings, but even in the high season it's possible to pick up last-minute deals for as little as UK£59/99. Charter flights to Crete also fly from Birmingham, Cardiff, Glasgow, Luton, Manchester and Newcastle. Contact the Air Travel Advisory Bureau (☎ 020 7636 5000, W www.atab.co.uk) for information about current charter flight bargains.

London is Europe's major centre for discounted fares. Some of the most reputable agencies selling discount tickets are:

**STA Travel** (☎ 0870 160 6070, W www.statravel .co.uk), 86 Old Brompton Rd, London SW7
**Trailfinders** (☎ 020 7937 1234, W www.trail finder.com), 215 Kensington High St, London W8
**Usit Campus** (☎ 0870 240 1010, W www.usit campus.co.uk), 52 Grosvenor Gardens, London SW1

Listings publications such as *Time Out*, the Sunday papers, the *Evening Standard* and *Exchange & Mart* carry advertisements for cheap fares. The *Yellow Pages* is worth scanning for travel agents' ads, and look out for the free magazines and newspapers widely available in London, especially *TNT*, *Footloose*, *Southern Cross* and *LAM* – you can pick them up outside the main train and tube stations.

Some travel agents specialise in flights for students aged under 30 and travellers aged under 26 (you need an ISIC card or an official youth card). Whatever your age, you should be able to find something to suit your budget.

Most British travel agents are registered with ABTA (Association of British Travel Agents). If you have paid for your flight through an ABTA-registered agent who then goes out of business, ABTA will guarantee a refund or an alternative. If an agency is registered with ABTA, its advertisements will usually say so.

## Continental Europe
Athens is linked to every major city in Europe by either Olympic Airways or the flag carrier of each country.

**France** Air France (☎ 0802 802 802) and Olympic Airways (☎ 01 44 94 58 58) have at least four Paris-Athens flights daily between them. Cronus Airlines (☎ 01 47 42 56 77) flies the same route four times weekly. Axon Airlines (☎ 01 44 71 07 08) have a daily flight to Athens with a later connection to Iraklio and a next-day connection to Hania. Olympic Airways also has three flights weekly from Marseille to Athens. Expect to pay from €320 to €427 plus taxes for return flights with any of these airlines in the high season.

Charter flights are much cheaper. You'll pay around €305 in the high season for a return flight from Paris to Iraklio or Hania. The fare to Athens drops to €230 in the low season. Reliable travel agents include:

**Air Sud** (☎ 01 40 41 66 66)
  18 Rue du Pont-Neuf, F-75001 Paris
**Atsaro** (☎ 01 42 60 98 98)
  9 Rue de l'Echelle, F-75001 Paris
**Bleu Blanc** (☎ 01 40 21 31 31)
  53 Avenue de la République, F-75011 Paris
**Héliades** (☎ 01 53 27 28 21)
  24–27 Rue Basfroi, F-75011 Paris
**La Grèce Autrement** (☎ 01 44 41 69 95)
  72 Boulevard Saint Michel, F-75006 Paris
**Nouvelles Frontières** (☎ 01 03 33 33)
  87 Boulevard de Grenelle, F-75015 Paris
**Planète Havas** (☎ 01 53 29 40 00)
  26 Avenue de l'Opéra, F-75001 Paris

**Germany** Air Greece has three flights a week from Iraklio to Stuttgart and four flights a week to Cologne in the summer, stopping at Thessaloniki. Iraklio is linked by Lufthansa to Frankfurt with a direct flight on Saturday and Sunday.

Atlas Reisewelt has offices throughout Germany and is a good place to start checking prices.

**The Netherlands** KLM-associate Transavia has direct flights between Amsterdam and Iraklio on Monday and Friday. Reliable travel agents in Amsterdam include:

**Budget Air** (☎ 020 627 12 51) Rokin 34
**Malibu Travel** (☎ 020 626 32 20, e postbus@ pointtopoint.demon.nl) Prinsengracht 230
**NBBS Reizen** (☎ 020-624 09 89) Rokin 66

## Turkey

Olympic Airways and Turkish Airlines share the İstanbul-Athens route, with at least one flight a day each. The full fare is US$250 one way. Olympic Airways also flies twice weekly between İstanbul and Thessaloniki (US$190). Students qualify for a 50% discount on both routes.

## Cyprus

Olympic Airways flies twice a week direct from Larnaka to Iraklio (CY£85.50). Olympic Airways and Cyprus Airways share the Cyprus-Greece routes. Both airlines have three flights daily from Larnaka to Athens. Cyprus Airways also flies from Pafos to Athens once a week in winter, and twice a week in summer.

## LAND
## Turkey

**Bus** There are daily connections between İstanbul and Athens. Varan/Bospor charges around US$65 for the one-way trip from Turkey.

**Train** There are daily trains between İstanbul and Athens (US$50) via Alexandroupolis and Thessaloniki. The service in Turkey to the Greek border is slow and there is usually a delay at the border. From Pythio to Athens, the service is via the comfortable Inter City train. Change at Thessaloniki or hop on a ferry to Crete in the northern capital.

**Car & Motorcycle** Crossing points for vehicles are at Kipi, 43km north-east of Alexandroupolis and at Kastanies, 139km north-east of Alexandroupolis. Kipi is more convenient if you're coming from İstanbul. The new Via Egnatia is slowly being built and sections of this fast, modern highway are already in operation in Turkey and Greece.

## Bulgaria

**Bus** There are three Sofia-Thessaloniki buses (US$18, six hours) daily with the 9am bus continuing on to Athens (US$41, 12 hours). Buses leave from Sofia's MATPU international bus station (☎ 02 952 5004) at Damian Gruev 23.

**Train** There's a daily Sofia-Thessaloniki train – the *Transbalkan* – connecting with OSE services to Athens. The *Transbalkan* leaves Sofia at 11pm and arrives in Thessaloniki (sleeper US$24, 8¼ hours) at 7.15am.

**Car & Motorcycle** The Bulgarian border crossing is at Promahonas, 145km north-east of Thessaloniki and 50km from Serres. There is an alternative crossing point at Ormenio in north-eastern Thrace.

## Albania

**Bus** There is a daily bus between Tirana and Athens (US$35, 24 hours) via Gjirokastra and Ioannina. The bus departs from in front of Skenderbeg Travel in Tirana at 5.30am daily.

**Car & Motorcycle** There are three crossing points between Albania and Greece. The main one is at Kakavia, 60km northwest of Ioannina; the second is at Krystallopigi, north-west of Kastoria. There is a third, little-used crossing at Sagiada 18km north of Igoumenitsa in Epirus.

## Former Yugoslav Republic of Macedonia

**Train** There is one train daily from Skopje (US$10, three hours). There is no passenger service between Bitola and Florina, despite the existence of a rail line.

**Car & Motorcycle** There are three border crossings between FYROM and Greece. One is at Evzoni, 68km north of Thessaloniki. This is on the main highway from Belgrade to Thessaloniki via Skopje. The second border crossing is at Niki, 16km north of Florina and the third, less-used crossing is at Doïrani, 70km north of Thessaloniki via the shores of Lake Doïrani.

## Western Europe

Overland travel between Western Europe and Greece is mainly undertaken by car and motorcycle owners these days. Most drivers and riders take their car or bike to one of the

*[Continued on page 99]*

**Phone numbers listed incorporate changes due in Oct 2002; see p61**

## Athens & Piraeus

The greater majority of travellers heading to Crete will be passing through Athens and Piraeus. While you can avoid Athens all together by heading straight to Piraeus, the following information will help you navigate what can at first sight seem a very confusing pair of cities.

### Athens Αθήνα

Athens seems a disorienting and noisy city at first and many choose not to linger, preferring to head straight for Crete or for some other Aegean island en route. This is a pity because Athens grows on you and is a city with an enormous wealth of history, and unlike many tourist resorts on the islands, Athens never shuts down. Unless you are flying to Crete directly, or taking a ferry from Thessaloniki or Rhodes, you will inevitably pass through the capital on your way to your destination.

### Orientation

Although Athens is a huge, sprawling city, nearly everything of interest to travellers is located within a small area bounded by Omonia Square (Plateia Omonias) to the north, Monastiraki Square to the west, Syntagma Square to the east and the Plaka district to the south. The city's two major landmarks, the Acropolis and Lykavittos Hill, can be seen from just about everywhere in this area. Syntagma is the heart of modern Athens; it's flanked by luxury hotels, banks and fast-food outlets and dominated by the old royal palace – home of the Greek parliament since 1935. The Plaka is the old quarter of Athens and probably the most attractive part of the city. Athens' two train stations are about 1km north of Omonia Square and are now linked to central Athens and Piraeus via the Athens Metro.

### Information

The main EOT tourist office (☎ 21 0331 0561) is close to Syntagma at Amerikis 2. It has a useful free map of Athens and information about ferry departures from Piraeus to Crete and to other islands. The office is open 9am to 7pm Monday to Friday and 9.30am to 2pm Saturday.

Most banks are near Syntagma and are open 8am to 2pm Monday to Thursday and 8am to 1.30pm Friday. Most banks now have ATM machines and some have currency exchange machines.

The most convenient – but busiest – post office is right on Syntagma Square. The handiest Internet cafe to Syntagma Square is the Sofokleus.com Internet Cafe at Stadiou 5, behind the Flocafe.

### Highlights

Everyone who comes to Athens visits the famous **Acropolis** and its **Parthenon** temple. A visit to the Acropolis should be coupled with a visit to the excellent **Archaeological Museum**. A walk up to **Lykavittos Hill** is a must. From the summit you will enjoy some of the most spectacular views in Athens. Pick up bric-a-brac or some unusual souvenirs at Athens' **flea market** and for some of the most atmospheric evenings in Athens wander around the **Plaka** district at night.

### Places to Stay & Eat

*Festos Youth & Student Guest House* (☎ 21 0323 2455, consolas@hol.gr, Filellinon 18) Dorm beds €10.50-12. Festos is a popular place with travellers despite being on one of the noisiest streets in Athens. There is a bar-cum-snack bar on the first floor.

*Student & Travellers' Inn* (☎ 21 0324 4808, fax 21 0321 0065, e students-inn@ath.forthnet.gr, Kydathineon 16) Dorm beds €16, singles/doubles €35/47. Possibly the best option in central Athens right in the heart of Plaka.

*Acropolis House Pension* (☎ 21 0322 2344, fax 21 0322 6241, Kodrou 6-8) Singles/doubles €45/55. This hotel is in a beautifully preserved 19th-century house and all rooms have central heating.

*Ouzeri Kouklis* (Tripodon 14) Mezedes €1.80-3.50. Kouklis serves only mezedes which are brought

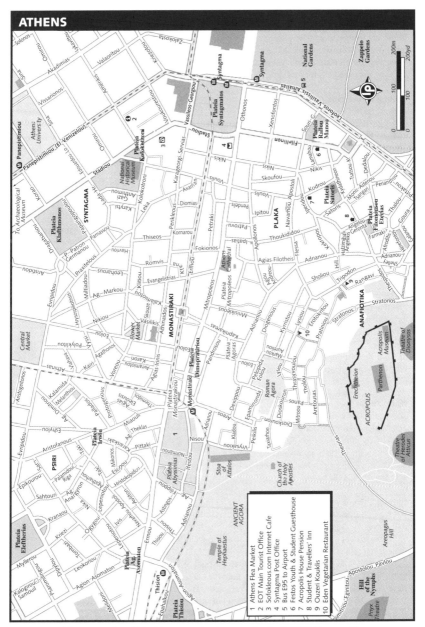

**ATHENS**

1 Athens Flea Market
2 EOT Main Tourist Office
3 Sofokleous.com Internet Cafe
4 Syntagma Post Office
5 Bus E95 to Airport
6 Festos Youth & Student Guesthouse
7 Acropolis House Pension
8 Student & Travellers' Inn
9 Ouzeri Kouklis
10 Eden Vegetarian Restaurant

## Athens & Piraeus

round on a large tray for you to take your pick. They include flaming sausages – ignited at your table – and cuttlefish as well as the usual dips.

*Eden Vegetarian Restaurant* (Lysiou 12) Mains €4.50-5.90. Eden has been around for years, substituting soya products for meat in tasty vegetarian versions of mousakas and other Greek favourites.

### Getting to/from the Airport

Athens' Eleftherios Venizelos airport, 27km east of Athens, opened in 2001. The only disadvantage is the greater distance from central Athens and the lack, as yet, of a Metro link.

Buses E95 and E96 to and from the airport leave both central Athens and the port of Piraeus every 20 minutes or so. The fare is a flat €3 and the journey takes around an hour – more if there is heavy traffic. A taxi to or from the airport and central Athens or Piraeus costs between €14.70-20.50.

### Piraeus Πειραιάς

Piraeus (pir-ay-**ahs**) is the port of Athens, the main port of Greece and one of the major ports of the Mediterranean. All ferries to Crete and most ferries to the Aegean Islands leave from Piraeus. The port is a busy, chaotic place especially during Greek holiday periods. Don't bother staying in Piraeus; the accommodation options in Athens are much better.

### Orientation & Information

Ferries to Crete all leave from the north-west corner of the harbour. If coming by metro to the Piraeus metro station, or train to the Peloponnisou station, turn right and walk about 200m. If arriving by train at the Larisis station, the Crete ferries are right in front of you as you exit the train station. The main ticket offices are in the central section of the harbour, though you can also buy tickets at agencies in the metro station.

Most main banks are in central Piraeus, though there is a handy ATM terminal on the Cretan ferries quay. EOT has a tourist office out of the way at Zea Marina. Stock up on tourist data from Athens or from the airport. The main post office is on the corner of Tsamadou and Filonos, just north of Plateia Themistokleous and you can check your email at the Surf Internet Café at Platanos 3, just off Iroön Polytehniou.

### Places to Eat

There are dozens of cafes, restaurants and fast-food places along the waterfront. The tiny *Restaurant I Folia* (Akti Poseidonos), opposite Plateia Karaïskaki, is a rough and ready place that does a bowl of gigantes beans for €2.50, calamari for €3.50 and mousakas for €3.20.

If you want to stock up on supplies before a ferry trip, head for the area just inland from Poseidonos. You'll find fresh fruit and vegetables at the market, open 8am to 8pm Monday to Friday, and 8am to 4pm Saturday.

### Getting There & Away

Bus No 049 runs from Omonia Square in Athens to the Main Harbour – for ferries to Crete. Bus No 040 leaves Syntagma Square for Piraeus also. The fare is €0.35. Bus E96 to and from the airport (€3) leaves every 20 minutes or so from near the main ferry ticket offices on Plateia Karaïskaki in Piraeus harbour.

The metro links Piraeus with Central Athens, including Syntagma Square and the Larisis train station. The fare is €0.45 to or from Piraeus. Both the Larisis and Peloponnisou train stations in Athens have connections to equivalent stations in Piraeus. Thus, if coming from Patra or Thessaloniki by train you can come to Piraeus directly. Check your train itinerary for its final destination.

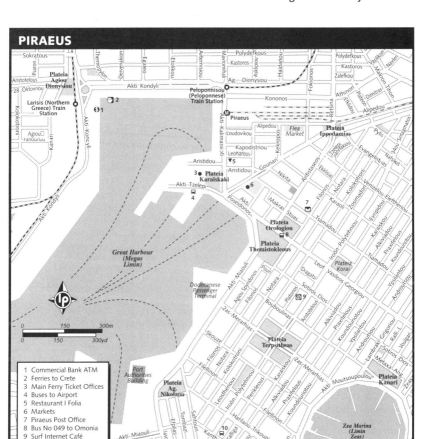

PIRAEUS

1  Commercial Bank ATM
2  Ferries to Crete
3  Main Ferry Ticket Offices
4  Buses to Airport
5  Restaurant I Folia
6  Markets
7  Piraeus Post Office
8  Bus No 049 to Omonia
9  Surf Internet Café
10  Bus No 040 to Syntagma

[Continued from page 95]

Italian ports such as Venice, Ancona, Bari or Brindisi and ship it across to Igoumenitsa or Patra. Passports are rarely required when crossing western European borders, the exception being the borders with Switzerland.

**Bus** There are no bus services to Greece from the UK, nor from anywhere else in northern Europe.

**Train** Unless you have a Eurail pass or are aged under 26 and eligible for a discounted fare, travelling to Greece by train is prohibitively expensive. In order to get to Crete, you can take a train to Brindisi in Italy and use your Eurail pass for a free passage to Patra in Greece. From Patra you can take a train directly to Piraeus harbour, or to Kalamata for your onward ferry connection to Crete.

**Car & Motorcycle** Almost all drivers to Greece now go by ferry via Italy from one of the four main ports serving Greece. From Venice, for example, it is now possible to reach Greece in as little as 18 hours via one of the new high speed car ferries. Crossing from Italy to Greece no longer requires border formalities and is preferred by the greater majority of drivers and riders heading to Greece.

It is still possible to travel to Greece via Slovenia, Croatia, Yugoslavia and the Former Yugoslav Republic of Macedonia, but the savings are not huge and are far outweighed by the distance involved and the necessity to now cross five borders.

It is feasible on weekends in summer to arrive in Patra by ferry in the morning and be on a high speed ferry to Crete by lunchtime, arriving in Iraklio at 6.30pm the same day. Otherwise, you can just as easily take an overnight ferry to Crete on the same day you arrive in Greece.

**Purchase Repurchase Schemes** It is hardly worth hiring a car to drive to Crete all the way from Western Europe since you can hire a car in Crete anyway. However, if you are resident outside the European Union and you plan to make an extended visit to Crete, or include other countries as part of your itinerary then it may be in your interest to look at the Purchase-Repurchase schemes to meet your transport needs.

Basically you lease a brand-new car for the duration of your stay at rates considerably below daily rental rates. The two major players are Peugeot and Renault, both French car manufacturers. This means in effect that you need to pick up your car in France, or for an extra premium from another designated European city.

You can then drive your car to more or less anywhere in Europe (including Greece of course) and return to a nominated French or European city of your choice (but not Athens). The most efficient way to get to Crete is to pick up your car (at no extra cost) from either Geneva or Nice airports and drive it to Venice or Ancona (1½ days) then take a ferry to Crete, via Piraeus, from there.

For further details on this excellent scheme contact the following agents:

**France**
**Peugeot** (☎ 01 49 04 81 56, fax 01 49 04 82 50)
**Renault** (☎ 01 40 40 32 32, fax 01 42 41 83 47)

**Australia**
**Peugeot** (☎ 02 9976 3000, fax 02 9976 2438, [e] enquiries@driveway.com.au, [w] www.drive away.com.au)
**Renault** (☎ 02 9299 3344, fax 02 9262 4590)

**Canada**
**Peugeot** (☎ 514 735 3083, fax 514 342 8801, [w] www.europauto.qc.ca)
**Renault**, (☎ 450 461 1149, fax 9450 461 0207)

**New Zealand**
**Peugeot** (☎ 09-914 9100, fax 09-379 4111)
**Renault** (☎ 09-525 8800, fax 09-525 8818)

**South Africa**
**Peugeot** (☎ 011-458 1600, fax 011 455 2818)
**Renault** (☎ 011 325 2345, fax 011 325 2840)

**USA**
**Peugeot** (☎ 1800 572 9655, fax 201 934 7501, [w] www.auto-france.com), (☎ 1800 223 1516, fax 212 246 1458, [w] www.europebycar.com), (☎ 914 825 3000, fax 914 835 5449, [w] www .kemwel.com)
**Renault** (☎ 1800 221 1052, fax 212 725 5375)

## SEA
## Domestic Ferries
Crete is well served by ferries and has mainland connections from Piraeus, Thessaloniki, Rhodes, Kalamata and Gythio plus a scattering of Cyclades islands and Kythira. There are many services in summer (May–October) but services in winter are considerably curtailed. Ferries are generally large car ferries and range in quality from 'comfortable' to luxurious.

**Routes** The hub of Greece's ferry network is Piraeus, the port of Athens. Ferries to Crete all depart from the western end of Piraeus' sprawling port. The departure points are convenient for the Larisis train station in Piraeus, but involve a 10-minute hike from either the Metro station or the Peloponnisou station nearby. From central Piraeus allow a good 15-20 minutes walking to reach the Crete ferry quays. Ferries leave here for Iraklio, Rethymno, Hania and Kissamos-Kastelli. Check the destination board at the stern of the ferry for your own route.

**Schedules** Ferry timetables change from year to year and season to season, and ferries

## Island Hopping to Crete

From Piraeus there are only two options for hopping off at other islands along the way to Crete. ANEN Lines' F/B *Myrtidiotissa* does a long 'milk run' via two Peloponnese ports and the islands of Kythira and Antikythira, while LANE Lines makes a stop in Milos in the western Cyclades on its thrice-weekly run to eastern Crete ports. From Thessaloniki, you have a choice of stopping off at Skiathos, Syros, Naxos, Mykonos or Santorini on Minoan Lines' F/B *El Greco* on its thrice weekly haul from one end of the Aegean to the other. You can head to any of these intermediate islands from Piraeus or elsewhere and pick up the Iraklio connection at your leisure. From Rhodes you have a choice of three islands to hop off at: Halki, Karpathos and Kasos, using LANE Lines' two- to three-times weekly connections from the Dodecanese.

꿰ᚨᛏᛎᚨᛊᛎᛎ ᚼ ᛁ ᚼ ᛎ ᚼᚨᛊᛑᚼᚼᛎᚨ ᚯ

are subject to delays and cancellations at short notice due to bad weather, strikes or boats simply conking out. No timetable is infallible, but the comprehensive weekly list of departures from Piraeus put out by the EOT in Athens is as accurate as humanly possible. The people to go to for the most up-to-date ferry information are the local port police *(limenarhio)*, whose offices are usually on or near the quayside.

There's a lot of information about ferry services on the Internet. Try the Web site at **w** www.ferries.gr with its useful search program and links.

Throughout the year there is at least one ferry a day from Piraeus to Crete. In summer the frequency can rise to three or four per day.

Travelling time can vary considerably from one ferry to another, depending on the ship and the route it takes. Before buying your ticket, check how many stops the boat is going to make, and its estimated arrival time.

**Costs** Prices are fixed by the government, and are determined by the distance travelled rather than by the facilities of a particular

boat. There can be big differences in the size, comfort and facilities of boats offering rival services on a given route, but the fares will be the same. You may find that differences in prices at ticket agencies are the result of some agents sacrificing part of the commission to qualify as a 'discount service'. The discount is seldom more than €1.

**Classes** The large ferries nominally have two classes – first and second – but the demarcation lines between them are blurred (see the boxed text 'Ferry Travel to Crete' later in this section). You pay instead for the quality of the cabin, or the choice between aircraft type seats or deck passage. Cabins range from two-berth outside cabins (first class), to four-berth inside cabins (second class). Aircraft-type seats can be very comfortable (Minoan's high speed boats) to bearable (most older boats). Deck class is hard and uncompromising and not usually custom-designed for deck-class sleepers. Modern ferry boats tend to have bare, exposed deck sections, but there are always wind-protected areas where you can set up temporary camp.

Deck class remains an economical way to travel, while a 1st-class ticket can cost almost as much as flying on some routes. Children under four travel for free, while children between four and 10 pay half fare. Full fares apply for children over 10. Unless you state otherwise when purchasing a ticket, you will automatically be given deck class. Prices quoted in this book are for deck class as this is what most travellers opt for.

**Ticket Purchase** Ferries are prone to delays and cancellations in bad weather, so it's best not to buy a ticket until it has been confirmed that the ferry is operating. If you need to reserve a car space, you may need to pay in advance. If the service is cancelled, you can transfer your ticket to the next available service with that company.

Agencies selling tickets line the waterfront of most ports, but there's rarely one that sells tickets for every boat, and often an agency is reluctant to give information about a boat it doesn't sell tickets for. This means

## Ferry Travel to Crete

It wasn't too long ago that ferry travel in Greece was a true ordeal. Deregulation of the once firmly closed domestic ferry market, a realisation by Greek ferry companies that 40-year-old grime buckets were no longer acceptable modes of travel and the aftershock of the F/B *Express Samaina* sinking in September 2000 have given the domestic and international ferry scene a much needed injection of quality.

Ferry services to and from Crete still differ in quality and service. The high speed boats of Minoan Lines linking Piraeus and Iraklio are by far the most comfortable means to get to and from the island. Both day and night services make the run to Crete or Piraeus in a flat six hours on modern, Western European standard monster ferries – notably the F/B *Festos Palace* and the almost identical F/B *Knossos Palace*. Minoan's competitors ANEK, while a comfortable option, still use older, smaller boats. Two smaller, ageing ANEK boats the F/B *Preveli* and the F/B *Arkadi* make the overnight run between Rethymno and Piraeus and are a popular choice among backpackers wishing to make landfall in central Crete. Larger ANEK boats also link the western Crete port of Souda which serves Hania, a convenient entry point for hikers wishing to tackle the Samaria Gorge.

The one-boat ANEN Lines of western Crete run a small ferry linking Piraeus and Gythio or Kalamata in the Peloponnese with Kissamos-Kastelli. It is a long haul to Kissamos (19 hours), so Iraklio may be a quicker option. To the east, LANE Lines links Piraeus with Agios Nikolaos and Sitia with a stop in Milos. Its two boats F/B *Vitsentzos Kornaros* and F/B *Ierapetra* are fairly old, but comfortable enough. From Crete they continue on to Kasos, Karpathos, Halki and Rhodes.

you have to check the timetables displayed outside each agency to find out which ferry is next to depart – or ask the port police. If you haven't purchased a ticket from an agency, ticket booths open up beside a ferry about an hour before departure.

### International Connections

**Cyprus & Israel** Two companies ply the route between the Israeli port of Haifa and Piraeus via Lemesos in Cyprus and Rhodes. One of the companies, Salamis Lines, also operates via Port Said in Egypt. From Rhodes you can connect with LANE services to Sitia and Agios Nikolaos in Crete. During July and August, Salamis Lines' F/B *Nisos Kypros* leaves Haifa at 8pm on Sunday, Port Said at 8pm on Monday and Lemesos at 4pm on Tuesday, reaching Rhodes at 11am on Wednesday.

Poseidon Lines operates a similar service throughout the year. The F/B *Olympia* sails from Haifa at 7pm on Monday and Lemesos at 2pm on Tuesday, arriving in Rhodes at 6.30am on Wednesday.

Salamis Lines has the higher fare structure of the two services. High-season deck-class

fares from Haifa or Port Said to Rhodes with Poseidon Lines is €97 and with Salamis Lines is €115; Poseidon from Lemesos to Rhodes charge €62 and Salamis Lines €76.50. An aircraft-style seat is an extra €9 while a bed in the cheapest cabin is an extra €30-40.

Information about both companies' schedules can be obtained from Viamare Travel Ltd (☎ 020 7431 4560, fax 431 5456, ⓔ ferries@viamare.com) at 2 Sumatra Rd, London NW6 1PU in the UK.

Sailing details, current tickets prices for both companies and bookings details can be found online at Ⓦ www.greekislands.gr/po seidon or at Ⓦ www.viamare.com/Salamis /index.html.

Departure tax from Lemesos is CY£15-18 when leaving by sea, however it's normally included in the cost of your ferry ticket.

**Turkey** You can not get to Crete directly from Turkey. You will have to cross from Marmaris in Turkey to Rhodes and pick up the three-times-weekly LANE ferry connections to eastern Crete. Between April and October there are three ferries

## Domestic Ferry Schedules

| departure city | destination city | boats per week | duration | fares |
|---|---|---|---|---|
| Antikythira | Kissamos-Kastelli | 5 | 2 hours | €6.50 |
| Gythio | Kissamos-Kastelli | 5 | 7 hours | €15.60 |
| Halki | Agios Nikolaos | 3 | 7 hours | €12.60 |
| Halki | Sitia | 2 | 5½ hours | €12.60 |
| Kalamata | Kissamos-Kastelli | 2 | 10 hours | €17.60 |
| Karpathos | Sitia | 3 | 6 hours | €11 |
| Karpathos | Agios Nikolaos | 3 | 7 hours | €13 |
| Kasos | Agios Nikolaos | 3 | 5½ hours | €8.50 |
| Kasos | Sitia | 3 | 4 hours | €8.50 |
| Kythira | Kissamos-Kastelli | 5 | 4 hours | €12.90 |
| Milos | Agios Nikolaos | 3 | 7½ | €16.30 |
| Milos | Sitia | 3 | 9½ hours | €16.30 |
| Naxos | Iraklio | 2 | 6¼ hours | €16.50 |
| Paros | Iraklio | 3 | 8½ hours | €16.50 |
| Piraeus | Agios Nikolaos | 3 | 12 hours | €23.20 |
| Piraeus | Hania | daily | 9 hours | €22 |
| Piraeus | Kissamos-Kastelli | 2 | 19 hours | €17.60 |
| Piraeus | Rethymno | daily | 10 hours | €22 |
| Piraeus | Sitia | 3 | 14½ hours | €24 |
| Rhodes | Agios Nikolaos | 3 | 10½ hours | €19 |
| Rhodes | Sitia | 3 | 10 hours | €20 |
| Santorini | Iraklio | 3 | 4 hours | €12 |
| Skiathos | Iraklio | 1 | 17½ hours | €31.50 |
| Syros | Iraklio | 1 | 8½ hours | €18 |
| Thessaloniki | Iraklio | 3 | 23 hours | €38 |
| Tinos | Iraklio | 1 | 8¾ hours | €20 |

daily from Marmaris to Rhodes and less-frequent services in winter. There are also daily hydrofoils to Rhodes (weather permitting) from April to October for around US$25.

**Italy** Crete is not linked to Italy by any direct ferry. However, the two ferry companies, Minoan Lines and ANEK, provide services to both Italy and Crete so you can easily book your outward and return tickets from Italy and Crete with either company to benefit from any discounts fares that may be on offer. From the mainland port of Patra – where most ferries from Italy dock – to Piraeus is a three-hour drive or longer by bus or train. More adventurous travellers could head from Patra to Kalamata,

or Gythio in the Peloponnese and take a ferry to Kissamos-Kastelli in far western Crete.

There are ferries to Greece from the Italian ports of Ancona, Bari, Brindisi, Trieste and Venice and most dock in Patra. In order to get to Crete you can take any train or bus to Athens and then Piraeus for a boat to Crete. There are buses from Patra to Athens (€10.90, three hours) every 30 minutes, with the last at 9.45pm. There are nine trains a day to Athens. Four are slow trains (€5, 4½ hours) and five are express intercity trains (€9, 3½ hours). The last intercity train leaves at 6pm, and the last slow train leaves at 8pm.

The following ferry services in this table are for the high season (July and August) and

## Ferry Services from Italy to Greece

| origin | destination | frequency | duration | one way (€) |
|--------|-------------|-----------|----------|-------------|
| Ancona | Patra | daily | 20-23 hours | 55-78 |
| Bari | Patra | daily | 15 hours | 37-48 |
| Brindisi | Patra | daily | 13 hours | 23-35 |
| Trieste | Patra | three per week | 37 hours | 71 |
| Venice | Patra | five per week | 18-30 hours | 70-75 |

prices are for one-way deck class. Deck class on these services means exactly that. If you want a reclining, aircraft-type seat, you'll be up for another 10 to 15% on top of the listed fares. Most companies offer discounts for return travel. Prices are about 30% less in the low season. Prices given here are the range of prices offered by different companies.

The following are the main companies that run ferries between Italy and Greece.

**Adriatica** (☎ 21 0429 0487, fax 21 0429 0490, W www.adriatica.it), Akti Miaouli & Flessa 85, GR-185 38 Piraeus, Greece

**ANEK** (☎ 2821 024 000, fax 2821 027 611, e anek@anek.gr, W www.anek.gr), Plastira & Apokoronou, Hania, GR-731 34, Greece

**Blue Star Ferries** (☎ 21 0422 5000, fax 21 0422 5265, W www.bluestarferries.com/english/), Akti Posidonos 26, GR-185 31, Piraeus, Greece

**Fragline** (☎ 21 0822 1285, 21 0823 7109, e fragline@internet.gr, W www.fragline.gr), Rethymnou 5a, GR-106 82 Athens, Greece

**Hellenic Mediterranean** (☎ 21 0422 5341, fax 21 0422 5317, e hml@otenet.gr, W www.greekislands.gr), Plateia Loudovikou 4, GR-185 10 Piraeus, Greece

**Minoan Lines** (☎ 21 0419 9900, fax 21 0413 5000, e booking-eta@minoan.gr, W www.minoan.gr), Akti Kondyli & Etolikou 2, GR-185 45 Piraeus, Greece

**Superfast Ferries** (☎ 21 0331 3252, fax 21 0331 0369, e info@superfast.com, W www.superfast.com), Alkyonidon 157, GR-166 73, Voula, Greece

**Ventouris Ferries** (☎ 21 0482 8001 fax 21 0481 3701, e info@ventouris.com, W www.ventouris.gr), Pireos 91, GR-185 41 Piraeus, Greece

There are distinct advantages and disadvantages between the various routes to and from Italy. Choose your route carefully based upon your own transport needs and budget. Ferries from southern Italian ports may be cheaper, but cost more to get to in terms of time, hotel accommodation, expensive Italian fuel and autostrada toll fees.

Ferries from northern Italian ports like Venice, Trieste and Ancona cost more on average, but involve considerably less travel expenses to reach and allow passengers the option of a mini-cruise before arriving in Greece.

### Venice to Corfu, Igoumenitsa & Patra

This route has become very popular over recent years as Venice is the closest Adriatic port to the main central European cities. Bookings are essential in the high season. Port facilities are chaotic-looking, but reasonably efficient. The train station is a 25-minute walk to the Stazione Marittima (international ferry terminal). Minoan Lines and Blue Star Ferries both offer good services on comfortable boats from Venice.

### Trieste to Corfu, Igoumenitsa & Patra

This route is better suited to travellers from Eastern Europe or Austria and offers the same logistical advantages as those afforded by travelling from Venice. Currently only one company (ANEK) runs ferries from Trieste, but you can make your booking to Crete through the same company as they also have services to Crete from Piraeus.

### Ancona to Corfu, Igoumenitsa & Patra

This route has become increasingly popular in recent years. There can be up to three boats daily in summer, and at least one a day year-round. It is a good mid-range port, but involves a slightly longer drive or train ride for travellers coming from central Europe. Superfast Ferries offer a high-speed link from Ancona to Patra. The train station is very close to the port. Other ferry companies such as Minoan and ANEK serve Corfu and Igoumenitsa as well.

**Bari to Corfu, Igoumenitsa & Patra** Bari is a popular southern port alternative to the busy Brindisi and involves somewhat less travelling or driving time to reach than Brindisi further south. It is still a long way down the Italian coastline, but is also served by the speedy, yet more expensive, Superfast Ferries company that offers a direct high-speed link to Patra. The train station is a fair hike from the port so you will need to take a cab. Other ferry companies also serve Corfu and Igoumenitsa.

**Brindisi to Corfu, Igoumenitsa & Patra** Brindisi has long been the port of preference for backpacker travellers on a Eurailpass or similar discount rail pass. Eurailpass holders get an (almost) free ride on Hellenic Mediterranean to the Greek mainland; port taxes are in addition. The crossing is short – eight hours to Igoumenitsa – and a further six hours to Patra. The ferry fleet tends to be smaller and older, but there is a wide choice of vessels and pre-bookings are rarely necessary. Drivers and bike riders have a long drive to reach Brindisi and will need an overnight somewhere along the way. Add fuel costs and road tolls and Brindisi is not the best option. Arrivals by train will have a 15-minute hike along Corso Garibaldi – lined with ferry ticket offices – to the port.

Also worth noting is that in high season Italian Ferries (☎ 0831 590 305) at Corso Garibaldi 96 in Brindisi operates a daily high-speed catamaran from Brindisi to Corfu (€90, 3¼ hours) leaving Brindisi at 2pm. The service continues to Paxi (€116, 4¾ hours).

## Yacht

Despite the disparaging remarks among backpackers, yachting is *the* way to see the Greek Islands. Nothing beats the peace and serenity of sailing the open sea, and the freedom of being able to visit remote and uninhabited islands.

### Warning

The information in this chapter is particularly vulnerable to change: Prices for international travel are volatile, routes are introduced and cancelled, schedules change, special deals come and go, and rules and visa requirements are amended. Airlines and governments seem to take a perverse pleasure in making price structures and regulations as complicated as possible. You should check directly with the airline or a travel agent to make sure you understand how a fare (and ticket you may buy) works. In addition, the travel industry is highly competitive and there are many lurks and perks.

The upshot of this is that you should get opinions, quotes and advice from as many airlines and travel agents as possible before you part with your hard-earned cash. The details given in this chapter should be regarded as pointers and are not a substitute for your own careful, up-to-date research.

The free EOT booklet *Sailing the Greek Seas*, although long overdue for an update, contains lots of information about weather conditions, weather bulletins, entry and exit regulations, entry and exit ports and guidebooks for yachties.

You can pick up the booklet at any GNTO/EOT office either abroad or in Greece.

The sailing season lasts from April until October. The best time to go depends on where you are going. The most popular time is between July and September, which ties in with the high season for tourism.

Unfortunately, it also happens to be the time of year when the *meltemi* is at its strongest. The meltemi is a northerly wind that affects the Aegean throughout the summer. It starts off as a mild wind in May and June, and strengthens as the weather hots up – often blowing from a clear blue sky. In August and September, it can blow at gale force for days on end.

If your budget won't cover buying a yacht there are several other options open to you. You can hire a bare boat (a yacht without a crew) if two crew members have a sailing certificate. Prices start at US$1300 per week for a 28-footer that will sleep six. It's an option only if two crew members have a sailing certificate; otherwise you can hire a skipper for an extra $100 per day.

Most of the hire companies are based in and around Athens. They include:

**Alpha Yachting** (☎ 21 0968 0486, fax 21 0968 0488, e mano@otenet.gr) Posidonos 67, GR-166 74 Glyfada

**Ghiolman Yachts & Travel** (☎ 21 0323 3696, fax 21 0322 3251, e ghiolman@travelling.gr) Filellinon 7, GR-105 57 Athens

**Hellenic Charters** (☎/fax 21 021 0988 5592, e hctsa@ath.forthnet.gr) Posidonos 66, GR-141 21 Alimos

**Kostis Yachting** (☎ 21 0895 0657, fax 21 0895 0995) Epaminonda 61, GR-166 74 Glyfada

**Vernicos Yachts** (☎ 21 0989 6000, fax 21 0985 0130, e info@vernicos.gr, w www.vernicos.gr) Posidonos 11, GR-141 21 Alimos 0989 6000

There are more yacht charter companies operating in Greece; the EOT can provide addresses.

## ORGANISED TOURS

The vast majority (80%) of travellers who decide to head for Crete opt for a package holiday. Flight/accommodation packages can be a remarkably good deal, costing far less than what you would pay if you booked your air fare and hotel room separately. The best deals can often pop up at the last-minute as tour operators struggle to fill charter flights and block-booked hotel rooms. Most of the offerings are for large resorts along the northern coast. For a less industrialised holiday experience, you can try one of the following companies:

**Diktynna Travel** (☎ 2821 041 458 or ☎ 2821 043 930, fax 43 930, e sales@diktynna-travel .gr) 6 Agiou Markou & Kanevaro, GR-731 00 Hania, Greece

**Greek Islands Club** (☎ 020 8232 9780, fax 8568 8330, e info@vch.co.uk), 10-12 Upper Square, Old Isleworth, Middlesex TW7 7BJ, UK

**Greek Options** (☎ 020 7233 5233, fax 020 7233 5100, e info@greekoptions.co.uk), Abford House, 15 Wilton Rd, London SW1V 1LT, UK

**Pure Crete** (☎ 020 8760 0879, fax 8688 9951, e info@pure-crete.com, w www.pure-crete .com) 79 George Street, Croydon, Surrey CRO 1LD, UK

**Simply Crete** (☎ 020 8541 2201, fax 020 8541 2280, crete@simply-travel.com, w www.simply -travel.com) Kings House, Wood St, Kingston upon Thames, Surrey KT1 1SG, UK

# Getting Around

## BUS

Crete is an easy place to travel around thanks to a comprehensive public transport system. A four-lane national highway skirts the north coast from Hania in the west to Agios Nikolaos in the east, and is being extended further west to Kissamos Kastelli. There are frequent buses linking all the major northern towns from Kissamos-Kastelli to Sitia. Less-frequent buses operate between the north-coast towns and resorts and places of interest on the south coast, via the mountain villages of the interior. Fares are fixed by the government, and are very reasonable by European standards.

Buses are operated by regional collectives known as KTEL (Kino Tamio Eispraxeon Leoforion). Every prefecture has its own KTEL, which operates local services within the prefecture and services to the main towns of other prefectures. A useful site is [w] www.ktel.org which has schedules for all the island's buses.

Larger towns usually have a central, covered bus station with seating, waiting rooms, toilets, and a snack bar selling pies, cakes and coffee. Large towns like Iraklio have more than one bus station, each serving different regions. In small towns and villages the 'bus station' may be no more than a bus stop outside a *kafeneio* or taverna which doubles as a booking office. Most booking offices have timetables in both Greek and Roman script. The timetables give both the departure and return times – useful if you are making a day-trip. Times are listed using the 24-hour-clock system.

Regular and reliable buses link the major northern towns from Kissamos-Kastelli to Sitia. These buses are generally in good shape and some are even air-conditioned. Buses do not have toilets on board and they don't have refreshments available, so make sure you are prepared on both counts. Smoking is prohibited on all buses in Greece; only the chain-smoking drivers dare to ignore the no smoking signs.

Most buses use the northern highway but there are at least one or two buses each day that use the old roads. The trip is more scenic but takes much longer so ask before you buy the ticket. In major towns it's best to buy your ticket at the station to make sure you have a seat but if you board at a stop along the way you buy the ticket from the conductor. When you buy a bus ticket, you will be given a seat number (look on the ticket). The seat number is indicated on the back of each seat, not on the back of the seat in front; this causes confusion among Greeks and tourists alike. Keep the ticket: it will be checked a few times en route. The bus stations in major towns keep long opening hours and are a good source of information. See the individual destination chapters for detailed bus timetable information.

## CAR & MOTORCYCLE

Crete is plenty big enough to warrant having your own vehicle which makes it possible to visit smaller, more out-of-the-way places. Roads have improved enormously in recent years but in many parts of the island, particularly in the south, you'll still find unpaved roads that are only suitable for jeeps. While it is now quite easy to bring you own vehicle from Europe, there are plenty of places to hire both cars and motorcycles.

If you explore the island by car or scooter, prepare to spend a fair amount of time poring over maps, since country roads are often unmarked. Road signs, when they exist, are usually marked in Greek and Latin letters except in remote locations. Even when written in Latin letters, the spelling of place names can vary wildly from the names on your map or in this book. Invest in a good map (Road Editions and Emvelia publish the most accurate maps of Crete), but even the best maps don't cover all the side roads.

Crete is well served by car ferries, but they are fairly expensive. For example, the price for a small vehicle from Piraeus to Crete (Hania or Iraklio) is €61.50; the charge for

## ROAD DISTANCES (KM)

| | Agia Galini | Agios Nikolaos | Anogia | Elafonisi | Hania | Hora Sfakion | Ierapetra | Iraklio | Kissamos-Kastelli | Kolymbari | Malia | Matala | Omalos | Paleohora | Plakias | Rethymno | Sitia | Spili | Tzermiado | Zakros |
|---|---|---|---|---|---|---|---|---|---|---|---|---|---|---|---|---|---|---|---|---|
| Agia Galini | --- | | | | | | | | | | | | | | | | | | | |
| Agios Nikolaos | 144 | --- | | | | | | | | | | | | | | | | | | |
| Anogia | 118 | 104 | --- | | | | | | | | | | | | | | | | | |
| Elafonisi | 224 | 314 | 218 | --- | | | | | | | | | | | | | | | | |
| Hania | 119 | 209 | 113 | 105 | --- | | | | | | | | | | | | | | | |
| Hora Sfakion | 45 | 215 | 119 | 70 | 70 | --- | | | | | | | | | | | | | | |
| Ierapetra | 137 | 36 | 140 | 352 | 247 | 182 | --- | | | | | | | | | | | | | |
| Iraklio | 75 | 69 | 35 | 247 | 142 | 148 | 105 | --- | | | | | | | | | | | | |
| Kissamos-Kastelli | 173 | 263 | 167 | 51 | 54 | 124 | 301 | 196 | --- | | | | | | | | | | | |
| Kolymbari | 144 | 234 | 138 | 65 | 25 | 95 | 261 | 167 | 14 | --- | | | | | | | | | | |
| Malia | 112 | 32 | 72 | 284 | 179 | 185 | 68 | 37 | 233 | 204 | --- | | | | | | | | | |
| Matala | 29 | 138 | 104 | 253 | 148 | 123 | 131 | 69 | 265 | 173 | 106 | --- | | | | | | | | |
| Omalos | 163 | 253 | 157 | 149 | 44 | 114 | 291 | 186 | 98 | 69 | 223 | 255 | --- | | | | | | | |
| Paleohora | 206 | 296 | 200 | 64 | 87 | 157 | 335 | 229 | 51 | 65 | 266 | 298 | 131 | --- | | | | | | |
| Plakias | 50 | 198 | 94 | 200 | 95 | 44 | 187 | 123 | 149 | 120 | 161 | 79 | 139 | 183 | --- | | | | | |
| Rethymno | 62 | 152 | 56 | 162 | 57 | 63 | 190 | 85 | 111 | 62 | 122 | 91 | 101 | 144 | 39 | --- | | | | |
| Sitia | 199 | 73 | 177 | 387 | 282 | 290 | 62 | 142 | 336 | 307 | 105 | 211 | 326 | 369 | 265 | 227 | --- | | | |
| Spili | 26 | 182 | 86 | 192 | 87 | 68 | 163 | 215 | 141 | 112 | 252 | 55 | 131 | 174 | 24 | 30 | 257 | --- | | |
| Tzermiado | 130 | 49 | 90 | 302 | 197 | 202 | 85 | 55 | 251 | 222 | 44 | 124 | 241 | 284 | 178 | 139 | 122 | 270 | --- | |
| Zakros | 235 | 106 | 211 | 421 | 316 | 322 | 98 | 176 | 370 | 341 | 138 | 229 | 360 | 405 | 285 | 259 | 36 | 289 | 155 | --- |

a large motorbike is about the same as the price of a 3rd-class passenger ticket.

In general, petrol in Greece is expensive, and the farther you get from a major city the more it costs. Prices vary from petrol station to petrol station. Unleaded petrol – available everywhere – may be as cheap as €0.67 per litre at big city discount places, but €0.79 to €0.90 is the normal range. Super is several cents more expensive. Diesel costs about €0.52 per litre.

See Documents in the Facts for the Visitor chapter for information on licence requirements in Crete.

See Useful Organisations in the Facts for the Visitor chapter for information about the Greek automobile club (ELPA).

### Road Rules

Few would be surprised to learn that Greece has one of the highest road fatality rates in Europe – it's a good place to practise your defensive driving skills! Overtaking is the biggest cause of accidents, so as a visitor you should familiarise yourself with the rules of the road. Slow-driving tourists in hire cars can often be a hazard to drivers used to the faster Greek driving manner and may cause impatient overtaking manoeuvres on the part of faster drivers.

Driving in the major cities is a nightmare of erratic one-way streets and irregularly enforced parking rules. Cars are not towed but parking tickets can be expensive. Parking for the handicapped is a rarity.

In Greece, as throughout Continental Europe, you drive on the right and overtake on the left. Major highways are four lanes, though some are still two lane highways with large hard shoulders. These hard shoulders are often used for driving in, especially when being overtaken. Be prepared to move over if someone wants to pass you.

Other regulations are that seatbelts must be worn in front and back seats, and you must travel with a first-aid kit, fire extinguisher and warning triangle. Carrying cans of petrol is banned. Outside built-up areas, traffic on a main road has right of way at intersections. In towns, vehicles coming from the right have right of way. Motorcyclists driving bikes of 50cc or more must wear helmets.

Offences and fines include:

Speed Limits (Cars) – 120km/h on highways, 90km/h on other roads and 50km/h in built-up areas. Drivers exceeding the speed limit by 20% are liable for a fine of €60; and by 40%, €150.
Speed Limits (Motorcycles) – 70km/h (up to 100cc), 90km/h (above 100cc).
Drink Driving – A blood alcohol limit of 0.05% will incur a fine of €150, and over 0.08% is a criminal offence.
Illegal overtaking – €300
Going through a red light – €300
Driving without a seat belt – €150
Motorcyclist not wearing a helmet – €150
Wrong way down one-way street – €150
Illegal parking – €30

The police can issue traffic fines, but payment cannot be made on the spot – you will be told where to pay. Reciprocal legal agreements between EU countries may well mean that an ignored parking fine will turn up in your mailbox at home a few weeks later. If you are involved in an accident and no-one is hurt, the police will not be required to write a report, but it is advisable to go to a nearby police station and explain what happened. A police report may be required for insurance purposes. If an accident involves injury, a driver who does not stop and does not inform the police may face a prison sentence.

**Warning** If you are planning to use a motorcycle or moped, check that your travel insurance covers you for injury resulting from a motorbike accident. Many insurance companies don't offer this cover, so check the fine print! You may now also be asked for a motorbike licence if you are planning to hire one.

## Rental
**Car** Hiring a car in Crete is more expensive than in other European countries but the prices have come down recently due to an increasingly competitive environment. It pays to shop around, especially if you'll be renting a car for a week or more. Although major international companies such as Hertz, Budget and Europcar have offices in most towns you'll usually get a better deal if you rent from a local company.

High-season weekly rates with unlimited mileage from a major company start at about €320 for the smallest models, such as a 900cc Fiat Panda. The rate drops to about €260 per week in winter. The many local companies are normally more open to negotiation, especially if business is slow. Their advertised rates are about 25% cheaper than those offered by the multinationals. VAT of 18% must be added to these prices. Then there are the optional extras, such as a collision damage waiver of €10 per day (more for larger models), without which you will be liable for the first €4400 of the repair bill (much more for larger models). Other costs include a theft waiver of at least €3 per day and personal accident insurance. It all adds up to an expensive exercise. Some companies offer much cheaper pre-booked and prepaid rates.

If you want to take a hire car onto a ferry, you will need advance written authorisation from the hire company. Unless you pay with a credit card, most hire companies will require a minimum deposit of €59 per day.

The minimum driving age in Greece is 18 years of age, but most car-hire firms require you to be at least 23 years old, although some will rent to 21 year olds.

See the Getting Around section of the relevant cities for details of car rental outlets.

**Motorcycle** Caution should be exercised when travelling by motorcycle. Roads change without warning from smooth and paved to cracked and pothole-ridden. Watch your speed. Greece is not the best place to initiate yourself into the world of motorcycling: many tourists have accidents every year. Experienced motorcyclists will find a lightweight Enduro motorcycle between 400 and 600cc ideal for negotiating Crete's roads.

Mopeds and motorcycles are available for hire wherever there are tourists to rent them. In many cases their maintenance has been minimal, so check the machine thoroughly before you hire it – especially the brakes: you'll need them! When you rent a moped, tell the shop where you'll be going to ensure that your vehicle has enough power to get you up Crete's steep interior hills.

Motorbikes are a cheap way to travel around. Rates range from €8.80 to €13.20 per day for a moped or 50cc motorbike to €20.50 per day for a 250cc motorbike. Out of season these prices drop considerably, so use your bargaining skills. By October it is sometimes possible to hire a moped for as little as €6 per day. Most motorcycle hirers include third party insurance in the price, but it is wise to check this. This insurance will not include medical expenses.

### Taxi

Taxis are widely available in Crete except in remote villages, and are relatively cheap by European standards. Large towns have taxi stands that post a list of taxi prices to outlying destinations, which removes any anxiety about over-charging. Otherwise you pay what's on the meter. You can negotiate with taxis to take you sightseeing for the day using the following prices as a guide: Flagfall is €0.73 followed by €0.18 per km (€0.40 per km outside town or between midnight and 5am). There's a €0.90 surcharge when the taxi is hired at the airport and a €0.45 surcharge if the taxi is hired at a bus station or port. Each piece of luggage weighing more than 10kg carries a surcharge of €0.15, and there's a surcharge of €0.90 for radio taxis. Rural taxis often do not have meters, so you should always settle on a price before you get in.

If your destination is at the end of a bumpy, unpaved road you'll pay considerably more – if you can find a taxi to take you there at all.

If you have a complaint about a taxi driver, take the cab number and report your complaint to the tourist police. Taxi drivers in Crete are, on the whole, friendly, helpful and honest.

### BICYCLE

Cycling has not caught on in Crete, which isn't surprising considering the hilly terrain. Tourists are beginning to cycle in Crete, but you'll need strong leg muscles. You can hire bicycles in most tourist places, but they are not as widely available as cars and motorbikes. Prices range from €3 to €9 per day, depending on the type and age of the bike. Bicycles are carried free on ferries.

### HITCHING

Hitching is never entirely safe in any country in the world, and we don't recommend it. Travellers who decide to hitch should understand that they are taking a small but potentially serious risk. People who do choose to hitch will be safer if they travel in pairs and should let someone know where they are planning to go. Greece has a reputation for being a relatively safe place for women to hitch, but it is still unwise to do it alone. It's better for women to hitch with a companion, preferably a male one. In Crete you don't hitch with your thumb up as in northern Europe, but with an outstretched hand, palm down to the road.

Some parts of Crete are much better for hitching than others. Getting out of major cities tends to be hard work; hitching is much easier in remote areas. On country roads, it is not unknown for someone to stop and ask if you want a lift even if you haven't asked for one. You can't afford to be fussy about the mode of transport – it may be a tractor or a spluttering old truck.

### WALKING

Unless you have come to Crete just to lie on a beach, the chances are you will do quite a bit of walking. You don't have to be a trekker to start clocking up the kilometres. The narrow, stepped streets of many towns and villages can only be explored on foot, and visiting the archaeological sites involves a fair amount of legwork.

See the What to Bring, Health, and Trekking sections in the Facts for the Visitor chapter for more information about walking.

## BOAT
### Ferry
In addition to the large ferries which ply between the large mainland ports and island groups, there are smaller boats linking the towns along the south coast, some of which are only accessible by sea.

In summer, there are daily boats from Paleohora to Hora Sfakion via Agia Roumeli, Sougia and Loutro that offer wonderful coastal views. Although the schedules change from year to year, there are usually two to three boats a day between Hora Sfakion and Agia Roumeli and one boat a day from Hora Sfakion to Paleohora. There are also three boats a week in the summer between Paleohora and Gavdos Island and a boat twice weekly between Paleohora and Gavdos Island.

There are also tourist boats connecting port cities with offshore islands. In the past these boats were always *caiques* – sturdy old fishing boats – but gradually these are being replaced by new, purpose-built boats, which are usually called express or excursion boats. Although it may be possible to negotiate with fishermen for trips on the caiques, it is illegal for fishing boats to take on passengers.

Some of the more popular excursions include Ierapetra to Hrysi Island, Agios Nikolaos to Spinalonga, and Kissamos-Kastelli to the Gramvousa Peninsula.

### Taxi Boat
Most southern port cities have taxi boats – small speedboats which operate like taxis, transporting people to places that are difficult to get to by land. Some owners charge a set price for each person, others charge a flat rate for the boat, and this cost is divided by the number of passengers. Either way, prices are usually quite reasonable.

## LOCAL TRANSPORT
### To/From the Airports
Olympic Airways operates buses to a few domestic airports (see individual entries in the appropriate chapters). Where the service exists, buses leave the airline office about 1½ hours before departure. In many places, the only way to get to the airport is by taxi. Check-in is an hour before departure for domestic flights.

### Bus
Local city buses operating from Iraklio, Rethymno, and Hania are designed to take people back and forth from the city suburbs and are not really practical for getting around the cities themselves. They are cheap and reliable if not terribly comfortable. Tickets are normally bought at kiosks *(periptera)*, or small shops and validated in a machine once you board the bus. Don't board a bus without a ticket.

## ORGANISED TOURS
Whether you want to see the island by boat, bus, jeep, bicycle, foot or on horseback, there's an organised tour for you. Organised tours can take you to otherwise inaccessible spots without having to hassle with buses, maps, bad roads, poorly marked roads, boat rentals or taxi drivers. The guide may provide you with fascinating insights into local culture and is right there to answer questions. The disadvantages are that you are locked into a pre-scheduled itinerary and, if you have limited time, there may not be a tour going to your destination on the days when you are available.

Most agencies have a tour schedule – Monday to the Samaria Gorge, Tuesday to Knossos etc. In large towns such as Hania, Agios Nikolaos, Iraklio or Rethymno travel agencies selling tours are abundant but they usually operate through one tour operator who provides the transport and guide. Shopping around is useless since the prices are set by the tour operator. Most agencies take children up to four-years-old free and give a 50% reduction to children between the ages of five and 15.

One of the most popular tours is to the Samaria Gorge, a trip you can arrange from almost any place on the island. The price ranges from €14.50 to €28 depending on your starting point, but it does not include the admission fee to the gorge or the boat trip from Agia Roumeli to Hora Sfakion. For a few euro less, most agencies also offer a Samaria Gorge 'easy way' that takes you from Agia Roumeli to the 'iron gates'. Unfortunately the route to the famous rock slabs is mostly hot and boring but you will get a taste of the gorge's majesty.

The Minoan Palace of Knossos is another tour favourite but taking a tour makes little sense if you're staying in Iraklio. From Hania or Agios Nikolaos the tour will cost €20.50 to €22 and includes a guide, transport and some free time for shopping and lunch in Iraklio. Admission to the site is not included.

Jeep safaris are a popular option if you're looking to get far off the beaten track. Although expensive (€36 to €50) you can reach delightfully out-of-the-way villages and sights. If the agency is sending out a procession of jeeps however, your main sight will be the dust from the vehicle ahead of you. Jeep safaris generally include lunch in a local taverna.

Depending on your location you may be able to take tours to the Dikteon Cave on the Lasithi Plateau as well as the towns, sights and beaches of Crete. There are also various village tours that lean heavily on shopping during the day and dinner/folk dancing shows at night. These tours can be worthwhile, especially if you have more money than time, but they can get crowded in the summer. Boat tours that include swimming operate from the harbours of Hania, Rethymno, and Agios Nikolaos as well as many south coast beaches. These tours can also get crowded but, unless you have your own boat, an organised tour is the only way to see remote beaches and islands.

## Organised Treks

**Trekking Hellas** (*☎ 21 0325 0853, fax 21 033 4548, Filellinon 7, Athens 105 57*) specialises in treks and other adventure activities for small groups. It offers two week-long treks that cover central and western Crete. See the Hania, Agios Nikolaos and Rethymno chapters for more information about organised treks.

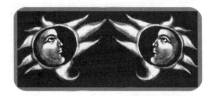

# Iraklio

The Iraklio region is the island's main point of entry for tourists and is undoubtedly the busiest. The twin poles of Cretan culture – mass tourism and Minoan archaeology – are amply represented in the region. The northern coast of Iraklio has surrendered lock, stock and barrel to package tourism. The eastern resorts of Malia and Hersonisos sum up for Cretans everything that is wrong with mass tourism. Yet behind the concrete sea-barrier of hotels, the island's most fascinating archaeological sites lie strewn throughout the nearly deserted interior. Knossos, Phaestos, Agia Triada, Gortyna and Malia are all within a day-trip from Iraklio. The southern coast is quieter than the northern coast; Matala is fairly developed but Keratokambos, Kastri and Arvi provide a more tranquil holiday experience.

## IRAKLIO Ηράκλειο
**postcode 710 01 • pop 115,124**
Hectic, noisy and traffic-ridden, Iraklio is often viewed as a grim necessity to be endured for the sake of archaeology. After the obligatory visit to the Archaeological Museum and Knossos, most visitors hurry away to more inviting spots.

Yet, as Crete's capital and Greece's 5th-largest city, Iraklio manages to achieve a certain urban sophistication despite its poor infrastructure. The city is prosperous; many neighbourhoods have been rebuilt and there are enough euros to go around to support a thriving cafe scene and lively nightlife.

The Archaeological Museum and the palace at Knossos are a window into Minoan culture but Iraklio abounds in other reminders of its turbulent history. The 14th-century Venetian walls and fortress underscore the importance of Iraklio (then called Candia) to the Venetians and many monuments date from Venetian occupation. Notice Morosini Fountain, the Venetian Loggia and Agios Markos Church.

## Highlights

- Exploring the ruins of the Minoan civilisation at Knossos, Gortyna and Phaestos
- Indulging in the lively nightlife and cafe scene of the island's capital, Iraklio
- Viewing artefacts at Iraklio's Archaeological Museum
- Unwinding on the lovely beaches of Matala, Kalamaki and Lendas on the south coast
- Enjoying the cool mountain air of Zaros

## History
Iraklio is believed to have been settled since the Neolithic age. Little is known about the intervening years but in AD 824. Iraklio was conquered by the Saracens and became known as Rabdh el Khandak (Castle of the Ditch), after the moat that surrounded their fortified town. It was reputedly the slave-trade capital of the eastern Mediterranean and the launching pad for the region's notorious pirates, who preyed upon unwary ships, looted them and sold the captive seamen into slavery.

Byzantine troops finally dislodged the Arabs after a siege which lasted almost a

113

IRAKLIO

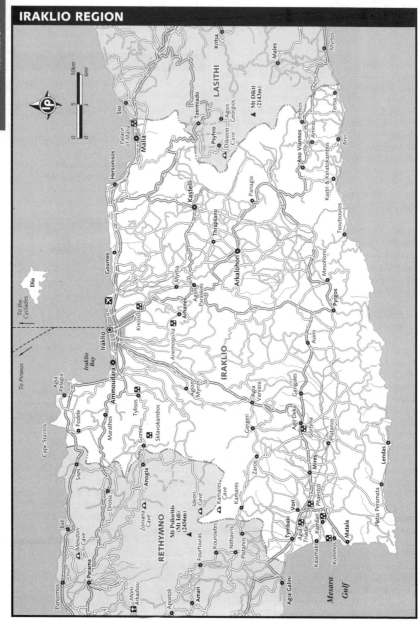

# IRAKLIO REGION

year in AD 961. The Byzantine leader Nikiforas Fokas made a lasting impression upon the Arabs by chopping off the heads of his prisoners and throwing them over the walls of the fortress.

The city became known as Handakas and remained the island's capital until Crete was sold to the Venetians in 1204. The Venetians also chose the city as the island's capital and named it Candia. The Venetians built magnificent public buildings and churches, and barricaded themselves inside the fortress when necessary to protect themselves against a rebellious populace.

Under the Venetians Candia became a centre for the arts and residence for painters such as Damaskinos and El Greco. When the Turks captured Constantinople the walls of Candia's fortress were fortified and extended in anticipation of the growing Turkish menace. Although the Turks quickly overran the island in 1645 it took them 21 years to penetrate the walls of Candia.

Other European countries sent defenders and supplies from time to time but it was mainly the strength of the walls that kept the Turks at bay. Pounding the walls with cannons proved ineffective so the Turks finally resorted to bribery. They managed to pay a Venetian colonel to reveal the weak points in the wall and thus were able to capture it in 1669. Casualties were high on both sides; the Venetian defenders lost 30,000 men and the Turks lost 118,000 men.

Under the Turks the city became known as Megalo Kastro (Big Castle). A cloud of darkness descended upon the city under Turkish rule. Artistic life withered away and most Cretans fled or were massacred.

On August 25 1898, a Turkish mob massacred hundreds of Cretans, 17 British soldiers and the British Consul in Iraklio. Within weeks, a squadron of British ships steamed into Iraklio's harbour and ended Turkish rule on Crete forever.

Hania became the capital of independent Crete at the end of Turkish rule in 1898, but Candia's central location soon saw it emerge as the commercial centre. It was renamed Iraklio and it resumed its position as administrative centre in 1971.

## How Did Iraklio Get Its Name?

After King Minos' wife, Pasiphae, gave birth to the Minotaur, her lover, the bull, went wild and laid waste to the Cretan countryside. He was out of control, tearing up crops and stamping down orchard walls. Fortunately, help was at hand in the form of iron-man Heracles, the man who killed a lion with his bare hands. His voyage to Crete to kill the bull was the seventh of his 12 mighty labours. Minos offered to help but Heracles would have none of it. As the monstrous animal belched flames and fumes, Heracles captured it single-handedly and took it away. The ancient Cretans were so grateful that they named Minos' port city after their superman. And that's how Iraklio (Iraklion, Heraklion) got its name.

The city suffered badly in WWII, when most of the old Venetian and Turkish town was destroyed by bombing.

## Orientation

Iraklio's two main squares are Plateia Venizelou and Plateia Eleftherias. Plateia Venizelou, recognisable by its famous Morosini Fountain (better known as the Lion Fountain), is the heart of the city and the best place from which to familiarise yourself with Iraklio's layout. The city's major intersection is a few steps south of the square. From here, 25 Avgoustou runs north-east to the harbour; Dikeosynis runs south-east to Plateia Eleftherias; Kalokerinou runs west to the Hania Gate; 1866 (the market street) runs south; and 1821 runs to the south-west.

Iraklio has three intercity bus stations. Station A, on the waterfront between the quay and 25 Avgoustou, serves eastern Crete. A special bus station which services Hania and Rethymno is opposite Station A. Station B, just beyond Hania Gate, serves Phaestos, Agia Galini and Matala. To reach the city centre from Station B walk through the Hania Gate and along Kalokerinou.

## Information

**Tourist Offices** EOT (☎ 281 022 8225, fax 281 022 6020) is just north of Plateia

Eleftherias at Xanthoudidou 1. The staff at the information desk hand out maps and photocopied lists of ferry and bus schedules. Opening times are 8am to 2pm Monday to Friday. In high season they also open on Saturday and Sunday. The tourist police (☎ 281 028 3190), Dikeosynis 10, are open from 7am to 11pm.

**Foreign Consulates** Foreign consulates in Iraklio include:

**Germany** (☎ 281 022 6288) Zografou 7
**Netherlands** (☎ 281 034 6202) Avgoustou 23
**UK** (☎ 281 022 4012) Papalexandrou 16

**Money** Most of the city's banks are on 25 Avgoustou, including the National Bank of Greece at No 35. It has a 24-hour automatic exchange machine, as does the Alpha Bank at No 94. There is a handy Ergo Bank ATM at Bus Station A. American Express is represented by Adamis Tours (☎ 281 034 6202, fax 281 022 4717, e adamis@her.forthnet.gr) at 25 Avgoustou 23. Opening hours are 8am to 2pm Monday to Saturday. Thomas Cook (☎ 281 024 1108) is represented by Summerland Travel, Epimenidou 30.

**Post & Communications** The central post office is on Plateia Daskalogianni. From Plateia Eleftherias go up Giannari and make a left on Zografou. Opening hours are 7.30am to 8pm Monday to Friday, and 7.30am to 2pm on Saturday. In summer, there is a mobile post office at El Greco Park, just north of Plateia Venizelou, which is open 8am to 6pm Monday to Friday and 8am to 1.30pm on Saturday. The OTE, on Theotokopoulou just north of El Greco Park is open 7.30am to 11pm daily.

**Email & Internet Access** Sportc@fe (☎ 281 028 8217) on the corner of 25 Avgoustou and Zotou has fast modern machines and serves up coffee, beers and soft drinks while you surf. Istos Cyber Cafe (☎ 281 022 2120) Malikouti 2, charges €3.80 an hour to use their computers and also scans, prints and faxes documents. There are half a dozen computers with fast connections. It's open 9am to 1am daily.

**Travel Agencies** Prince Travel (☎ 281 028 2706) at 25 Avgoustou 30 is an excellent source of information on cheap flights. It's a friendly office that stores luggage and has plenty of useful advice about Iraklio. It's open 9am to 6pm Monday to Friday. Adamis Tours (see Money earlier in this section) is also a reputable travel agency.

For the latest ferry schedules and all advice on boat transport go to Arabatzoglou (☎ 281 022 6697), at 25 Avgoustou 54. It's open 9am to 7pm Monday to Friday.

**Bookshops** The Planet International Bookshop (☎ 281 028 1558) on the corner of Hortatson and Kydonias stocks most of the books recommended in this book and has a large selection of Lonely Planet guides. It's open 8.30am to 2.30pm Monday, Wednesday, Saturday; and 8.30am to 2pm and 5pm to 9.30pm Tuesday, Thursday and Friday. Road Editions (☎/fax 281 034 4610) at Handakos 29 has the best selection of maps in Iraklio as well as a good range of Lonely Planet titles.

**Laundry** There are two self-service laundrettes: Laundry Washsalon (also has left-luggage facilities) at Handakos 18 and Inter Laundry at Mirabelou 25, near the Archaeological Museum. Both charge around €6 for a wash and dry.

**Luggage Storage** The left-luggage office at Bus Station A charges €1 per day and is open 6.30am to 8pm daily. Other options are Prince Travel (☎ 281 028 2706) at 25 Avgoustou 30, which also charges €1.50, Washsalon (see Laundry) which charges €1.50 and the youth hostel at Vyronos 5 which charges €1.50.

**Medical Services** The modern University Hospital (☎ 281 039 2111) at Voutes, 5km south of Iraklio, is the city's best equipped medical facility. The Apollonia Hospital (☎ 281 022 9713), inside the old walls on Mousourou, is more convenient.

## Things to See
**Archaeological Museum** This outstanding museum (☎ 281 022 6092, Xanthoudidou 1;

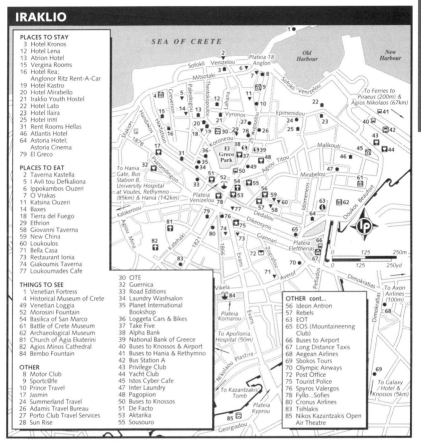

**IRAKLIO**

**PLACES TO STAY**
3 Hotel Kronos
12 Hotel Lena
13 Atrion Hotel
15 Vergina Rooms
16 Hotel Rea;
   Anglonor Ritz Rent-A-Car
19 Hotel Kastro
20 Hotel Mirabello
21 Iraklio Youth Hostel
22 Hotel Lato
23 Hotel Ilaira
25 Hotel Irini
31 Rent Rooms Hellas
46 Atlantis Hotel
64 Astoria Hotel;
   Astoria Cinema
79 El Greco

**PLACES TO EAT**
2 Taverna Kastella
5 I Avli tou Defkaliona
6 Ippokambos Ouzeri
7 O Vrakas
11 Katsina Ouzeri
14 Baxes
18 Tierra del Fuego
29 Ethrion
58 Giovanni Taverna
59 New China
60 Loukoulos
71 Bella Casa
73 Restaurant Ionia
74 Giakoumis Taverna
77 Loukoumades Cafe

**THINGS TO SEE**
1 Venetian Fortress
4 Historical Museum of Crete
49 Venetian Loggia
52 Morosini Fountain
54 Basilica of San Marco
61 Battle of Crete Museum
62 Archaeological Museum
81 Church of Agia Ekaterini
82 Agios Minos Cathedral
84 Bembo Fountain

**OTHER**
8 Motor Club
9 Sportc@fe
10 Prince Travel
17 Jasmin
24 Summerland Travel
26 Adamis Travel Bureau
27 Porto Club Travel Services
28 Sun Rise
30 OTE
32 Guernica
33 Road Editions
34 Laundry Washsalon
35 Planet International
   Bookshop
36 Loggeta Cars & Bikes
37 Take Five
38 Alpha Bank
39 National Bank of Greece
40 Buses to Knossos & Airport
41 Buses to Hania & Rethymno
42 Bus Station A
43 Privilege Club
44 Yacht Club
45 Istos Cyber Cafe
47 Inter Laundry
48 Pagopiion
50 Buses to Knossos
51 De Facto
53 Aktarika
55 Sousouro

**OTHER cont...**
56 Ideon Antron
57 Rebels
63 EOT
65 EOS (Mountaineering
   Club)
66 Buses to Airport
67 Long Distance Taxis
68 Aegean Airlines
69 Sbokos Tours
70 Olympic Airways
72 Post Office
75 Tourist Police
76 Spyros Valergos
78 Fyllo...Sofies
80 Cronus Airlines
83 Tsihlakis
85 Nikos Kazantzakis Open
   Air Theatre

*admission €4.40; open 8am-7pm Tues-Sun, 12.30pm-7pm Mon, closes 5pm end Oct-start Apr)* is second in size and importance only to the National Archaeological Museum in Athens. If you are seriously interested in the Minoans you will want more than one visit. Even a fairly superficial perusal of the contents requires half a day.

The exhibits, arranged in chronological order, include pottery, jewellery, figurines and sarcophagi as well as some famous frescoes, mostly from Knossos and Agia Triada. All testify to the remarkable imagination and advanced skills of the Minoans.

Unfortunately, the exhibits are not very well explained. If they were, there would be no need to part with €6.50 for a copy of the glossy illustrated guide by the museum's director.

Room 1 is devoted to the Neolithic and Early Minoan periods.

Room 2 has a collection from the Middle Minoan period. Among the most fascinating exhibits are the tiny, glazed colour reliefs of Minoan houses from Knossos, called the 'town mosaic'.

Room 3 covers the same period with finds from Phaestos, including the famous

**Phaestos Disk**. (See the boxed text later in this chapter.) The symbols inscribed on this 16cm diameter disk have not been deciphered. Here, also, are the famous **Kamares pottery vases**, named after the sacred cave of Kamares where the pottery was first discovered. Case 40 contains fragments of 'eggshell ware', so called because of its fragility. The four large vases in case 43 were part of a royal banquet set. They are of exceptional quality and are some of the finest examples of Kamares pottery.

Exhibits in Room 4 are from the Middle Minoan period. Most striking is the 20cm black stone **Bull's Head**, which was a libation vessel. The bull has a fine head of curls, from which sprout horns of gold. The eyes of painted crystal are extremely lifelike. Also in this room are relics from a shrine at Knossos, including two fine **snake goddess** figurines. Snakes symbolised immortality for the Minoans.

Room 5 contains pottery, bronze figurines and seals. Other exhibits include vases imported from Egypt and some Linear A and B tablets. The Mycenaean Linear B script has been deciphered and the inscriptions on the tablets displayed here have been translated as household or business accounts from the palace at Knossos.

Room 6 is devoted to finds from Minoan cemeteries. Especially intriguing are two small clay models of groups of figures that were found in a tholos tomb. One depicts four male dancers in a circle, their arms around each other's shoulders. The dancers may have been participating in a funeral ritual. The other model depicts two groups of three figures in a room flanked by two columns. Each group features two large seated figures, who are being offered libations by a smaller figure. It is not known whether the large figures represent gods or departed mortals. On a more grisly level, there is a display of the bones of a horse, which had been sacrificed as part of Minoan worship.

The finds in Room 7 include the beautiful bee pendant found at Malia. It's a remarkably fine piece of gold jewellery depicting two bees dropping honey into a comb. Also in this room are the three celebrated vases from Agia Triada. The **Harvester Vase**, of which only the top part remains, depicts a light-hearted scene of young farm workers returning from olive picking. The **Boxer Vase** shows Minoans indulging in two of their favourite pastimes – wrestling and bull-grappling. The **Chieftain Cup** depicts a more cryptic scene: a chief holding a staff and three men carrying animal skins.

Room 8 holds the finds from the palace at Zakros. Don't miss the gorgeous crystal vase that was found in over 300 pieces and was painstakingly put together again by museum staff. Other exhibits include a beautiful elongated libation vessel decorated with shells and other marine life.

Room 10 covers the postpalatial period (1350–1100 BC) when the Minoan civilisation was in decline and being overtaken by the war-like Mycenaeans. Nevertheless, there are still some fine exhibits, including a child (headless) on a swing in case 143.

Room 13 is devoted to Minoan sarcophagi. However, the most famous and spectacular of these, the **sarcophagus from Agia Triada**, is upstairs in Room 14 (the Hall of Frescoes). This stone coffin, painted with floral and abstract designs and ritual scenes, is regarded as one of the supreme examples of Minoan art.

The most famous of the Minoan frescoes are also displayed in Room 14. Frescoes from Knossos include the **Procession Fresco**, the **Griffin Fresco** (from the Throne Room), the **Dolphin Fresco** (from the Queen's Room) and the amazing **Bull-Leaping Fresco**, which depicts a seemingly double-jointed acrobat somersaulting on the back of a charging bull. Other frescoes here include the two lovely **Frescoes of the Lilies** from Amnisos and fragments of frescoes from Agia Triada. There are more frescoes in Rooms 15 and 16. In room 16 there is a large wooden model of Knossos.

**Historical Museum of Crete** This museum (☎ 281 028 3219, Lysimahou Kalokerinou 7; admission €3; open 9am-5pm Mon-Fri, 9am-2pm Sat in high season, 9am-

3pm Mon-Sat in low season), just back from the western waterfront, houses a fascinating range of bits and pieces from Crete's more recent past. The ground floor covers the period from Byzantine to Turkish rule, displaying plans, charts, photographs, ceramics and maps. On the 1st floor is the only El Greco painting on display in Crete – View of Mt Sinai and the Monastery of St Catherine (1570). Other rooms contain fragments of 13th- and 14th-century frescoes, coins, jewellery, liturgical ornaments, and vestments and medieval pottery.

The 2nd floor has a reconstruction of the **library of author Nikos Kazantzakis** and displays letters, manuscripts and books.

## Nikos Kazantzakis – Crete's prodigal son

Crete's most famous contemporary literary son is Nikos Kazantzakis. Born in 1883 in Iraklio, the then Turkish-dominated capital city of Crete, Kazantzakis spent his early childhood in the ferment of revolution and change that was creeping upon his homeland. In 1897 the revolution that finally broke out against Turkish rule forced him to leave Crete for studies in Naxos, Athens and later Paris. It wasn't until he was 31, in 1914, that he finally turned his hand to writing by translating philosophical books into Greek. For a number of years he travelled throughout Europe – Switzerland, Germany, Austria, Russia and Britain – thus laying the groundwork for a series of travelogues in his later literary career.

Nikos Kazantzakis was a complex writer and his early work was heavily influenced by the prevailing philosophical ideas of the time. The nihilistic philosophies of Nietzsche influenced his writings throughout which Kazantzakis is tormented by a tangible metaphysical and existentialist anguish. His relationship with religion was always troubling – his official stance being that of a non-believer, yet he always seemed to toy with the idea that perhaps God did exist. His self-professed greatest work is his *Odyssey* a modern day epic loosely based on the trials and travels of the ancient hero Odysseas (Ulysses). A weighty and complex opus of 33,333, 17 iambic verses, *Odyssey* never fully vindicated Kazantzakis' aspirations to be held in the same league as the Ancient Greeks' Homer, the Romans' Virgil or the Renaissance Italians' Tasso.

Ironically it was much later in his career where Kazantzakis belatedly turned to novel writing that his star finally shone. It was through works like *Christ Recrucified* (1948), *Kapetan Mihalis* (1950) and *The Life and Manners of Alexis Zorbas* (1946) that he became internationally known. This last work gave rise the image of the ultimate, modern Greek male 'Zorba the Greek', immortalised in the Anthony Quinn and Melina Mercouri movie of the same name, and countless restaurants throughout Crete and Greece in general. Kazantzakis died in Freiburg, Germany on 26 October 1957 while on yet another of his many travels. Despite resistance from the Orthodox Church, he was given a religious funeral and buried in the southern Martinenga Bastion of the old walls of Iraklio. Among the writer's more optimistic quotes – *Happy is the man who before dying has the good fortune to travel the Aegean Seas. Nowhere else can one pass so easily from reality to the dream.* (Nikos Kazantzakis 1883–1957).

MARTIN HARRIS

Phone numbers listed incorporate changes due in Oct 2002; see p61

Another room is devoted to Emmanouil Tsouderos, who was born in Rethymno and who was Prime Minister in 1941. Some dramatic photographs of a ruined Iraklio are displayed in the **Battle of Crete** section. There is an outstanding **folklore collection** on the 3rd floor.

**Other Attractions** Iraklio burst out of its **city walls** long ago but these massive fortifications, with seven bastions and four gates, are still very conspicuous, dwarfing the concrete structures of the 20th century. Venetians built the defences between 1462 and 1562. You can follow the walls around the heart of the city for views of Iraklio's neighbourhoods, but it is not a particularly scenic city. The 16th-century **Rocca al Mare** (☎ 281 024 6211, Iraklio Harbour; admission €1.50; open 8am-6pm Mon-Sat, 10am-3pm Sun), another Venetian fortress, stands at the end of the Old Harbour's jetty. The Venetian fortress stopped the Turks for 22 years and then became a Turkish prison for Cretan rebels. The exterior is most impressive with reliefs of the Lion of St Mark. The interior has 26 overly restored rooms and good views from the top.

Several other notable vestiges from Venetian times survive in the city. Most famous is **Morosini Fountain** on Plateia Venizelou, which spurts water from four lions into eight ornate U-shaped marble troughs. The fountain, built in 1628, was commissioned by Francesco Morosini while he was governor of Crete. Opposite is the three-aisled 13th-century **Basilica of San Marco**. It has been reconstructed many times and is now an exhibition gallery. A little north of here is the attractively reconstructed 17th-century **Venetian Loggia**. It was a Venetian version of a gentleman's club; the male aristocracy came here to drink and gossip. It is now used as government offices.

The delightful **Bembo Fountain**, at the southern end of 1866, is shown on local maps as the Turkish Fountain, but it was actually built by the Venetians in the 16th century. It was constructed from a hotchpotch of building materials including an ancient statue. The ornate edifice next to the fountain was added by the Turks, and now functions as a snack bar.

The former **Church of Agia Ekaterini** (☎ 281 028 8825, Monis Odigitrias; admission €1.50; open 9am-1.30pm Mon-Sat, 5pm-8pm Tues, Thur & Fri), next to Agios Minos Cathedral, is now a museum housing an impressive collection of icons. Most notable are the six icons painted by Mihail Damaskinos, the mentor of Dominikos Theotokopoulos (El Greco).

The **Battle of Crete Museum** (☎ 281 0034 6554, cnr Doukos Beaufort & Hatzidaki; admission free; open 9am-1pm) chronicles this historic battle through photographs, letters, uniforms and weapons.

You can pay homage to Crete's most acclaimed contemporary writer, Nikos Kazantzakis (1883–1957), by visiting his **tomb** at the Martinenga Bastion (the best-preserved bastion) in the southern part of town. The epitaph on his grave, 'I hope for nothing, I fear nothing, I am free', is taken from one of his works.

## Places to Stay

As the island's capital and business centre, Iraklio's accommodation opportunities are weighted toward the needs of business travellers. Hotels tend to be bland but they are clustered in the centre of town, convenient to public transport. The closest beach resort to Iraklio is Ammoudara, 2km west of town.

## Places to Stay – Budget

**Camping** The nearest camp sites are at Gouves and Hersonisos.

*Camping Creta* (☎ 2897 041 400, fax 2897 041 792, Gouves) Person/tent €3.50/2.70. Camping Creta is 16km east of Iraklio along the main road to Agios Nikolaos and then 2km left to the beach. The camping grounds are in a flat, shadeless area but there is a sand and pebble beach.

*Camping Hersonisos* (☎/fax 2897 022 902, Anisaras) Person/tent €3.50/2.70. This camping ground is 22km east of Iraklio, 3km before Hersonisos. The camping ground is on the sandy beach and features traditional-style buildings.

**Hostels** *Iraklio Youth Hostel (☎ 281 028 6281, fax 281 022 2947, Vyronos 5)* Bed in single-sex dorm €7.40, doubles/triples €17.60/25. This is a GYHA establishment is a clean, well-run place, though a little on the quiet side. Luggage storage is available for €1.50 per piece and breakfast and dinner are served, if required.

**Domatia** There are few domatia in Iraklio and not enough cheap hotels to cope with the number of budget travellers who arrive in the high season.

*Rent Rooms Hellas (☎ 281 028 8851, fax 281 028 4442, Handakos 24)* Dorm bed €6.80, doubles/triples/quads €22/26.50/ 31.70. Many travellers prefer the livelier atmosphere at this de facto youth hostel that has a roof garden and a bar. Luggage storage is free.

*Hotel Mirabello (☎ 281 028 5052, fax 281 022 5852, e mirabhot@otenet.gr, Theotokopoulou 20)* Singles/doubles €22/ 29.50, with bath €29.50/35.30. One of the most pleasant low-priced places is the Mirabello on this quiet street in the centre of town. The rooms are immaculate. Try to get a room with a balcony.

*Hotel Lena (☎ 281 022 3280, fax 281 024 2826, Lahana 10)* Singles/doubles €23.50/32.50, doubles with bath €38.20. Renovated in 2001, Hotel Lena now has comfortable and airy rooms, either with air-conditioning or fan, phones and double-glazed windows.

*Vergina Rooms (☎ 281 024 2739, Hortatson 32)* Doubles/triples €20.50/26.50. The pleasant Vergina Rooms is a turn-of-the-century house with a small courtyard, spacious high-ceilinged rooms and lots of character. Bathrooms are on the terrace and hot water is available upon request.

*Hotel Rea (☎ 281 022 3638, fax 281 024 2189, Kalimeraki-Handakos)* Singles/doubles €19/23.50, doubles/triples with bath €26.50/35.30. This handy place is clean, quiet and friendly.

## Places to Stay – Mid-Range
*Hotel Kronos (☎ 281 028 2240, fax 281 028 5853, e kronosht@otenet.gr, Venizelou 2)*

Singles/doubles €32.30/41. This is as close to the sea as you can get in Iraklio without actually being in the water. The large, twin-bedded rooms are in excellent condition with sparkling tile floors and white walls. All rooms have balconies, some with views of the sea and double-glazed windows.

*Atrion Hotel (☎ 281 022 9225, fax 281 022 3292, Hronaki 9)* Singles/doubles €54.30/63.40 including buffet breakfast. This is a business-like establishment with few concessions to frivolity. The large, well-furnished rooms have air-con on demand, TVs with international stations and modern bathrooms but the most attractive feature of the hotel is the enclosed garden-terrace.

*Hotel Irini (☎ 281 022 6561, fax 281 022 6407, Idomeneos 4)* Singles/doubles €47/ 61.60. This is a modern establishment with 59 large, airy rooms with TV (local stations only), radio, telephone and air-con. Most of the Mediterranean-style rooms have balconies enlivened by plants and flowers.

*Hotel Kastro (☎ 281 0284 185, fax 281 022 3622, w www.kastro-hotel.gr, Theotokopoulou 22)* Singles/doubles €26.40/ 35.20 including breakfast. The Kastro has comfortable amenities including a great rooftop terrace with chairs for sunbathing. The rooms are large, contain telephones and have air-con.

*Hotel Ilaira (☎ 281 022 7103, fax 281 024 2367, Ariadnis 1)* Singles/doubles €41/52.80. The best feature of Hotel Ilaira is the rooftop terrace with a panoramic view of the ports and fortress. The pleasant stucco and wood rooms have telephones, some have TVs and others have small balconies with sea views.

*El Greco (☎ 281 028 1071, fax 281 028 1072, 1821 St 4)* Singles/doubles €51/65 including breakfast, air-con €7.40 extra. Near Morosini Fountain, El Greco has a no-nonsense look. Nonetheless, the location is good, the rooms are in decent shape and some have TVs and air-con.

## Places to Stay – Top End
*Galaxy Hotel (☎ 281 023 8812, fax 281 021 1211, e galaxyir@otenet.gr, Dimokratias 67)* Singles/doubles €65/88. Although

not in the town centre, Galaxy offers a lot of amenities. There's a swimming pool large enough to swim laps, a sauna and very comfortable rooms with air-con on demand, TVs with international stations, telephones, hair dryers, safes and balconies.

***Hotel Lato*** (*☎ 281 022 8103, fax 281 024 0350,* **e** *info@lato.gr, Epimenidou 15)* Singles/doubles €67/140 including buffet breakfast. This three-star superior hotel overlooking the fortress offers excellent value. The sound-insulated comfortable rooms have air-con, Web browser, pay TV, telephone, radio and balconies with views of the sea.

***Atlantis Hotel*** (*☎ 281 022 9103, fax 281 022 6265,* **e** *atlantis@atl.grecotel.gr, Ygias 2)* Singles/doubles €70.50/100 including buffet breakfast. The Atlantis is located on a quiet street near the harbour. This gleaming, modern hotel has an indoor swimming pool, health club, sauna and solarium. The rooms are spacious and well-appointed with air-con on demand.

***Astoria Hotel*** (*☎ 281 034 3080, fax 281 022 9078,* **e** *astoria@her.forthnet.gr, Plateia Eleftherias 11)* Singles/doubles €83.70/106 including buffet breakfast. This is the businessperson's hotel of choice. It's in the thick of the action on Plateia Eleftherias, convenient to all public transport and equipped with a rooftop swimming pool.

## Places to Eat

Iraklio has restaurants to suit all tastes and pockets from excellent fish tavernas to exotic international cuisine. The business-like temperament of the city also allows for a wider choice of formal dining options, unlike the rest of the island. Note that the majority of restaurants are closed on Sunday. You may be relegated to self-catering, looking for a Hotel restaurant or heading to one of the fast-food outlets around the Morosini Fountain.

## Places to Eat – Budget

***Loukoumades Cafe*** (*☎ 281 034 6005, Dikeosynis 8)* Loukoumades €1.50. Open 5am-midnight. This cafe has the best *loukoumades* (honey-dipped fritters) in Iraklio.

Workers, shopkeepers and business people drift in an out all day for their loukoumades fix, but, on a scale of one to 10, the ambience is minus six.

***O Vrakas*** (*☎ 69 7789 3973, Plateia Anglon)* Mains €2.90-3.50. Vrakas is a small streetside ouzeri that grills fresh fish al fresco in front of diners. It's cheap and unassuming and the menu is limited, but still very popular with locals. Grilled octopus (€3.22) with ouzo is a good choice.

## Places to Eat – Mid-Range

***Tierra del Fuego*** (*☎ 281 028 9542, Theotokopoulou 26)* Open 8pm-midnight Mon-Sat. Mexican food is trendy in Crete right now making this place popular with a hip, young crowd. If you don't have your heart set on authenticity, you'll be amused by the Cretan versions of Mexican standards.

***Ippokambos Ouzeri*** (*☎ 281 028 0240, Mitsotaki 2)* Mains €3.50-5.30. This place is as good as taverna-style eating gets. The interior is attractively decorated with cooking pots but most people prefer to squeeze onto one of the sidewalk tables. Whether you opt for vegetarian mezedes or baked squid, you'll find the food fresh and savoury.

***I Avli tou Defkaliona*** (*☎ 281 024 4215, Kalokerinou 8)* Mains €3.80-6.20. Open 8pm-4am Mon-Sat. Its wicker chairs, red-checked tablecloths and plastic grapevines put diners in a cheery mood intensified by delicious food. After the tourists leave at around 11pm, the locals pile in, the owner takes out his accordion and the festivities commence.

***Taverna Kastella*** (*☎ 281 028 4432, Sofokli Venizelou 3)* Grills €3.80-6.80. Open 9.30am-12.30am Mar-Nov. This place has good food but a better setting. The taverna is right on the water offering a spectacular view of the Venetian fortress. Come at the end of the day and enjoy the sunset over an ouzo and mezedes.

***Katsina Ouzeri*** (*☎ 281 022 1027, Marineli 12)* Mezedes €1.50-4.40. Open 7pm-1am Tues-Sun. This is an old neighbourhood favourite. Most people come for the lamb and pork, roasted in a brick oven, or the excellent stewed goat. Portions are hearty and the atmosphere is convivial.

*Bella Casa (☎ 281 028 5681, Zografou 16)* Mains €4.40-7.30. Open noon-5pm & 8pm-1am Mon-Sat. Bella Casa is set in a stunning turn-of-the-century villa with a small terrace-garden on the street. The stylish rooms are air-conditioned in the summer allowing you to savour a wide assortment of richly flavoured Greek and Italian dishes without working up a sweat.

*Baxes (☎ 281 027 7057, Gianni Hronaki 14)* Mains €3.20-5. Open 11am-2am. Baxes is now run by country folk. This simple restaurant offers special-occasion cooking. Lamb and goat are stewed for hours or roasted in a brick oven just the way Cretans cook them.

*Giakoumis Taverna (Theodosaki 5-8)* Mayirefta €2.30-4.40. Open noon-3pm & 7pm-10pm Mon-Sat. Theodosaki is lined with tavernas catering to the market on 1866 and this is one of the best. There's a full menu of Cretan specialties and turnover is high, which means that the dishes are freshly cooked.

*Restaurant Ionia (☎ 281 028 3213, Evans 3)* Mayirefta €2.60-4.40. Open 7pm-midnight Mon-Sat. At the intersection of Evans and Giannari, this is the place for good Cretan home-cooking. Choose your meal from the pots and pans of food on display, sit down and prepare to enjoy a scrumptious meal.

## Places to Eat – Top End

*Ethrion (☎ 281 028 9542, Almyrou 2)* Mains €5.30-8.80. Open 7.30pm-1am Mon-Sat. When you're ready for a more formal dining experience head to Ethrion on the corner of Almyrou and Akrolcondos. This upscale restaurant serves a full menu of well-prepared Greek specialties. Linen tablecloths and a grand piano set a romantic tone for a meal on the plant-filled terrace.

*Giovanni Taverna (☎ 281 034 6338, Koraï 12)* Seafood platter for 2 €32.30. Open noon-2.30pm & 7.30pm-midnight Mon-Sat. This is a splendid place with two floors of large, airy rooms and, in summer, outdoor eating on a quiet pedestrian street. The food is a winning Mediterranean combination of Greek and Italian specialties.

*Loukoulos (☎ 281 022 4435, Koraï 5)* Grills €13-16. Open noon-3pm & 7pm-midnight Mon-Sat. Loukoulos offers luscious Mediterranean specialties served on fine china and accompanied by soft classical music. You can either choose the elegant interior or dine on the outdoor terrace under a lemon tree.

*New China (☎ 281 024 5162, Koraï 1)* Set menu for 2 €30. Open noon-3pm & 7pm-midnight Mon-Sat. No city can call itself truly cosmopolitan without a Chinese restaurant and Iraklio is no exception. New China has an extensive menu of competent Chinese dishes slightly altered to please local palates.

## Entertainment

The best time to engage in cultural pursuits is during the Iraklio Summer Arts Festival that presents international guest orchestras and dance troupes as well as local talent. Concerts and stage productions are offered sporadically throughout the rest of the year; the tourist office of Iraklio will have the latest schedules.

*Nikos Kazantzakis Open Air Theatre (☎ 281 024 2977, Jesus Bastion)* Box office open 9am-2.30pm and 6.30pm-9.30pm daily. The main venue for Iraklio's cultural scene is this immense open-air theatre. It is the main site for Iraklio's Summer Arts Festival when musicians, actors and dancers perform under the stars. There are special events the rest of the year and, when not being used by live performers in the summer, it's used as an open-air cinema.

Iraklio has about half a dozen cinemas but the most centrally located is the *Astoria Cinema (☎ 281 022 6191, Plateia Eleftherias)*. It screens new-release movies in their original language, which is usually English.

**Cafes & Bars** The bars and cafes around Plateia Venizelou are as hyped-up as the nonstop crowds milling around the Morosini Fountain. The pedestrian area of Koraï and Perdikari is lined with stylish kafeneia that attract a before-disco crowd eager to see and be seen. The old buildings along Handakos street contain relaxed bars and cafes with cosy interiors and enclosed patios more suitable for conversation than people-watching.

**Fyllo...Sofies** (☎ 281 028 0732, Plateia Venizelou) Open noon-midnight. This place has a restaurant downstairs and a rooftop bar that is a great perch to watch the goings-on around the Morosini Fountain directly below. A subdued crowd chats in comfortable chairs around a replica of the famous Four Lions Fountain.

**De Facto** (☎ 281 034 2007, Kantanoleon 2) Open noon-midnight. Although busy all day, this is one of the most fashionable bars in town early in the evening when it offers ringside seats to the evening promenade around Morosini Fountain. It's also very gay-friendly.

**Guernica** (☎ 281 028 2988, Apokoronou Kritis 2) Open 10am-midnight. Guernica boasts traditional decor and contemporary rock that mix well to create one of Iraklio's hippest bar/cafes. The terrace-garden of this rambling old building is a delight in summer and in winter you can warm up next to the fireplace.

**Take Five** (☎ 281 022 6564, Akroleondos 7) Open 10am-midnight. This is an old favourite on the edge of El Greco Park that doesn't get going until after sundown when the outside tables fill up with a diverse crowd of regulars. It's a gay-friendly place; the music and ambience are low-key.

**Jasmin** (☎ 281 028 8880, Handakos 45) Open noon-midnight. This is a friendly bar/cafe with a back terrace that specialises in herbal tea but also serves alcoholic beverages. The nightly DJs play rock and world music as well as techno.

**Aktarika** (☎ 281 034 1225, Dedalou 2) Open 10am-1am. This is a large airy upscale place next to the Morosini Fountain that bustles day and night. It has a great balcony and is a good place to come early in the evening for people-watching. The DJ plays jazz, rock and world music.

**Pagopiion** (☎ 281 034 6028, Plateia Agiou Titou) Open 8am-midnight. This is a former ice factory and the most original bar/restaurant on the island. The restaurant serves dishes with names like 'Roll With Me, Baby' pasta and Arm Agadon peppers. At around 10pm a DJ comes to spin jazz, rock and techno. It's gay-friendly.

**Ideon Antron** (☎ 281 024 2041, Perdikari 1) Open 10am-1am. On trendy Koraï with its rows of post-modern kafeneia, this is a throwback to the past. The stone interior with its shiny wood bar creates a relaxed, inviting place.

**Sousouro** (☎ 281 022 6510, Androgeo 9) Open 6pm-1am. Sousouro has a quieter ambience than other places in the neighbourhood. Sit outside and watch the scene around Koraï or retreat to the artsy interior where a pianist entertains most evenings.

**Rebels** (Cnr Koraï & Perdikari) This was one of the pioneers in the neighbourhood and is the most obvious 'designer' bar. Marble-topped tables and hanging lamps with Japanese patterns create a decor that blends badly with the relentless techno pounding in the background.

**Discos** Iraklio has the smartest and most sophisticated discos on the island. The following venues open around midnight and close near dawn. The cover charge runs from €4.40 to €5.90 and includes a drink.

**Privilege Club** (Doukos Beaufort 7) Iraklio's smart set packs this dancing club that can easily hold 1000 people. Like many of Crete's dancing clubs, there's international music (rock, techno etc) until about 2am when the Greek music takes over.

**Yacht Club** (☎ 281 034 3500, Doukos Beaufort 9) Next door is the club that attracts a smartly dressed assortment of young locals and visitors. The clubs vie to attract the most chic from the chic crowd.

You may not want to buy real estate on Leoforos Ikarou just down from Plateia Eleftherias, but this action-packed street serves up the wildest nightlife in town. There is a wide range of similar discos and clubs. The music is a contemporary mix of rock, techno and Greek. Many close during the week and move to Ammoudara in the west.

## Shopping
Iraklio is where the money is, so it's a good place to pick up the latest Cretan fashions,

replace a suitcase or shop for luxury goods. Dedalou is a pedestrian shopping street lined with some of the classier tourist shops but the market street, 1866, is a lot more fun. This narrow street is packed on most days and stalls spill over with sponges, herbs, fruits, vegetables, utensils, T-shirts, nuts, honey, shoes and jewellery. For gold and silver jewellery, head to Kalokerinou or the busy commercial 25 Avgoustou. Kalokerinou is also a good street to buy embroidery. There are no department stores in Iraklio.

*Tsihlakis (☎ 281 028 2045, '1821' 96)* For leather goods try this store that offers a wide selection of handbags and ladies shoes, some of which are handmade by local artisans.

*Spyros Valergos (☎ 281 028 5019, '1866' 5)* This is a good stop on colourful 1866 street for ceramics, clothing, statues and icons.

## Getting There & Away

**Air – International** Olympic Airways flies to Larnaka from Iraklio (€148, twice weekly).

Cronus Airlines offers direct connections to Paris and, in association with its partner Aegean Airlines, one-stop connections to Cologne/Bonn, Munich, Rome and Stuttgart. Its office (☎ 281 034 3366) is at '1821' 10.

KLM-associate Transavia flies direct between Amsterdam and Iraklio on Monday and Friday. Transavia is represented by Sbokos Tours (☎ 281 022 9712), Dimokratias 51.

Iraklio has lots of charter flights from all over Europe. Prince Travel (☎ 281 028 2706), 25 Avgoustou 30, advertises cheap last-minute tickets on these flights. Sample fares include London for €88 and Munich for €125.

**Air – Domestic** Olympic Airways (☎ 281 022 9191) at Plateia Eleftherias 42, has at least six flights daily to Athens (€80) from Iraklio's Nikos Kazantzakis airport (☎ 281 024 5644). It also has flights to Thessaloniki (€97, two weekly), Rhodes (€80, two weekly) and Santorini (€56, two weekly).

Aegean Airlines (☎ 281 034 4324, fax 281 034 4330) at Leoforos Dimokratias 11, has flights to Athens (€70, three daily), Thessaloniki (€90, two daily) and Rhodes (€75, one daily).

Axon Airlines (☎ 281 033 1310, fax 281 022 2297) at Ethnikis Andistasis 134, has flights to Athens (€70, two daily).

**Bus** There are buses every half-hour (hourly in winter) to Rethymno (€5.60, 1½ hours) and Hania (€10.90, three hours) from the Rethymno/Hania bus station opposite Bus Station A. Following is a list of other destinations from Bus Station A (☎ 281 024 5020, fax 281 034 6284, ℮ ktelirla@otenet.gr, ⓦ www.ktel.org /iraklio/en/):

| destination | duration | fare | frequency |
| --- | --- | --- | --- |
| Agia Pelagia | 45 mins | €2.20 | 5 daily |
| Agios Nikolaos | 1½ hours | €4.50 | half-hourly |
| Arhanes | 30 mins | €1.20 | 15 daily |
| Hersonisos/ Malia | 1 hour | €2 | half-hourly |
| Ierapetra | 2½ hours | €6.80 | 7 daily |
| Lasithi plateau | 2 hours | €4.50 | 2 daily |
| Milatos | 1½ hours | €3.50 | 1 daily |
| Sitia | 3½ hours | €9.40 | 5 daily |

Buses leave Bus Station B for:

| destination | duration | fare | frequency |
| --- | --- | --- | --- |
| Agia Galini | 2½ hours | €5 | 7 daily |
| Anogia | 1 hour | €2.30 | 6 daily |
| Matala | 2 hours | €5 | 9 daily |
| Phaestos | 2 hours | €4.10 | 8 daily |

**Taxi** There are long-distance taxis (☎ 281 021 0102 or ☎ 281 021 0168) from Plateia Eleftherias, opposite the Astoria Hotel and Bus Station B, to all parts of Crete. Sample fares include Agios Nikolaos (€34), Hania (€69) and Rethymno (€43). A taxi to the airport costs around €6.

**Ferry** Minoan Lines (☎ 0801-7500, ⓦ www .minoan.gr) and ANEK both operate ferries every evening each way between Iraklio and Piraeus (10 hours). They depart from both Piraeus and Iraklio between 7.45pm and

8pm. Fares are (€21.70 deck class and (€41.70 for cabins. The Minoan Lines' high speed boats, the F/B Festos Palace and F/B Knossos Palace, are much more modern and more comfortable than their ANEK rivals.

In summer and from Friday to Sunday Minoan Lines runs six-hour day services. Boats depart Iraklio and Piraeus at 12.30pm and arrive at 6.30pm. This is by far the most convenient way to get to and from Crete. The boats are fast and less troubled by meltemi-prone seas.

Minoan also has a three times weekly service to Thessaloniki (€38, 23 hours) departing at 1pm from Iraklio and arriving in Thessaloniki at noon. The boat stops at Santorini and Mykonos and depending on the schedule also at Naxos, Paros Syros, Tinos and Skiathos.

The travel agencies on 25 Avgoustou are the place to get information and buy tickets. Iraklio's port police can be contacted on ☎ 281 024 4912.

## Getting Around

**To/From the Airport** Bus No 1 goes to/from the airport every 15 minutes between 6am and 1am for €0.60. It leaves from outside the Astoria Hotel on Plateia Eleftherias.

**Bus** Local bus No 2 goes to Knossos every 10 minutes from Bus Station A (€0.80, 20 minutes). It also stops on 25 Avgoustou and 1821.

**Car & Motorcycle** Most of Iraklio's car and motorcycle-hire outlets are on 25 Avgoustou. You'll get the best deal from local companies like Sun Rise (☎ 281 022 1609) at 25 Avgoustou 46, Loggeta Cars & Bikes (☎ 281 028 9462) at Plateia Kallergon 6, next to El Greco Park, Motor Club (☎ 281 022 2408), at Plateia 18 Anglon or Ritz Rent-A-Car at the Hotel Rea, which has discounts for hotel guests. The airport has a full range of car-rental companies including Hertz, Eurodollar and Europcar.

**Bicycle** Mountain bikes can be hired from Porto Club Travel Services (☎ 281 028 5264) 25 Avgoustou 20.

## KNOSSOS Κνωσός

Knossos (k-nos-**os**), 5km south of Iraklio, was the capital of Minoan Crete. Nowadays it's the island's major tourist attraction. The road leading up to the famous site (☎ 281 023 1940, Knossos; admission €4.40; open 8am-7pm Apr-Oct, to 5pm in winter) is an uninspiring gauntlet of souvenir shops and fruit juice stands but the palace is magnificent. Thanks to a beautiful site surrounded by green hills and shaded by pine trees it is Crete's most evocative location.

The ruins of Knossos were uncovered in 1900 by the British archaeologist Sir Arthur Evans. Heinrich Schliemann, the legendary discoverer of ancient Troy, had had his eye on the spot (a low, flat-topped mound), believing an ancient city was buried there, but had been unable to strike a deal with the local landowner. Arthur Evans was a well-travelled journalist, museum curator and classicist with an interest in ancient scripts when he came across some ancient stones engraved with what appeared to be hieroglyphic writing.

Learning that the stones came from Crete, Evans set sail in 1894. Still thinking that the low, flat-topped mound that interested Schliemann might contain the key to his hieroglyphics, Evans acquired a share of the site that, significantly enough, gave him exclusive rights to the excavation. He returned five years later and began digging with a group of Cretan workmen.

The flat-topped mound was called Kefala and the vanished palace that it contained emerged quickly. The first treasure to be unearthed was a fresco of a Minoan man followed by the discovery of the Throne Room. The archaeological world was stunned. Until he began his excavations no one had suspected that a civilisation of this maturity and sophistication had existed in Europe at the time of the great Pharaohs of Egypt. Some even speculated that it was the site of the lost city of Atlantis to which Plato referred many centuries later.

You will need to spend about four hours at Knossos to explore it thoroughly. There is absolutely no signage, so unless you have a travel guide, or hire a guide, you will have no idea what you are looking at. To beat the crowds and avoid the oppressive heat, it's best to get there as soon as the site opens and visit the Throne Room first before the tour buses arrive. The cafe at the site is expensive – you'd do better to bring a picnic along.

## History

The first palace at Knossos was built around 1900 BC but most of what you see dates from 1700 BC after the Old Palace was destroyed by an earthquake. It was then rebuilt to a grander and more sophisticated design. The palace was partially destroyed again sometime between 1500 and 1450 BC and inhabited for another 50 years before it was devastated once and for all by fire.

The New Palace was not erected helter-skelter but carefully designed to meet the needs of a complex society. There were domestic quarters for the king or queen, residences for officials and priests, homes of common folk and burial grounds. Public reception rooms, shrines, workshops, treasuries and storerooms were built around a paved courtyard in a design so intricate that it may have been behind the legend of the Labyrinth and the Minotaur.

Until recently it was possible to enter the royal apartments, but in early 1997 it was decided to cordon this area off before it disappeared altogether under the continual pounding of feet. Extensive repairs are under way but it is unlikely to be open to the public again.

## The Myth of the Minotaur

King Minos of Crete invoked the wrath of Poseidon when he failed to sacrifice a magnificent white bull sent to him for that purpose. Poseidon's revenge was to cause Pasiphae, King Minos' wife, to fall in love with the animal. In order to attract the bull, Pasiphae asked Daedalus, chief architect at Knossos and all-round handyman, to make her a hollow, wooden cow structure. When she concealed herself inside, the bull found her irresistible. The outcome of their bizarre association was the Minotaur: a hideous monster who was half-man and half-bull.

King Minos asked Daedalus to build a labyrinth in which to confine the Minotaur and demanded that Athens pay an annual tribute of seven youths and seven maidens. This was by way of compensation for the Athenians having killed Minos' son Androgeos at games where he had participated and had been victorious. The hapless youths were fed to the Minotaur in order to satisfy the monster's huge appetite.

The Athenians became enraged by the tribute demanded by Minos. The Athenian hero, Theseus, vowed to kill the Minotaur and sailed off to Crete posing as one of the sacrificial youths. On arrival, he fell in love with Ariadne, the daughter of King Minos, and she promised to help him if he would take her away with him afterwards. She provided him with the ball of twine that he unwound on his way into the labyrinth and used to retrace his steps after slaying the monster. Theseus eventually fled Crete with his now bride-to-be Ariadne.

## Exploring the Site

Numerous rooms, corridors, dogleg passages, staircases, nooks and crannies, prohibit a detailed walk description of the palace. However, Knossos is not a site where you'll be perplexed by heaps of rubble, trying to fathom whether you're looking at the Throne Room or a workshop. Thanks to Evans' reconstruction, the most significant parts of the complex are instantly recognisable (if not instantly found). While you wander you will come across many of Evans' reconstructed columns. Most are painted deep brown-red with gold-trimmed black capitals. These, like all Minoan columns, taper at the bottom.

Strategically placed copies of Minoan frescoes help infuse the site with the artistic spirit of these remarkable people. The Minoan achievements in plumbing equal their achievements in painting; drains and pipes were carefully placed to avoid flooding, taking advantage of centrifugal force. It

appears that at some points water ran uphill, demonstrating a mastery of the principle that water finds its own level. Also notice the placement of light wells and the relationship of rooms to passages, porches, light wells and verandas, which kept rooms cool in summer and warm in winter.

The usual entrance to the palace complex is across the Western Court and along the **Corridor of the Procession Fresco**. The fresco depicted a long line of people carrying gifts to present to the king; only fragments remain. A copy of one of these fragments, called the **Priest King Fresco**, can be seen to the south of the Central Court.

An alternative way to enter is to have a look at the Corridor of the Procession Fresco, then walk straight ahead to enter the site from the northern end. If you do this you will come to the **theatral area**, a series of steps whose function remains unknown. It could have been a theatre where spectators watched acrobatic and dance performances,

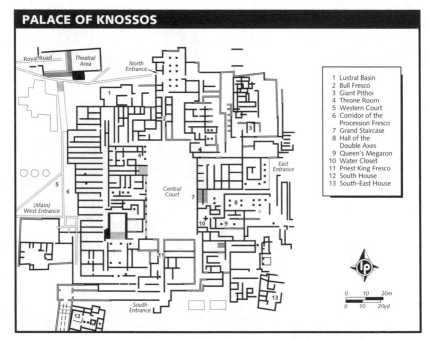

**PALACE OF KNOSSOS**

Royal Road — Theatral Area — North Entrance

1  Lustral Basin
2  Bull Fresco
3  Giant Pithoi
4  Throne Room
5  Western Court
6  Corridor of the
   Procession Fresco
7  Grand Staircase
8  Hall of the
   Double Axes
9  Queen's Megaron
10  Water Closet
11  Priest King Fresco
12  South House
13  South-East House

(Main) West Entrance

Central Court

East Entrance

South Entrance

0    10    20m
0    10    20yd

Nightclub advertising, Iraklio

Archaeological Museum, Iraklio

Inside the Iraklio Cathedral

A street cobbler mending shoes, Iraklio

'1866' Street market stall, Iraklio

Iraklio Archaeological Museum

An aerial view of the Venetian Castle on the harbour, Iraklio

Watching the world go by at Cafe Terrace, Iraklio

Circular Minoan tomb, Kamalari

or the place where people gathered to welcome important visitors arriving by the Royal Road.

The **Royal Road** leads off to the west. The road, Europe's first (Knossos has lots of firsts), was flanked by workshops and the houses of ordinary people. The **Lustral Basin** is also in this area. Evans speculated that this was where the Minoans performed a ritual cleansing with water before religious ceremonies.

Entering the **Central Court** from the north, you will pass the relief **Bull Fresco** which depicts a charging bull. Relief frescoes were made by moulding wet plaster, and then painting it while still wet.

Also worth seeking out in the northern section of the palace are the **giant pithoi**. Pithoi were ceramic jars used for storing olive oil, wine and grain. Evans found over 100 of these huge jars at Knossos (some were 2m high). The ropes used to move them inspired the raised patterns that adorn the jars.

Once you have reached the Central Court, which in Minoan times was surrounded by the high walls of the palace, you can begin exploring the most important rooms of the complex.

From the northern end of the west side of the palace, steps lead down to the **Throne Room**. This room is fenced off but you can still get a good view of it. The centrepiece, the simple, beautifully proportioned throne, is flanked by the **Griffin Fresco**. Griffins were mythical beasts regarded as sacred by the Minoans.

The room is thought to have been a shrine, and the throne the seat of a high priestess, rather than a king. Certainly, the room seems to have an aura of mysticism and reverence rather than pomp and ceremony. The Minoans did not worship their deities in great temples but in small shrines, and each palace had several.

On the 1st floor of this side of the palace is the section Evans called the **Piano Nobile**, for he believed the reception and staterooms were here. A room at the northern end of this floor displays copies of some of the frescoes found at Knossos.

Returning to the Central Court, the impressive **grand staircase** leads from the middle of the eastern side of the palace to the royal apartments, which Evans called the **Domestic Quarter**. This section of the site is now cordoned off. Within the royal apartments is the **Hall of the Double Axes**. This was the king's megaron, a spacious double room in which the ruler both slept and carried out certain court duties. The room had a light well at one end and a balcony at the other to ensure air circulation.

The room takes its name from the double axe marks on its light well. These marks appear in many places at Knossos. The double axe *(labrys)* was a sacred symbol to the Minoans, and the origin of our word 'labyrinth'.

A passage leads from the Hall of the Double Axes to the **queen's megaron**. Above the door is a copy of the **Dolphin Fresco**, one of the most exquisite Minoan artworks. A blue floral design decorates the portal. Next to this room is the queen's bathroom, complete with terracotta bathtub and a **water closet**, touted as the first ever to work on the flush principle; water was poured down by hand.

## Getting There & Away
Regular buses operate from Iraklio. See Iraklio's Getting Around section for details.

## AMMOUDARA Αμμουδάρα
**postcode 710 02 • pop 1083**
Ammoudara lies about 4km west of Iraklio and is the closest beach to the city. Long, sandy and wide, the beach is relatively uncrowded, making Ammoudara an alternative place to stay if you want to escape big-city Iraklio. The discos and nightlife of Ammoudara lure tourists and residents of Iraklio alike during the summer.

## Orientation
The town lies along the main road from Iraklio. The strip of hotels begins at Candia Maris in the east and ends at the Hotel Dolphin Bay in the west. Although it may seem that the beach is completely barricaded by hotels, in fact there are entrances next to the Agapi Beach Hotel and the Candia Maris Hotel.

## Places to Stay

Ammoudara is dominated by large resort hotels but there are a few domatia scattered about.

*Rent Rooms* (☎ 281 025 0723, Ammoudara) Singles/doubles €26.50/32.50. Rent Rooms is in central Ammoudara across the street from the luxury Candia Maris Hotel.

*Hotel Sun* (☎ 281 025 1790, fax 281 0251 161, Ammoudara) Singles/doubles €32.50/38.20. Also fairly central is this hotel that has a small swimming pool and simple rooms.

*Agapi Beach* (☎ 281 025 0502, fax 281 0258 731, Ammoudara) Singles/doubles €85/140 in high season includes half-board. This place is in the middle of the hotel strip right on the beach and has two outdoor swimming pools, three tennis courts, air-conditioning and a water sports centre.

## Places to Eat

*Golden Wheat Chinese Restaurant* (Ammoudara) Set meal for 2 €28-32. Open 6.30pm-midnight Mon-Sat. The dining scene in Ammoudara is uninspiring but you could try here for crispy duck and fried noodles with shrimp at a reasonable price.

## Entertainment

*Bachalo* (Linoperamata) Open 11pm-dawn June-Sept. This is the hottest disco in the region and generates high-voltage glamour on summer evenings. It's in Linoperamata, 2km west of Ammoudara.

*Banana Club* (Ammoudara) In the centre of Ammoudara try this club across the street from the Candia Maris Hotel. It has occasional live music.

## Getting There & Away

The No 6 bus from Iraklio stops in front of the Cretan Beach Hotel and the Agapi Beach Hotel in Ammoudara. By taxi it costs about €4.50.

## TYLISOS Τύλισος

The minor Minoan site at the village of Tylisos (til-is-os), (☎ 281 022 6092, Tylisos; admission €1.50; open 8.30am-3pm daily) 13km south of Iraklio, is only for the insatiable enthusiast. Three villas dating from different periods have been excavated. Buses from Iraklio to Anogia go through Tylisos. They also go past another Minoan site at **Sklavokambos**, 8km closer to Anogia. The ruins date from 1500 BC and were probably the villa of a district governor.

# South Central Iraklio Region

The highway that runs from Tymbaki to Pyrgos divides the northern portion of the Iraklio prefecture from the southern coastal resorts. Along the highway are busy commercial centres, such as Agia Varvara, Tymbaki, Mires, Agii Deka and Pyrgos that market the agricultural produce from the surrounding region. Although these towns hold little interest for tourists they do give a sense of the dynamism of the Cretan economy. Of more interest to travellers are the extraordinary archaeological sites of Phaestos, Agia Triada and Gortyna which trace almost 3000 years of ancient history from Minoans through the Romans to the early Christians.

When you get tired of poking around ancient ruins the south coast beaches of Matala, Kalamaki and Lendas beckon with long stretches of sandy beach. Further to the east are the more deserted beach communities of Arvi, Kastri and Keratokambos and the lovely mountain village of Ano Viannos.

## VORI Βώροι
### postcode 704 00 • pop 742

The pleasant unspoilt village of Vori, 4km east of Tymbaki, is composed of a main square surrounded by winding streets of whitewashed houses. The main attraction here is the outstanding **Museum of Cretan Ethnology** (☎ 2892 091 112, Vori; admission €3; open 10am-6pm in summer, 9am-3pm Mon-Fri Nov-Mar) that provides a fascinating insight into traditional Cretan culture. The detailed explanations are in

English, the first part of the exhibits deals with the herbs, flora and fauna that form the basis of the Cretan diet. There are descriptions about how snails, crabs and eels were gathered and eaten. Other exhibits include farm implements such as ploughs and grinding mills as well as beautiful weavings, wicker furniture, woodcarvings and musical instruments. A guide is available for €3. The museum is well-signposted from the main road.

There are a few *tavernas* around the main square and *Pension Margit (☎ 2892 091 128, fax 2892 091 539, Vori)* is signposted 400m up from the museum. Rates are €20.50 in this comfortable pension in a pine and palm tree shaded garden.

## MIRES Μοίρες
**postcode 704 00 • pop 4500**
This busy market town is an inevitable stop if you're changing buses from Iraklio en route to the south coast. It's a good place to pick up supplies in the many stores lining the main street. There's a post office on the main street and the OTE is on the street immediately south of the bus station. Also around the bus station is the Commercial Bank of Greece with an ATM and a Eurobank with an ATM. Check your email at Internet Cafe Escape (☎ 2892 024 163) on the main street. Access time costs €3.50 per hour.

*Rent Rooms Gortys (☎ 2892 022 528, Mires)* Doubles €23.50. If you have to stay overnight you'll find this place signposted 150m up from the bus station.

There are 13 buses a day from Iraklio (€3.50, 1¼ hours).

## ARCHAEOLOGICAL SITES
The south central region of Crete is blessed with a trio of important archaeological sites – Phaestos, Agia Triada and Gortyna – and a cluster of minor sites, spanning Cretan history from the Minoans to the Romans. For the visitor this is a boon, though getting from one to the other will ideally require private transport or joining a comprehensive sites tour from Iraklio. Either way, allow some time to see the sites and consider basing yourself here for a day or two.

## Gortyna Γόρτυνα
The archaeological site of Gortyna *(gor-tih-nah), (☎ 2892 031 144, Gortyna; admission €2.30; open 8am-7pm)*, also called Gortyn or Gortys, 46km south-west of Iraklio, is the largest in Crete and one of the most fascinating. There's not much here from the Minoan period because Gortyna was little more than a subject town of powerful Phaestos until it began accumulating riches (mostly from piracy) under the Dorians. By the 5th century BC it was as influential as Knossos. When Crete was under threat from the Romans the Gortynians cleverly made a pact with them and, when the Romans conquered the island in 67 BC, they made Gortyna the island's capital. The city blossomed under Roman administrators who endowed it with lavish public buildings such as a Praetorium, amphitheatre, public baths, a music school and temples. Except for the 7th-century-BC Temple of the Pithian Apollo and the 7th-century-AD Church of Agios Titos, most of what you see in Gortyna dates from the Roman period. Gortyna's centuries of splendour came to an end in AD 824 when the Saracens raided the island and destroyed the city.

The vastness of the site indicates how important Gortyna city was to the Romans. The city sprawls over a square kilometre of plains, foothills and the summit of Mt Agios Ioannis. As for most Roman cities, water was an important resource. The Romans needed water for their elaborate systems of fountains and public baths. At one time there must have been ducts and an aqueduct that brought water from the springs of Votomos, 15km away. There also must have been streets and a town square, but these have not been excavated.

Although Italian archaeologist Federico Halbherr first explored the site in the 1880s, excavations are still going on. There is a fenced area north of the main road with a large number of ruins outside the fenced area both north and south of the main road from Agii Deka.

Beginning south of the main road you'll first come to **Temple of the Pythian Apollo** that was the main sanctuary of pre-Roman

Gortyna. Built in the 7th century BC, the temple was expanded in the 3rd century BC and converted into a Christian basilica in the 2nd century AD. Nearby is the **Praetorium** that was the palace of the Roman governor of Crete, an administrative building with a basilica and a private residence. Most of the ruins date from the 2nd century AD and were repaired in the 4th century. To the north is the 2nd century **Nymphaeum**, a **public bath** supplied by an aqueduct bringing water from Zaros. It was originally adorned with statues of nymphs. South of the nymphaeum is the **amphitheatre**, which dates from the late 2nd century AD.

The most impressive monument within the fenced area is **Church of Agios Titos**, which is the finest early-Christian church in Crete. It was probably built on the site of an earlier church but this construction dates from the 6th century. The stone cruciform church has two small apses and contains three levels. The surviving apse provides a hint of the magnificence of this church many centuries ago. Nearby is the **Odeion**, a theatre built around the 1st century BC. Behind the Odeion is a plane tree that, according to legend, served as a love nest for Zeus and Europa.

Beyond the Odeion is the star attraction – the stone tablets engraved with the 6th century BC **Laws of Gortyna**. The stone tablets containing the laws, written in 600 lines in a Dorian dialect, were the earliest law code in the Greek world. Ancient Cretans were preoccupied with the same issues that drive people into court today – marriage, divorce, transfers of property, inheritance and adoption as well as criminal offences. Dorian legal theories are interesting but the main value of these remarkable tablets is the insight they provide into the social organisation of pre-Roman Crete. It was an extremely hierarchical society, divided into slaves and several categories of free citizens, each of whom had strictly delineated rights and obligations.

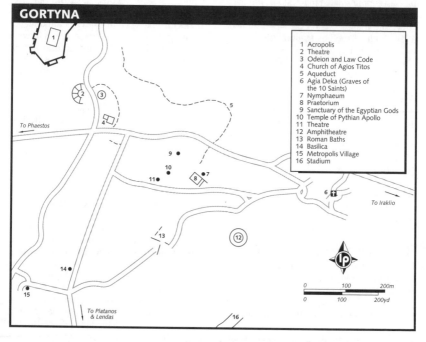

**GORTYNA**

1 Acropolis
2 Theatre
3 Odeion and Law Code
4 Church of Agios Titos
5 Aqueduct
6 Agia Deka (Graves of the 10 Saints)
7 Nymphaeum
8 Praetorium
9 Sanctuary of the Egyptian Gods
10 Temple of Pythian Apollo
11 Theatre
12 Amphitheatre
13 Roman Baths
14 Basilica
15 Metropolis Village
16 Stadium

To Phaestos

To Iraklio

To Platanos & Lendas

0    100    200m
0    100    200yd

It's a bit of a hike but it's worth visiting the **Acropolis** at the top of the hill in the north-west corner of the site. Following the road along the stream near the Odeion you will come to a gate beyond the theatre that marks the start of the path to the top. In addition to a birds-eye view of the entire site, the acropolis contains impressive sections of the pre-Roman ramparts.

## Phaestos Φαιστός

The Minoan site of Phaestos (*fes-tos*), (☎ 2982 042 315, *Festos; admission €3.50; open 8am-7pm, to 5pm in winter*) 63km from Iraklio, was the second most important palace-city of Minoan Crete. With amazing all-embracing views of the Mesara Plain and Mt Psiloritis, Phaestos has the most awe-inspiring location of all the Minoan sites. The layout of the palace is similar to Knossos, with rooms arranged around a central court.

Pottery deposits indicate that the site was inhabited in the Neolithic era around 4000 BC when the first settlers established themselves on the slopes of Kastri Hill. The first palace was built around 2000 BC and then destroyed by the earthquake that levelled many Minoan palaces. The ruins were covered with a layer of lime and debris that formed the basis of a new palace that was begun around 1700 BC. It too was destroyed in the catastrophe that befell the island in 1450 BC. In the intervening centuries Phaestos was the political and administrative centre of the Mesara Plain. Ancient texts refer to the palace's importance and note that it minted its own coins. Although Phaestos continued to be inhabited in later centuries, it fell into decline as Gortyna rose in importance. Under the Dorians Phaestos headed a league of cities that included Matala and Polyrrinia in western Crete. The leagues battled continuously and Phaestos was defeated by Gortyna in the 2nd century BC.

Excavation of the site began in 1900 by Professor Federico Halbherr of the Italian School of Archaeology, which is continuing the excavation work. In contrast to Knossos, Phaestos has yielded very few frescoes; it seems the palace walls were mostly covered

### The Phaestos Disk

This 3600-year-old terracotta tablet, about 16cm in diameter is an inscrutable relic from the Minoan archives. It was discovered at Phaestos in 1908 and has remained the object of much interpretational speculation ever since. The disk consists of a pictographic script made up of 241 'words' written in a continuous linear format from the outside of the disk to the inside (or the other way round). It has so far resisted all attempts at decipherment. The simplistic pictogrammes in most cases are easily identifiable – parts of the body, animal, tools etc – and bear only a passing similarity to the other scripts of Crete, Linear A and Linear B. Given that no other similar script has ever been discovered and that it is quite possible that the disk is an import from outside Crete, eventual decipherment in the foreseeable future seems highly unlikely.

with a layer of white gypsum. There has been no reconstruction of these ruins. The difficulty of visualising the structure of the palace is further compounded by the fact that the site includes remains of the Old Palace and the New Palace.

**Exploring the Site** Past the ticket booth, the **Upper Court** that was used in both the old and new palaces contains remains of buildings from the Hellenistic era. A stairway leads down to the **Theatral Area** that was once the staging ground for performances. The seats are at the northern end and the southern end contains the **west facade of the Old Palace**. The 15m-wide **grand stairway** leads to the **Propylon**, which was a porch. The steps of the stairway are thicker and higher in the middle to produce an impressive effect. Below the Propylon are the **storerooms** that still contain pithoi storage urns. The square hall next to the storerooms is thought to have been an **office**, where tablets containing Linear A script were found beneath the floor in 1955. South of the storeroom a **corridor** led to the west side of the **Central Court**. South of the corridor is a **lustral basin,** rooms with benches and a **pillar**

IRAKLIO

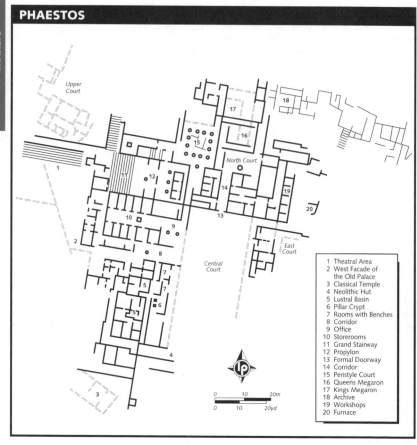

## PHAESTOS

Upper Court

North Court

Central Court

East Court

1 Theatral Area
2 West Facade of the Old Palace
3 Classical Temple
4 Neolithic Hut
5 Lustral Basin
6 Pillar Crypt
7 Rooms with Benches
8 Corridor
9 Office
10 Storerooms
11 Grand Stairway
12 Propylon
13 Formal Doorway
14 Corridor
15 Peristyle Court
16 Queens Megaron
17 Kings Megaron
18 Archive
19 Workshops
20 Furnace

0   10   20m
0   10   20yd

**crypt** similar to that at Knossos. The Central Court is the centrepiece of the palace, affording spectacular views of the surrounding area. It is extremely well preserved and gives a good sense of the magnificence of the palace. Porticoes with columns and pillars once lined the long sides of the Central Court. Notice the **Neolithic hut** at the south-western corner of the Central Court. The best preserved parts of the palace complex are the reception rooms and private apartments to the north of the Central Court, where excavations continue. Enter through the **Formal Doorway** with half columns at either side,

the lower parts of which are still *in situ*. The corridor leads to the north court; the **Peristyle Court**, which once had a paved veranda, is to the left of here. The royal apartments (**Queen's Megaron** and **King's Megaron**) are north-east of the Peristyle Court but they are currently fenced off. The celebrated Phaestos Disk was found in a building to the north of the palace. It now resides in Iraklio's Archaeological Museum.

### Agia Triada Αγία Τριάδα
Agia Triada (ag-**i**-a tri-**a**-da) is a small Minoan site (☎ 2892 091 564, Agia Triada;

*admission €2.90; open 8.30am-3pm)* 3km west of Phaestos in an enchanting landscape surrounded by hills and orange groves. Like the site of Phaestos it appears that Agia Triada has been occupied since the Neolithic era.

Masterpieces of Minoan art such as the 'Harvester's Vase', the 'Boxer Vase' and the 'Chieftain's Cup', now in the Iraklio Archaeological Museum, were found here but the palace was clearly not as important as the palace at Phaestos. Its principal building was smaller than the other royal palaces although it was built to a similar design.

This, and the opulence of the objects found at the site, indicate that it was a royal residence, possibly a summer palace of Phaestos' rulers.

After the entrance, you will first pass the ruins of a **Minoan House** before reaching the **shrine** that dates from the early 14th century BC. It once contained a frescoed floor painted with octopuses and dolphins. The floor is now in the Archaeological Museum of Iraklio. North-west of the shrine is a paved courtyard that Italian excavators called the **Court of Shrines**. Notice the **magazines and workshops** in the south-west

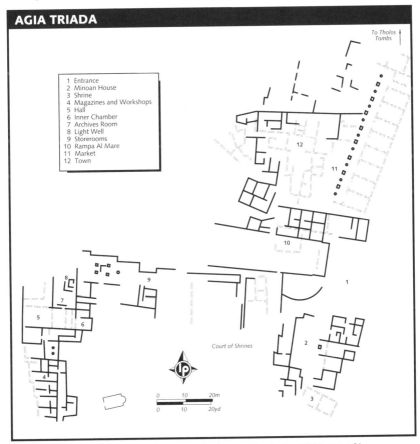

**AGIA TRIADA**

To Tholos Tombs

1 Entrance
2 Minoan House
3 Shrine
4 Magazines and Workshops
5 Hall
6 Inner Chamber
7 Archives Room
8 Light Well
9 Storerooms
10 Rampa Al Mare
11 Market
12 Town

Court of Shrines

0    10    20m
0    10    20yd

wing of the palace; the 'Chieftain's Cup' was found in one of these rooms. North of the workshops you will come to a **hall** and then the **inner chamber** that contains a raised slab that might have supported a bed, indicating that these were the residential quarters. This part of the palace had rooms for entertainment and rooms for business. The **archives room** once contained over 200 sealstones, which were probably used to fasten documents, and a wall painting of the wild cat of Crete that is now in the Archaeological Museum of Iraklio. The **Rampa al Mare** ramp that runs beneath the north side of the palace is thought to have run down to the sea at one point. A path leads from the fenced site along the hillside to a Minoan **cemetery** that dates from around 2000 BC. There are two circular beehive tombs.

The road to Agia Triada takes off to the right about 500m from Phaestos on the road to Matala. There is no public transport to the site.

### Kommos Κόμμος

The archaeological site of Kommos, 12km south-west of Mires along a beautiful beach, is still being excavated by American and Canadian archaeologists. Although the site is fenced off it's easy to get an idea of it from the outside. Kommos is believed to have been the port for Phaestos and contains a wealth of Minoan structures. It's even possible to spot the layout of the ancient town with its streets and courtyards, and the remains of workshops, dwellings and temples. Notice the Minoan road paved in limestone that leads from the southern section inland towards Phaestos; the ruts in the road were from Minoan carts and a sewer on its northern side are still visible.

**Getting There & Away** There are eight buses a day from Iraklio's Bus Station B to Phaestos (€4, 1½ hours), six from Agia Galini (€1.50, 40 minutes) and five from Matala (€1.20, 30 minutes). Buses to Phaestos also stop at Gortyna. Services are halved in winter. There is no public transport to Agia Triada and the site is about a 5km walk from any major nearby village.

Kommos is 3km north of Matala and makes for a pleasant walk.

### MATALA Μάταλα
postcode 702 00 • pop 132

Matala (**ma**-ta-la), on the coast 11km southwest of Phaestos, was once one of Crete's best known hippie hang-outs. When you see the dozens of eerie caves speckling the rock slab on the beach's edge, you'll see why 60s hippies found it like groovy, man. The caves were originally Roman tombs cut out of the sandstone rock in the 1st century AD and have been used as dwellings for many centuries. The soft rock allowed cave-dwellers to carve out windows, doors and beds.

The caves are all that remains of ancient Matala that probably served as a port for the great Minoan centre of Phaestos. Matala enjoyed a burst of activity under the Romans that lasted from 67 BC until the Arab conquest in the 9th century. During those centuries Matala was the port for Gortyna. Excavations around Matala have revealed coins from Gortyna, vases and amphorae.

These days, Matala is a decidedly tacky tourist resort packed out in summer and bleak and deserted in winter. The turtles like it, however. Matala and the area around it is a popular nesting ground for *Caretta Caretta* sea turtles. The Sea Turtle Protection Society has a booth near the car park. The sandy beach below the caves is one of Crete's better ones and the resort is a convenient base to visit Phaestos and Agia Triada.

### Orientation & Information

Matala's layout is easy to fathom. The bus stop is on the central square, one block back from the waterfront. There is a mobile post office just past the car park on the right as you enter the village. The OTE is beyond here in the beach car park. There is no tourist office but Monza Travel (☎ 2892 045 757, fax 2892 045 763), on the right as you enter town, rents rooms, apartments, cars and bikes, changes money and arranges for boat excursions. There is a laundry on the left as you enter the village and a bookshop with English-language books and newspapers diagonally opposite the Hotel Zafiria.

## The Hippy Connection

Long before Mykonos was hip and Ios was hot, Matala was host to a colony of flower children and alternative lifestylers in the late 1960s and early 1970s who made Matala their very own pied-à-terre. The hippies turned the caves into a modern troglodyte city – moving ever higher up the cliff to avoid sporadic attempts by the local police to evict them. Singer Joni Mitchell was among a number of hippies who lived in the caves. In 'Carey' from her 1970's album *Blue* she sang: *...but let's not talk about fare-thee-wells now, the night is a starry dome and they're playin' that scratchy rock and roll beneath the Matala Moon.*

Drawn by the lure of free cave accommodation, a gorgeous beach, a smattering of low-key, cheap tavernas, free love and copious pot Matala's hippies came in droves and hung around – wearing little more than headbands and guitars. Today, the caves are still there, but they are now fenced off. The hippies have traded places with the would-be hip, and buses and cars now come in droves. The beach is still gorgeous, but the tavernas are rather more expensive. As one ex-hippy put it 'Things ain't just cool no more...like, man!'

Check email at the Coffee Shop (☎ 2892 045 460) or at Zafiria Internet (2892 045 498). Both charge around €4.40 per hour.

## Things to See & Do

Forget about museums, monuments and archaeological sites. Matala is about the beach and the **caves** *(admission €1.50; open 8am-7pm June-Sept)*. The caves are fenced off at night. The beach is great for swimming and has pine trees along the edge that cast some shade. You can rent a lounge chair for €2.40 a day. If you feel more energetic, **pedalboats** cost €7.50 an hour and **canoes** are €4.50 an hour.

For a less crowded beach head to **Kokkini Ammos** (Red Beach). It's a 30 minute scramble south over the rocks and attracts a smattering of nudists. At the furthest end

of the village along the beach is a market street with woodcarvings, jewellery, ceramics and small fruit stands selling local products.

## Places to Stay

There are several pleasant options in Matala proper including one handy camping ground. The street running inland and at right angles from the main drag is lined with budget accommodation.

**Matala Community Camping** *(☎/fax 2892 045 340, Matala)* Person/tent €3.50/2.60. This is a reasonable place just back from the beach.

**Pension Andonios** *(☎ 2892 045 123, fax 2892 045 690, Matala)* Singles/doubles €11.70/17.60, double/triple apartments €23.50/26.40. Opposite Fantastic, this pension has attractively furnished rooms and apartments.

**Fantastic Rooms to Rent** *(☎ 2892 045 362, fax 2892 045 292, Matala)* Doubles/triples €17.60/23.50. One of the cheapest accommodation options in Matala is this place, on the road leading inland. The comfortable rooms have a bathroom.

**Silvia Rent Rooms** *(☎ 2892 045 127, Matala)* Doubles/triples €23.50/29.50. On the same street you'll find Silvias. The nine rooms each have a fridge.

**Hotel Frangiskos** *(☎ 2892 045 380, Matala)* Singles/doubles with bath €26.50/35.50, €5 extra for air-con. The C-class hotel is on the left as you head out of Matala. The hotel is somewhat bland but it has a swimming pool. Breakfast is an extra €4.50 per day.

**Hotel Europa** *(☎ 2892 045 113, Matala)* Singles/doubles €26.50/29.50. On the right as you head out of the village is an attractive building of whitewashed walls and pine.

**Hotel Zafiria** *(☎ 2892 045 366, fax 2892 045 725, ⓔ zafiria@forthnet.gr, Matala)* Singles/doubles €29.50/38 including breakfast. The sprawling Hotel Zafiria takes up a whole block on Matala's main street. At the hotel there is a spacious lobby-bar and rooms have balconies, sea views and telephones.

## Places to Eat

Eating in Matala is not an experience in haute cuisine, but you won't starve.

*Taverna Manolis* (☎ *2892 045 122, Matala*) Grills €5.50-6.50. Split over two sides of the main street, this largish restaurant serves up standard fare.

*Lions* (☎ *2892 045 108, Matala*) Daily special €5.30-8.80. Overlooking the beach, Lions has been a popular place for quite a while. Food is better than average.

*Restaurant Zafiria* (☎ *2892 045 455, Matala*) Mains €5.30-8.80. A little more expensive than other places, this eatery has reasonably good food, though its location overlooking the car park is not the best.

For self-caterers, there's a *minimarket* across the street from the Hotel Zafiria.

## Getting There & Away

There are eight buses a day between Iraklio and Matala (€5, two hours), five a day between Matala and Phaestos, (€1.20, 30 minutes), eight a day between Mires and Matala (€1.20, 30 minutes) and one a day between Matala and Malia (€6.50, 2¾ hours) via Hersonisos.

## AROUND MATALA

When Matala fills up in the summer, travellers head to **Pitsidia,** a sleepy little village 5km north-east of Matala. There's not much to do here except meet other travellers and book a horse riding tour from **Melanouri Horse Farm** (☎ *2892 045 040)* that offers lessons and beach rides through the surrounding region. A horse trek and picnic to the **Odigitria monastery** is €35. There is no post office or OTE. You can rent cars or motorcycles from Monza Travel Agency (☎ 2832 045 275). All buses to Matala stop in Pitsidia; the bus stop is in the centre of the village in front of Hotel Aretousa.

*Komos Beach camp site* (☎ *2892 042 332, Komos Pitsidion*) Person/tent €3.50/2.50. This camping ground is at Komos Beach, about 4km before Matala on the road from Phaestos.

*Hotel Aretousa* (☎ *2892 045 555, Pitsidia*) Singles/doubles €20.50/23.50. This small hotel is on the main road.

*Rent Rooms Babis* (☎ *2892 045 273, Pitsidia*) Singles/doubles €23.50/28. Also on the main road, this place has a large taverna on the ground floor and rooms above.

## KAMILARI Καμηλάρι
postcode 704 00 • pop 339

Built on top of three hills, Kamilari provides a complete escape into traditional Cretan village life. Its proximity to Kalamaki Beach makes it attractive to visitors, plus there's an important Minoan tomb just outside village. Since the village is only 2.5km west of Phaestos, it's a good base to explore the beaches and archaeological sites of the southern coast.

## Orientation & Information

There's no tourist office but in the centre of the village Moto Auto Store (☎/fax 2892 042 690) rents cars, motorcycles, rooms and apartments. It's open 8am to 1pm and 5pm to 9pm Monday to Saturday.

## Things to See

The circular **Minoan Tomb** of Kamilari dates from 1900 BC and is extraordinarily well-preserved with stone walls still standing 2m high. Archaeologists believe that outside the circular tomb there were five small rooms that were used for burial rites. Clay models depicting the funerary rituals were unearthed by excavators and are now in the Archaeological Museum of Iraklio. The road to the tomb is clearly indicated at the entrance to Kamilari. It is a good 30-minute walk out to the tomb located in the middle of fields about 3km from the village.

## Places to Stay & Eat

Kamilari is becoming popular with travellers so there are a number of accommodation opportunities.

*Pension Koula* (☎ *2892 041 689, fax 2892 045 689, Kamilari*) Singles/doubles €17.50/20.50. At the entrance to the village is Pension Koula with tidy rooms and a shady garden.

*Studios Pelekanos* (☎ *2892 042 690, Kamilari*) Singles/doubles €23.50/26.50.

Next door is this neat and clean place with large rooms that have a fridge and air-con.

*Apartments Ambeliotisa (☎/fax 2892 042 690, e ambeliotisa@mir.forthnet.gr, Kamilari)* Studios/apartments €23.50/26.50. This place has furnished studios and apartments all of which have air-con and heating for winter visitors. The pink and white stucco building has a stone fireplace, veranda and an outdoor barbecue.

*Taverna Mylonas (☎ 2892 042 156, Kamilari)* Mains €2.70-5. This place has good home-cooked Cretan food in the centre of the village. A hearty mixed platter goes for €5.90.

### Getting There & Away
There is one morning bus daily from Iraklio via Mires (€4.50, 1½ hours).

## KALAMAKI Καλαμάκι
**postcode 702 00 • pop 133**
The wide, sandy beach that stretches for many kilometres in either direction is Kalamaki's best feature and makes for a beautiful walk. Located 2.5km south-west of Kamilari, tourism is in its embryonic stage in Kalamaki after the recent opening of a paved road all the way to the beach. The good news is that you won't feel crowded but, unfortunately, the beach is lined with a string of half-finished concrete structures. It's a quiet place to stay however and the swimming is good.

### Orientation & Information
There is one main road leading into the village square that is right behind the beach. There is no post office, tourist office or OTE but Monza Travel (☎/fax 2892 045 692, e papam@mir.forthnet.gr) is a friendly, informative office that handles car and bike rentals, hotel reservations and air and boat tickets. It also organises various excursions around Crete ranging in price from €23 for a tour to the local archaeological sites to €47 for a jeep safari. Monza Travel is on the main square and is open 9am to 2pm and 5pm to 10pm daily from Easter to October. Umbrellas and beach chairs are available for rent on the beach but most tavernas lining the beachfront promenade offer them for free if you eat at their establishment.

### Places to Stay
*Kostas Rent Rooms (☎/fax 2892 045 692, e papam@mir.forthnet.gr, Kalamaki)* Singles/doubles €14.70/20.50. All rooms have fridges, coffee making equipment and enjoy a communal patio. Kostas Rooms is on the main square above Monza Travel.

*Rooms Nefeli (☎ 2892 045 211, Kalamaki)* Double studios €38.20. On the right when you enter the village you'll come to a brand new three-storey building. There is a communal kitchen and fridge for guests' use.

*Pension Galini (☎ 2892 045 042, fax 2892 023 442, Kalamaki)* Singles/doubles €29.50/35.50. One of the most attractive places to stay in Kalamaki is about 100m from the sea. The spacious rooms with balconies are furnished in pine and some have fully equipped kitchens. There's also a rooftop terrace with a view of the sea.

### Places to Eat
*Yiannis (☎ 2892 045 685, Kalamaki)* Mezes platter €5.60. Virtually hidden from sight and one block back from the beach on the main inland street, Yiannis plies his trade quietly and without fuss, producing no-nonsense mezedes at a cheap price. A free glass of raki is offered to all diners.

*Taverna Avra (☎ 2892 045 052, Kalamaki)* Fish €29.50kg. At the northern end of the beachfront, this is a good spot for fresh fish and Cretan home cooking. It is open all year.

### Getting There & Away
There's one morning bus daily from Iraklio via Mires (€4.90, two hours)

## LENDAS Λέντας
**☎ 2892 • postcode 704 00 • pop 77**
The narrow pebbly beaches of Lendas would not be anyone's idea of an idyllic getaway, but the village that clings to the cliff over the beach has a pleasant view over the Libyan Sea. The demands of tourism have seen Lendas expand into a more sizeable village, but it retains an appealing intimacy.

Within walking distance there's an archaeological site and the Dytikos naturist beach.

## Orientation & Information

As you enter the village from the main road there's a left fork that takes you to the eastern car park and a right fork that takes you to the main square. The bus stops outside the eastern car park. In the main square you'll find Monza Travel Agency, an exchange place and a supermarket. There is no post office, bank or OTE. To get to Dytikos follow the main road west for 1km or the path alongside the coastal cliffs.

## Things to See

The archaeological site of **Lebena** is right outside the village. Lebena was a health spa that the Romans visited for its therapeutic springs. Only two granite columns remain of a temple that dates from the 4th century BC. Next to the temple was a treasury with a mosaic floor that is still visible. Very little else is decipherable and the springs have been closed since the 1960s.

## Places to Stay & Eat

*Rent Rooms Zorbas* (☎ 2892 095 228, *Lendas*) Apartments €25, rooms without/with sea view €18/15 with bath. The right fork from the main road takes you down to the restaurant.

*Rent Rooms El Greco* (☎ 2892 095 322, *Lendas*) Singles/doubles with bath €18/22. Rooms have balconies with sea views. There's a taverna here too.

*Eva's Rooms* (☎ 2892 095 244, *Lendas*) Doubles €14. Eva's is next to the main square.

## Getting There & Away

There's a daily afternoon bus from Iraklio (€5, three hours)

## ANO VIANNOS  Άνω Βιάννος
**postcode 700 04 • pop 941**

Ano Viannos, 65km south of Iraklio, is a delightful village built on the southern flanks of Mt Dikti. Steep, cobbled streets lead up from the main road to a thicket of lanes bedecked with flowers and overhung

with trees. From the top of the village there are panoramic views over the region. The air is cooler than it is along the overheated coast and the village gets very little tourism, which makes it a pleasant stop or overnight stay.

## Orientation & Information

There is only one main road that passes through the village. The post office is next to the restored church and signs from the village centre direct you up to the Agia Pelagia Church. There is an Agricultural Bank and ATM on the eastern side of the village.

## Things to See

The **Folklore Museum** (☎ 2895 022 778, *Ano Viannos; admission €1.50; open 10am-2pm*) has a wealth of exhibits explaining traditional Cretan culture. There are colourful costumes, musical instruments, wine and olive presses, weavings and a collection of farm implements. It is on the western edge of the village.

The village's 14th-century **Church of Agia Pelagia** (*Ano Viannos; admission free; open 9am-8pm in high season*) is a tiny structure. The interior walls, covered with luscious frescoes by Nikoforos Fokas, are in need of restoration but can still be appreciated. The blues, rusts, oranges and greens of the frescoes create an otherworldly effect that perfectly suits the spiritual nature of their subjects. Follow signs from the main street, but it's a steep and tiring climb up to the church.

## Places to Stay & Eat

Ano Viannos has one accommodation option. *Taverna & Rooms Lefkes* (☎ 2895 022 719, *Ano Viannos*) Singles/doubles with bath €12/15. It's 50m downhill from the large church. The rooms are over the taverna that has good Cretan specialties and a pleasant shady terrace.

## Getting There & Away

Public transport is poor. There are two buses a week from Iraklio to Ano Viannos (€6.20, 2½ hours) and two a week to Ierapetra (€2.80, one hour) via Myrtos.

## KASTRI & KERATOKAMBOS

Καστρί & Κερατόκαμπος
**postcode 700 04 • pop 130**
From Ano Viannos it's a 13km, very winding road south, to the unspoilt and now contiguous villages of Kastri and Keratokambos, where there's a pleasant tree-lined beach and not much else. The one road that runs along the beach contains a few domatia and tavernas. The tranquillity of this tiny resort is its chief asset. Many Germans have moved in and bought property here. If you like peace and quiet and have a few books to read, this is your kind of place.

## Orientation & Information

There's no bank, post office, OTE, car rental agency or any other reminder of the outside world. There is a minimarket and you can exchange money and rent cars at Taverna Kriti.

## Places to Stay & Eat

*Filoxenia Appartments* (☎ 2895 051 371, *Kastri*) Double studios €35.30. Wrapped in a flower-shaded garden, Filoxenia's two- to three-person studios are beautiful. Equipped with kitchenette and fridge, they make an ideal mid-range accommodation option.

*Komis Studios* (☎ 2895 051 390, fax 2895 051 593, e pervass@otenet.gr, *Keratokambos*) Rooms €73.50. Ecologically sound and aesthetically pleasing, Komis Studios offers 15 three-level apartments exquisitely decorated in a rustic style but with the comforts of air-con, telephone and TV. The units use wind and solar power and the sewage is treated biologically.

*Taverna Nikitas* (☎ 2895 051 477, *Keratokambos*) Grills €4-5. By the sea in the centre of Keratokambos, this place offers delicious grills. Roast lamb and pork (€5) is recommended.

*To Livyko* (☎ 2895 051 290, *Keratokambos*) Grills €3.80-5.60. Next door to Nikitas is this equally good waterside taverna. Cypriot-style kondosouvli (€4.70) is a good dish.

*Morning Star Taverna* (☎ 2895 051 209, *Kastri*) Mains €4.10-4.70. Grills and fish feature here with a mixed fish grill (€3.80).

Tasty artichoke stew (€3) is a good choice for vegetarians.

*Taverna Kriti* (☎ 2895 051 231, *Kastri*) Fish €26.50-35.30kg. This place offers excellent fish dishes as well as a wide range of grills and Cretan specials.

## Getting There & Away

There's no public transport available to Keratokambos. The 8km road to Arvi in the east is driveable in a conventional vehicle.

## ARVI Αρβη

**postcode 700 04 • pop 298**
The turn-off for Arvi is 4km east of Ano Viannos. Arvi is bigger than Keratokambos, but only gets visitors during July and August. Hemmed in by cliffs, Arvi is a suntrap where bananas grow in abundance. Like Keratokambos, it's a good place to escape the hectic summer resort scene, but it sees relatively few foreign visitors and is not quite as cosmopolitan as Kastri and Keratokambos to the west.

## Orientation & Information

The main street skirts a long sand and pebble beach. It's a 15-minute walk inland to Moni Agiou Androniou, a 19th-century monastery on a hillside. There is no bank, post office or OTE in Arvi.

## Places to Stay & Eat

*Pension Kolibi* (☎ 2895 071 250, *Arvi*) Doubles/triples with bath €29.50/32. This immaculate pension is in a quiet setting 1km west of Arvi overlooking a pebbly beach.

*Pension Gorgona* (☎ 2895 071 353, *Arvi*) Doubles with bath €28. This pension on the main street has pleasant rooms.

*Hotel Ariadne* (☎ 2895 071 300, *Arvi*) Singles/doubles with bath €14.70/22. Further west, Hotel Ariadne has well-kept rooms. The restaurant here is reasonable and food is par for the course with a mixture of grills and fish on offer. Mains €3-4.50.

*Apartments Kyma* (☎ 2895 071 344, *Arvi*) Apartments €23.50. At the eastern end of the village you'll find these luxurious apartments.

***Taverna Diktina*** (☎ *2895 071 249, Arvi*)
Mains around €4.50. This place features
vegetarian food such as beans or stuffed
tomatoes, both for €3.

## Getting There & Away

There is no public transport to Arvi. The
8km coastal dirt road between Arvi and
Kastri-Keratokambos is driveable.

# Central Iraklio Region

Although most travellers zip through the region that lies between Iraklio and the south
coast, several sights make it well worth a
stop, but you need your own wheels to explore the region. Mt Psiloritis lies to the
west in the Rethymno region; its eastern
slopes taper down to a series of high
plateaus and deep caves. The most famous
cave is the Ideon Andron (Ideon Cave)
which was either the birthplace of Zeus or
his playground as a young child, depending
on which legend you believe. There's not
much to see in the cave and there are no
paved roads, but if you have a motorcycle
or a jeep, take the main road south from
Anogia and follow the signs to the cave.

The main roads leading south from Iraklio pass through a series of bustling commercial centres and villages that see very
few tourists. There are no hotels or domatia
in this region. Arhanes, with a couple of interesting Minoan sites nearby, makes a
worthwhile stop and Zaros is a good base to
explore the surrounding region.

## ZAROS Ζαρός

**postcode 700 02 • pop 2239**

If the name rings a bell, it's probably because your litres of mineral water are labelled 'Zaros'. Known for its spring water
and bottling plant, Zaros (46km south of
Iraklio) is a traditional town where many
men and women still wear black. Various
excavations in the region indicate that the
Minoans and the Romans settled here, lured
by the abundant supply of fresh water. The

spring water from Zaros also supplied the
great Roman capital of Gortyna. Byzantine
monasteries are nearly as abundant as the
spring water. You can visit the monasteries
of Agios Andonios Vrondisios, Agios
Nikolaos, Odigitria, Apezano and Kardio-
tissa; Hotel Idi in Zaros has full details on
treks to all the monasteries.

## Orientation & Information

The business end of Zaros is at the southern
entrance of the town. The post office and a
supermarket are across the street from the
police station. There's no OTE or Internet
cafe. You can change money at the Hotel Idi.

## Things to See & Do

The Zaros **bottling plant** is on the northern
end of town past the Hotel Idi. They will
usually allow you to take a look at the packaging and bottling operations inside. A
short distance before the bottling plant you
will come to a lovely shady park, **Votomos**,
with a small lake and a children's playground, which makes a great picnic stop.

If you have your own wheels the Byzantine monasteries and traditional villages that
are tucked away in the hills are worth exploring. Take the road that leads west from
Zaros and you'll see a sign directing you to
**Moni Agiou Nikolaou**, which is at the
mouth of the Agios Nikolaos Gorge. The
monastery still houses several monks and
the church contains some 14th-century
paintings. A few kilometres beyond Moni
Agiou Nikolaou is the **Moni Agiou Ando-
niou Vrondisiou** that is notable for its 15th-
century Venetian fountain. The monastery
also has a church with excellent examples
of early 14th-century frescoes from the Cretan School of Fresco Painting.

The drive to the monasteries and beyond
to the traditional mountain villages of
Vorizia and Kamares is particularly scenic.
From Kamares or Vorizia you can hike inland and up to Mt Psiloritis. From here you
have a choice of heading westwards along
the E4 trail down the mountain to Fourfouras or eastwards along the same trail
down to the Nida Plateau. From here there
is a paved road to the village of Anogia. See

the boxed text on 'Hiking on Mt Psiloritis' in the Rethymno & Central Crete chapter.

## Places to Stay & Eat

*Hotel Idi (☎ 2894 031 301, fax 2894 031 51, e votomos@otenet.gr, Zaros)* Singles/doubles €29.50/44 including breakfast. One kilometre outside the village, Hotel Idi is surrounded by trees and greenery and makes for a restful, rural escape. The rooms are pleasant and traditional. The hotel is open all year and has a swimming pool, tennis courts, gymnasium, jacuzzi and sauna.

*Studios Keramos (☎/fax 2894 031 352, Zaros)* Singles/doubles €20.50/23.50. Close to the village centre is this homey hostelry run by friendly Katerina. She has decorated her cosy establishment with a display of Cretan crafts, weaving, baskets and pottery. The studios are large with TV, kitchenette and air-con and include a copious traditional Cretan breakfast.

*Votomos (☎ 2894 031 666, Zaros)* Trout €17.60kg. Open 11am-midnight daily Mar-Oct, Sat & Sun Nov-Feb. Trout is the speciality at this superb fish restaurant affiliated with the Hotel Idi. You'll see the trout gliding through a huge freshwater reserve so you'll know they're fresh.

## Getting There & Away

There are two afternoon buses daily from Iraklio (€3, one hour).

## ARHANES Αρχάνες

postcode 701 00 • pop 4000

Known for its excellent wine, Arhanes, 16km south of Iraklio, lies in the heart of Crete's principal grape-producing region. The fertile basin of Arhanes has been settled since the Neolithic period. The ancient Minoans built a grand palace that was an administrative centre for the entire Arhanes basin. The palace was destroyed, rebuilt and destroyed again along with the other great Minoan palaces. The town came back to life under the Mycenaeans, flourishing until the Dorian conquest of Crete in 1100 BC. Today Arhanes is a quiet and obviously prosperous town with meticulously restored old houses and neatly laid out squares. The

main reason to visit is for the excellent archaeological museum but there is no place to stay in town.

## Orientation & Information

The bus stop is across the street from a restored church. Uphill from the bus stop and a right fork is another small square. Signs direct you to the post office, and the OTE is in a pastel building next to a taxi stand. Nearby is a small park surrounded by tavernas and a Creta Bank.

## Things to See

Only scraps of the palace (signposted from the main road) remain. The **Archaeological Museum of Arhanes** *(Arhanes; admission €1.50; open 8.30am-2.30pm Wed-Mon)* has some interesting finds from the archaeological excavations that have been taking place for the last three decades in numerous sites around the region. The exhibits, including **larnakes** (coffins) and **musical instruments** from Fourni are well displayed and extremely informative. On display also is an ornamental dagger from the **Anemospilia** temple that was only uncovered in 1979. See the boxed text 'Murder in the Temple' in 'The Minoans' special section.

## Getting There & Away

There are buses hourly from Iraklio (€1, 30 minutes).

## AROUND ARHANES
## Vathypetro Villa

Vathypetro Villa *(Arhanes; admission free; open 8.30am-3pm)* is 5km south of Arhanes and is well-signposted from the town. Dating from 1600 BC the villa was probably the home of a prosperous Minoan noble. The villa complex included storerooms, where wine and oil presses, a weaving loom and a kiln were discovered. Although the doors to the rooms with the wine press and oil press are locked you can catch a glimpse of the tools through the barred windows. There is no public transport to the site although several travel agencies in Iraklio include a visit as part of their tour itinerary.

From the bus stop in Arhanes follow signs up a steep trail to the Minoan burial grounds at **Fourni**. The round stone 'beehive tombs' form the most extensive Minoan cemetery in the island and date from about 2500 BC. One of the tombs contained the remains of a Minoan noble woman whose jewellery is on display in the Archaeological Museum of Iraklio.

# North-Eastern Coast

Ever since the national road along the northern coast opened in 1972, the coast between Iraklio and Malia has seen a frenzy of development. A concrete wall of hotels, schnitzel outlets and tacky souvenir shops lines every stretch of sandy beach here. There's not much here for individual travellers since the hotels deal almost exclusively with package tour operators who block-book hotel rooms many months in advance. The prices for individual travellers are relatively steep, compared with the discounts package-tourists receive, and service is likely to be indifferent for those without the clout of a tour operator behind them. The main centres here are Hersonisos and Malia. The Minoan palace at Malia is the only site of cultural interest.

## MALIA Μάλια
**postcode 700 07 • pop 2459**

The township of Malia is a highly commercialised resort that developed in the 1970s because of its long sandy beach. It's crowded and noisy but there's plenty to do and it's within easy reach of the fascinating Minoan Palace of Malia. The spread-out settlement is distinctly divided into two parts by the main through road: the rowdy, northern side (New Malia) and the quieter and more relaxed southern side (Old Malia). It's hardly worth making Malia your base given its extremely rowdy reputation. If you do, stick to the south side and you may well be pleasantly surprised.

## Orientation & Information

New Malia is packed with hotels, restaurants, travel agencies and nightlife; south of the main road is Old Malia, or the 'village'. The post office is near the main road at 28 Oktovriou 2 and the OTE is uphill about 500m and signposted from the Old Malia.

## Mass Tourism

Although none of the resorts along the north-eastern coast would win any beauty contests, Hersonisos and Malia set a new standard of dreariness. In both resorts, the local population has retreated to pleasant little hill villages behind the main road and left the lower beachfront towns to wallow in sleazy commercialism. From frozen fish in the seaside restaurants to imported 'Cretan' ceramics and machine-made weavings in souvenir shops, nothing is authentic. Unlike the rest of the island, the music in bars and tavernas is either Western or the most Westernised Greek music available.

Don't understand Greek letters? Don't worry. You won't see a single one in Hersonisos and Malia. All signs are in Latin letters. Fish and chip stands, cafes with names like 'Cheers' and 'Union Jack', video bars playing British sitcoms seem designed to shield visitors from the horrible realisation that they are actually in a foreign country.

Although Hersonisos and Malia are often considered identical examples of atrocious overdevelopment, there are subtle differences between the two resorts. Both places chase bargain-hunting package tourists but Hersonisos has a few luxury hotels on the outskirts. The crowds are young in both towns but in Malia, you'll feel decrepit if you're over 22. Both places assume that you will consume copious quantities of alcohol. In Hersonisos you drink to get drunk, dance and wake up with a stranger while at Malia you drink to get drunk, fall down and wake up on the pavement. If that sounds good to you, you know where to go, but try to visit Crete someday.

There are plenty of places to change money on the main road. Charlie's Travel (☎ 2897 033 834) is a good source of information and sells excursions to all destinations on the island. Check email at Internet Cafe Malia (☎ 2897 029 563, e netmail@hrs.forth net.gr) at Dimokratias 78, in New Malia.

## Places to Stay & Eat

*Sofia Rent Rooms (☎ 2897 031 873, Dimokratias 76)* Doubles €17.60. Given the lack of decently priced places on the north side, this place is one option. Rooms are basic, the neighbourhood is noisy and the owners somewhat indifferent.

*Kalimera Apartments (☎ 2897 02 211, Old Malia)* Doubles €35.30. A much better, though more expensive option are these fully equipped apartments in the old village of Malia. Call in to the Kalimera Taverna to contact the owner.

*Argo (☎ 2897 031 636, Old Malia)* Doubles €35.30. You could also try this place that is right on the main road and has reasonable rooms.

*Espera (☎ 2897 031 086, Old Malia)* Doubles €44; studios €58.70. Signposted in the old village is this fourth, also quieter option.

For eating, forget the north side of Malia. There is nothing worth casting even a glance at. Head to Old Malia.

*Kalimera Taverna (☎ 2897 031 618, Old Malia)* Cypriot-style mezedes for two €20.50. This beautiful and tasteful taverna in the warren of Malia's old village backstreets is an excellent choice. Other than the popular Cypriot mezedes, there is a range of mouth-watering and imaginative dishes, such as octopus in wine, saganaki, mussels or sardines all costing between €1.90 and €4.70.

*San Giorgio Restaurant (☎ 2897 032 211, Old Malia)* Grills €3.50-6.20. The most obvious eatery is this brightly painted restaurant that spills out into the main square in the old village. The rowdy crowd rarely make it up this far, so you can dine on good Cretan food in peace.

## Entertainment

Discos, bars and nightclubs are as ephemeral as the youthful tourists who patronise them.

There are bars and discos on every corner, none of which particularly stand out. Bars commonly sell every permutation of British and Irish beers and ciders at very cheap prices (€1.50 a pint). 'Entertainment' frequently consists of street brawls; steer clear if you see one brewing.

## Getting There & Away

There are buses from Iraklio every 30 minutes (€2.40, one hour).

**PALACE OF MALIA** Ανάκτορα Μαλίων
The Palace of Malia (☎ 2897 031 597; admission €2.40; open 8.30am-3pm daily), 3km east of Malia, was built at about the same time as the two other great Minoan palaces at Phaestos and Knossos. The first palace was built here around 1900 BC and rebuilt after the earthquake of 1700 BC. What you see is the remains of the newer palace where many exquisite artefacts from Minoan society were found. Excavation began in 1915 by Greek archaeologists and is being continued by French archaeologists. Because the ground plan has been well-preserved, it's an easy site to comprehend. Any bus going to/from Iraklio along the north coast can drop you at the site.

## Exploring the Site

Entrance to the ruins is from the **West Court.** Head south through the **Magazines** and at the extreme southern end you'll come to the eight circular pits which archaeologists think were **grain silos.** To the east of the pits is the main entrance to the palace which leads to the southern end of the **Central Court.** Moving north-east you'll come to the **Kernos Stone,** a disk with 24 holes around its edge. Archaeologists have yet to ascertain its function, but it probably had a religious purpose. Adjacent is the **Grand Staircase** which might have led to a shrine. To the north is the **Pillar Corridor** with interconnecting rooms and next to it is the **Pillar Crypt** with the Minoan double-axe symbol engraved on the pillars. The impressive **Central Court** is 48m long and 22m wide and contains remains of the Minoan

## PALACE OF MALIA

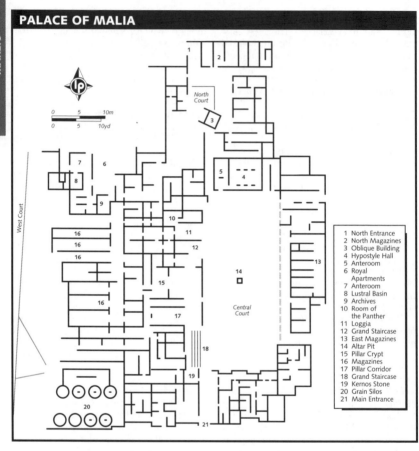

North Court

North

Central Court

West Court

1 North Entrance
2 North Magazines
3 Oblique Building
4 Hypostyle Hall
5 Anteroom
6 Royal
   Apartments
7 Anteroom
8 Lustral Basin
9 Archives
10 Room of
   the Panther
11 Loggia
12 Grand Staircase
13 East Magazines
14 Altar Pit
15 Pillar Crypt
16 Magazines
17 Pillar Corridor
18 Grand Staircase
19 Kernos Stone
20 Grain Silos
21 Main Entrance

columns. Notice the pit in the exact centre of the courtyard, which may have been an altar.

At the northern end of the western side of the court is the **Loggia**, which was probably used for ceremonial purposes. Next to the Loggia is the **Room of the Panther** in which a 17th-century-BC stone axe shaped like a panther was found. North-west are the **Royal Apartments** with a **Lustral Basin**. At the north end of the central court is the **Hypostyle Hall** with benches on the side indicating that it may have served as a kind of council chamber. Other rooms include the

**archives room** in which tablets containing Linear A script were found. On your way out through the north entrance notice the pithoi in the **North Court**.

## HERSONISOS Χερσόνησος
**postcode 710 02 • pop 747**

Hersonisos, 27km east of Iraklio, began its days as a small fishing village on a hill, but those days are long past. Like Malia, it too is a mecca to package tourism with a long coastal strip of neon-lit restaurants and look-alike hotels. The beach is sandy but packed with lounge chairs and umbrellas.

There is always something to do in Hersonisos; there are plenty of excursions to all parts of the island and an action-packed nightclub scene.

## Orientation & Information

The coastal road from Iraklio to Agios Nikolaos, which runs through the elongated village, is Eletheriou Venizelou. Most travel agencies, banks and services are located along here. The OTE office is north of Eletheriou Venizelou and the post office is in the centre of town on Digeni Akrita. There is also a beachfront road of tavernas, hotels and nightclubs. There is no tourist office but Hermes Rent a Bike (☎ 2897 032 271) is a good source of information.

Uphill from the main road is the village of Koutouloufari, which is touristy but retains the atmosphere of a traditional village.

## Places to Stay & Eat

Most hotels only deal with groups. For decent accommodation and the chance of a night's sleep without noise pollution, head for Koutouloufari.

*Elen Mari Apartments (☎ 2897 025 525, Koutouloufari)* 2-3 person apartments €35.30-44. This is by far the best option. The fully equipped studios are neat and very new-looking and some have great views over Hersonisos.

*Sergiani (☎ 2897 022 514, Plateia Eleftheriou Venizelou)* Mezedes €2-5.70. Enjoying a good night view over Hersonisos,

Sergiani offers up original dishes like village mushrooms (€4.40) or shrimps with ouzo (€6.50).

*Emmanuel Taverna (☎ 2897 021 022, Plateia Eleftheriou Venizelou)* Mains €5.30-7. Run by a Greek-Australian family, this homely taverna specialises in spit-roast meats and oven-cooked dishes. The owner recommends lamb in rose wine with bay leaves (€6.70), or pork with orange and Grand Marnier (€6.50).

*Rahati (☎ 2897 029 303, Evropis 86)* Breakfast €2.80. Open 8am-midnight. After a hard night take breakfast at this neat, Dutch-run establishment. Munch on cakes and apples pies and wake up with a strong coffee.

## Entertainment

Most people come to Hersonisos for the nightlife. As soon as the sun goes down, the bars fill up, the discos crank up their volume and the whole resort turns into one vast party. Like Malia, the nightspots, bars and discos wax and wane in popularity from one year to the next. No place particularly stands out and all of them deliver a pounding mix of booze, rock 'n' roll, retro, disco, techno, house, garage and sometimes…garbage. Forget Greek entertainment. Hersonisos is for non-Greeks out for frantic fun.

## Getting There & Away

There are buses from Iraklio every 30 minutes (€1.90, 45 minutes).

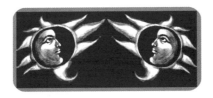

# Rethymno & Central Crete

Rethymno is Crete's most mountainous prefecture containing Mt Psiloritis in the east and bordered by the Lefka Ori in the west. Since most of the prefecture is composed of barren mountains and hills, only 537 sq km are cultivated out of the 1496 sq km in the prefecture. The rocky region is perfect for raising livestock which is the main occupation of Rethymno, although olives and olive oil are also produced.

The prefecture is divided into four provinces: Rethymno, with Rethymno town as its capital; Agios Vasilios, with its capital at Spili, the coastal resorts of Agia Galini and Plakias, as well as Moni Preveli; Amari with its capital at the town of the same name; and, Mylopotamos, with its capital at Perama. Mylopotamos also includes the northern coastal resorts of Panormos and Bali, and the inland towns of Anogia and Zoniana, as well as the Ideon Cave.

## RETHYMNO Ρέθυθμνο
**postcode 741 00 • pop 23,355**

Rethymno (**Reth**-im-no) is Crete's third-largest town. Conveniently located on the northern coast between Hania and Iraklio, Rethymno makes a good port of entry and base for explorations of the northern coast. With a long sandy beach running eastwards from the old quarter, the town has become a popular package holiday destination in recent years. The main attraction, though, is the old Venetian-Ottoman quarter that occupies the headland beneath the massive Venetian *fortezza* (fortress).

The old quarter is a maze of narrow streets, graceful wood-balconied houses and ornate Venetian monuments, with minarets adding a touch of the Orient. Architectural similarities invite comparison with Hania, but Rethymno has a character of its own and boasts of being the most culturally aware city in Crete.

A 16th-century fortress stands on Palekastro Hill, the site of the city's ancient acropolis. Many buildings once stood within

its massive walls but now only a church and a mosque survive intact. The ramparts offer good views, while the site has lots of ruins to explore. Pride of place among the many vestiges of Venetian rule (from 1210–1645, when the Turks took over) goes to the Rimondi Fountain with its spouting lion heads, and the 16th-century Loggia. At the southern end of Ethnikis Andistasis is the well-preserved Porto Guora (Great Gate), a remnant of the Venetian defensive wall.

## History

The name Rethymno means 'stream of water' and evidence now found in the city's

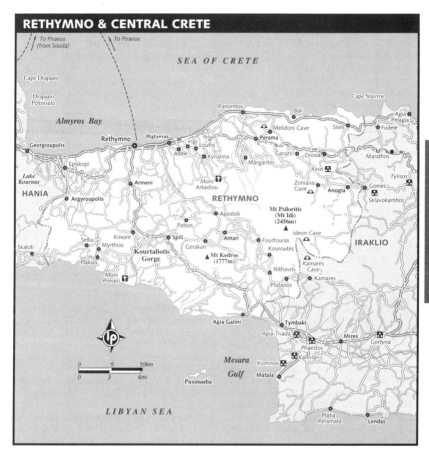

RETHYMNO & CENTRAL CRETE

archaeological museum indicates that the site of modern Rethymno has been occupied since Late Minoan times. In the 3rd and 4th centuries BC, 'Rithymna' emerged as an autonomous state of sufficient stature to issue its own coinage. Ancient Rithymna probably lay under Palekastro Hill but its remains have never been excavated, although later Roman mosaics have been found underneath the modern town.

The town prospered once more under the Venetians, who ruled from 1210 until 1645, and made Rethymno into an important commercial centre based upon the export of

wine and oil from the region. The town flourished artistically under the Venetians and became the seat of a Venetian Prefect. The Venetians built a harbour, Mandraki, and began fortifying the town in the 16th century against the growing threat from the Turks. The best military architect of the era, Sammicheli designed thick outer walls of which only the Porto Guora survives. The walls did not stop the city from being sacked by the pirate Barbarossa in 1538.

The Venetians then built the massive fortress on the hill, that nevertheless was unable to withstand the Turkish assault of

## Pandelis Prevelakis – Rethymno's Son

Iraklio has Kazantzakis but Rethymno has Prevelakis. The writer and poet Pandelis Prevelakis was born in Rethymno in 1908. He painted an exquisite portrait of his birthplace in the book *The Tale of a Town*. One of the most moving passages of the book deals with the expulsion of the Turkish community of Rethymno in 1923 after the failed Greek invasion of Smyrna. Riots broke out as Greek refugees from Smyrna waited to move into homes that anguished Turks were destroying. Prevelakis is also known as a poet and for his critical writings on Kazantzakis.

1646, and collapsed after a 22-day siege. Rethymno was an important seat of government under the Turks but it was also a centre of resistance to Turkish rule. The Turks inflicted severe reprisals upon the town for its role in the uprising of 1821 but the resistance continued.

Turkish forces held the town until 1897, when it was taken by Russia as part of the occupation of Crete by the Great Powers. Rethymno became an artistic and intellectual centre after the arrival of a large number of refugees from Smyrna in 1923. The city has a campus of the University of Crete, attracting a student population that keeps the town alive outside the tourist season.

### Orientation

The city's old quarter occupies the headland north of Dimakopoulou, which runs from Plateia Vardinogianni on the west side to Plateia Iroön on the east (becoming Gerakari en route). Most of the good places to eat and sleep are to be found here, while banks and government services are just to the south on the edge of the new part of town.

The beach is on the eastern side of town, curving around from the delightful old Venetian harbour in the north. El Venizelou is the beachfront street. Curving parallel one block back is Arkadiou, the main commercial street. The old quarter's maze of twisting and curving streets make it an easy place to get lost, especially since street signs are a rarity.

Coming from the south, the best way to approach is through the Porto Guora onto Ethnikis Andistasis. This busy shopping street leads to the Rimondi Fountain, the old quarter's best known landmark. The area around here is thick with cafes, restaurants and souvenir shops.

If you arrive in Rethymno by bus, you will be dropped at the bus terminal at the western end of Igoumenou Gavriil, about 600m west of the Porto Guora. If you arrive by ferry, the old quarter is as far away as the end of the quay. If you are driving into town from the expressway, there are three possible exit points. The car park opposite the park is a convenient spot to stop and check things out.

### Information

**Tourist Offices** Rethymno's municipal tourist office (☎ 2831 029 148) is on the beach side of El Venizelou, opposite the junction with Kallergi. It's open 8.30am to 2.30pm Monday to Friday. The tourist police (☎ 2831 028 156) occupy the same building and are open from 7am to 10pm every day.

**Money** Banks are concentrated around the junction of Dimokratias and Pavlou Koundouriotou. The National Bank is on Dimokratias, on the far side of the square opposite the town hall. The Credit Bank (Pavlou Koundouriotou 29) and the National Mortgage Bank, next to the town hall, have 24-hour automatic exchange machines. Both banks have ATMs also.

**Post & Communications** The OTE is at Koundouriotou 28, and the post office is a block south at Moatsou 21. In summer there is a mobile post office about 200m southeast of the tourist office on El Venizelou. You can check your email at Galero (☎ 2831 054 345) on Plateia Rimini, open 7am to late at €3.50 per hour.

# RETHYMNO

**PLACES TO STAY**
5 Rooms Lefteris
7 Hotel Ideon
11 Palazzo Vecchio
13 Hotel Fortezza
34 Palazzo Rimondi
38 Olga's Pension
41 Hotel Veneto & Restaurant
45 Garden House
46 Rooms to Rent Anda
48 Park Hotel
51 Rethymno Youth Hostel
55 Rent Rooms Sea Front

**PLACES TO EAT**
1 Sunset
6 Fanari
9 Taverna Castro
12 Taverna O Pontios
16 Knosos
30 Taverna Kyria Maria
33 Avli
37 Stella's Kitchen
42 Taverna Old Town
44 Gounakis Taverna & Bar

**THINGS TO SEE**
2 Entrance to Fortress
4 Archaeological Museum
29 Loggia
31 Rimondi Fountain
39 Nerantzes Mosque
43 Historical & Folk Art Museum
49 Porto Guora
58 Kara Musa Pasha Mosque

**OTHER**
3 Zaharias Theodorakis
8 Notes
10 Cinema Asteria
14 Opera Club
15 ANEK
17 Ferries to Piraeus
18 Nitro Music Bar
19 Metropolis NYC
20 Fortezza Disco
21 The Pirate
22 Dolphin Cruises
23 Zourbakis Cruises
24 Rock Club Cafe
25 International Press Bookshop
26 Paradise Dive Centre

27 Public Toilet
28 Xenia
32 Galero
35 Motor Stavros
36 Ilias Spondidakis
   Bookshop
40 Figaro
47 Katerina Karaoglani
50 I Melissa
52 Laundry Mat
53 The Happy Walker
54 Ellotia Tours
56 Municipal Tourist Office;
   Tourist Police
57 Xenia
59 National Mortgage Bank
60 Town Hall
61 OTE
62 Credit Bank
63 National Bank of Greece
64 EOS
65 Halkiadakis Supermarket
66 Post Office
67 Olympic Airways
68 Hospital
69 Bus Station

**RETHYMNO & CENTRAL CRETE**

Fortress

Kefalogianni
Makedonias
Plateia Plastira
Himaras
Katehaki
Mesologiou
Melissinou
Salaminos
Smyrnis
Arabatzoglou
Paleologou
Vernardou
Nikiforou Foka
Koroneou
Riga Fereou
Plateia Iroon Polytehniou
Parallaki Leoforos
Venetian Harbour
SEA OF CRETE
Ferry Quay
Soliou
Arkadiou

National Stadium
Plateia Vardinogianni
Dimakopoulou
Ethnikis Antistasis
Tombazi
Plateia Martyron
Koundourotou
Gerakari
Varda Kallergi
El Venizelou
Plateia Iroon
Marouli

Alexandrou
Kefalogiannidon
Vlastou Sifi
Igoumenou Gavriil
Igoumenou Gavriil
Iliakaki
Timoleondos Vassou
Koumoundourou
Khari
Dimitrakaki
Moatsou
Daskalaki
Dimokratias

Municipal Park

To University of Crete (3km) & Hania (57km)

To Elizabeth Camping (3km) & Iraklio (85km)

0    100    200m
0    100    200yd

**Travel Agencies** Ellotia Tours (☎ 2831 024 533, fax 2831 051 062, **e** elotia@ ret.forthnet.gr), at Arkadiou 161, is a helpful office that handles boat and plane tickets, changes money, rents cars and motorcycles and books excursions. It's open 9am to 9pm daily March to November. Olympic Airways office (☎ 2831 027 353) is at Koumoundourou 5 in the new town.

**Bookshops** The International Press Bookshop (☎ 2831 024 111) Petihaki 15, stocks English novels, travel guides and history books. The Ilias Spondidakis bookshop (☎ 2831 054 307) Souliou 43, stocks novels in English, books about Greece, CDs and tapes of Greek music and has a small second-hand section.

**Laundry** The Laundry Mat self-service laundry (☎ 2831 056 196) at Tombazi 45, next door to the youth hostel, charges €7.50 for a wash and dry.

**Toilets** There is a reasonable public toilet in the centre of Rethymno in a side street just off Arkadiou.

## Things to See

The **Archaeological Museum** (☎ 2831 029 975, Fortezza; admission €1.50; open 8.30am-3pm daily) is opposite the entrance to the fortress and was once a prison. The exhibits are well labelled in English and contain Neolithic tools, Minoan pottery excavated from nearby tombs, Mycenaean figurines and a 1st-century-AD relief of Aphrodite, as well as an important coin collection.

There are also some excellent examples of blown glass from the classical period. Various displays outline the history of archaeological excavations in the region.

Rethymno's excellent **Historical & Folk Art Museum** (☎ 2831 023 398, Vernardou 28-30; admission €3; open 9.30am-2.30pm Mon-Sat) gives an excellent overview of the region's rural lifestyle with a collection of old clothes, baskets, weavings and farm tools whose purpose would remain obscure if the exhibits were not so well labelled.

The main gate of the 16th-century **Fortress** (☎ 2831 028 101, Paleokastro Hill; admission €2.70; open 8am-7pm daily) is opposite the Archaeological Museum on the eastern side of the fortress but there were once two other gates on the western and northern sides for the delivery of supplies and ammunition.

Barracks, the arsenal and storerooms were on the southern side, gunpowder was stored on the northern side and the centre once contained a cathedral which the Turks converted into a mosque. The ramparts offer good views of the town and the coast.

Pride of place among the many vestiges of Venetian rule in the old quarter goes to the **Rimondi Fountain** with its spouting lion heads and Corinthian capitals, built first in 1588 and rebuilt in 1626 by Rimondi. One of Rethymno's other major landmarks is the 16th-century **Loggia**, once a meeting house for Venetian nobility.

At the southern end of Ethnikis Andistasis is the well-preserved **Porto Guora** (Great Gate), a remnant of the defensive wall that was once topped with the symbol of Venice: the Lion of St Mark, now in the Archaeological Museum. Around the Porto Guora lies a network of old streets built by the Venetians and rebuilt by the Turks.

Other Turkish legacies in the old quarter include the **Kara Musa Pasha Mosque** which has a vaulted fountain and the **Nerantzes Mosque**, which was converted from a Franciscan church in 1657. The minaret was built in 1890.

## Trekking

For a varied program of regular and mountain walks in the region, try **The Happy Walker** (☎/fax 2831 052 920, **e** info@happy walker.nl, **W** www.happywalker.nl, Tombazi 56; day walks from €22). Most walks start in the early morning when a minibus picks you up at the hotel and takes you to the beginning of your walk. The walks are usually about 14km along farm roads and donkey paths. Favourite spots include the Bon Ripari Castle with a view of the Lefka Ori, Pikris, wild flowers around Kare, the ancient city of Eleftherna, the pottery village of Margarites and Moni Elias. Walks finish with lunch in a local taverna at a price of €8.80 including wine and dessert.

Rethymno's chapter of the **EOS** (☎ 2831 057 766, Dimokratias 12) can give good advice on mountain climbing in the region.

## Diving

**The Paradise Dive Centre** (☎ 2831 026 317, fax 2831 020 464, e pdcr@otenet.gr, El Venizelou 76) has activities and a PADI course for all grades of divers.

**The Dolphin Diving Centre** (☎ 2831 071 703, Hotel Rethymno Mare, Rethymno) also offers the same services.

## Courses

The University of Crete in Rethymno runs four-week **summer courses in Modern Greek** during July (☎ 2831 077 278, fax 2831 077 308, e moderngreek@phl.uoc .gr, Rethymno). Contact the university for full details.

## Organised Tours

Lying in the centre of the Cretan coast, Rethymno is well placed for boat excursions. Along the harbour front there are several companies that offer boat trips.

**The Pirate** (☎ 2831 051 643, fax 2831 024 729, Rethymno Harbour) Day-trips adults/children under 12 €26.50/14.70 including lunch. The most conspicuous company on the waterfront, the Pirate offers swimming and fishing trips along the coast on an old schooner.

**Zourbakis Cruises** (☎ 2831 057 032) Five-hour trip €20.50. This operator takes you for a cruise on a modern sailboat.

**Dolphin Cruises** (☎ 2831 057 666) Adults/children under 12 €20.50/13.20. This company offers a day trip to Georgioupolis.

## Special Events

The city's main cultural event is the annual Renaissance Festival that runs during July and August, featuring dance, drama and films as well as art exhibitions. Some years there's a Wine Festival in mid-July held in the municipal park, that offers a good opportunity to sample local wine and cuisine for about €3. Ask the tourist office for details.

## Places to Stay

Rethymno's accommodation scene has something for everyone. Because it's a dynamic commercial centre, many hotels are open all year. Those who want to lounge around a resort will head east from the town centre to find an endless string of hotels. Within the town centre, there's an ample supply of restored mansions and friendly pensions to immerse yourself in the town's fascinating history. There are buses every half-hour from Rethymno centre.

**Camping** *Elizabeth Camping* (☎ 2831 028 694, fax 2831 050 401, Mysiria) Person/tent €5/3.50. The nearest camping ground is near Mysiria beach 3km east of Rethymno. The site has a taverna, snack bar and minimarket. There is a communal fridge, iced water 24 hours a day, free beach umbrellas and loungers and a beach BBQ every Saturday night. An Iraklio-bound bus can drop you here.

**Hostels** *Rethymno Youth Hostel* (☎ 2831 022 848, e manolis@yhrethymno.com, w www.yhrethymno.com, Tombazi 41) Beds €5.30. The hostel is friendly and well run with free hot showers. Breakfast is available and there's a bar in the evening. There is no curfew and the place is open all year.

**Domatia** *Rent Rooms Sea Front* (☎ 2831 051 981, fax 2831 051 062, e elotia@ret .forthnet.gr, El Venizelou 45) Singles/doubles with bath €20.50/26.50. This is a delightful pension with six studio apartments but each one is fresh and cheerful. The best part is that you're right across the street from the beach; the worst part is that the front rooms can be noisy at night.

*Olga's Pension* (☎ 2831 028 665, Souliou 57) Singles/studios €20.50/29.50. The friendly Olga's is tucked away on touristy but colourful Souliou. A network of terraces, all bursting with greenery, connects a wide range of rooms, some with bath and sea views and others without.

RETHYMNO & CENTRAL CRETE

*Rooms Lefteris* (☎ *2831 023 803, Kefalogianni 25-26)* Singles/doubles with bath €23.50/29.50. Tranquillity is not the selling point here but anyone who wants to be in the centre of Rethymno's nightlife has come to the right place. All rooms are pleasant. The front rooms have stunning sea views although they can be noisy at night.

*Rooms for Rent Anda* (☎ *2831 023 479, Nikiforou Foka 33)* Singles/doubles €27/33. This is a great choice if you have kids because it's just a short walk from Rethymno's municipal park. The prettily furnished rooms have private bathrooms but no other amenities. The owner will gladly help you with anything you need.

*Garden House* (☎ *2831 028 586, Nikiforou Foka 82)* Doubles/triples with bath €32.50/47. On a quiet street in Rethymno's old town, this is an impeccably maintained 600-year-old Venetian house retaining many of its original features including impressive doors and a gorgeous grape-arboured garden. The rooms are simple, comfortable and tasteful.

*Park Hotel* (☎ *2831 029 958, Igoumenou Gavriil 9)* Singles/doubles €32.50/41 including breakfast. The only missing ingredient here is an elevator to take you to rooms that are spread over two floors. The rooms are comfortable with air-con, TV, telephone, sound-proofing and balconies offering a view of the municipal park.

**Hotels – Mid-Range** *Hotel Fortezza* (☎ *2831 055 551, fax 2831 054 073,* e *mliodak@ret.forthnet.gr, Melissinou 16)* Singles/doubles €55.80/70.50 including buffet breakfast. This is an isle of calm in a busy neighbourhood. Housed in a refurbished old building in the heart of the old town, the tastefully furnished rooms have TVs, telephones and air-con on demand. After a day of roaming through Rethymno, it's pleasant to relax by the swimming pool.

*Hotel Ideon* (☎ *2831 028 667, fax 2831 028 670,* e *ideon@otenet.gr, Plastira 10)* Singles/doubles €50/75 including buffet breakfast. To spare you the long walk to Rethymno's beach, the modern Hotel Ideon provides you with a swimming pool. Other amenities in this polished establishment include rooms with air-con, safes, radios, telephones and balconies.

*Hotel Veneto* (☎ *2831 056 634, fax 2831 056 635,* e *info@veneto.gr,* w *www.veneto .gr, Epimenidou 4)* Studio/suite €85/105. The oldest part of Hotel Veneto dates from the 14th century and it has preserved many of its traditional features without sacrificing modern comforts. The eye-catching rooms of polished wood floors and ceilings also have air-con, TVs, telephones, safes and kitchenettes.

**Hotels – Top End** *Palazzo Vecchio* (☎ *2831 035 352, fax 2831 025 479, Plateia Iroön Polytehniou & Melissinou)* Double studios €73.50. Located in a quiet neighbourhood near the Fortezza, Palazzo is a small boutique hotel for those who like it quiet but exclusive. There is a small swimming pool around which you can take the inclusive breakfast.

*Palazzo Rimondi* (☎ *2831 051 289, fax 2831 051 013, Xanthoulidou 21 & Trikoupi 16)* Suites 2-5 persons €50-79.30. In the heart of the old city, these exquisite studios, each individually decorated have kitchenettes. A large continental breakfast is included in the room rate.

## Places to Eat

The waterfront along El Venizelou is lined with amazingly similar tourist restaurants staffed by fast-talking waiters desperately cajoling passers-by into eating at their establishments. The situation is much the same around the Venetian Harbour, except that the setting is better and the prices higher. The most authentic places are in the web of side streets inland from the harbour.

*Stella's Kitchen* (☎ *2831 028 665, Souliou 55)* Breakfast €4.50-5.90. Open 8am-midnight. This tiny, homey spot on one of Rethymno's oldest streets, serves up tasty snacks and a few meals. It's a good bet for breakfast as well. There are only a few tables however, so you may have to take the food away.

*Taverna O Pontios* (☎ *2831 057 624, Melissinou 34)* Mains €2.70-4.50. Open noon-2.30pm & 6pm-midnight. This place proves once again that some of the best Cretan food comes from places that look like upgraded street stalls. A convivial group of locals comes here for the delicious cheese-stuffed calamari among other dishes.

***Taverna Old Town*** (☎ *2831 026 436, Vernardou 31)* Set menus for 2 persons €12.30-15.30. Open noon-3pm & 7pm-midnight. This is a good spot to come after an exploration of the Historical and Folk Art Museum right across the street. The traditional Cretan food is well prepared and there are good value set-price menus with wine.

***Gounakis Taverna*** (☎ *2831 028 816, Koroneou 6)* Mains €3.50-5.60. Open 8pm-1am. This is a fun place, worth visiting for its food as much as for its music. The plain interior contains a small stage that attracts some of Rethymno's finest folk musicians and the cooking is delicious. (See Entertainment later in this section.)

***Knosos*** (☎ *2831 025 582, Limani)* Fish platter for 2 persons €35.30. Of all the harbourside restaurants, only at the diminutive Knosos can you guarantee fresh fish and honest service at a reasonable price. Most popular fish dish is *tsipoura* (€29.50kg).

***Avli*** (☎ *2831 026 213, Xanthoudidou 22)* Salads €5-7.40. Open noon-2.30pm & 6pm-midnight. There's no better place in town than Avli for a romantic evening out. The food is superb and this former Venetian villa has an idyllic enclosed garden for dining alfresco.

***Sunset*** (☎ *2831 023 943, Periferiakos)* Set fish menu for 2 persons €36. Open noon-midnight. Let the tourists eat elbow to elbow on Venizelou street. Sunset is on the other side of the Venetian fortress where all is calm. You can feast on decent Cretan dishes while seated right along the water. Come at sunset, of course.

***Taverna Kyria Maria*** (☎ *2831 029 078, Moshovitou 20)* Cretan dishes €2.40-6.50. Open 8am-1am. For authentic atmosphere try here. Wander inland down the little side streets to Kyria Maria, behind the Rimondi Fountain. This cosy, traditional taverna has outdoor seating under a leafy trellis with twittering birds. All meals end with a complimentary dessert and shot of raki.

***Taverna Castro*** (☎ *2831 022 666, Melissinou 17)* Grills €5.90-11.50. Open noon-midnight. A little off the beaten track, Taverna Castro often has space when others are full. The enclosed garden-terrace provides a soothing setting for decent Cretan dishes, or even eastern favourites like chicken curry (€6.20).

***Fanari*** (☎ *2831 054 849, Kefalogianni 15)* Mezedes €1.80-4.70. Open noon-midnight. Tourists rarely wander over this way, but this is as typical a taverna as you're likely to find in Rethymno. The mezedes are original, the fish is fresh, carnivores will love the grilled steak and the home-made wine is surprisingly good.

***Veneto Restaurant*** (☎ *2831 056 634, Epimenidou 4)* Mains €5.30-10. Under the hotel of the same name, the very atmospheric and upper-market Veneto has a generic Mediterranean menu and includes some Ancient Greek dishes like lamb chops in wine, honey, sesame oil and thyme (€12.30). Lobster spaghetti for two (€44) is another special treat.

Self-caterers might make a note of the well-stocked and always busy ***Halkiadakis supermarket*** *(Hatzidaki 20)* on the southern side of town.

## Entertainment

**Bars & Discos** The bars and cafes along El Venizelou fill up on summer evenings with pink-skinned tourists, dazed from the sun and nursing tropical drinks. The ambience is comfortable but soporific. Rethymno's livelier nightlife is concentrated in the streets around the Venetian harbour where a cluster of bars, clubs and discos create a carnivalesque atmosphere.

***Gounakis Bar*** (☎ *2831 028 816, Koroneou 6)* Open 8pm-1am. If you love drinking cheap wine and listening to live Cretan folk music, this is the place to go. There's music and impromptu dancing most nights. (See Places to Eat earlier in this section.)

***Nitro Music Bar*** (☎ *2831 027 205, Nearhou 26)* Open 10pm-dawn. In the heart of Rethymno's nightlife district, this is a crowded, friendly dance club with music programming that leans toward techno early in the evening and Greek music later on.

***Fortezza Disco*** *(Nearhou 20)* Open 11pm-dawn. This is the town's showpiece disco. It's big and flashy with three bars, a laser show and a well-groomed international crowd that starts drifting in around midnight.

***Opera Club*** *(Salaminos 30)* Open 11pm-dawn. Formerly a cinema, now a huge dance club, the OC has hired an attractive multilingual staff in an effort to capture the tourist market. The sounds are contemporary international.

***Rock Club Cafe*** *(☎ 2831 031 047, Petihaki 8)* Open 9pm-dawn. RCC is having its moment in the sun as Rethymno's trendiest hang-out. The crowd of young professionals that fills the club nightly may move on soon but right now this is where the action is.

***Metropolis NYC*** *(☎ 2831 Nearhou 24)* Open 10pm-7am. The DJ spins hits from the '60s for a crowd that comes to tank up on cocktails before hitting the discos.

***Notes*** *(☎ 2831 029 785, Himaras 27)* Open 10am-midnight. Notes is a quiet bar/cafe with a polished wood bar, and was opened by a musician who has an excellent selection of Greek music. It's a good place to escape the crowds along El Venizelou.

***Figaro*** *(☎ 2831 029 431, Vernardou 21)* Open noon-midnight. Housed in an ingeniously restored old building, Figaro is an atmospheric bar which attracts a subdued crowd for drinks, snacks and rock music.

**Cinema** *Cinema Asteria (☎ 2831 022 830, Melissinou 21)* is a small open-air cinema showing late-release movies. It's open from 9pm daily and entrance costs €3.60.

## Shopping

The shopping section of Rethymno is relatively compact and contains a wide assortment of stores selling everything from souvenirs to jewelled watches. The waterfront promenade of El Venizelou has plenty of souvenir shops sandwiched between the restaurants but you'll find higher quality merchandise, including jewellery shops, on Arkadiou.

Souliou is a narrow pedestrian street crammed with stores of every kind and makes a wonderful stroll. Don't miss the Thursday market on Dimitrakaki for fresh produce, clothing and odds and ends.

***Xenia*** *(☎ 2831 022 045, Arkadiou 32 & 265)* Open 8.30am-8pm Mon-Sat. A Cretan summer may make it difficult to think about leather outerwear but the suede and leather here is buttery soft and is made into elegant ladies' suits, jackets and coats.

***Zaharias Theodorakis*** *(☎ 2831 022 738, Katehaki 4)* Open 10am-8pm Mon-Sat. Zaharias Theodorakis turns out onyx bowls and goblets on the lathe at his small workshop.

***Katerina Karaoglani*** *(☎ 2831 024 301, Nikiforou Foka 7)* Open 10am-11pm Mon-Sat. Friendly Katerina Karaoglani makes her pottery in the store. You'll find the standard blue-glazed Cretan ceramics of a better quality than the tourist shops deliver.

***I Melissa*** *(☎ 2831 029 601, Ethnikis Andistasis 23)* Open 9am-8pm Mon-Sat. In addition to hand-made icons, Melissa sells candles, incense, oil lamps and other fragrant substances.

## Getting There & Away

**Bus** There are numerous services to both Hania (€5.30, one hour) and Iraklio (€5.60, 1½ hours). There's a bus in each direction every half-hour in summer and every hour in winter. In summer there are also four buses a day to Plakias (€3.10, one hour); four to Agia Galini (€4.25, 1½ hours); one to Omalos (€8.50, two hours); three to Moni Arkadiou (€1.80, 30 minutes) and two to Preveli (€2.80, 1¼ hours). The morning bus to Plakias continues to Hora Sfakion (€4.70, two hours). Services to these destinations are greatly reduced in winter.

**Ferry** ANEK (☎ 2831 029 221, fax 2831 055 519, W www.anek.gr) operates a ferry between Rethymno and Piraeus leaving Rethymno and Piraeus at 7.30pm daily. Tickets are available from the company's office at Arkadiou 250. Deck-class tickets cost €22 and a berth in a tourist-class cabin is €32.50.

## Getting Around

**Car, Motorcycle & Bicycle** Most of the car hire firms are grouped around Plateia Iroön. Motor Stavros (☎ 2831 022 858), at Paleologou 14, has a wide range of motorcycles and also rents bicycles.

# Around Rethymno

The hinterland villages of Rethymno make for pleasant scooter or motorbike excursions. The hills are not too taxing, the roads not too busy and the scenery is pleasantly verdant. There are at least a couple of villages to the south-west of Rethymno that make for an ideal afternoon jaunt.

## EPISKOPI Επισκοπή
**postcode 700 08 • pop 873**

Episkopi, 23km south-west of Rethymno, is a pretty, traditional town of winding lanes and tiny houses, overlooking the valley. One main road runs through town with a smaller road running parallel to the main road. There is no OTE but there is a post office past the BP station on the right.

As a market centre for the region's produce Episkopi is busy and prosperous although most men and women are still clad in traditional black Cretan garb.

The town is a good place to experience Cretan life and attracts few tourists although there are a few domatia.

*Loutraki* (☎ *2831 061 677, Episkopi)* Singles/doubles €17.50/20.50. Rooms are basic but comfortable enough. The bathroom is shared.

*Rent Rooms Irene* (☎ *2831 061 325, Episkopi)* Singles/doubles €18/21. Close to the centre of the village these rooms have private baths and simple but comfortable facilities.

From Monday to Friday there are two buses daily from Rethymno to Episkopi (€1.20, 30 minutes).

## ARGYROUPOLIS Αργυρούπολη
**postcode 740 55 • pop 396**

When the summer heat becomes too intense even for the beach, you'll find a natural, outdoor air-conditioning system at Argyroupolis, 25km south-west from Rethymno. The lower village of this two-village town is a watery oasis formed by mountain springs that keeps the temperature markedly cooler than the coast. Running through aqueducts, washing down walls, seeping from stones and pouring from spigots, the gushing springwater supplies the entire city of Rethymno.

Towering chestnut and plane trees and luxuriant vegetation create a shady, restful spot, perfect for lingering over lunch in one of the local tavernas.

Argyroupolis, is built on the remains of the ancient city of Lappa so there's also plenty to explore. The villagers maintain a traditional lifestyle, largely undisturbed by tourism but are proud of their heritage and eager to show you around.

## History

Although legend has it that Agamemnon built Lappa, most likely it was founded by the Dorians. The inland city was safe from piracy and was bordered by a fertile valley in the north and protective mountains to the south and west. The city flourished but, along with the town of Lyttos, became a centre of resistance to rule from Knossos in the 3rd century BC.

When Lyttos was destroyed by Knossos in 220 BC its vanquished inhabitants took refuge in Lappa, which together with Polyrrinia succeeded in securing peace in western Crete with the help of Philip V of Macedonia. Lappa's knack for being on the right side of political struggles continued when it supported Octavian in his winning battle with Mark Antony. As Emperor, Octavian rewarded Lappa by erecting elaborate public buildings in the town. He built a reservoir in 27 BC that is still in use today and excavations have revealed a Roman floor mosaic, Roman baths and Roman tombs.

The city prospered until its destruction by the 9th-century Saracens and then enjoyed a second life under the Venetians who built villas and churches in this cool mountain hideaway. Archaeologists are continuing to excavate in the area and are turning up remnants of Lappa's history from its origins to its eventual destruction by the Saracens.

## Orientation & Information

The town is divided into two parts. The main square and old town is in the upper part, which is connected to the water wheels of lower Argyroupolis by a good paved road, or a steep, concrete-paved street.

There is no post office, OTE, tourist office or travel agency but the Lappa Avocado Shop just off the main square is a good source of information on the town and will provide visitors with maps. You can change money here and pick up a supply of their excellent avocado-based creams and soaps.

## Things to See

**Upper Town** The main square is marked by the 17th-century Venetian **Church of Agios Ioannis** *(Argyroupolis; admission free; open 8am-8pm daily)*. Passing through the stone archway opposite the church with the Lappa Avocado Shop on the left you will enter the old town where Roman remnants are scattered amid the Venetian and Turkish structures.

The main stone street will take you past a **Roman gate** on the left with the inscription 'Omnia Mundi Fumus et Umbra' (All Things in This World are Smoke and Shadow). In a few metres a narrow street to the right leads down to a 3rd-century-BC **marble water reservoir** with seven interior arches.

Returning to the main road and continuing in the same direction past grapevines and apricot trees you will see on the left a **Roman mosaic floor**, dating from the 1st century BC. With 7000 pieces in six colours, the well-preserved floor is a good example of design from the Geometric Period. The same road takes you back to the stone-arched entrance.

**Lower Town** The centre of the lower town is formed by a group of tavernas clustered around the tumbling springs. A path from the bottom of the town leads you to a **Roman bath** and a water-driven **wooden fulling machine** which was used to thicken cloth by moistening and beating it. Nearby is **St Mary's Church** *(Argyroupolis; admission free; open 8am-8pm daily)*, built on a temple devoted to Neptune. Another path from the village centre takes you to the **St Nikolas Church** *(Argyroupolis; admission free; open 9am-7pm daily)* inside a cave, and **waterfalls**.

**Other Sights** North of the upper town a footpath on the right takes you about 50m to a **Roman Necropolis** with hundreds of tombs cut into the cliffs. The shady path leads on to a **plane tree** that is supposed to be 2000 years old and is so large that the path runs right through it. There are benches around the tree and mountain springs.

## Places to Stay & Eat

*Rooms Argyroupolis (☎ 2831 081 281, Argyroupolis)* Singles/doubles €19/21. This place is about 500m uphill from the lower town, and has rooms with scenic views over the valley.

*Mikedakis (☎ 2831 081 225, Argyroupolis)* Singles/doubles €17.60/22. This is a charming place, half-buried behind trees and flowering bushes that offers spectacular views of the area from its balconies.

*Agia Dynamis (Argyroupolis)* Mains €3-5. This place is surrounded by waterfalls and fountains and offers good value meals.

## Getting There & Away

From Monday to Friday there are two buses daily from Rethymno (€1.60, 40 minutes).

# The Hinterland

The Amari Province is the heartland of Crete and the repository of its culture. The province's capital at Amari is surrounded by some of the most tranquil and untouched villages on the island while the hills and valleys of Mt Psiloritis create breathtaking views.

From the legend of Zeus to the horrifying bloodbath at Moni Arkadiou, Crete's tormented history took shape under the shadow of the looming Mt Psiloritis, now crisscrossed by shepherds' trails and goats' tracks. You will need your own wheels to do justice to the province which is poorly served by public transportation, although there are three buses a day from Rethymno to Amari.

## SPILI Σπήλι
**postcode 740 53 • pop 710**

Spili (**Spee**-lee) is a gorgeous mountain village with cobbled streets, rustic houses and plane trees. Its centrepiece is a unique Venetian fountain which spurts water from 19 lion heads. Bring along your own water containers and fill up with the best water on the island.

Despite its distance from the coast, Spili is no longer an undiscovered hideaway. Tourist buses on their way to the southern coast bring a fair amount of visitors to Spili during the day but in the evening the town belongs to the locals. Spili is a great base for exploring the region and deserves more than a passing look-in.

### Orientation & Information
The post office and bank are on the main street. The OTE is up a side street, north of the central square. The bus stop is just south of the square.

### Places to Stay & Eat
*Green Hotel* (☎ 2832 022 225, Spili) Doubles with private bath €19. Across from the police station on the main street, this is a homey place practically buried under plants and vines that also fill the interior. Rooms are attractive.

*Heracles Rooms* (☎ 2832 022 111, fax 2832 022 411, Spili) Singles/doubles with private bathroom €23.50/29.50. Signposted from the main road are these excellent rooms which are sparkling and beautifully furnished. Each room has large insect screens on the door. Breakfast is available for €3-5.90 per person.

*Costas Inn* (☎ 2832 022 040, fax 2832 022 043, Spili) Doubles/triples with bath €35.30/44. Further along, on the left, Costas Inn has well-kept, ornate rooms with satellite TV, radio and the use of a washing machine.

*Taverna Costas* (☎ 2832 022 040, Spili) Cretan dishes €2.50-4.50. Under the inn of the same name this popular eatery is a very good choice. Food products including wine are organic. Try the traditional sweets for dessert.

*Taverna Stratidakis* (☎ 2832 022 006, Spili) Mayirefta €2.50-4.70. Opposite Costas Inn, this place serves excellent traditional Greek dishes. The specials of the day are in pots at the back of the room. Enjoy a rabbit lunch (€4.70) on the balcony overlooking olive and plane trees.

### Getting There & Away
Spili is on the Rethymno-Agia Galini bus route.

## AROUND SPILI
Most people come to the alluring little village of Patsos to visit the nearby **Church of Agios Antonios** in a cave above a picturesque gorge.

The cave was an important sanctuary for the Minoans and the Romans, and is still a pilgrimage destination on 17 January. You can drive here from Rethymno, or you can walk from Spili along a scenic 10km dirt track.

To reach the track, walk along 28 October, passing the lion fountain on your right. Turn right onto Thermopylon and ascend to the Spili-Gerakari road. Turn right here and eventually you will come to a sign for Gerakari. Take the dirt track to the left, and at the fork bear right. At the crossroads turn right, and continue on the main track for about one hour to a T-junction on the outskirts of Patsos. Turn left to get to the cave.

Heading west then south towards the coast at Plakias you will pass through the dramatic **Kourtaliotis Gorge** through which the river Megalopotamos rumbles on its way to the sea at **Preveli Beach**. About 8km before Plakias there is a turnoff to the left for Preveli Beach and **Moni Preveli**.

## AMARI VALLEY Κοιλάδα Αμαρίου
If you have your own transport you may like to explore the enchanting Amari Valley, south-east of Rethymno, between Mts

**Phone numbers listed incorporate changes due in Oct 2002; see p61**

Psiloritis and Kedros. This region harbours around 40 well-watered, unspoilt villages set amid olive groves and almond and cherry trees. The valley begins at the picturesque village of **Apostoli**, 25km southeast of Rethymno. The turn-off for Apostoli is on the coast 3km east of Rethymno. The road forks at Apostoli and then joins up again 38km to the south, making it possible to do a circular drive around the valley; alternatively, you can continue south to Agia Galini.

The road to **Apostoli** follows a wild and deserted gorge bordered by high cliffs and is spectacularly scenic. Apostoli makes a good rest stop; there's a taverna on the right side of the road that serves good chewy bread and has beautiful views over the valley, but there's no other place in Apostoli to pick up supplies. Taking the left fork from Apostoli you'll come to the village of **Thronos** with its Church of the Panagia constructed on the remains of an early Christian basilica. The 14th-century frescoes are faded but extraordinarily well-executed; the oldest are in the choir stalls. Ask at the kafenion next door for the key.

Returning to Apostoli continue along the main road south. The next town is **Agia Fotini** which is a larger town with a supermarket. The road twists and turns along the scenic valley before it comes to **Meronas**, a little village with big plane trees, and a fine Church of the Panagia. The oldest part of the church is the knave which was built in the 14th century. The southern side of the church with its elegant portal was added under the Venetians. The highlight of the church is the beautifully restored 14th-century frescoes.

The road continues south to **Gerakari**, an area known for its delicious cherries. From Gerakari a new road continues on to Spili which affords sweeping views of the valley.

## MT PSILORITIS Ορος Ψειλορίτης

The imposing Mt Psiloritis, also known as Mt Idi, dominates the Amari Province and at 2456m is the highest mountain in Crete. The eastern base of Mt Psiloritis is the **Nida Plateau** a wide open expanse used for sheep grazing and lying in between a circle of imposing mountains. The winding, 22km paved road leading up to the plateau from Anogia is carpeted with wild flowers in the early spring and you'll notice many *mitata* (round stone shepherd's huts) along the

### Hiking on Mt Psiloritis

From the Nida Plateau you can join the east-west E4 trail for the ascent to the summit of Psiloritis known as **Timios Stavros** (Holy Cross). The return trek to the summit can be done in about seven hours from Nida. While you don't need to be an alpine mountaineer to complete the trek, it is a long slog and the views from the summit may be marred by heat haze, or not uncommon cloud cover. Shortly after leaving Nida a spur track leads to the Ideon Cave itself, which is at an altitude of 1495m. Along the way to the summit a number of mitata provide occasional sheltering opportunities, should the weather turn inclement, while at the summit of Psiloritis itself is a twin-domed, small dry-stone chapel.

An alternative access, or exit route begins (or ends) at Fourfouras on the edge of the Amari Valley and a further 3½ hours trek to the west from the summit. There is a prominent EOS-run mountain refuge about halfway along this trail. From Fourfouras you can find onward transport, or continue to follow the E4 to Spili. A third access/exit route from the mountain runs to the south and meets the village of Kamares (five hours). Halfway along this track you will pass the **Kamares cave** in which a large collection of painted Minoan urns was found and which is a popular day trek in its own right for visitors to the southern side of Psiloritis.

The best map for anyone planning to walk in this region is the 1:100,000 *Kreta Touristikkarte* published by Harms Verlag. (See Maps in the Facts about Crete chapter.)

Matala Beach is edged by cliffs sporting man-made caves that date back to prehistoric times.

Market stalls on '1866' Street, Iraklio

Dolphin mural, Palace of Knossos

Agios Minos Cathedral, Iraklio

Display of delicious honey, Rethymno

Shot up road sign for Rethymno province

Moni Arkadiou, with its triple-belled tower

The exit of Kourtaliotiko Gorge, Preveli

Enjoying a game of backgammon, Rethymno

Nightlife on Arkadhiou Street, Rethymno

way. The mountain's historically important feature is the **Ideon Cave** the place where, according to legend, the god Zeus was reared. The cave may have been inhabited in the early Neolithic period but is now being excavated and was closed to visitors at the last count.

## MONI ARKADIOU Μονή Αρκαδίου

This 16th-century monastery *(Arkadi; admission free; open 8am-1pm & 3.30pm-8pm)* stands in attractive hill country 23km south-east of Rethymno. The most impressive building of the complex is the Venetian baroque church. Its striking facade has eight slender Corinthian columns and is topped by an ornate triple-belled tower. This facade used to feature on the old 100 drachma note.

In November 1866 the Turks sent massive forces to quell insurrections which were gathering momentum throughout the island. Hundreds of men, women and children who had fled their villages used the monastery as a safe haven. When 2000 Turkish soldiers staged an attack on the building, the Cretans, rather than surrender, set light to a store of gun powder. The explosion killed everyone, Turks included, except one small girl. This sole survivor lived to a ripe old age in a village nearby. A bust of this woman, and the abbot who lit the gun powder, stand outside the monastery.

The exterior of Moni Arkadiou (which is still a working monastery) is coldly impressive but the Venetian church inside dates from 1587 and has a richly decorated Renaissance facade. On the right of the church there is a stairway that leads to a small museum commemorating the history of the monastery.

There's a small **museum** *(Arkadi; admission €2; open 8am-1pm & 3.30pm-8pm daily)*.

## Getting There & Away

There are buses from Rethymno to the monastery (€1.60, 30 minutes) at 6am, 10.30am and 2.30pm, returning at 7am, noon and 4pm.

# The North Coast

The Mylopotamos Province has some of the more dramatic scenery in northern Crete. The coastline east of Rethymno is indented and pockmarked with watery caves and isolated coves that are only accessible by boat. The chief resorts along the north coast are Bali and Panormos. The hilly interior contains a scattering of villages and farming towns that are just beginning to attract some tourism. Within this region you will find some of Crete's most outstanding crafts, including the pottery at Margarites and the textiles at Anogia.

## PANORMOS Πάνορμος
**postcode 740 57 • pop 372**

Panormos is one of the lesser known resorts on the northern coast despite the fact that it has a couple of sandy beaches and is easy to get to from Rethymno. While the beaches are not the most pristine – there is a fair bit of flotsam and jetsam at times and the water is a bit murky – the village does have a relaxed folksy atmosphere and makes for a quieter alternative to the occasionally claustrophobic scene immediately east of Rethymno and the more sporty scene at Bali 10km further east.

The village was built on the site of an ancient settlement of which little is known. Coins found here indicate that the village flourished from the 1st to the 9th centuries AD when it was destroyed by the Saracens. There was once an early Christian basilica of Agia Sofia, probably built around the 6th century, and there are the ruins of a Genoese castle on the harbour.

### Orientation & Information

The bus stop is on the main road outside of town. The post office is one block behind the remains of the Genoese castle. There is no bank or OTE.

### Places to Stay & Eat

*Lucy's Pension (☎ 2834 051 212, fax 2834 051 434, Panormos)* Singles/doubles €23.50/29.50. Lucy is to the right as you enter the village from the main highway.

Phone numbers listed incorporate changes due in Oct 2002; see p61

RETHYMNO & CENTRAL CRETE

*Hotel Kirki* (☎ *2834 051 225, fax 2834 051 013, Panormos*) Singles/doubles €30/38. In the village but closer to the main road is a B-class hotel with modern rooms.

*Panormos Beach Hotel* (☎ *2834 051 321, Panormos*) Singles/doubles €32.50/41. Once the best accommodation in town is this friendly hotel across the road from the beach. It has a pool in an interior garden and attractive studios with balconies.

*To Steki tou Sifaka* (☎ *2834 051 230, Panormos*) Mezedes €2-5.20. This small, cosy taverna-cum-ouzeri is on a paved street a block back from the waterfront. Courgettes and potatoes, or stuffed courgettes (€3.80) are among the recommended vegetarian mezedes on offer.

## Getting There & Away
Buses between Rethymno and Iraklio stop on the main road outside of town.

## BALI Μπαλί
**postcode 740 57 • pop 203**
Bali, 38km east of Rethymno and 51km west of Iraklio, has one of the most stunning settings on the northern coast. No less than five little coves are strung along the indented shore, marked by hills, promontories and narrow, sandy beaches. Helter-skelter development around the coast has somewhat marred the natural beauty of Bali and the narrow beaches can become crowded in the summer, but it's a great place to rent a boat and get the full effect of the dramatic landscape.

The name Bali has nothing to do with its tropical namesake in Indonesia; rather the name means 'honey' in Turkish, for excellent honey was once collected and processed here. In antiquity the place was known as Astali, though no traces of ancient Astali now remain.

## Orientation & Information
Bali is a rather spread-out settlement and it is a long walk from one end of Bali to the other – 25 minutes or more – so plan your accommodation and eating options accordingly. The village is punctuated by a series of coves and attendant hotels and restaurants starting with Paradise Beach, followed by Kyma Beach, and then Bali Beach. The ensuing port has a small, but popular swimming area, but the last and best beach is Evita Beach at the far northern end. Walkers can take a short cut along a coastal path from the port, while riders and drivers must make a circuitous approach over the clifftops.

There is no bank or post office but you can change money at Racer Rent-a-Car on the left as you enter town or in one of the travel agencies clustered around the coves. You can check your email at the Posto Cafe (☎ 2834 094 003) on the port, where access time costs €3 per hour.

## Activities
There is a wide variety of water sports activities available in Bali.

*Diving Centre Ippokambos* (☎ *2834 094 193, Bali; dives €50/59 including equipment*) Based at Evita Beach, this company offers a 'discover scuba diving' dive and boat dives.

*Water Sports Lefteris* (☎ *2834 094 102, Bali*) will rent you a pedal boat for €6 an hour, a small canoe for €4.50 an hour, a sailboat for €36 for two hours and a jet ski for €18 for 15 minutes. Paragliding costs €30 for a 15-minute flight. On the port, Lefteris also offers day-long and sunset cruises.

## Places to Stay & Eat
There is little budget accommodation in Bali, most of it being designed for couples or families on holiday. A lot of the accommodation is also taken over by packaged holiday groups, so pre-booking is a good idea in high season.

*Apartments Ikonomakis* (☎ *2834 094 125, Bali*) Singles/doubles €26.50/38.50. This place is on a quiet street slightly inland from the port. Rooms are quite comfortable and are centrally placed.

*Evita Rent Rooms* (☎ *2834 094 250, Bali*) Singles/doubles €26.50/38.50. Overlooking the beach of the same name, Evita has cosy rooms with a fridge. This place is sometimes block-booked by tour companies.

*Sunrise Apartments* (☎ *2834 094 267, Bali*) Doubles €28. Right on Evita Beach,

Sunrise Apartments is among the cheaper options. The rooms are very pleasant and the owners will pick up guests from Iraklio airport.

***Rose Apartments*** *(☎ 2834 094 440, fax 2834 094 256)* Studios doubles/quads €44/59. On the left shortly after you enter Bali are these very tasteful new studios. Complete with air-conditioning, kitchenette, umbrella-equipped balconies and enjoying ample parking, Rose Apartments is one of the better independent accommodation choices in Bali for two or more persons.

***Katerina Rooms*** *(☎ 2834 094 513)* Studios for 2-3 persons €36. Next door to Rose Apartments are these older studios with similar facilities, though the furnishings are older. There is a kitchenette in most rooms.

There is a wealth of cafes and restaurants clustered along the coves.

***Kyma Restaurant*** *(☎ 2834 094 240, Bali)* Mains €3.80-5.90. The Kyma, right on Kyma beach, serves good value meals in a pleasant setting. The chef recommends his oven-baked vegetables (€3.50).

***Panorama*** *(☎ 2834 094 217, Bali)* Mains €3.80-5.90. Overlooking the port, this is another good choice. A filling mixed platter costs €5.90.

***Taverna Karavostasi*** *(☎ 2834 094 267, Bali)* Mains €3-5.60. Belonging to Sunrise Apartments, this cosy little eatery 30m back from Evita beach offers simple home cooking and snacks. Okra with lamb (€4.50) is one of their more requested dishes.

## Entertainment
***Highway Club*** *(Bali)* One of the liveliest dance clubs in Bali, the Highway Club is at the entrance to town. It's an open-air space decorated as a tropical garden.

***Volcano*** *(Bali)* Also popular, Volcano is at the top of the hill overlooking the church.

***On The Rocks*** *(Bali)* Across from the church, this place caters more to teenagers.

## Getting There & Away
Buses between Iraklio and Rethymno drop you at the main road, from where it is a 2km walk to the port of Bali.

## Getting Around
Racer Rent-a-Car (☎ 2834 094 149, fax 2834 094 249) has an office at the entrance to town and one at the port and offers good deals on rentals.

# MARGARITES Μαργαρίτες
**postcode 740 52 • pop 328**
Known for its fine pottery, this tiny town is invaded by tour buses in the morning but it's a brief interlude. By the afternoon all is calm and you can enjoy wonderful views over the valley from the taverna terraces on the main square.

## Orientation & Information
There is only one road that runs through town to the town square which is dominated by giant eucalyptus trees. The bus stop is in front of a taverna on the main square and you'll see many ceramic shops on the main street as well as the side streets. There is no bank, post office or travel agency.

## Places to Stay & Eat
***Irini Apartments*** *(☎ 2834 092 494,* e *piterm@hotmail.com, Margarites)* Singles/doubles €19/25. The only accommodation in town is Irini Apartments which has rooms with kitchenettes. It is on the southern side of the village, on the left as you come from Rethymno.

***Dionysios*** *(☎ 2834 092 100, Margarites)* Just off the main street in a little alleyway, this is a good shop to buy ham, sausage and blackberry pies. Across the street is a cheese shop with big wheels of local cheese.

## Getting There & Away
There are two buses daily, Monday to Friday from Rethymno (€2, 30 minutes).

# ANOGIA Ανώγεια
**postcode 740 51 • pop 2223**
If ever there was a village in Crete that embodies the quintessential elements that make up the 'real' Crete, it is Anogia, a bucolic village perched on the flanks of Mt Psiloritis 37km south-west of Iraklio. Enjoying a more temperate climate than you'll find on the coasts, Anogia is well-known

for its rebellious spirit, its determination to hang on to its undiluted Cretan character, its sheep-rearing moustachioed men and its stirring music.

During WWII Anogia was a centre of resistance to the Germans, who massacred all the men in the village in retaliation for their role in sheltering Allied troops and aiding in the kidnap of General Kreipe. Today, Anogia is the centre of a prosperous sheep husbandry industry and a burgeoning tourist trade, bolstered as much by curious Greeks as by foreign travellers seeking a Crete away from the hype of the coastal resorts. If you come to Anogia, plan to stay a few days; you never know what might happen.

## Orientation & Information

The town is spread out on a hillside with the textile shops in the lower half and most accommodation and businesses in the upper half. There's an Agricultural bank with an ATM, a post office and an OTE in the upper village. Moving between the upper and lower villages often involves some steep climbing.

## Special Events

At any given time there is likely to be some event – official or not – taking place in Anogia. Spontaneous, lively *mandinades* (rhyming couplets) sessions take place at any time, but particularly during the sheep shearing season in July. Copious amounts of raki are drunk when mandinades are composed and sung – with pistol shots ringing into the night air.

A wedding in Anogia is a very special event. Everyone gets dressed up, parades through the village to the accompaniment of

### Anogia's Musical Heritage

Anogia has produced a disproportionate number of musically talented sons: the much-loved and now long-lamented singer and lyrist Nikos Xylouris was from Anogia and his house is maintained as a kind of musical shrine in the lower village of Anogia. His idiosyncratic brother Psarandonis has since taken up the reins and is wildly popular among Cretans nationwide, while Psarandonis' son Georgos Xylouris plays music both at home in Crete and in Australia where he has lived on and off over the years.

Vasilis Skoulas, the latest in a long line of lyra players from the same family, now proudly plays lyra and sings on the world stage as well as to fellow Cretans.

More recently the talented, but capricious Georgos Tramoundanis, who goes by the stage name of Loudovikos ton Anogion (Ludwig from Anogia) has been selling his brand of folksy, ballad-style Cretan compositions to audiences all over Greece. His concerts often start at the ungodly hour of 4am.

Lyre player Vasilis Skoulas with his instrument

STELLA HELLANDER

live music and dances all night in the village square (see the boxed text 'A Cretan Affair').

In late July each year the Yakinthia Festival is held in and around Anogia. This is a musical, cultural and theatrical festival. There are displays, lectures, theatrical presentations and open-air concerts – usually on makeshift stages in sheep paddocks on the slopes of Mt Psiloritis. Sheer magic! Look around for posters in Anogia from mid-July onwards, or check the Internet ( **e** info@yakinthia.com, **w** www.yakinthia .com) for current details.

## Places to Stay
Domatia make up the bulk of the accommodation options. Most are in the upper village, thus enjoying not only the view to the north, but also the cooling breezes.

*Rooms Aris* (☎ 2834 031 460, fax 2834 031 058, Anogia) Singles/doubles €17.60/20.50. In the upper village, Rooms Aris enjoys perhaps the best views in Anogia. Rooms are clean and cosy and the owners are very friendly. Bathrooms are shared.

*Hotel Aristea* (☎ 2834 031 459, Anogia) Singles/doubles €20.50/26.50. Next door to Rooms Aris is another place enjoying good views. Aristea has simple but well-outfitted rooms with private bathrooms.

*Rent Rooms Arkadi* (☎ 2834 031 055, Anogia) Doubles/triples €23.50/26.50. On the busy main street in the upper village, Arkadi offers comfortable accommodation with fridges but shared bathrooms.

*Rent Rooms Psiloritis* (☎ 2834 031 194, Anogia) Rooms €29.50. Downhill from Arkadi this place has simple, homey rooms.

*Rent Rooms Kitros* (☎ 2834 031 429, Anogia) Doubles €26.50. In the lower village, this is the only accommodation. Rooms are reasonably priced and are close to the much more atmospheric lower village.

## Places to Eat
Eating in Anogia can be a bit of a hit and miss affair. Some of the attractive looking restaurants in the lower village square offer little more than dull permutations of spaghetti and chunks of char-grilled lamb. However there is some salvation.

*Taverna Ta Skalomata* (☎ 2834 031 316, Anogia) Mains €2.40-4.50. The oldest restaurant in town, Ta Skalomata provides a wide variety of Cretan dishes at very reasonable prices. Zucchini with cheese and aubergine (€3.20) is very tasty, as is their home-baked bread. It is on the eastern side of the upper village and enjoys great evening views.

*Taverna Kitros* (☎ 2834 031 429, Anogia) Mains €3-5.60. In the lower village this eatery does a presentable job of dishes like lima beans *(gigandes)* in oil (€3), or lamb and potatoes (€5.60). The home-made wine is very good too.

*Delina* (☎ 2834 031 701, Anogia) Mezedes €2.40-5.50. The queen of tavernas in Anogia, the capacious Delina is owned and occasionally patronised by internationally renowned Cretan lyra player Vasilis Skoulas. The mezedes are high-class as are the grills and salads. The taverna is about 2km outside of Anogia on the road to the Nida Plateau.

## Getting There & Away
There are five buses daily from Iraklio (€2.50, one hour); and two buses daily Monday to Friday from Rethymno (€3.40, 1¼ hours).

## AROUND ANOGIA
The roads leading north-west from Anogia to the small commercial centre of Perama are stunning and pass through a series of cosy villages and bustling market towns along the foothills of Mt Psiloritis. The northern road takes you to the village of **Axos** with the kind of lazy Cretan ambience that has made it a popular stop for tour buses from Iraklio and Rethymno.

During the day the village is quiet but at night the few tavernas with open-air terraces host 'Cretan folklore evenings' for the tourists. Following this rural road you'll come next to the pretty, shady town of **Garazo** which has a couple of tavernas, a post office and a bank.

The route continues north and crosses the highway to arrive at **Melidoni** with a fascinating cave to explore. Over 300 villagers

RETHYMNO & CENTRAL CRETE

## A Cretan Affair

Cretans from all over Crete will come to Anogia if they know a wedding is in the air. It is truly an unforgettable experience. While many rituals take place during the days prior to the wedding day, they usually occur in the homes of the bride and groom. On the day of the wedding the fun for observers really starts at the groom's house where a large group of family and friends gather to accompany the groom with a musical procession through the village to the bride's house.

The staccato rattle of a machine gun, or the crack of pistols fired into the air signal the start of the groom's walk. At the bride's house, the groom's party is met with more machine gun fusillades as well as wine, lamb and chunks of watermelon. Thereafter the combined groom's and bride's parties make their way to the church for the actual ceremony. After the ceremony the parties retire for food and drink and then the music and dancing begins in the village square. It doesn't end until the sun comes up the following day. A wedding in Anogia is a wildly colourful event, not often repeated elsewhere. Ask around if you are in Anogia on the weekend; you might just witness an event never to be forgotten.

took refuge from the Turkish army in the cave in 1824. When the villagers refused orders to emerge, the Turks threw burning materials through a hole in the top of the cave and everyone was asphyxiated. After paying homage to the martyrs at a monument, you can wander through a series of chambers filled with stalactites and stalagmites.

The southern route from Anogia to Perama is equally scenic. The largest town in the region is **Zoniana**, where everyone seems to be dressed in black and driving pick-up trucks. Look for signs to the **Sendoni Cave**.

Whether named after a rebel or a robber according to local legend, Sendoni is the most spectacular cave on the island. Stalactites, stalagmites and strange rock formations make the visit an eerie experience. The front of the cave was a hideout for Greek fighters against the Turks but most of the large cave was undisturbed. Walkways make exploration easier but it's still important to watch your step.

# The South Coast

The Agios Vasilios Province begins at Armeni in the north and ends at the southern coast. It is a region of gently rolling hills and pretty drives along good roads. As you near the coast the scenery becomes more dramatic and takes in marvellous views of the Libyan Sea. The capital of the province is Spili and the south includes the beach resorts of Agia Galini, Plakias and for the striking Moni Preveli and its attendant beach annexe.

Heading south from Rethymno, there is a turn-off to the right to the Late Minoan **Cemetery of Armeni**, 2km before the modern village of Armeni. Some 200 tombs were carved into the rock between 1300 and 1150 BC in the midst of an oak forest. The curious feature of this cemetery is that there does not seem to have been any sizeable town nearby which would have accounted for so many tombs. Pottery, weapons and jewellery excavated from the tombs are now on display at the Archaeological Museum in Rethymno.

## PLAKIAS Πλακιάς
### postcode 740 60 • pop 139
The south coast town of Plakias was once a tranquil fishing village before it became a retreat for adventurous backpackers. Fortunately the package tour operators have not yet totally destroyed the ambience and relaxed outlook of this south coast village and it still remains a popular traveller destination. Plakias offers a good range of independent accommodation, some pretty decent eating options, a brace of good regional walks, a large sandy beach and enough nightlife to keep the nightbirds singing until dawn. All in all, Plakias is one of the better choices for independent travellers looking for a hang-out in Crete.

## Orientation & Information

It's easy to find your way around Plakias. One street skirts the long sandy beach and another runs parallel to it one block back. The bus stop is at the middle of the waterfront. Plakias doesn't have a bank nor a stand-alone ATM, but Monza Travel Agency (☎ 2832 031 882, fax 2832 031 883), near the bus stop, offers currency exchange. Finikas Travel (☎ 2832 031 785) is also a good source of information and rents cars. It's open 9am to 7pm daily. In summer there is a mobile post office on the waterfront and a laundrette in the centre of the village. Check your email at the one PC in the Ostraco Bar (☎ 2832 031 710) for €4.50 per hour.

## Activities

Plakias is an excellent base to explore the surrounding region since you don't have to walk very far out of town to find yourself in the middle of fields and greenery. There are well-worn paths uphill to Myrthios overlooking the sea and to the scenic village of Sellia, the Moni Finika, Lefkogia, and a lovely walk along the spectacular Kourtaliotis Gorge to Moni Preveli. An easy 30-minute path to Myrthios village above Plakias begins just before the youth hostel. A booklet and map of walks around Plakias is on sale at the minimarket by the bus stop (€3.50).

**Phoenix Diving Club** (☎ 2832 031 206, Plakias) near the Ostraco Bar offers day-long scuba diving programs and a certification course as well as snorkelling trips. Here are some of the options the club offers: open water diving course (€250), discover scuba diving (€5), shore dive – tull equipment (€30) and snorkelling (€10).

For return trips to Moni Preveli, there is an excursion boat, the **Venus Express** (€7.50, departs 10am daily Apr-Oct). Ask at the supermarket across from Taverna Christo for bookings.

## Places to Stay

**Camping** *Camping Apollonia* (☎ 2832 031 318, Plakias) Person/tent €3.80/2.20. On the right of the main approach road to Plakias, this place has a restaurant, mini-market, bar and swimming pool. While the site is at least shaded, it all looks rather scruffy and run down.

**Hostel** *Youth Hostel 2832 Plakias* (☎ 2832 032 118, **e** info@yhplakias.com, **w** www .yhplakias.com). Dorm beds €6. Open Apr-Oct. For independent travellers this is *the* place to stay in Plakias. Manager Chris from the UK has created a very packie-friendly place with spotless dorms, green lawns, volley ball court and Internet access. Partying is much in evidence here helped along by Chris' eclectic music collection. Many guests stay for up to a month. Follow the signs from the waterfront. The hostel is tucked away in the olive trees behind the town, a 10-minute signposted walk from the bus stop.

**Domatia** There is a wide range of independent domatia on offer. Most are signposted on a communal wooden sign board next to Monza Travel. Try these for starters.

*Pension Kyriakos* (☎ 2832 031 307, fax 2832 031 631, Plakias) Doubles €20.50. 'If you don't like raki, stay away from here', says owner Kyriakos. His small, clean rooms have only coffee making facilities, but that is made up for by ample raki, supplied by the gregarious owner.

*Morfeas Rent Rooms* (☎/fax 2832 031 583, Plakias) Singles/doubles with bath €20.50/29.50; studios €35.30-53. Close to the bus stop and above a supermarket, Morfeas has light, airy and attractively furnished rooms with fridge, phone and air-con. It has, in addition, new studios for 2 to 4 persons with self-catering facilities.

*Ippokambos* (☎ 2832 031 525, Plakias) Studios €23.50. The large clean rooms here have flower-bedecked balconies and fridges but no cooking facilities other than gas rings to make coffee or tea.

*Pension Thetis* (☎ 2832 031 430, fax 2832 031 987, Plakias) Double studios €29.50. Thetis is a very pleasant, family-oriented set of studios. Rooms have fridge and cooking facilities. There's a cool and shady garden to relax in.

RETHYMNO & CENTRAL CRETE

**Phone numbers listed incorporate changes due in Oct 2002; see p61**

*Pension Afrodite* (☎ 2832 031 266, *Plakias*) Doubles/triples with bath €29.50/ 38.20. Rooms here are spotless. Head inland to Monza Travel Agency, turn left at the T-junction and then take the first right and you will come to the pension on the left after 100m.

*Castello* (☎/fax 2832 031 112, *Plakias*) Double studios €35.30. It is the relaxed owner Christos and his cool and shady garden with ample car parking that makes this place a haven. All rooms are cool, clean, fridge-equipped and enjoy cooking facilities. After the beach, sip on a cold beer in the garden with Christos and the other guests.

**Hotels** *Hotel Livykon* (☎ 2832 031 216, fax 2832 031 420, *Plakias*) Singles/doubles €17.60/23.50. This fairly ordinary hotel with OK rooms is on the seafront. The room rate does at least include air-conditioning.

*Horizon Beach* (☎ 2832 031 476, fax 2832 031 176, *Plakias*) Singles/doubles €32.50/41. Horizon Beach is right outside the town centre in a quiet location overlooking the beach.

*Alianthos Beach* (☎ 2832 031 851, fax 2832 031 197, e *alianthosbeach@hotmail .com, Plakias*) Singles/doubles €44/58.70. This hotel is at the western end of the beach and has a pool and air-conditioned rooms with TV and fridge.

*Neos Alianthos Garden* (☎ 2832 031 280, fax 2832 031 282, e *alianthos@otenet .gr, w www.alianthos.gr, Plakias*) Singles/ doubles €47/61.60 This place is at the entrance to town next to the road overlooking the sea. It's comfortably furnished in traditional Cretan style and has two pools.

## Places to Eat

With one or two exceptions most of the waterfront restaurants that tout picture menus are mediocre and bland. Choose assiduously.

*Nikos Souvlaki* (☎ 2832 031 921, *Plakias*) Mixed grill €4.70. Popular with packies and just inland from Monza Travel Agency, this is a good souvlaki place, where a monster mixed grill of gyros, souvlaki, sausage, hamburger and chips won't break the bank.

*Kri Kri* (☎ 2832 032 223) Pizzas (€3.50-6.75). Pizzas don't come any better than at Kri Kri, near the bus stop. The vegetarian-designed 'rustic' pizza (€4) is a good choice from its long list of pizza combos.

*Taverna Sofia* (☎ 2832 031 333, *Plakias*) Cretan specials €3-5.90. In business since 1969, Sofia's is a solid choice. Check the meals on display from the trays in the window. The jovial gastronome owner recommends lamb in yogurt (€5.90).

*Taverna Christos* (☎ 2832 031 472, *Plakias*) Mains €3.50-9. One of the best waterfront tavernas, is this romantic terrace overlooking the sea. It has a good choice of main dishes.

*O Tasomanolis* (☎ 2832 031 129, *Plakias*) Fish €32.50kg. On the western end of the beach try O Tasomanolis for an excellent array of local specialities as well as fish.

*Siroko* (☎ 2832 032 055, *Plakias*) Mains €3.50-5.60. Further along from Tasomanolis, Siroko is a family-run place popular with travellers. Try the lamb in egg and lemon sauce (€5.60) or a mixed seafood grill (€7). Vegetarians are also catered for.

## Entertainment

Plakias has a good nightlife scene in the summer. Travellers tend to gravitate to a couple of key hang-outs.

*Ostraco* (☎ 2832 031 710, *Plakias*) Night-cruisers usually hit Ostraco between 10pm and 1am for '70s and '80s retro rock. Ostraco is also Plakias' Internet cafe. Send emails if sculling vodkas gets you down.

*Meltemi* (*Plakias*) Long drinks €4.10. Just out of earshot of Plakias' sleepers on the eastern side, Meltemi kicks in at around 2am. Be prepared for a long night!

## Getting There & Away

Plakias has good bus connections in summer, but virtually none in winter. A timetable is displayed at the bus stop. Summer services have five buses a day to Rethymno (€3.10, one hour) and one to Hora Sfakion. In winter there are two buses a day to Rethymno, one on Sunday. It's possible to get to Agia Galini from Plakias by catching a Rethymno bus to the Koxare junction (referred to as Bale on timetables) and waiting for a bus to Agia Galini.

## Getting Around

Odyssia (☎ 2832 031 596), on the waterfront, has a large range of motorcycles and mountain bikes. Cars Allianthos (☎ 2832 031 851) is a reliable car-hire outlet.

## AROUND PLAKIAS
### Myrthios Μύρθιος
postcode 740 60 • pop 224

This pleasant village is perched on a hillside overlooking Plakias and the surrounding coast. Apart from taking in the views, the main activity is walking, which you'll be doing a lot of unless you have your own transport.

**Places to Stay & Eat** *Niki's Studios & Rooms* (☎ 2832 031 593, Myrthios) Singles/doubles with bath €13.20/19, studio for 2 people €26.50. The comfortable Niki's is one of the domatia options in the village. It is just below Restaurant Panorama.

*Restaurant Panorama* (☎ 2832 032 077, Myrthios) Mains €4-5. This place lives up to its name; it has great views. It also does good food, including vegetarian dishes and delicious desserts.

*Plateia* (☎ 2832 031 560, Myrthios) Mains €3.50-5.50. Preferred by Greeks, Plateia has equally good views and food that appeals to a more discerning local palate. Pork with vegetables (€5) is a good bet.

### Moni Preveli Μονή Πρέβελη

The well-maintained Moni Preveli (☎ 2832 031 246, Preveli; admission to monastery & museum €2; open 8am-7pm mid-Mar–May, 8am-1.30pm & 3.30pm-7.30pm June-Oct) stands in splendid isolation high above the Libyan Sea. From the car park outside the monastery, there's a lookout with a panoramic view over the southern coast. It might be worthwhile making the trip for the view alone but the monastery itself has an interesting history. The origins of the monastery are unclear because most historical documents were lost in the many attacks inflicted upon it over the centuries. The year '1701' is carved on the monastery fountain but it may have been founded much earlier.

Like most of Crete's monasteries, it played a significant role in the islanders' rebellion against Turkish rule. It became a centre of resistance during 1866, causing the Turks to set fire to it and destroy surrounding crops. After the Battle of Crete in WWII, many Allied soldiers were sheltered here by Abbot Agathangelos before their evacuation to Egypt. In retaliation, the Germans plundered the monastery.

The monastery's **museum** contains a candelabra presented by grateful British soldiers after the war. Built in 1835, the church is worth a visit for the wonderful icon screen containing a gaily painted *Adam and Eve in Paradise* by the monk Mihail Prevelis.

From the road to the monastery, a road leads downhill to a large car park from where a steep foot track leads down to Preveli Beach.

**Getting There & Away** In summer there are two buses a day from Rethymno to Moni Preveli.

### Preveli Beach Παραλία Πρέβελη

Preveli Beach – known officially as Paralia Finikodasous (Palm Beach) – at the mouth of the Kourtaliotis Gorge, is one of Crete's most photographed and popular beaches. The river Megalopotamos meets the back end of the beach before it conveniently loops around its assorted bathers and empties into the Libyan Sea. It's fringed with oleander bushes and palm trees and used to be popular with freelance campers before even that simple pleasure was officially outlawed. The beach is mainly sand, has some natural shade at either end – though umbrellas and loungers can be hired – and enjoys cool and clean protected water which is ideal for swimming and skin-diving. If you don't bring your own supplies, there are a couple of seasonal snack bars.

Walk up the palm-lined banks of the river and you'll come to cold, freshwater pools ideal for a swim. Hire a pedal boat, if you

RETHYMNO & CENTRAL CRETE

## The Prevelly Way

In August 1941 Australian soldier Geoff Edwards was caught up in the Battle of Crete and cornered by invading German troops. Rescued by a shepherd in the harsh mountains of southern Crete he was delivered to the safety and protection of the monks of the Preveli monastery. He was eventually evacuated on the HMS *Thresher* and found his way back to Western Australia after the war.

In gratitude for his rescue by the monks at Preveli he built and dedicated a chapel at a settlement in the south of Western Australia that he called Prevelly. St John the Theologian Chapel of Prevelly was consecrated and given to the monks and villagers surrounding the Preveli Monastery while various units from the Australian Army contributed funds and material for the furnishing of the chapel. The opening ceremony took place in 1979.

Over the years Mr Edwards contributed various memorial gifts to the monastery including an annual student scholarship for a university student from the prefectures of Hania, Rethymno and Iraklio, and a Memorial Water Fountain which was built in the grounds of the Preveli Monastery. In 2000, he established a Shrine of Peace and Remembrance overlooking the Libyan Sea near the monastery. His book *The Road to Prevelly* documents his experiences and is on display in the monastery's museum.

feel less strenuous. A steep path leads down to the beach from a car park below Moni Preveli, or you can drive to within several hundred metres of the beach by following a signposted 5km dirt road (driveable) from a stone bridge to the left just off the Moni Preveli main road. From the end of the dirt road walk west along a 500m access track over the headland and you're home.

You can get to Preveli from Plakias by boat in summer for €8.80 return or by taxi boat from Agia Galini for €17.50 return.

### Beaches between Plakias & Preveli

Between Plakias and Preveli Beach there are several secluded coves popular with freelance campers and nudists. Some are within walking distance of Plakias, via Damnoni Beach. To reach them ascend the path behind the Plakias Bay Hotel. Just before the track starts to descend, turn right into an olive grove.

At the first T-junction turn left and at the second turn right. Where six tracks meet, take the one signposted to the beach. Walk to the end of Damnoni Beach and take the track to the right, which passes above the coves. Damnoni Beach itself is pleasant out of high season, despite being dominated by the giant Hapimag tourist complex.

### AGIA GALINI Αγία Γαλήνη
postcode 740 56 • pop 1009

Agia Galini (A-ya Ga-**lee**-nee) is another erstwhile picturesque fishing village which this time really has gone down the tubes due to an overdose of tourism.

Hemmed in against the sea by large sandstone cliffs and phalanxes of hotels and domatia, Agia Galini is rather claustrophobic – an ambience which is made worse by an ugly cement-block littered harbour.

Before the advent of mass tourism Agia Galini was a port of the ancient settlement of Sybritos. At the turn of the century it was populated by families from nearby mountain villages who built a cluster of white houses around the harbour.

The late 19th-century village is the core of Agia Galini's would-be appeal even though the shoulder to shoulder crowds at the height of the season obscure the village's undeniable charm and character. Still, it does boast 340 days of sunshine a year, and some places do remain open out of season.

It's nonetheless a convenient base to visit Phaestos and Agia Triada, and although the town beach is more dirt than sand, there are boats to better beaches. Ultimately, you would be better off further to the east at Kalamaki.

## Orientation & Information

The bus station is at the top of Eleftheriou Venizelou, the main street, which is a continuation of the approach road. The central square, which overlooks the harbour, is downhill from the bus station. On the way, you'll walk past the post office as well as a number of hotels and domatia. The OTE is on the square. There is no bank but you can change money at Cretan Holidays (☎ 2832 091 241) as well as many other places. There is a laundry just off the main square open 10am to 2pm and 5pm to 10pm daily.

To find the beach follow the rocky path leading left from the harbour. Check your email at Cosmos Internet (☎ 2832 091 262, e damvax@yahoo.com). It's open from 9am until late and charges €3.50 per hour.

## Organised Tours

*Monza Travel* (☎ 2832 091 278) offers boat excursions to Preveli for €15, a day-long fishing excursion for €21, and a boat trip to the lovely beach of Agios Pavlos for €9.

*Cretan Holidays* offers minibus tours to Knossos for €35.30, a tour of southern Crete that includes Zaros and Phaestos for €29.50 and a tour of western Crete that includes Moni Arkadiou, Lake Kournas and Rethymno for €32.50.

## Places to Stay

There is no shortage of places to stay in Agia Galini at every price level. However, you may have trouble finding the room of your dreams at the height of the season. The village is a popular destination for the package-tour market and up to 90% of the hotels and studios are pre-booked by tour operators. Still, you will generally find that the price-quality ratio is quite high, and you can always bargain.

**Camping** *Agia Galini Camping* (☎ 2832 091 386, Agia Galini) Person/tent €3.80/2.30. This camping ground is next to the beach, 2.5km east of the town. It is signposted from the Iraklio-Agia Galini road. The site is well-shaded and has a restaurant, snack bar and minimarket.

**Domatia** *Candia Rooms* (☎ 2832 091 203, Agia Galini) Singles/doubles with bath €14.70/17.50. This place has very basic rooms. To get there take the first left opposite the post office.

*Areti* (☎ 2832 091 240, Agia Galini) Singles/doubles with bath €17.60/29.50. This place with pleasant balconied rooms is on the road to the village.

*Agapitos* (☎ 2832 091 164, Agia Galini) Singles/doubles €20.50/26.50, 5-person apartment with patio €35.30. This place boasts studios with fans.

*Stohos Rooms* (☎ 2832 091 433, Agia Galini) Double/triple studios €36/39. This is the only accommodation on the beach.

**Hotels** *Hotel Rea* (☎ 2832 091 390, fax 2832 091 196, Agia Galini) Singles/doubles €20.50/26.50. Nearer to the beach is a small, modern hotel that offers tidy rooms. You will find it at the bottom of the main road on the right.

*Hotel Selena* (☎ 2832 091 273, Agia Galini) Singles/doubles with private bathroom €29.50/35.30. Open all year. The rooms here are D-class. To reach the hotel, walk downhill from the bus station, turn left after the post office, take the second right and turn left at the steps.

*Hotel Kissandros* (☎/fax 2832 091 406, Agia Galini) Singles/doubles €20.50/23.50 including continental breakfast. On the right side of the main road is a pretty, white building overhung with vines that has a roof garden and small rooms with sea views.

*El Greco* (☎ 2832 091 187, fax 2832 091 491, Agia Galini) Singles/doubles €38.20/48.50. At the hilltop leading into town, this newish hotel offers rooms with sea views.

*Hotel Astoria* (☎ 2832 091 253, fax 2832 091 153, Agia Galini) Singles/doubles €45/53 including small buffet breakfast. Hotel Astoria often has rooms available when other places are booked. It's a sleek, modern hotel with air-conditioned rooms that have views of the sea or the mountains.

## Places to Eat

*Restaurant Megalonisos* (Agia Galini) Mains €2.40-3.80. Open 9am-midnight.

Phone numbers listed incorporate changes due in Oct 2002; see p61

RETHYMNO & CENTRAL CRETE

Near the bus stop, this is one of the town's cheapest restaurants, if not the friendliest.

*Medousa Taverna (☎ 2832 091 487, Agia Galini)* Grills €4.50-5.50. Open noon-2am Apr-Oct. In the town centre, this taverna is owned by a German/Greek couple and presents a menu of specialties from both countries.

*La Strada (☎ 2832 091 053, Agia Galini)* Mains €5-6. Open noon-3pm & 6pm-midnight. This pizzeria is on the first street left of the bus station and has excellent pizzas, pastas and risottos.

*Onar (☎ 2832 091 288, Agia Galini)* Mezedes €1.70-5.30. Open 8am-1am Mar-Nov. Meaning 'dream' in Homeric Greek, Onar overlooks the harbour and is a good place to come for breakfast, mezedes or cocktails.

*Alikes (☎ 2832 091 343, Agia Galini)* Snacks €2.70-3.80. Open 9am-1am. At the end of the harbour near the beach, this is a quiet cafe/bar, half-buried behind flowering plants. The location is tops, but the service is pretty underwhelming.

*Madame Hortense (☎ 2832 091 215, Agia Galini)* Mains €6.20-11.80. Open 11am-midnight. The most elaborate restaurant/bar is on the top floor of the three-level Zorbas complex on the harbour. Cuisine is Greek Mediterranean, with a touch of the East. Try chicken in curry sauce (€6.50).

For self-catering there is a *supermarket* up the street from the bus station on the left side and a *bakery* down the street from the bus station on the right side.

## Entertainment

Agia Galini's nightlife centres are all clustered together within a shot glass' throw of each other. Among the more popular watering holes are the following.

*Jukebox Club (Agia Galini)* Open from 8pm daily in summer, weekends only in winter. Jukebox plays Greek music after 2am while happy hour is from 10pm-midnight.

*Paradiso Club (Agia Galini)* Open 8pm in summer, weekends only in winter. Paradise has a rooftop garden-bar. Happy hour is 8pm-11.30pm.

*Escape Club (Agia Galini)* Open 11pm in summer, weekends only in winter. Escape Club plays '70s, '80s and '90s rock. Cocktails go for around €4.50.

*Zorbas (☎ 2832 091 215, Agia Galini)* Fronting the eastern side of the harbour, this is another popular venue covering two floors – cafeteria downstairs, bar next floor up.

## Getting Around

Mano's Bike (☎ 2832 091 551), opposite the post office, rents scooters and motorcycles, and Monza Travel (☎ 2832 091 278) rents cars.

## Getting There & Away

**Bus** The story is the same as at the other beach resorts: heaps of buses in summer, skeletal services in winter. In peak season there are seven buses a day to Iraklio (€4.90, 2½ hours), five to Rethymno (€4.25, 1½ hours), six to Matala (€2, 45 minutes) and six to Phaestos (€1.40, 40 minutes). You can get to Plakias by taking a Rethymno-bound bus and changing at Koxare (Bale).

**Taxi Boat** In summer there are daily taxi boats from the harbour to the beaches of Agios Giorgios, Agios Pavlos and Preveli (Palm Beach). These beaches, which are west of Agia Galini, are difficult to get to by land. Both are less crowded than, and far superior to, the Agia Galini beach. Departures are between 9.30am and 10.30am.

# Hania & Around

Hania is the largest town in western Crete and the capital of its prefecture. This part of the island has some of Crete's most spectacular sights including the Samaria Gorge, the Lefka Ori Mountains and Mt Gingilos in the rugged interior. The rocky southern coast is dotted with laid-back beach communities such as Paleohora and Sougia and the nearly deserted west has two of Crete's finest beaches – Falasarna in the northern corner and Elafonisi in the southern corner. Near the town of Hania is the Akrotiri Peninsula with several interesting monasteries and a few beach resorts.

The prefecture is divided into five provinces: Sfakia that extends from the Lefka Ori mountain range to the south coast; Kydonia, which includes the town of Hania; Kissamos, which covers the western third of the prefecture; Selino in the southwestern corner; and Apokoronas in the east. Each province is distinctive. You'll always have something to do from mountain climbing, gorge-trekking and scuba diving to lazing on the beach and exploring Venetian architecture.

Kydonia includes Hania and the Akrotiri Peninsula and is western Crete's most populous province with 93,460 inhabitants. The coastline is highly developed, especially the stretch west of Hania, but it's possible to find more isolated spots on the Akrotiri Peninsula. The most outstanding geographical feature in the Hania region is Souda Bay, the largest natural harbour of the Mediterranean, which is now used as a naval base.

## HANIA Χανιά
### postcode 731 00 • pop 50,077

Hania is Crete's most evocative city with a wealth of buildings from its former Venetian and Turkish overlords scattered throughout its narrow, stone streets. Don't be discouraged by the carapace of modern development that presses around the Old Town. Remnants of Venetian walls still border a web of atmospheric streets that tumble

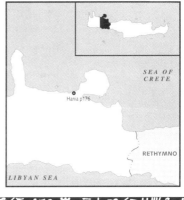
onto a magnificent harbour. The Venetian townhouses along the harbourside promenade have been restored and converted into *domatia*, restaurants, cafes and shops.

The massive fortifications built by the Venetians are still impressive. The western wall is the best-preserved section, running from the fortress to the Siavos bastion. It was built in 1538 as part of a defence system when the Turks were looking to expand their real estate holdings in the Mediterranean. The engineer, Michele Sanmichele, also designed Iraklio's defences. The lighthouse at the entrance to the harbour looks in need of tender loving care these days, but makes a fine silhouette against the sky, especially at sunset.

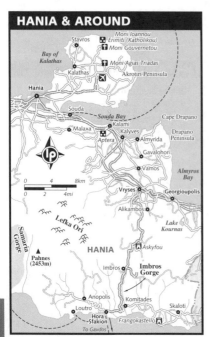

## HANIA & AROUND

Hania's war-torn history has left it with only a few impressive monuments but the city wears its scars proudly. Walk along Zambeliou, Theotokopoulou and Angelou streets in the old quarter and you'll come across roofless Venetian buildings turned into gracious outdoor restaurants. Many of the timber houses that date from Turkish rule have been restored. Even during the height of the tourist season when the buildings are festooned with technicolour beach towels and similar claptrap, Hania retains the exoticism of a city caught between East and West.

Hania is famous for its wonderful old Venetian quarter but there's lots more to discover in Crete's second city and former capital. Hania has a lively tradition of artisanship making it a great shopping city, and the inner harbour is ideal for relaxing in a cafe and watching the passing promenade. The covered food market was modelled after the one in Marseilles and presents a colourful panoply of Cretan products. To escape the crowds, take a stroll around the Splantzia quarter, a delightful tangle of narrow streets and little squares, or head out to the beach. Nea Hora is the town beach, just west of the fortress, but the water is not particularly clean. For better swimming, keep heading west and you'll come to Oasis Beach which becomes Kalamaki Beach after about 5km.

## History

Neolithic people first settled on Kastelli Hill east of the port in Hania Harbour and were followed by the early Minoans who arrived around 2200 BC and founded a settlement known as Kydonia. Great seamen, the Minoans built a harbour and Kydonia became an important port. Little excavation work has been done, but the finding of clay tablets with Linear B script has led archaeologists to believe that Kydonia was both a palace and an important town, that is buried under the modern city of Hania.

Kydonia met the same fiery fate as most other Minoan settlements in 1450 BC, but soon re-emerged as a force. Although little has been excavated that dates from the millennium preceding the Roman conquest in 69 BC, the town was mentioned by classical Greek writers as an important city. When the Romans stormed Crete, the town put up a heroic but futile resistance.

It continued to flourish under the Romans with Kastelli Hill serving as a Roman Acropolis. Its prosperity continued during the early Christian years and it became the seat of a bishopric.

Not much is known about the early Byzantine years (around AD 330) through to the beginning of Venetian rule in 1204. It appears that the Byzantines recognised the port's strategic importance and built a fortress here out of the remains of ancient Kydonia. It is possible that the name Hania dates from this period.

Although the Venetians bought Crete from Boniface Monferatico in 1204, they failed to consolidate their control over Hania and lost it in 1266 to the Genoese. When the Venetians finally wrested this important harbour town from the Genoese in 1290 they made sure that they wouldn't lose it again. They invested considerable time and money in fortifying Hania, constructing massive walls around the town. The first walls were built in the 14th century around Kastelli Hill, and in the 16th century the Venetians walled the entire town as a defence against the pirates who were plaguing the Cretan coast.

By the 17th century the Turks had replaced pirates as the main threat. The growing menace from the east threatened all of Venetian rule and, after a gruelling two-month siege, the Turks conquered Hania in 1645, giving them a foothold on the island. The Turks made Hania the seat of the Turkish Pasha, and turned the churches into mosques. Turkish rule lasted until 1898 during which time the architectural style of the town changed, becoming more Oriental with wooden walls and latticed windows.

The Great Powers made Hania the island capital in 1898 and it remained so until 1971, when the administration was transferred to Iraklio. The WWII Battle of Crete largely took place on the coast west of Hania and the city was nearly destroyed by the German bombardment that was followed by a fire. Fortunately, enough remains so that Hania is still characterised as Crete's most beautiful city.

## Orientation
The station for local buses is on Kydonias, two blocks south-west of Plateia 1866, one of the city's main squares. From Plateia 1866 to the Venetian Port is a short walk north up Halidon. The main hotel area is to the left as you face the harbour, where Akti Koundourioti leads around to the old fortress on the headland. The headland separates the Venetian Port from the crowded town beach in the quarter called Nea Hora. Zambeliou, which dissects Halidon just before the harbour, was once Hania's main thoroughfare. It's a narrow, winding street, lined with craft shops, hotels and tavernas.

Boats to Hania dock at Souda, about 7km south-east of town. There are frequent buses to Hania (€0.90) as well as taxis (€8.80).

## Information
**Tourist Offices** Hania's EOT (☎ 2821 092 943, fax 282 092 624) is at Kriari 40, close to Plateia 1866. It is well-organised and considerably more helpful than most. Opening hours are 7.30am to 2.30pm Monday to Friday. The tourist police (☎ 2821 053 333) are at Kydonias 29. The tourist police office is open 7.30am to 2.30pm Monday to Friday.

**Money** The National Bank of Greece on the corner of Tzanakaki and Giannari, and the Alpha Bank at the junction of Halidon and Sakalid have 24-hour automatic exchange machines. There are numerous places to change money outside banking hours. Most are willing to negotiate their commission, so check around.

**Post & Communications** The central post office is at Tzanakaki 3. It is open 7.30am to 8pm Monday to Friday and 7.30am to 2pm Saturday. The OTE is next door at Tzanakaki 5. Opening times are 7.30am to 10pm daily.

**Internet Resources** Internet access is available at Vranas Studios (☎ 2821 058 618) on Agion Deka (see Places to Stay). The cost is €3 per hour and it's open 9am to 11pm daily. Access is also available at Internet C@fe (☎ 2821 073 300) on Theotokopoulou 53, open 8am to 3am for €3.50 per hour.

**Travel Agencies** Tellus Travel (☎/fax 282 091 500) at Halidon 108 is centrally located and rents cars, changes money, arranges air and boat tickets and sells excursions. It's open 9am to 7pm Monday to Friday.

**Bookshops** The George Haïkalis Bookshop (☎ 2821 042 197), on Plateia Venizelou, sells English-language newspapers, books and maps. The range is not great and the display is rather haphazard.

**Laundry** The town has two laundrettes: Laundry Fidias at Kallinikou and Afroditi at Agion Deka 18. The price is €5.90 to wash and dry about 6kg of clothes.

**HANIA & AROUND**

# HANIA

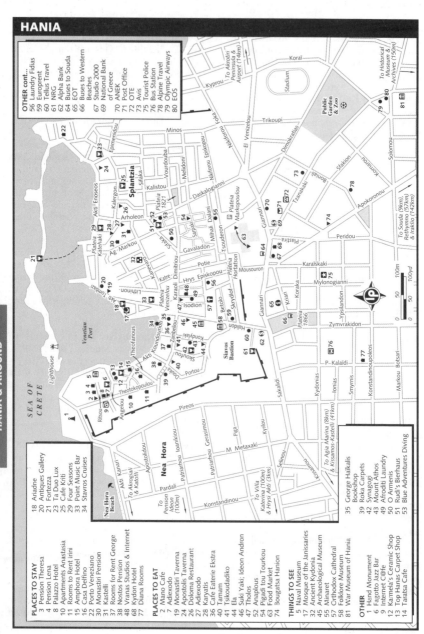

Swimming at Preveli Beach

Traditional mountain lamb barbecue, Anogia

Late night feast on the slopes of Mt Psiloritis, Anogia

Chapel at Preveli monastery

Street vendor, Rethymno

Display tapestry, Rethymno

Rethymno waterfront at night

'Father I'm sure I had the ring when I left home.' An earnest discussion during the ceremony, Anogia.

Waves beating at the sea wall, Hora Skafion

Church detail, Rethymno

**Left Luggage** Luggage can be stored at the main bus station on Plateia 1866 for €1.50 per day.

## Things to See

Hania's **Archaeological Museum** (☎ 2821 090 334, Halidon 30; admission €1.50; open 8am-4.30pm Tues-Sun) is housed in the 16th-century Venetian Church of San Francisco that became a mosque under the Turks, a movie theatre in 1913 and a munitions depot for the Germans during WWII. The Turkish fountain in the grounds is a relic from the building's days as a mosque. The museum houses a well-displayed collection of finds from western Crete dating from the Neolithic to the Roman era. To the left as you enter the museum you'll see artefacts from 3400 BC to 1200 BC. Notice the tablets with Linear A script. Next you'll see vases from the Geometric era (1000–700 BC), and of the Hellenistic and Roman exhibits, the statue of Diana is particularly impressive. In the same section there are vases, idols and jewellery excavated from western Crete. Before leaving the museum, stop in the courtyard and notice the marble fountain decorated with lions' heads from the Venetian period.

The **Naval Museum** (☎ 2821 091 875; Akti Koundourioti; admission €1.80; open 10am-4pm) has an interesting collection of model ships, naval instruments, paintings and photographs. The museum is housed in the fortress on the headland.

Hania's interesting **Folklore Museum** (☎ 2821 090 816, Halidon 46B; admission €1.50; open 9am-3pm & 6pm-9pm Mon-Fri) contains a selection of crafts and implements including weavings with traditional designs.

The **Historical Museum and Archives** (☎ 2821 052 606, Sfakianaki 20; admission free; open 9am-1pm Mon-Fri) traces Crete's war-torn history with a series of exhibits focusing on the struggle against the Turks. There are also exhibits relating to the German occupation and a folklore collection.

## Trekking & Mountain Climbing

**Alpine Travel** (☎ 2821 050 939, fax 2821 053 309, ⓔ alpin@cha.forthnet.gr, ⓦ www

.alpine.gr, Boniali 11-19; open 9am-2pm Mon-Fri & after 7pm some evenings), in the Boniali complex, offers many trekking programs. The owner, George Andonakakis, helps run Hania's chapter of the EOS (☎ 2821 044 647, Tzanakaki 90), and is the person to talk to for information about serious climbing in the Lefka Ori. George can provide information on Greece's mountain refuges, the E4 trail and climbing and trekking in Crete in general.

**Trekking Plan** (☎/fax 2821 060 861, ⓔ sales@cycling.gr, ⓦ www.cycling.gr, Agia Marina) on the main road next to the Santa Marina Hotel, offers treks to the Agia Irini Gorge, the Imbros Gorge and climbs of Mt Gingilos, among other destinations for about €44. For mountain bikers they offer a one-day guided tour for €32 while for racing cyclists an all-in eight-day program for €170. See also the 'Head to the Hills' special section in the Facts for the Visitor chapter.

## Mountain Biking

**Trekking Plan** (see earlier) offers a full program of mountain bike tours at varying levels of difficulty for prices that begin at €25.

## Scuba Diving

**Blue Adventures Diving** (☎ 2821 040 608, fax 282 040 608, Daskalogianni 69) offers a PADI certification course for €325 and dives around Hania for €65 including equipment.

## Horse Riding

In Tersanas on the Akrotiri Peninsula, the **Horseriding Club** (☎ 2821 039 360, Tersanas) offers lessons or trail rides for €13.50.

It also provides a half-day monastery ride (4½ hours) across Akrotiri that costs €39 for a minimum of two people. English saddles are available.

If you'd like to stay, studios, including breakfast, dinner and a few hours riding per day, are available for €205 per person per week.

Rooms are also available for singles/ doubles at €20.50/26.50 a night.

HANIA & AROUND

## Children's Activities

If your five-year-old has lost interest in Venetian architecture before the end of the first street, the place to head is the **public garden** between Tzanakaki and Dimokratias. There's a playground, a small zoo with a resident *kri-kri* and a children's resource centre that has a small selection of books in English.

## Organised Tours

***Tony Fennymore*** (☎ 2821 087 139, ☎ 69-7253 7055, **e** *FennysCrete@hotmail.com*, **w** *www.fennyscrete.ws*) 2-hr walking tours €10.30. From Apr-Jul & Sept-Oct. Historian Tony Fennymore is a wealth of information about Hania's history and culture. Tours begin at the 'Hand' monument on Plateia Talo at the north end of Theotokopoulou. He also runs various guided minibus tours around the region. His witty and indispensable walking guide *Fenny's Hania* (€7.40) is available at Roka Carpets (see Shopping).

There is a number of boat trips that run from Hania and take you to the nearby island of Agii Theodori and the east coast of Hania Bay. The tours include swimming and snorkelling.

***Stavros Cruises*** (☎ 69-4914 045, *Akti Koundourioti*) Cruises €17.60, children under 10 free. This is one good company that offers full-day cruises from Hania.

## Special Events

In addition to the religious and historical events that are celebrated throughout the island, the town of Hania commemorates the Battle of Crete with athletics competitions, folk dancing and ceremonial events during the last week of May.

## Places to Stay

Hania's Venetian quarter is chock-full of family-run hotels and pensions housed in restored Venetian buildings.

The western end of the harbour is a good place to look but it can be noisy at night. Most hotels in town are open all year. Resorts can be found along the strip of beach that runs west of the town centre.

## Places to Stay – Budget

**Camping** *Hania Camping* (☎ 2821 031 138, fax 282 033 371, *Agii Apostoli*) Person/tent €3.80/3. The nearest camping ground is this one 3km west of town on the beach. The site is shaded and has a restaurant, bar and minimarket. Take a Kalamaki Beach bus (every 20 minutes) from the south-east corner of Plateia 1866 and ask to be let off at the camping ground.

**Domatia** *Diana Rooms* (☎ 2821 097 888, *P Kalaïdi 33*) Singles/doubles with bath €14.70/20.50. If you want to hop straight out of bed and onto an early morning bus bound for the Samaria Gorge, the best rooms around the bus station are here. They are light, airy and clean.

***Rooms for Rent George*** (☎ 2821 088 715, *Zambeliou 30*) Singles/doubles with bath €14.70/20.50. If it's character you're after, you can't do better than this 600-year-old house dotted with antique furniture.

***Pension Lena*** (☎ 2821 086 860, **e** *lena chania@hotmail.com, Ritsou 3*) Singles/doubles €26.50/32.50. Lenas is a friendly pension in an old Turkish building. There is a communal kitchen and owner Lena from Hamburg makes guests feel very welcome.

***Villa Katerina*** (☎ 2821 095 183 or 98 940, *Selinou 78*) Doubles from €26.50. This place has a range of rooms including some attractively furnished doubles.

***Rooms to Rent Irini*** (☎ 2821 093 909, *Theotokopoulou 9*) Doubles with bath €35.30. Irini has clean, simply furnished rooms.

***Pension Theresa*** (☎/fax 282 092 798, *Angelou 2*) Singles/doubles €38.20/44. Three storeys of antique-furnished rooms in a creaky old house make this the most atmospheric pension in Hania. Even if you don't snag a room with a view, there's always the stunning vista from the rooftop terrace.

***Monastiri Pension*** (☎ 2821 054 776, *Ag Markou 18*) Doubles with bathroom €32.50. This pension has a great setting right next to the ruins of the Santa Maria de Miracolioco monastery in the heart of the old kastelli. Rooms are simple with shared bathrooms but some have a sea view. There's a convenient communal kitchen for preparing meals. Rooms are fair value.

*Apartments Anastasia* (☎ 2821 088 001, fax 282 046 582, Theotokopoulou 21) Studios €38.20. These are stylish well-equipped studios.

## Places to Stay – Mid-Range

*Kastelli* (☎ 2821 057 057, fax 282 045 314, Kanevaro 39) Singles/doubles €26.50/29.50, apartments €47-58.70 depending on size. On the quieter, eastern end of the harbour, Kastelli has renovated apartments with high ceilings, white walls and pine floors. There's no TV or telephone, but some rooms have attractive views.

*Palazzo Hotel* (☎ 2821 093 227, fax 282 093 229, Theotokopoulou 54) Singles/doubles €35.30/58.70. Outside the old town, on a pedestrian street at the western end of the old harbour, is this restored mansion with wrought iron balconies and wooden shutters. The pine-floored rooms have air-con, fridges, safes and telephones but there's no elevator.

*Nostos Pension* (☎ 2821 094 740, fax 282 094 743, Zambeliou 42-46) Singles/doubles with bathroom €41/64.50. Mixing Venetian style and modern fixtures, this is a 600-year-old building that has been modelled into classy split-level rooms/ units, all with kitchen. Try to get a room in front for the view of the harbour.

*Vranas Studios* (☎/fax 282 058 618, e vranas@yahoo.com, w www.vranas.gr, Agion Deka 10) Studios €53. This place is on a lively pedestrian street and has spacious, immaculately maintained studios with kitchenettes. All rooms have polished wooden floors, balconies, TVs and telephones. Air-con is also available.

## Places to Stay – Top End

*Porto Veneziano* (☎ 2821 027 100, fax 282 027 105, e portoven@otenet.gr, w www.porto-veneziano.gr, Akti Enosis) Singles/doubles €60/76 including buffet breakfast. At the harbour's eastern edge, this is a stylish and comfortable hotel offering large rooms with TV, telephone and air-con. The light fresh decoration is cheerful and there's an interior garden for relaxing.

*Amphora Hotel* (☎ 2821 093 224 fax 282 093 226, e reception@amphora.gr, w www .amphora.gr, Parodos Theotokopoulou 20) Singles/doubles €60/85 including buffet breakfast. This is Hania's most historically evocative hotel. It is located in an immaculately restored Venetian mansion with rooms around a courtyard. There's no elevator and no air-con but the rooms are elegantly decorated and some have views of the harbour. Front rooms can be noisy in the summer.

*Kydon Hotel* (☎ 2821 052 280, fax 282 051 790, e kydon@cha.forthnet.gr, Plateia Agoras) Singles/doubles €82/97 including buffet breakfast. The Kydon is slick, modern and comfortable. The carpeted rooms are soundproof and have satellite TV, fridges, safes, hairdryers and modem ports. There's air-con on demand plus free parking.

*Casa Delfino* (☎ 2821 093 098, fax 282 096 500, e casadel@cha.forthnet.gr, w www.casadelfino.com, Theofanous 7) Doubles €117, apartment €205 with buffet breakfast. This modernised 17th-century mansion features a splendid courtyard of traditionally patterned cobblestones and 19 individually decorated suites. The apartment is huge, palatial and split-level; it sleeps up to four people.

**Nea Hora** *Pension Ideon* (☎ 2821 070 132, Patriarhou Ioanikiou 17) Singles/doubles €18.50/31. This friendly, well-kept pension is one block in from the beach.

*Rooms Stelisia* (☎ 2821 075 785, Papanikoli 3) Singles/doubles €24/€37. The modern Rooms Stelisia has a taverna downstairs and simple, pleasant rooms with balconies and air-con.

*Danaos* (☎ 2821 096 021, fax 282 096 022, Akti Papanikoli 7, Nea Hora) Inside/sea-view rooms €43/50. The best feature of this rather bland, modern hotel is its location across the road from Nea Hora Beach. The functional rooms have balconies and telephones.

## Places to Eat

Dining along Hania's scenic harbour has an undeniable appeal but the restaurants are

HANIA & AROUND

nearly all fronted by touts who can be very insistent and annoying. Avoid these generally mediocre and often over-priced restaurants and head for the back streets. The best Cretan tavernas are housed in roofless Venetian ruins scattered in the streets of Splantzia and the Old Town. Halidon is a good place to grab a snack.

## Places to Eat – Budget

The two restaurants in the *food market* are good places to seek out traditional cuisine. Their prices are almost identical. You can get a solid chunk of swordfish with chips for €4.50. More adventurous eaters can tuck into a bowl of garlic-laden snail and potato casserole for €3.80.

*Bougatsa Hanion* (☎ 2821 043 978, *Apokoronou 37)* Slice of bougatsa €1.80. For a treat try the excellent *bougatsa tyri* (filo pastry filled with local myzithra cheese) that comes sprinkled with a little sugar.

*Mano Cafe* (☎ 2821 072 265, *Theotokopoulou 62)* Continental breakfast €3.70. Open 8am-midnight. This is a tiny place and has very little seating, but offers good value breakfasts and snacks.

*Doloma Restaurant* (☎ 2821 051 196, *Kalergon 8)* Mayirefta €3-4.70. Open 7.30pm-1am Mon-Sat. This unpretentious restaurant is half-hidden amid the vines and foliage that surround the outdoor terrace. It's a relaxed spot to escape the crowds and the traditional cooking is faultless.

## Places to Eat – Mid-Range

*To Karnagio* (☎ 2821 053 336, *Plateia Katehaki 8)* Cretan specialities €3.50-7.60. Open noon-1am. This place is on every Haniot's short list of favourite restaurants. Its sprawling outdoor terrace near the harbour makes it appealing to tourists but it has not sacrificed one whit of authenticity.

*Cafe Eaterie Ekstra* (☎ 2821 075 725, *Zambeliou 8)* Vegetarian dishes €3.50-4.20. Open 8am-10pm. This is a friendly, casual eatery located right in the heart of Hania's bustling old town but the cooking is a modern take on traditional Cretan dishes. There are good value set-price menus and their original salads are excellent.

*Pigadi tou Tourkou* (☎ 2821 054 547, *Sarpaki 1-3)* Mains €5.80-8. Open 7pm-midnight Wed-Mon. This restaurant occupies a former steam bath from the 19th century. Owned by Briton Jenny Payavia, the restaurant features mouth-watering Middle Eastern specialties such as *lahma mashuri* – grilled, herbed and spiced minced meat with pine nuts on skewers (€8), or devil's (chilli) prawns (€11.30).

*Anaplous* (☎ 2821 041 320, *Sifaka 34)* Open 7pm-1am. Cretan dishes €4-6. With four crumbling walls and no roof, Anaplous has nevertheless achieved a surprising stylishness with a few strategically placed urns and some potted plants. A subdued crowd comes here for traditional Cretan dishes and the occasional guitar playing.

*Apostolis Taverna* (☎ 2821 045 470, *Enoseos 6)* Seafood platter for 2 €23.40. Open noon-midnight. In the quieter eastern harbour, this is a good address for fish and Cretan dishes. Service is friendly and efficient, there's a good wine list and a view over the harbour.

*Monastiri Taverna* (☎ 2821 055 527, *Akti Tombazi)* Mezedes €2.50-8.80. One of the few waterfront restaurants that gets the general thumbs up from discerning diners, Monastiri on the eastern side of the harbour dishes up fish and excellent Cretan fare. Try lamb in oil and wine sauce (€7) or *staka* with eggs (€5.10).

*Tamam* (☎ 2821 058 639, *Zambeliou 49)* Vegetarian specials €3-5.50. Open 1pm-12.30am. Locals find most Old Town restaurants too touristy but Tamam has inspired a loyal following among the trendy set. Housed in old Turkish baths, this atmospheric place presents a superb array of vegetarian specialties.

*Ela* (☎ 2821 074 128, *Kondylaki 47)* Special dishes €6.20-9.40. Open noon-1am. Dating from the 14th century, the building of Ela was first a soap factory, then a school, distillery and cheese-processing plant. Now Ela serves up a well-executed array of Cretan specialties while local musicians create a lively ambience on summer evenings.

*Tholos* (☎ 2821 046 725, *Agion Deka 36)* Meat dishes €7-13.20. Open noon-midnight.

The fish dishes are good but the speciality at Tholos is meat. The restaurant prides itself on its cooked-to-order steaks and tender veal.

**Tsikoudadiko** (☎ 2821 072 873, Zambeliou 31) Cretan specials €4-7.50. Open noon-midnight. Tsikoudadiko has all the signs of being a tourist trap, including a tout outside ready to hook all passers-by and the dreaded 'international' food. Despite all that, the kitchen turns out honest Cretan cooking and the roofless plant-filled interior is a delight.

**Adiexodo** (☎ 2821 098 882, Angelou 36-38) Mezedes €2-5.90. Open noon-3pm & 7pm-midnight. The back-to-basics cuisine at Adiexodo provides a richly satisfying meal. Locals come here for the food and the live music on summer nights, packing the tables inside and outside on the narrow pedestrian street.

**Karyatis** (☎ 2821 055 600, Katehaki 12) Italian mains €8.80-11.80. Open noon-3pm & 6pm-midnight. You may hear the strains of Italian opera emanating from even before you come to the wide outdoor patio. The Greek dishes are standard but the pizza and pastas are well above average.

## Places to Eat – Top End

**Akrogiali** (☎ 2821 071 110, Akti Papanikoli 20, Nea Hora) Open 7pm-midnight Mon-Sat. Fish €32.50kg. Most people consider Akrogiali the best seafood restaurant in Hania. The fish is so fresh it's practically wiggling on the plate and the accompaniments are superb. The light airy restaurant opens onto the seafront giving you a great view of the sunset.

**Katofli** (☎ 2821 098 621, Akti Papanikoli 13, Nea Hora) Mains €5.90-11.80. Open noon-3pm & 7pm-midnight. The rustic decor at Katofli makes a pleasant backdrop for the excellent seafood. Try the *kakavia* (fish soup) and wash it down with one of the restaurant's good local wines.

**Suki Yaki** (☎ 2821 074 264, Halidon 28) Open noon-midnight. Set menu for two €25-35. This elaborate Chinese-Thai restaurant offers an intriguing change from Cretan food. The menu is varied and you can eat in the courtyard under an ancient plane tree. There's also an extensive wine list of local and imported wines.

## Entertainment

**Cafes/Bars** Funky rock and roll joints play the dominant role in Hania's nightlife scene but there are also some cosy spots for jazz, light rock and Cretan music. When Haniotes want to party the night away in a disco, they're likely to head out to Platanias, a coastal resort about 11km west of Hania. Try these for something more local.

**Cafe Kriti** (☎ 2821 058 661, Kalergon 22) Open 6pm-1am. Music starts after 8.30pm. This is a rough-and-ready joint with a decorative scheme that relies on saws, pots, old sewing machines and animal heads, but it's the best place in Hania to hear live Cretan music.

**Ideon Andron** (☎ 2821 095 598, Halidon 26) Open noon-midnight. In the middle of busy, touristy Halidon, this place offers a more sophisticated atmosphere. It has discreet music, a garden setting and serves up good mezedes.

**Fagotto Jazz Bar** (☎ 2821 071 887, Angelou 16) Open 7pm-2am. Black-and-white photographs of jazz greats line the walls here. It's housed in a restored Venetian building and offers the smooth sounds of jazz and light rock. Sometimes there's a live jazz group in summer.

**Point Music Bar** (☎ 2821 057 556, Sourmeli 2) Open 9.30pm-2am. This is a good rock bar for those allergic to techno. When the interior gets steamy you can cool off on the 1st-floor balcony overlooking the harbour.

**Taratsa Cafe** (☎ 2821 074 960, Akti Koundourioti 54) Open 8am-1am. On the waterfront, this place plays rock music at a volume that renders conversation possible only for lip readers but you can escape to the outdoor terrace.

**Ariadne** (☎ 2821 050 987, Akti Tombazi 2) Open 10am-1am. Formerly a disco, Ariadne has taken on a sleek modern look and now uses its excellent sound system to play a variety of music. Usually there's jazz early in the evening and rock later on.

HANIA & AROUND

There's a wide range of beverages on offer and some mezedes.

**Fortezza** (☎ *2821 046 546, Old Harbour*) Open 10am-1am Apr-Oct. This cafe/bar/restaurant installed in the old Venetian ramparts is the best place in town for a sunset drink. A free barge takes you across the water from the bottom of Sarpidona to the sea wall wrapping around the harbour. From the rooftop bar, there's a splendid view of the Venetian harbour.

**Four Seasons** (☎ *2821 055 583, Akti Tombazi 29*) Open 10am-1am. Drinks around €5.90. This rock bar on the harbour attracts a fashionable group of young Haniotes. The harbourside terrace is always full and the atmosphere is friendly.

**Ta Duo Lux** (☎ *2821 052 519, Sarpidona 8*) Open 10am-midnight. If Che Guevara was alive and in Hania, he'd feel at home in this 'alternative cafe'. The music is Latin American, there's plenty of reading material of a counter-cultural nature strewn about, and the cosy seating is perfect for plotting revolutions.

**Rudi's Bierhaus** (☎ *2821 050 824, Sifaka 26*) Open 6pm-midnight Tues-Sun. Austrian Rudi Riegler packs this tiny bar with fine Belgian *guezes* and *krieks* as well as other excellent beers. He also serves some of the best mezedes in town.

**Synagogi** (☎ *2821 096 797, Skoufou 15*) Housed in a roofless Venetian building that was once a synagogue, Synagogi serves up fresh fruit juices, coffee, drinks and snacks. The stone and wooden interior is stunning and there's a good selection of rock music playing in the background.

**Discos** NRG (☎ *2821 072 768, Halidon 2*) Open midnight-5am. Most people head out to the sizzling nightlife at Platanias but if you want to party in town, take the first narrow passage on Halidon next to the Hania Exchange Bank and you'll come to Hania's main disco. The crowd runs from 18 to 21 and the music is deep house and techno.

## Shopping

Hania offers the best combination of souvenir hunting and shopping for crafts on the island. The main street is Halidon, which is impossible to avoid since it connects the inner town with the harbour. Skrydlof is 'leather lane' with good quality handmade boots, sandals and bags. There's also an outdoor market Saturday mornings from 7am to 7pm on Minoös where you can pick up fruits, vegetables, local products and cheap clothes.

**Roka Carpets** (☎ *2821 074 736, Zambeliou 61*) You can watch Mihalis Manousakis weave his wondrous rugs on a 400-year-old loom using methods that have remained essentially unchanged since Minoan times. This is one of the few places in Crete where you can buy genuine, handwoven goods. Prices begin at €23.50 for a small rug.

**Karmela's Ceramic Shop** (☎ *2821 040 487, Angelou 7*) Karmela's produces ceramics using ancient techniques and also displays unusual jewellery handcrafted by young Greek artisans.

**Top Hanas Carpet Shop** (☎ *2821 058 571, Angelou 3*) This place specialises in old Cretan *kilims* (flat-woven rugs) that were traditional dowry gifts; prices start at €88.

**Hania District Association of Handicrafts Showroom** (☎ *2821 056 386, Akti Tombazi 15*) The embroidery, weaving and ceramics are well-executed but the sculptures of Greek mythological figures are unusually fine.

**The Antiques Gallery** (☎ *69-9442 7070, Akti Tombazi 1*) Next to the Mosque of the Janissaries, most of the stuff here is too bulky to tuck into your suitcase, but, in addition to framed paintings and old furniture, there are more unusual odds and ends dating from the Turkish occupation.

**O Armenis** (☎ *2821 054 434, Sifaka 29*) The owner Apostolos Pahtikos has been making traditional Cretan knives since he was 13. You can watch him work as he matches the blade to the carefully carved handle. A finely honed kitchen knife costs €14.70.

**Mount Athos** (☎ *2821 088 375, Kondylaki 12*) Mount Athos offers handmade icons but the best deals are had on the handmade chess sets using figures from Greek mythology.

*Studio 2000 (☎ 2821 043 214, Plateia Agoras 15)* Catering to Cretan tastes for both popular and folk music, Studio 2000 is a good place to pick up a wide range of cassettes or CDs.

## Getting There & Away

**Air** Olympic Airways has at least four flights a day to Athens (€53-76.60). There are also two flights a week to Thessaloniki (€103.30). The Olympic Airways office (☎ 2821 057 701) is at Tzanakaki 88.

Aegean Airlines (☎ 2821 063 366, fax 282 063 669) at the airport on the Akrotiri Peninsula, 14km from Hania, has three daily flights to Athens (€55).

Axon Airlines (☎ 2821 020 928) also at Hania airport, has flights to Athens twice daily (€70).

**Bus** Buses depart from Hania's bus station for the following destinations:

| destination | duration | fare | frequency |
|---|---|---|---|
| Elafonisi | 2 hours | €7.40 | 1 daily |
| Falasarna | 1½ hours | €4.90 | 2 daily |
| Hora Sfakion | 2 hours | €4.90 | 3 daily |
| Iraklio | 2½ hours | €10 | half-hourly |
| Kastelli-Kissamos | 1 hour | €3.10 | 14 daily |
| Kolymbari | 45 mins | €2 | half-hourly |
| Lakki | 1 hour | €2 | 4 daily |
| Moni Agias Triadas | 30 mins | €1.30 | 3 daily |
| Omalos (for Samaria Gorge) | 1 hour | €4.50 | 4 daily |
| Paleohora | 2 hours | €4.90 | 4 daily |
| Rethymno | 1 hour | €5.30 | half-hourly |
| Sougia | 2 hours | €4.50 | 1 daily |
| Stavros | 30 mins | €1.20 | 6 daily |

**Ferry** Ferries for Hania dock at Souda, about 9km east of town. ANEK (☎ 2821 027 500) opposite the food market, has boats to Piraeus (€20.50, 10 hours) each evening at 8.30pm. Souda's port police (☎ 2821 089 240) can also be contacted.

## Cretan Knives

Given the island's unruly history, it's not surprising that Cretans have a highly developed tradition of knife-making. Traditional Cretan dress for men always includes a knife, often white-handled, as an accessory to the standard black shirt, trousers and boots outfit. Knives have acquired a power that borders on the mystical. Older Cretans believe that knives made during Holy Week offer protection from evil spirits. In eastern Crete, it's considered bad luck to give a knife as a present, while in western Crete, it's considered good luck for the best man or godfather at a wedding to be presented with a knife.

Although the Minoans certainly produced knives, the current method probably developed under Turkish rule. At that time, the handles were made from buffalo horn or mountain goat antlers but since horns became rarer, cutlers sometimes use cattle bones. Unfortunately, customers are also becoming more scarce and the cutlers' craft is slowly disappearing.

A good Cretan knife is hard to find now but you can always make your own. Here's how:

1. If you don't have a goat horn, get a good slab of cattle bone.
2. Boil it for four to five hours in water, ashes and lime.
3. Carve it into shape.
4. Forge a stainless steel blade with a single edge.
5. Emboss the knife with designs or a verse from a *mandinada*.
6. Find some oleander wood for the sheath. Make sure to cut it when the moon is waning or it will soon be oozing worms.
7. Split the wood in the middle and carve out the interior to fit the blade.
8. Cut a thin piece of leather into shape and glue it to the sheath.
9. Fit handle, blade and sheath together, tuck it into your black trousers and look for some *raki·*

HANIA & AROUND

Phone numbers listed incorporate changes due in Oct 2002; see p61

## Getting Around

**To/From the Airport** There is no airport bus and a taxi to the airport from the town centre costs about €11.80. A taxi to Kissamos-Kastelli costs around €23.50 and a taxi to Kolymbari around €14.70.

**Bus** Local buses (blue) leave for the port of Souda from outside the food market; buses for the western beaches leave from the main bus station on Plateia 1866.

**Car, Motorcycle & Bicycle** Hania's car hire outlets include Avis (☎ 2821 050 510), Tzanakaki 58 and Europrent (☎ 2821 040 810 or 27 810), Halidon 87. Most motorcycle hire outlets are on Halidon.

# Around Hania

## SOUDA BAY Ορμός Σούδας

The harbour of Souda is one of Crete's largest and the port of entry if you come to Hania by ferry. The Venetians built a castle at the entrance of Souda Bay, which they held until 1715, even though the Turks had already seized the rest of the island. Souda is now the site of the Greek navy's main refitting station and sees a sizeable military presence in the area.

## SOUDA Σούδα

**postcode 732 00 • pop 5507**
The town of Souda sprang up 130 years ago under Turkish rule but little remains from that period. The town today is pretty uninteresting but is unavoidable if you arrive or leave Hania by ferry. There is a wealth of services including travel agencies, banks and stores all clustered close to the main square and within a three-minute walk of the ferry quay itself. Accommodation and dining opportunities are limited and you are much better off in Hania.

## Orientation & Information

The main street of Souda is 3 Septemvriou that runs parallel to the harbour. The harbour opens onto a large square with travel agencies and cafes. The National Bank of Greece is on the square and has an ATM. At the port is a 24-hour exchange machine. Also on the main square is Gelasakis Travel Centre which changes money, handles air and boat tickets and rents cars. It's open 7.30am to 9pm daily. The post office is on 3 Septemvriou about 100m right from the main square. The OTE is on the same street about 20m right from the main square.

## Places to Stay & Eat

**Hotel Parthenon** (☎ 2821 089 245, Souda) Doubles €27. Right across from the main square is this hotel; there's also a taverna downstairs that serves souvlaki and grills.

## Getting There & Away

Souda is about 9km east of Hania. There are frequent buses to Hania (€0.75) that meet the ferries. There are also taxis (€5.90).

## AROUND SOUDA

About 1km west of Souda, there is an immaculate **military cemetery**, where about 1500 British, Australian and New Zealand soldiers who lost their lives in the Battle of Crete are buried. Beautifully situated at the water's edge, the rows of white headstones make a moving tribute to the heroic defenders of Crete. The buses to Souda port that depart from outside the Hania food market on Giannari can drop you at the cemetery.

## AKROTIRI PENINSULA

Χερσόνησος Ακρωτήρι
The Akrotiri (ak-roh-**tee**-ree) Peninsula, to the east of Hania, is a barren, hilly stretch of rock covered with scrub. There are a few coastal resorts, Hania's airport and a naval base on Souda Bay. There are few buses and the poorly signposted roads meander about making it a difficult region to explore. However, it's a good place to escape the crowds and the peninsula contains a few interesting monasteries.

**Monasteries** If you haven't yet had your fill of Cretan monasteries, there are three on the Akrotiri Peninsula. The impressive 17th-century **Moni Agias Triadas** (Akrotiri; admission €1.20; open 6am-2pm, 5pm-7pm *daily)* was founded by the Venetian monks Jeremiah and Laurentio Giancarolo. The brothers were converts to the Orthodox faith. There was a religious school here in the 19th century and it is still an active monastery with an excellent library. The church is worth visiting for its altar piece as well as its Venetian-influenced domed facade. The monastery is known for its excellent *Agiotriaditiko* wine.

The 16th-century **Moni Gouvernetou** *(Our Lady of the Angels; Akrotiri; open 8am-12.30pm, 4.30pm-7.30pm daily)* is 4km north of Moni Agias Triadas. The monastery may date as far back as the 11th century at a time when an inland sanctuary was an attractive refuge from coastal pirates. The building itself is disappointingly plain but the church inside has an ornate sculptured Venetian facade. This monastery is also still in use.

From Moni Gouvernetou, it's a 15-minute walk on the path leading down to the coast to the ruins of **Moni Ioannou Erimiti** known also as **Moni Katholikou**. The monastery, which has been in disuse for many centuries is dedicated to St John the Hermit who lived in the cave behind the ruins. Near the entrance to the cave, there's a small pond whose water is believed to be holy. On the feast day of St John (7 October), there's a festival here that begins with a vigil the previous evening. His grave is at the end of a cave at the bottom of a rock staircase.

There are three buses a day (except Sunday) to Moni Agias Triadas from Hania (€1.30).

## Kalathas Καλαθάς
postcode 731 00 • pop 121
Kalathas is a tiny beach resort 10km north of Hania that closes down completely in the winter. In the summer the two sandy beaches lined by pine trees can fill up, but Kalathas remains a pretty place to spend the day. It is the preferred weekend haunt of Haniots, many of whom own summer and weekend houses nearby.

**Places to Stay** There are a number of accommodation options, most of which cater to walk-in clients. Rates for cheaper places run from €23.50 to €38. Two of the better places to stay are as follows.

*Esplanade Apartments (☎ 2821 064 253, fax 2821 069 810, e espland@otenet.gr, Kalathas)* Studios €58.70. This is an attractive two-storey structure with a swimming pool. Studios are roomy, light and breezy and have phone, TV and kitchenette. Internet access is available to guests.

*Georgi's Blue Apartments (☎ 2821 064 080, e info@blueapts.gr, w www.blueapts .gr, Kalathas)* Studios €70.50. Signposted to the left off the main road from Hania, Georgi's is a tasteful, rather upmarket complex of rooms and apartments. All are very well furnished and have phone, satellite TV, fridge, kitchenette. There is a guests' swimming pool.

Three kilometres north of Kalathas is the small beach settlement of Tersanas, signposted off the main Kalathas-Stavros road. You could also try looking here for a place to stay.

*Georges' Studios (☎ 2821 039 684, Tersanas)* Studios €41. The studios are a little on the small size, but this neat accommodation block a 10-minute walk from Tersanas is a good option. The studios have the usual kitchenette and bathroom facilities and are in a very quiet location.

**Getting There & Away** Buses from Hania to Stavros stop at Kalathas.

## Stavros Σταυρός
postcode 731 00 • pop 95
The village of Stavros, 6km north of Kalathas, is little more than a scattering of houses and a few hotels located behind Stavros Cove. It's the kind of place you go in order to really unwind and relax. There is no village 'scene' to speak of as most houses, restaurants and accommodation are spread over a fairly wide area. The main cove is a narrow strip of sandy beach dominated by a mammoth rockshelf that served as a backdrop for a scene in the movie *Zorba the Greek*.

There is some accommodation near the beach, but it is shared with a few package travellers who prefer Stavros' quiet lifestyle to the frenetic scene further west of Hania. There are quite a few more hotels and domatia on the rocky outpost about a kilometre west of the beach. Most cater to both packaged and independent travellers.

**Places to Stay** *Villa Eleana Apartments* (*☎/fax 282 039 480, Stavros*) Apartments €47. Hidden away somewhat, but prominently signposted, you could try Villa Eleana which has very roomy, clean apartments with kitchenette, fridge and telephone. Most rooms have a sea view. There is also a swimming pool for guests.

*Blue Beach* (*☎ 2821 039 404, fax 282 039 406, e vepe@cha.forthnet.gr, Stavros*) Doubles €47. Right on the beach, Blue Beach is a low-key resort hotel that welcomes independent travellers. The rooms are comfortable and there is a pool for guests. Air-con is an extra €7.30.

## Getting There & Away

There are six buses a day from Hania (€2.40, 45 minutes). If you're coming by car from Hania follow signs to the airport and then signs to Stavros.

## THE GULF OF HANIA

The coastline west of Hania between the Akrotiri and Rodhopou peninsulas and forming the Gulf of Hania is a non-stop strip of hotels, domatia, souvenir shops, travel agencies, minimarkets and restaurants. This is not the place to come if you're looking for a quiet, relaxing holiday, but the nightlife is good and there are plenty of banks, travel agencies, and car rental outlets along the main road. The strip is almost continuous along the coast for about 13km. Along the road you will pass through former villages that have become little more than entertainment strip malls.

The first strip-mall community you will meet is **Agia Marina** 9km from Hania. While it caters primarily to package tourists, you will find a clutch of undistinguished domatia along the main road. The beach tends to be packed with lines of identical loungers and umbrellas and the water

is rather murky and uninspiring. Nonetheless, Agia Marina is the first port of call for the Hania nightclubbers who head out this way in search of action.

Next along is **Platanias**, 12km from Hania and almost indistinguishable from Agia Marina. It is also a community of mid-range accommodation, fast food grills, bars, clubs and shops. Platanias is made up of a busy main strip and an old town that sprawls over a steep hill on the south side of the road. The streets of the old town are picturesque but touristy and there are great views from the top. The beach, as at Agia Marina, is crowded and mediocre.

Marginally better is the more open **Gerani** at the far end of the strip and 13km from Hania. The western end beach is less crowded, but like much of the beach scene along the Gulf of Hania, it's no great shakes and is better for sunbathing than for enjoyable swimming.

## Places to Stay

*Haris Hotel* (*☎ 28211 068 816, fax 2821 068 393, Agia Marina*) Singles/doubles €42/60. This is a small hotel on Agia Marina beach with air-conditioning and a swimming pool.

*Ilianthos Village Apartments* (*☎ 28211 060 667, fax 2821 060 721, Agia Marina*) Singles/doubles €50/68. The best accommodation in this large resort on a wide stretch of beach. It has a swimming pool, air-con, children's facilities and wheelchair access.

*Lola's* (*☎ 28211 068 345, Platanias*) Singles/doubles €18/20.50. For domatia try Lola's close to Platanias beach and over a snack bar.

*Filoxenia* (*☎ 28211 048 502, Platanias*) Singles/doubles €24/30. This fairly decent hotel, while taking in package tourists, usually has room for independent travellers.

*Alfa* (*☎ 28211 073 571, Gerani*) Singles/doubles €18/27. Alfa is accommodation on a modest level. Rooms are comfortable, if a little small.

*Creta Paradise Hotel* (*☎ 28211 061 315, fax 2821 061 134, Gerani*) Singles/doubles €73.50/94. The best hotel in Gerani has a swimming pool, tennis courts, children's playground and is on the beach.

## Places to Eat

*Maria's Restaurant* (☎ 28211 068 888, *Kato Stalos)* Mains €3-5.50. For a good feed try Maria's on the eastern edge of Agia Marina that serves Cretan and Mediterranean food on a plant-filled terrace. Try the local meat pie.

*Mylos (Platanias)* Grills €3,50-6.50. The best restaurant in the area is this one on the main road. Located in an old flour mill the ambience is pleasant, and the food a notch above the generally bland establishments nearby.

## Entertainment

*Patatrak Club (Agia Marina)* For nightlife this joint is popular with the local crowd as much for the medieval decor as for its selection of Greek songs and its location right on the beach.

*Splendid Cocktail & Dancing Bar* (*Platanias)* Open 9am-1am Apr-Oct. From morning breakfasts to late-night cocktails and dancing, this place does brisk business, especially at night when the interior is wall-to-wall with locals and visitors.

*Utopia (Platanias)* Open 7pm-2am. Utopia is a relaxed cocktail bar that attracts people of all ages who enjoy music from the '60s, '70s and '80s.

## Getting There & Away

Buses running between Hania and Kastelli-Kissamos stop in Platanias, Gerani and Agia Marina.

# Eastern Hania

This north-eastern corner of Hania prefecture contains some of its more interesting sights, such as the island's only freshwater lake, Lake Kournas, and beach resorts such as Kalyves, Almyrida and Georgioupolis,

---

## The Good Oil

The olive has been part of life in the eastern Mediterranean since the beginnings of civilisation. Olive cultivation can be traced back about 6000 years. It was the farmers of the Levant (modern Syria and Lebanon) who first spotted the potential of the wild European olive (Olea europaea) – a sparse, thorny tree that was common in the region. These farmers began the process of selection that led to the more compact, thornless, oil-rich varieties that now dominate the Mediterranean.

Whereas most Westerners think of olive oil as being just cooking oil, to the people of the ancient Mediterranean civilisations it was much more. It was almost inseparable from civilised life itself. As well as being an important foodstuff, it was burned in lamps to provide light, it could be used as a lubricant and it was blended with essences to produce fragrant oils.

The Minoans were among the first to grow wealthy on the olive and western Crete remains an important olive-growing area, specialising in high-quality salad oils. The region's showpiece, Kolymbari cooperative, markets its extra-virgin olive oil in both the USA (Athena brand) and Britain (Kydonia brand).

Locals will tell you that the finest oil is produced from trees grown on the rocky soils of the Akrotiri Peninsula, west of Hania. The oil that is prized above all others, however, is agoureleo, meaning unripe, which is pressed from green olives.

Few trees outlive the olive. Some of the fantastically gnarled and twisted olive trees that dot the countryside of western Crete are more than 1000 years old. The tree known as dekaoktoura, in the mountain village of Anisaraki (near Kandanos on the road from Hania to Paleohora) is claimed to be more than 1500 years old.

Many of these older trees are being cut down to make way for improved varieties. The wood is burnt in potters' kilns and also provides woodturners with the raw material to produce the ultimate salad bowl for connoisseurs. The dense yellow-brown timber has a beautiful swirling grain.

which are more intimate villages than the resorts that spread along the coast west of Hania. There's also the restored village of Vamos and the ancient site of Aptera as well as off-the-beaten-track villages such as Plaka and Gavalohori.

## GEORGIOUPOLIS Γεωργιούπολη
**postcode 730 07 • pop 608**
Although it is no longer the secret getaway that it once was, Georgioupolis retains the ambience of a languid seaside village. Its most attractive feature is the eucalyptus trees lining the residential streets that fan out from the main square.

Located at the junction of the Almyros River and the sea, Georgioupolis is a nesting area for the endangered loggerhead sea turtle as well as hordes of mosquitoes in the summer. Georgioupolis was named after Prince George, High Commissioner of Crete from 1898 to 1906, who had a hunting lodge here. In classical times it was known as Amphimalla and was the port of ancient Lappa.

### Orientation & Information
The main street leads from the highway to the centre of Georgioupolis and contains a number of travel agencies, tavernas and services. Ethon (☎ 2825 061 432, fax 2825 061 269), on the main square, is a good place to change money and rent wheels. It's open 8am to 1pm and 4pm to 9pm daily March to November. There's a Cooperative Hania Exchange Bank, on the main road into the village before the main central square, and an ATM just as you enter the village.

There's no post office or OTE in Georgioupolis but there is Internet access at Alchemist Gift Shop (☎ 2825 061 732, [e] alchemist@otenet.gr, [w] www.otenet.gr/alchemist), that costs €4 for one hour. The shop is open 9am to noon daily March to November. It's on the left side of the main road heading from the square to the small port. There are two beaches, a long narrow stretch of hard-packed sand east of town and a smaller beach to the north of the river and port.

### Things to See & Do
The **marshes** surrounding the riverbed are known for their wildlife, especially egrets and kingfishers that migrate into the area in April. At the foot of the main street in Georgioupolis there's **Yellowboat** (€6 an hour per person) rents pedalboats and canoes to go up the river where you can see turtles, fish, birds and ducks.

### Places to Stay
*Andy's Rooms (☎ 2825 061 394, Georgioupolis)* Doubles with fridge €29.30, studios €35.20-47. To the right of the main road is Andy's Rooms, which provides mosquito nets for guests.

*Hotel Gorgona (☎ 2825 061 341, Georgioupolis)* Singles/doubles €35/42, breakfast €3. South of the village centre along the beach is Hotel Gorgona. This is a quiet place with three floors of large rooms surrounded by flowering plants and palm trees.

*Egeon (☎ 2825 061 161, fax 2825 061 171, Georgioupolis)* Doubles €29.30, studios with fridge €35.20. To the left of the main road is Egeon. The friendly owner, Polly, has installed ceiling fans and screened windows in the rooms, while some have air-con.

*Christina Rooms and Studios (☎ 2825 061 165, Georgioupolis)* Doubles €29.30. Near to Egeon is Christina that has well-maintained doubles with a kitchenette and ceiling fans.

*Apartments Sofia (☎ 2825 061 325, Georgioupolis)* Studios €38.10. This is a tidy white building with blue balconies overlooking the sea.

*Nicolas Hotel (☎ 2825 061 375, fax 2825 061 011, Georgioupolis)* Doubles €41 including breakfast. On the main road entering the village, Nicolas Hotel has doubles attractively furnished in pine.

*Zorba's Rooms (☎ 2825 061 381, fax 2825 061 018, Georgioupolis)* Doubles €30. Across the street from Andy's Rooms, Zorba's has rooms with fridge and a handy taverna downstairs.

*Pilot Beach Hotel (☎ 2825 061 002, fax 2825 061 397, [e] info@pilot-beach.gr, Georgioupolis)* Singles/doubles €64.60/85.

For more luxury try this hotel on the beach outside Georgioupolis with air-con, tennis courts and a swimming pool.

## Places to Eat

*Poseidon Restaurant* (☎ *2825 061 026, Georgioupolis)* Fish €29.30kg. Open 6pm-midnight Mar-Nov. The best meal can be had at Poseidon, which is signposted down a narrow alley to the left as you come into the village on the main road. The chef is happy to explain the varieties of fish on the menu, all of which are fresh and excellent.

*Zorba's Taverna* (☎ *2825 061 381, fax 061 018, Georgioupolis)* Mains €3.50-5. Downstairs from the rooms of the same name, the taverna serves up honest cooking with a predictable range of menu items.

*Taverna Plateia* (☎ *2825 061 567, Georgioupolis)* Mains €3.50-5.30. Just south off the main square, Plateia is unassuming and pretty reasonable with a range of Cretan dishes as well as grills.

*Edem Cocktail Bar and Restaurant (Georgioupolis)* Greek specials €2.60-6.75. Edem stretches along the beach and has a large swimming pool open to the public. Try the 'Greek plate' for two persons (€17.60).

## Entertainment

There's a lively bar scene in Georgioupolis.

*Cafe Avgi (Georgioupolis)* On the main square, this is a popular place for a drink.

*Georgioupolis Beach Hotel* (☎ *2825 061 567, Georgioupolis)* This bar presents live Cretan music from 8.30pm every Tuesday evening in the summer.

There are two or three discos that start trading late in the evening. Some places don't open until July.

*Nembo (Georgioupolis)* Nembo opens its doors at 10.30pm and is just south off the main square.

## Getting There & Away

Buses between Hania and Rethymno stop on the highway outside Georgioupolis.

## LAKE KOURNAS Λίμνη Κουρνάς

Lake Kournas is 4km inland from Georgioupolis and is a lovely, restful place to pass an afternoon. It is about 1.5km in diameter, 45m deep and is fed by underground springs. There's a narrow sandy strip around the lake, but no beaches as such and you can only walk two-thirds of the way around the lake. The crystal-clear water is great for swimming and changes colour according to the season and time of day. You can rent **pedalboats** and **canoes** (€5.90 per hour) and view the turtles, crabs, fish and snakes that make the lake their home.

There are a number of tavernas around the lake and a few simple places to stay.

*Taverna Omorfi Limni* (☎ *2825 061 665, Lake Kournas)* Rooms with bath €17.60. The rooms are smallish but comfortable enough. There is a decent taverna attached as well.

*Limni* (☎ *2825 061 674, Lake Kournas)* Doubles €17.60. Limni is at the turn off for the lake. The double rooms are fine but have no fridge.

*Nice View Apartments & Studio* (☎ *2825 061 315, Lake Kournas)* Singles/doubles €23.50/29.30. On a hill overlooking the lake, this place has spectacular views.

*To Mati tis Limnis* (☎ *2825 061 695)* Mains €3-5. The 'Eye of the Lake' taverna on the shore of the lake is cool and shady and does good Cretan dishes such as rabbit casserole with onions or filling cheese pies *(mizythropittes)*.

The lake is below **Kournas Village**, which is a steep 5km up a hill overlooking the lake. It's a traditional village of whitewashed stone houses and a couple of kafeneia. There's no place to stay but you can get a delicious meal of roasted meat and Cretan specialities at *Taverna Kanarinia* (☎ *2825 096 325, Kournas)* at the end of the village.

As you enter the village there's an excellent **ceramics shop** (☎ *2825 096 434, Kournas)*, run by friendly Kostas Tsakalakis, that sells exquisite vases and dishes at reasonable prices. It's open from 9am to 8.30pm.

## Getting There & Away

There's a tourist train that runs from Georgioupolis to Lake Kournas in the summer, but no other public transport.

HANIA & AROUND

## KALYVES Καλύβες
**postcode 730 03 • pop 175**
Originally a farming village, Kalyves has now become a good-sized resort. Located 18km east of Hania on Souda Bay, Kalyves is popular with Greeks on holiday as well as international guests. The town is spread out along both sides of the main road and boasts a long sandy beach as well as an appealingly low-key village ambience.

### Orientation & Information
All services are located along the main road. The post office and the OTE are on the main road and there's an Agricultural Bank with an ATM. The sandy beach stretches from the centre of Kalyves east to Kalyves Beach Hotel. West of the centre the coast is rockier and most of the domatia are located at this end. Kalyves Travel Agency (☎ 2825 031 473) is in the centre of the village and is a good place to rent cars, change money, find accommodation and book excursions throughout the region. It's open 8.30am to 1.30pm and then 5.30pm to 10pm daily April to October.

### Places to Stay & Eat
Most of the private domatia are clustered at the western end of the village.

*Maria* (☎ 2825 031 519, *Kalyves*) Singles/doubles €17.60/25. Maria has small rooms with a kitchenette and sea view.

*Kalyves Beach Hotel* (☎ 2825 031 825, fax 2825 031 134, e kalbeach@otenet.gr, *Kalyves*) Singles/doubles €55.80/64.60. Open Apr-Oct. Most people stay at this luxurious hotel at the eastern end of town that has a fully-equipped spa, an indoor and outdoor pool and air-conditioned rooms.

*Provlita Taverna* (☎ 2825 031 835, *Kalyves*) Fixed-price daily meal with wine €5.60. For a good meal on the seaside try here. It is on the western side of the village.

*The Old Bakery* (*Kalyves*) Stop in the centre of Kalyves for scrumptious cakes and home-made breads and biscuits.

### Getting There & Away
There are four buses (two on weekends) daily to Kalyves from Hania (€1.80, 45 minutes).

## ALMYRIDA Αλμυρίδα
**postcode 73 008 • pop 74**
The village of Almyrida lies 4km east of Kalyves but it's considerably less developed. It is nonetheless a good spot to hang out for a few days and would probably prove more popular for independent travellers than the more tourist-oriented Kalyves. Almyrida is a popular spot for windsurfing because of its long, exposed beach and there are at least a couple of outfits catering to the bands of itinerant windsurfers who pass through. History buffs might note that there are the remains of an early Christian basilica at the western end of the village.

There's only one road through the village that runs along the beach. There's no post office or bank, but Flisvos Tours (☎/fax 2825 031 337) Almyrida, is open 8am to 2pm and 5pm to 9.30pm March to November. Located on the main road, Flisvos Tours changes money, rent cars, scooters and mountain bikes and is a good source of information.

There's a **water sports centre** (☎ 2825 032 062) outside Hotel Dimitra where you can **windsurf** or rent a **kayak** (€8.80 per hour) or a **catamaran** (€20.50 per hour).

### Places to Stay & Eat
*Rooms Marilena* (☎ 2825 032 202 *Almyrida*) Doubles €20.50. Popular with the windsurfing fraternity is this neat set of smallish but spotless rooms all with fridge and cooking ring upon request.

*Hotel Dimitra* (☎ 2825 031 956, fax 031 995, *Almyrida*) Singles/doubles €44/50 including breakfast. The best hotel in Almyrida has a pool, tennis courts and excellent food.

The beach road is lined with tavernas. Try this one for starters.

*Psaros* (☎ 2825 031 401, *Almyrida*) Special fish dishes €6.50-9.40. Open noon-midnight. Psaros has excellent fish and overlooks the beach.

## PLAKA Πλάκα
**postcode 730 08 • pop 231**
If you have your own wheels it's a pretty drive up to the village of Plaka. The winding

lanes and low-rise white buildings are a world away from the tourist bustle along the coast. With elderly men dozing in kafeneia and a main square shaded by eucalyptus trees, Plaka offers a glimpse of a traditional Cretan farming village. Scenes from the film *Zorba the Greek* were filmed in the main square.

*Studios Koukourou (☎ 2825 031 145, fax 2825 031 879, Plaka)* Studios with kitchenettes €29.30. Signs at the entrance direct you to Studios Koukourou. The owner Eva Papadomanolakos has gone to a lot of trouble to create a typically Cretan atmosphere for her guests and has decorated her place with a variety of tropical plants and flowers. There's also a roof garden with panoramic views over the coast.

## APTERA Απτερα

The ruins of the ancient city of Aptera *(admission €1.50; open 8am-2.30pm Tues-Sun)*, about 3km west of Kalyves, is spread out over two hills that loom over Souda Bay. Founded in the 7th century BC, Aptera was one of the most important city-states of western Crete and was continuously inhabited until an earthquake destroyed it in the 7th century AD.

It came back to life with the Byzantine reconquest of Crete in the 10th century and became a bishopric. In the 12th century, the monastery of St John the Theologian was established; the reconstructed monastery is the centre of the site.

The site is still being excavated but you can see Roman cisterns, a 2nd-century-BC Greek temple and massive defensive walls. At the western end there's a Turkish fortress, built in 1872, with a panoramic view of Souda Bay. The fortress was built at a time when the Cretans were in an almost constant state of insurrection as part of a large Turkish fortress-building program. Notice the 'Wall of the Inscriptions' that was probably part of a public building and was excavated in 1862 by French archaeologists. The Greek Ministry of Culture is continuing to restore the site, installing signs and paths.

There are no cafes or snack bars at the site, but a few tavernas on the way up such

as *Ta Aptera (☎ 2825 031 313, Aptera)* that serves dishes for €2.30-3.50. There's no public transport to the site so private transport or taxi are your only options.

## VAMOS Βάμος
### postcode 730 08 • pop 618

The 12th-century village of Vamos, 26km south-east of Hania, was the capital of the Sfakia province from 1867 to 1913 and was the scene of a revolt against Turkish rule in 1896. It is now the capital of the Apoko ronas province. In 1995 a group of villagers banded together to preserve the traditional way of life of Vamos. They persuaded the EU to fund a renovation project to showcase the crafts and products of the region and develop a new kind of tourism in Crete. They restored the old stone buildings of the village using traditional materials and crafts and turned them into guest houses. They opened stores and cafes where visitors could taste regional products and staged periodic exhibitions and musical evenings.

Vamos is a pleasant stop in this corner of Crete, though the authentic village theme is a little over-rated and artificial. The guest house accommodation, while undoubtedly very tasteful, is rather expensive and seems pitched at well-heeled Cretans on 'country weekends' rather than travellers on more modest budgets.

### Orientation & Information

As you approach on the main road from Hania you'll see the *Taverna I Sterna tou Bloumosifi* (Bloumosifi's Cistern), on the right. The OTE is 20m further on the right and the post office is on Mariakaki, off to the right. The village square is 50m up from Bloumosifi's Cistern. The tourist office (☎/fax 2825 023 100, **w** www.travelgreece .com/crete/xania/vamos) is between the taverna and the main square, on the left. Opening hours are unreliable but if it is open you can change money, rent cars and book excursions here.

### Places to Stay & Eat

Accommodation in Vamos consists mainly of the aforementioned stone cottages, though some less expensive rooms are available in a larger communal building. Most can accommodate up to four people, but there's one two-bedroom cottage that accommodates up to seven people.

*Traditional Guesthouses* (☎ 2825 229 32, Vamos) Cottages €73.50-132. The stone cottages contain kitchens, fireplaces and TVs and are decorated with traditional furniture and fabrics. The *Parthenagogio*, or Virgin's School, is a tastefully decorated building with eight double rooms. This is a cheaper option than the cottages themselves.

*I Sterna tou Bloumosifi* (☎ 2825 022 932, Vamos) Mains €2.40-5.30. This old stone taverna is one of the better eating places in the village. For an unusual dish try tagliatelle and rooster (€5.30).

*Liakoto* (☎ 2825 023 251, Vamos) Snacks €3-4.50. Part of the Bloumosifi's business operation, Liakoto is a cafe-cum-art gallery serving light snacks. It is close to the main cluster of stone cottages. Walk up the hill for 100m, turn right and walk a further 100m until you find it.

*Myrovolo Wine Store & General Store* (☎ 2825 022 996, Vamos) You can buy Cretan products at this little shop next door to Liakoto.

## Getting There & Away

There's a daily bus to Vamos from Hania (€2, 45 minutes).

## AROUND VAMOS

The village of **Gavalohori**, 25km south-east of Hania, makes a pleasant stop if you're exploring the region. The main attraction is the **Folklore Museum** (☎ 2825 023 222, Gavalohori; admission €1.50; open 10am-1.30pm, 5-8pm daily), which is located in a renovated building that was constructed during Venetian rule and then extended by the Turks. The main architectural feature is the stone arches that divide the ground floor of the house into bedrooms, a kitchen, a room for a wine press and a storage room. The exhibits are well-labelled in English and include examples of pottery, weaving, woodcarving, stonecutting and other Cretan crafts. Notice examples of *kapaneli*, which

is intricately worked silk lace. There is also a historical section of the museum that documents Cretan struggles for independence.

**Women's Cooperative** (☎/fax 2825 022 038, Gavalohori; open 9am-8pm daily) This shop is another highlight of a visit to Gavalohori. It sells examples of kapaneli made by local women. Prices for lacework items range from €8.80 to €1100 depending on the size of the piece; the quality is excellent. The cooperative is on the main square; signs direct you to the nearby Folklore Museum and **Byzantine wells**, **Venetian arches** and **Roman tombs** about 1.5km above the village.

## VRYSES Βρύσες
**postcode 730 07 • pop 570**

Most travellers just pass through Vryses, 30km south-east of Hania, on their way to or from the south coast but this cool, pleasant and sizeable village deserves more time. There's not much to do here but the rivers Voutakas and Vrysanos run through the centre of the village watering the giant plane trees along the banks. When the coast is sweltering you can cool off in the shade in one of the riverside tavernas under the trees. Vryses is a market centre for the region's agricultural products and is a relatively new settlement, dating back to 1925.

## Orientation & Information

Buses stop at the crossroads in the village centre, which is marked by a monument commemorating Cretan independence. Following the main street right across the river takes you to tavernas, stores, a supermarket and the National Bank of Greece that has an ATM. Following the main street left, you'll come to the post office and OTE about 100m up the road.

## Places to Stay & Eat

*Spyridakis* (☎ 2825 051 206, Vryses) Studios €29.50. The only domatia is in the centre of Vryses and has large, comfortable studios with a fridge and kitchenette.

*Taverna Progoulis* (☎ 2825 051 086, Vryses) Grills €5. This taverna has average food, but its tables under the river trees make for a pleasant lunchtime interlude.

Decorative wedding bread, Hania

Fortezza restaurant sign, Hania

Hand Statue, Hania

A 'laterna' player in the street of Hania

The Pension Nora, Hania

PAUL HELLANDER

Traditional knifemaker Apotolos Pahtikos, Hania

DIANA MAYFIELD

Battle of Crete reminders near Askyfou

JOHN ELK III

The lighthouse at Hania was built by the Venetians in the 16th century.

DIANA MAYFIELD

Mosque of the Janissaries, Hania

NEIL SETCHFIELD

Sea sponges for sale, Hania

## A Cretan Feast

Here are a few ideas for putting together an original Cretan meal. Serve it with some chilled Chardonnay or rose or, better still, a few shots of Cretan raki.

*Dakos* (rusk salad): you will need the big round Cretan rusks (twice-baked bread dough) for this one to get the best effect. Look for them in your Greek delicatessen. Briefly run the rusks under cold running water for a couple of seconds to soften them up. Place them on a small dish and drizzle some olive oil over each one; top with very finely chopped fresh tomatoes, cottage or feta cheese and sprinkle over a pinch of oregano and serve.

*Kakavia* (fish soup): well-known throughout the Aegean Islands, this dish is particularly popular in the north-east coast of Crete. You will need 1.5kg of a large fish (red snapper, grouper, sea bass etc); 500g of any small fish; two tomatoes; a sprig of parsley; a bunch of celery, two onions; two potatoes; four tablespoons of olive oil; salt, pepper; juice of two lemons. Scale and clean the fish, sprinkle with salt and lemon juice and set aside. Bring a good amount of water to boil in a large pan; add the oil, whole tomatoes, coarsely chopped onion and celery, the salt and pepper and bring to the boil. After ten minutes add the small fish and cook until it dissolves. Strain the soup and add the big fish and potato cubes and cook for about 20 minutes. Add the remaining lemon juice and serve.

*Hohlii boubouristi* (pan-simmered snails): you'll need 500g of good quality cooking snails for this classic Cretan dish. Wild snails, nurtured on Crete's aromatic herbs are the best. Clean the snails by boiling them for a short while in salted water to release the froth. Clean the orifice of each snail with a small knife to remove any membrane or debris. Put a thin layer of salt in a frying pan and place one layer of snails (open side down) in the pan. Slowly cook for five minutes and then add olive oil and cook for a further 10 minutes. Finally pour in three tablespoons of vinegar and one tablespoon of rosemary leaves. Serve the snails with the juice of the pan. Eat the snails with toothpicks.

*Ofti salata* (roast potato salad): for this unusual cooked salad you will need some handy, hot barbecue coals, two medium-sized potatoes, one onion, half a cup of wrinkled olives, salt, black pepper, olive oil and lemon juice. Wrap the washed potatoes in aluminium foil along with the onion and the olives. Place the parcel in the barbecue embers until cooked. When ready (15-20 minutes) remove, slice the potatoes and onion and place, along with the olives, into a salad bowl. Pour over the olive oil and lemon juice and sprinkle with salt and cracked black pepper.

**HANIA & AROUND**

***Vryses Way*** (☎ *2825 051 705, Vryses*) Gyros €1.50. At the crossroads in the town centre, this is a modest establishment that serves excellent *gyros*, pittes and yogurt with honey, which is a speciality of the town.

## Getting There & Away

There are three buses daily from Hania to Hora Sfakion that stop at Vryses (€1.30, 30 minutes).

## ASKYFOU Ασκύφου

**postcode 730 13 ● pop 377**

The road south from Vryses takes you across the war-torn plain of Askyfou which was the scene of one of the most furious battles of the Cretan revolt of 1821. The Sfakiot forces triumphed over the Turks in a bloody battle here, that is still recounted in local songs. More than a century later the plain was the scene of more strife as Allied troops retreated across the plateau towards their evacuation point in Hora Sfakion. The central town of the region is Askyfou that stretches out on either side of a hill. The post office is at the top of the hill with a minimarket and several tavernas with fairly cheap rooms to rent.

As you enter Askyfou from Hania, one sign after another directs you to the **military museum** (☎ *2825 095 289, Askyfou; admission free; unreliably open 8am-7pm Mon-Sat*), which turns out to be the gun and military odds and ends collection of Georgios Hatzidakis. The Sfakian is eager to show you around his collection, which includes various artefacts from wars of the 20th century.

## Places to Eat

***Taverna Askyfou*** (☎ *2825 095 291, Askyfou*) Mains €2.40-4.50. Try this place. It's nothing flash, but it's easy to find on the main road and the food is mainly grills and a few Cretan mayirefta dishes.

***O Barba Geronymos*** (☎ *2825 095 211, Askyfou)* Mains €2.50-4.50. This one is next to the bakery and has similar menu offerings to Taverna Askyfou.

## IMBROS GORGE Φαράγγι Ιμπρου

The Imbros Gorge, 57km south-east of Hania, is less hiked than its illustrious sister at Samaria but is just as beautiful. Cypresses, holm-oaks, fig and almond trees gradually thin to just cypresses and Jerusalem sage deep within the gorge. The narrowest point of the ravine is 2m wide while the walls of rock reach 300m. At only 8km the Imbros walk is also much easier on

the feet. You can begin from the southern end of the gorge at the village of Komitades, but most people begin in the little mountain village of Imbros. Both places are used by gorge-hikers and have plenty of minimarkets and tavernas to fuel up. There's nowhere to stay in Imbros village but there are a few domatia in Komitades. If you start from Imbros you'll find the well-marked entrance to the gorge next to a taverna, just outside Imbros village on the road to Hora Sfakion. The track is easy to follow as it traces the stream bed past rockslides and caves. The gorge path ends at the village of Komitades, where you can either walk or take a taxi to Hora Sfakion (5km).

## Getting There & Away

There are three daily buses from Hania to Hora Sfakion (€3.70, 1½ hours) that stop at Imbros village. Buses from Hora Sfakion to Hania stop at Komitades or take a taxi for about €8.80. The gorge is open daily all year. There is no admission fee.

# Western Crete

Hania is the largest town in western Crete and the capital of its prefecture. This part of the island has some of Crete's most spectacular sights including the Samaria Gorge, the Lefka Ori Mountains and Mount Gingilos in the rugged interior. The rocky southern coast is dotted with laid-back beach communities such as Paleohora, Sougia, Loutro and Hora Sfakion, and the nearly deserted west has two of Crete's finest beaches – Falasarna in the northern corner and Elafonisi in the southern corner. Near the town of Hania is the Akrotiri Peninsula with several interesting monasteries and a few beach resorts.

The prefecture is divided into five provinces: Sfakia that extends from the Lefka Ori mountain range to the coast; Kydonia which includes the town of Hania; Kissamos which covers the western third of the prefecture; Selino in the south-western corner; and Apokoronas in the east. Each province is unique, so you'll always have something to do – from mountain climbing, gorge-trekking and scuba diving, to lazing on the beach and exploring Venetian architecture.

## Sfakia Hinterland

The province of Sfakia extends from the Omalos Plateau down to the southern coast and includes the Lefka Ori Mountains with the spectacular Samaria Gorge. It is Crete's most mountainous region and the most culturally interesting.

Sfakia was the centre of resistance during the island's long centuries of domination by foreign powers, its steep ravines and hills making effective hideaways for Cretan revolutionaries. The Sfakian people are renowned for their fighting spirit which, even in the recent past, has turned family against family in the form of murderous vendettas that have depopulated many of the region's villages.

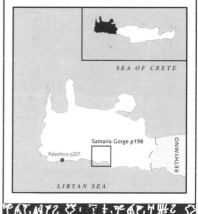

## Highlights

- Trekking the spectacular Samaria Gorge
- Taking a slow loop around the Ennia Horia villages
- Relaxing on beaches such as Elafonisi and Frangokastello
- Visiting remote Gavdos Island – Europe's most southerly point
- Roaming the Gramvousa Peninsula and its beaches, fit for a prince and princess

SEA OF CRETE

Samaria Gorge p198

Paleohora p207

RETHYMNO

LIBYAN SEA

### Road to Omalos

The road from Hania to the beginning of the Samaria (Sa-ma-**ria**) Gorge is one of the most spectacular routes in Crete. It heads through orange groves to the village of Fournes. A left fork leads to **Meskla**, twisting and turning along a gorge offering beautiful views. Although the bottom part of the town is not particularly attractive with boarded-up buildings, the road becomes more scenic as it winds uphill to the modern, multi-coloured **Church of the Panagia**. Next to it is a 14th-century chapel built on the foundations of a 6th-century basilica that might have been built on an even earlier Temple of Aphrodite. At the entrance to

WESTERN CRETE

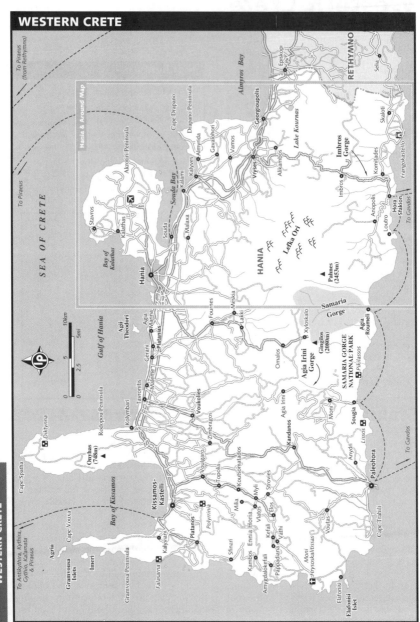

# WESTERN CRETE

the town a sign directs you to the **Chapel of Metamorfosis Sotiros** (Transfiguration of the Saviour) which contains 14th-century frescoes. The fresco of the Transfiguration on the south wall is particularly impressive. The main road continues to the village of **Lakki** (**La**-kee), 24km from Hania. This unspoilt village in the Lefka Ori affords stunning views wherever you look. The village was a centre of resistance during the uprising against the Turks, and in WWII.

***Taverna & Rooms Seli*** *(☎ 2821 067 316, Lakki)* Singles/doubles with shared bathroom €14.70/17.60. This place has comfortable rooms and serves good value meals.

***Rooms for Rent Nikolas*** *(☎ 2821 067 232, Lakki)* €15/18 Across the street, this place has similar rooms and a downstairs restaurant. Both have magnificent views over the valley.

## OMALOS Ομαλός
**postcode 730 05 • pop 12**

Most tourists only hurry through Omalos, 36km south of Hania, on their way to the Samaria Gorge but this plateau-settlement deserves more. During summer, the air is bracingly cool here compared to the steamy coast and there are some great mountain walks in the area. After the morning Samaria rush, there's hardly anyone on the plateau except goats and shepherds.

### Orientation & Information

Omalos is little more than a few hotels on either side of the main road that cuts through the plateau. There is no bank, post office, OTE or travel agency and the village is practically deserted in the winter. The town is about 4km before the entrance to the Samaria Gorge.

### Places to Stay & Eat

Generally, Omalos hotels are open when the Samaria Gorge is open. Most hotels have restaurants that do a bustling trade serving breakfast to hikers and are open at meal times the rest of the day.

***Hotel Neos Omalos*** *(☎ 2825 067 269, fax 2825 067 190, Omalos)* Doubles €23.50.

This is the poshest hotel with comfortable modern rooms that include satellite TV.

***Elliniko*** *(☎ 2825 067 169, Omalos)* Doubles €20.50. This is the nearest to the Samaria Gorge and has simple double rooms. There is also an attached restaurant.

***Hotel Exari*** *(☎ 2825 067 180, fax 2825 067 124, Omalos)* Rooms €20.50. Exari was recently renovated and has pleasant, well-furnished rooms as well as a restaurant. The owners give walkers lifts to the start of the Samaria Gorge.

***Hotel Gingilos*** *(☎ 2825 067 181, Omalos)* Singles/doubles €11.80/17.60. This is the friendliest Hotel in Omalos. Rooms are rather barely furnished but are large and very clean.

***Kallergi Hut*** *(☎ 2825 033 199, Omalos)* Bunk bed €4.50. The EOS (Greek Mountaineering Club) maintains this hut located in the hills between Omalos and the Samaria Gorge. It has 45 beds, electricity (but no hot water) and makes a good base for exploring Mt Gingilos and surrounding peaks.

### Getting There & Away

There are four daily buses to Omalos from Hania (one hour, €4.50).

## SAMARIA GORGE
Φαράγγι της Σαμαριάς

A visit to this stupendous gorge *(☎ 2825 067 179; admission €3.50; open 6am-3pm, May 1-mid-Oct most years, depending on the amount of water in the gorge)* is an experience to remember. The gorge is enveloped in the scent of pine. Along the way you might see owls, eagles or vultures. If you're extremely lucky you might spot the *lammergeier* (bearded vulture), harrier eagle or golden eagle – all endangered species. The gorge's inaccessibility has saved it from the twin evils of Cretan wildlife – timber-cutting and livestock-grazing. As a result, the gorge is teeming with life. There's an incredible number of wildflowers, at their best in April and May. Watch for rare peonies that flourish in the dampness of the gorge. The gorge is home to the *zouridha* (Cretan polecat) and the kri-kri, a wild goat that survives in the wild

WESTERN CRETE

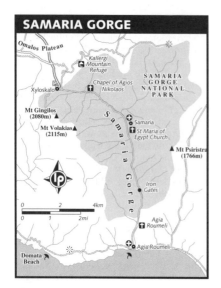

**SAMARIA GORGE**

only here and on the islet of Kri-Kri. The gorge was made a national park in 1962 to save the kri-kri from extinction but you're unlikely to see one of these timid animals.

At 18km long, Samaria is supposedly the longest gorge in Europe. Beginning just below the Omalos Plateau, it was carved out by the river that flows between Mt Psiristra (1766m) and Mt Volakias (2115m). The best way to see the gorge is on a trek but bear in mind that you won't be alone. The gorge attracts several thousand visitors a day in July and August making it uncomfortably crowded at times.

There's a small **museum** (☎ 2825 067 140; Omalos admission €0.60; open 9am-2pm March-Nov) at the entrance to the gorge with exhibits relating to the ecology of the gorge. It's interesting if you have time to spare, but hardly essential. There's also a snack bar and souvenir shop at the entrance to the gorge.

The trek from Xyloskalo to Agia Roumeli takes six hours to complete on average. That is, if you are reasonably fit and don't hang around too much. Early in the season it's sometimes necessary to wade through the stream. Later, as the flow drops,

it's possible to use rocks as stepping stones. An early start helps to avoid the worst of the crowds, but during July and August even the earliest bus from Hania can be packed.

The trek begins at Xyloskalo, the steep wooden staircase that gives access to the Samaria Gorge. The towering wall of rock on the right is **Mt Gingilos**. There is a **Visitors Centre** at Xyloskalo (☎ 2825 67 140; admission (€0.60; open 8am-6pm) with informative displays in Greek, English and German on the flora and fauna of the region. It's worth spending some time here before you make the walk.

You'll descend swiftly – about a kilometre in the first two kilometres of the walk. There are springs of fresh mountain water and several toilets and drinking fountains en route. The route levels out after the **Chapel of Agios Nikolaos** on the right and you'll be amid pines and cypresses. The gorge is wide and open until you reach the abandoned village of Samaria, the inhabitants of which were relocated when the gorge became a national park. The warden's office is in the abandoned village and just south is the **Saint Maria of Egypt church**, after whom the gorge is named. The walk becomes rockier, the path twists and turns and the scenery becomes more spectacular as the rock walls rise majestically on either side. The path narrows until, at the 12km mark, the walls are only 3.5m apart – the famous **Iron Gates**. After a few more kilometres you'll reach the almost abandoned village of Old Agia Roumeli where there are stands selling overpriced drinks. The last kilometre is the dullest, but finally you arrive at the small resort of **Agia Roumeli**, where you can grab some lunch at the Kri Kri restaurant or wade into the sparkling sea.

Hold on to your ticket as it will be collected at the end of your hike in order to help wardens keep track of the people in the gorge. Swimming and spending the night in the gorge is forbidden.

### Getting There & Away
There are excursions to the Samaria Gorge from every sizeable town and resort in Crete. Most travel agents have two excursions:

## A Short Survival Guide to the Gorge

The Samaria Gorge hike is not a Sunday stroll; it is long and, at times, hard. Do not attempt it if you are not used to walking. If you find that the going is too tough within the first hour, there are park wardens with donkeys who will take you back to the beginning. They will be on the look out for stragglers.

Rugged footwear is essential for walking on the uneven ground, which is covered by sharp stones. Don't attempt the walk in unsuitable footwear – you will regret it. The track from Xyloskalo to Agia Roumeli is downhill all the way and the ground makes for generally uneven walking. You'll also need a hat and sunscreen. There's no need to take water. While it's inadvisable to drink water from the main stream, there are plenty of springs along the way spurting delicious cool water straight from the rock. There is nowhere to buy food, so bring something to snack on.

'Samaria Gorge Long Way' and 'Samaria Gorge Easy Way'. The first comprises the regular trek from the Omalos Plateau to Agia Roumeli; the second starts at Agia Roumeli and takes you as far as the Iron Gates and then back again. Although undoubtedly an easier hike, you miss the best part of the gorge which lies near the top.

Obviously it's cheaper to trek the Samaria Gorge under your own steam. Hania is the most convenient base. There are buses to Xyloskalo (Omalos) (€4.50, one hour) at 6.15am, 7.30am, 8.30am and 1.45pm. There's also a direct bus to Xyloskalo from Paleohora (€4.55, 1½ hours) at 6am.

# Sfakia Coast

## HORA SFAKION Χώρα Σφακιών
**postcode 730 01 • pop 366**
Hora Sfakion (**Ho**-ra Sfa-ki-**on**) is the small coastal port where the hordes of walkers from the Samaria Gorge spill off the boat and onto the bus. As such, in high season it can seem like Piccadilly Circus at rush hour. Most people pause only long enough to catch the next bus out but the town makes a relaxing stay for a few days. Under Venetian and Turkish rule Hora Sfakion was an important maritime centre and, as capital of the Sfakia region, the nucleus of the Cretan struggle for independence. The Turks inflicted severe reprisals on the town's inhabitants for their rebelliousness in the 19th century after which the town fell into an economic slump that lasted until the arrival of tourism a couple of decades ago. Hora Sfakion played a prominent role during WWII when thousands of Allied troops were evacuated by sea from the town after the Battle of Crete.

### Orientation & Information
The ferry quay is at the eastern side of the harbour. Buses leave from the square on the north-eastern side. The post office and OTE are on the square, and the police station overlooks it. There is no tourist office and no tourist police. You can change money at many places advertising their services. Sfakia Tours (☎ 2825 091 130) next to the post office is a good source of information; they can change money, rent cars and find accommodation. There is no parking in the village itself but there is a large car park immediately outside the village as well as an extra one nearer the ferry terminal. Cars cost €0.60 per day. There is a useful web site about the village of Hora Sfakion at **W** www.sfakia-crete.com.

### Things to See & Do
There is not a lot to do in Hora Sfakion other than sit around, eat and drink and watch passengers boarding and disembarking from the ferries that run along the south coast. There are two beaches in town, one in front of the promenade and another less crowded beach at the town's western end. A third beach called **Ilingas** is about 2km west of Hora Sfakion just off the road up to Anopolis.

WESTERN CRETE

## Vendettas

Cretans are a distinct breed, formed from the various races that have occupied the island over the millennia. However, ethnic and religious homogeneity has not brought harmony. Cretans are notorious throughout Greece for murderous vendettas that have lasted for generations and caused hundreds of Cretans to flee the island.

Particularly prevalent in Sfakia, a vendetta can start over the theft of some sheep, an errant bullet at a wedding or anything deemed an insult to family honour. The insult is avenged with a murder, which must be avenged with another murder and so on. Modernity has somewhat stemmed the carnage but, ironically, prosperity and increased mobility have allowed would-be avengers to pursue their targets across Greece.

### Places to Stay & Eat

Accommodation in the village is of reasonable quality and value.

*Sofia Rooms* (☎ 2825 091 213, fax 2825 091 259, Hora Sfakion) Singles/doubles with shared bath €14.70/17.60. This is the cheapest place to stay and is one block back from the harbour. There is a communal fridge for guests' use.

*Hotel Samaria* (☎ 2825 091 261, fax 2825 091 161, Hora Sfakion) Singles/doubles with bathroom €14.70/20.50. This decent hotel is on the waterfront.

*Rooms Stavris* (☎ 2825 091 220, fax 2825 091 152, e info@sfakia-crete.com, Hora Sfakion) Singles/doubles €17.60/19. Up the steps at the western end of the port, Hotel Stavris has clean rooms with private bathroom.

*Hotel Xenia* (☎ 2825 091 202, fax 2825 091 491, Hora Sfakion) Singles/doubles from €26.50/35.30 including breakfast. Close to the fishing-boat dock, this place has spacious fridge-equipped rooms overlooking the sea.

*Alkyon* (☎ 2825 091 180, fax 2825 091 330, Hora Sfakion) Singles/doubles €17.60/35.30. The Alkyon has 16 modern rooms of white walls and pine furniture.

*Livikon* (☎ 2825 091 211, fax 2825 091 222, Hora Sfakion) Singles/doubles €35.30/38.20 in high season. Some of the better accommodation is on the waterfront. Livikon has large, brightly decorated rooms with stone floors and sea views.

The adjoining hotels Samaria and Livikon have a *taverna* (☎ 2825 091 320) downstairs that has a good selection of mayirefta and vegetarian dishes. Main dishes cost €2.70-4.20.

### Getting There & Away

**Bus** There are three buses a day from Hora Sfakion to Hania (€4.50, two hours). In summer only there are two daily buses to Plakias (€3.50, 1¼ hours) via Frangokastello, leaving at 10.30am and 5.30pm and two to Rethymno (€5.30, two hours) at 10.30am and 7.30pm.

**Boat** In summer there are daily boats from Hora Sfakion to Paleohora (€8, three hours) via Loutro, Agia Roumeli and Sougia. The boat leaves at 10.30 am and 12.30pm. There are also three or four boats a day to Agia Roumeli (€4.50, one hour) via Loutro (€1.50, 15 minutes). From May to June there are boats to Gavdos Island on Friday, Saturday and Sunday leaving at 10.30am and returning at 2.45pm (€8). From July to August there is an extra boat on Thursday and from September to October there are boats on Saturday and Sunday only.

## FRANGOKASTELLO

Φραγκοκάστελλο
**postcode 730 01• pop 22**

Frangokastello, 82km south-east of Hania, boasts one of the finest stretches of beach on the south coast and a well-preserved fort, a scattered settlement, an eventful history and even ghosts. The wide, white-sand beach beneath the 14th-century fortress is nearly deserted and slopes gradually into shallow warm water making it ideal for kids. Development has been kept to a minimum with most accommodation set back from the shore leaving the natural beauty untouched. Frangokastello is popular with day-trippers, but is an ideal retreat for those who wish to get away from it all for a while.

## History

The striking sand-coloured fortress was built by the Venetians to protect the coast from pirates and to deal with chronically rebellious Hora Sfakion 14km to the west. The Sfakian region continued to pose problems for the Turkish occupiers several centuries later. The legendary Sfakian patriot Ioannis Daskalogiannis led a disastrous rebellion against the Turks in 1770 and was persuaded to surrender at the Frangokastello Fortress. He was flayed alive. On May 17 1828, 385 Cretan rebels, led by Hadzi Mihalis Dalanis, made a heroic last stand at the fortress in one of the bloodiest battles of the Cretan struggle for independence. About 800 Turks were killed along with Dalanis and the Cretan rebels.

## Orientation & Information

There's no actual village centre in Frangokastello, just a series of domatia, tavernas and residences that stretch on either side of the main road from Hora Sfakion to the fortress which marks the end of the settlement. There's no bank, post office or OTE, but there are card phones and a couple of minimarkets for supplies. The bus stops at several spots along the strung-out settlement's long main road.

## Places to Stay & Eat

*Fata Morgana* (☎/fax 2825 092 077, Frangokastello) Singles/doubles €14.70/20.50. This beachside taverna has reasonable rooms to rent near the fortress. It is also the only place you can step out of the water and into your lunch plate. Mains €3.20-5.

*Artemis Rooms* (☎/fax 2825 092 096, Frangokastello) Doubles €23.50. Artemis Rooms has large doubles (with fridge) overlooking the beach.

*Stavris Rooms* (☎ 2825 092 250, fax 2825 091 152, e info@sfakia-crete.com, Frangokastello) Double studios €26.50. This place is on the right as you enter the town from Hora Sfakion. The rooms have balconies and sea views and there is a handy minimarket across the road.

*Corali Rooms to Rent* (☎ 2825 092 033, fax 2825 092 368, Frangokastello) Singles/doubles €23.50/26.50. Corali is conveniently located near the fortress and a minimarket.

*Oasis* (☎ 2825 092 136, fax 2825 092 242, Frangokastello) Double rooms/studios €23.50/26.50. Oasis has studios and rooms overlooking the beach about a kilometre before the fortress.

*Vrahos Rooms & Apartments* (☎ 2825 092 219, fax 2825 092 034, Frangokastello) 4-person apartments €35.30. This is also on the right as you enter town and has a taverna downstairs. The owner has other houses to rent from €35.30-50.

## The Spirits of Frangokastello

The bloodshed of 17 May 1828 gave rise to the legend of the *Drosoulites*. The name comes from the Greek word *drosia* meaning 'moisture', which in itself could refer to the dawn moisture that is around when the ghosts are said to appear, or the misty content of the spirits themselves. It's said that around dawn on the anniversary of the decisive battle, or in late-May, a procession of ghostly figures materialises around the fort and marches to the sea. The phenomenon has been verified by a number of independent observers.

Although locals believe the figures are the ghosts of slaughtered rebels, others theorise that it may be an optical illusion created by certain atmospheric conditions and that the figures may be a reflection of camels or soldiers in the Libyan Desert. When questioned about the ghostly phenomenon, locals are understandably a little shy, but remain convinced that something does in fact happen. Most claim that the older residents of Frangokastello have seen the apparitions. Whether you will depends on your luck – or belief in ghosts.

*Restaurant Kriti* (☎ *2825 092 214, Frangokastello*) Grills €4.50-5.90. This is a beautifully designed structure across from the fortress, elaborately outfitted with several terraces and a forest of potted plants. Try *sfakiano tsigaristo* – a local lamb or goat pilaf dish (€5.90).

## Getting There & Away
In July and August only, there are two daily buses from Hora Sfakion to Plakias (€3.50, 1¼ hours) via Frangokastello (€1.50, 25 minutes). From Hania there's a daily afternoon bus (€5.30, 2½ hours) and there is a daily bus from Rethymno (€4.90, 1¼ hours). A taxi (☎ 2825 092 109) to/from Hora Sfakion costs about €14.70.

## LOUTRO Λουτρό
**postcode 731 36 • pop 52**
The small but rapidly expanding fishing village of Loutro (Loo-**tro**) lies between Agia Roumeli and Hora Sfakion. The town is little more than a crescent of houses and domatia bordering a narrow beach. It's a pleasant, lazy resort that is never overwhelmed with visitors although it can get busy in July and August.

Loutro is the only natural harbour on the south coast of Crete and is accessible by boat or on foot. Its advantageous geographical position was appreciated in ancient times when it was the port for Phoenix and Anopolis. According to legend, St Paul was on his way to Loutro when he encountered a storm that blew him off course past Gavdos Island and on to eventual shipwreck in Malta.

## Orientation & Information
There's no bank, post office or OTE but there are many places to change money at the western end of the beach. The boat from Hora Sfakion docks in the centre of the beach but the boat from Agia Roumeli docks at the far western end in front of the Sifis Hotel. You can buy boat tickets at a stall on the beach that is open an hour before each departure.

## Activities
Loutro is a good base for boat excursions along the south coast. There are two boats a week to **Gavdos Island** that cost €41 including food and soft drinks. There are also excursion boats that do a **sunset cruise** or a **dolphin sightseeing cruise** for €13.50.

### Walks Around Loutro

Loutro is also a good base for walks. It's a half-hour walk west to **Phoenix** (or Finix), an important settlement for the Romans and Byzantines now a cluster of stark, white houses set against rust-coloured cliffs on a narrow cove.

To get there, go past Sofia Rooms, bear left, go through a wooden fence and follow signs to the E4 European footpath. The path takes you over a plain and past a Turkish castle before descending to Phoenix.

From Phoenix, the path continues over cliffs and hills to **Likkos**, a wide cove with three tavernas clustered at the eastern end. Barren cliffs loom over a wide shadeless beach with caves and rocks on either end. The next cove is **Marmara Beach**. It's a long, hot walk from Likkos (over an hour) which is why most people come on excursion boats from Hora Sfakion.

An extremely steep path leads up from Loutro to the village of **Anopolis** which was the scene of Daskalogiannis' great rebellion against the Turks. Now it is a tranquil and traditional mountain village that gets few visitors.

From Loutro it's a moderate hour-long walk along a coastal path to the celebrated **Sweet Water Beach** named after freshwater springs which seep from the rocks. Freelance campers spend months at a time here. Even if you don't feel inclined to join them, you won't be able to resist a swim in the translucent sea. There is a taverna on the western end of the beach that sells drinks and snacks and rents sun umbrellas.

Hotel Porto Loutro is a good source of information for boat schedules and there's a stall in front where you can rent **canoes** for €2 an hour or €6 a day. **Taxi boats** leave from in front of Hotel Porto Loutro, charging €12 to Sweet Water Beach and €20.50 to Hora Sfakion.

### Places to Stay & Eat
*Restaurant and Rent Rooms Ilios (☎ 2825 091 160, Loutro)* Rooms €23.50. You could try here at the eastern end of the beach.

*Rooms Sofia (☎ 2825 091 354, Loutro)* Doubles/triples €23.50/29.50. These rooms are over the Sofia Minimarket one street in from the beach.

*Sifis Hotel (☎ 2825 091 346, fax 2825 091 447, Loutro)* Singles/doubles €26.50/ 35.20, breakfast included. Open Apr-Oct. Sifis Hotel has pretty, well-kept rooms with air-con, fridge and sea views.

*Faros ☎/fax 2825 091 334, Loutro)* Doubles/triples €35.30/41. New in 2000, these spacious, airy rooms a stone's throw from the beach have air-con, fridges and balconies.

*Apartments Niki (☎/fax 2825 091 259, Loutro)* Apartments €36. These apartments have beautifully furnished four-person studios with beamed ceilings and stone floors.

The beachfront is lined with *tavernas* that maintain reasonably good standards.

### Getting There & Away
Loutro is on the main Paleohora-Hora Sfakion boat route. From April to October there are three boats a day from Hora Sfakion (€1.50), three boats from Agia Roumeli (€3), and one boat a day from Paleohora (€7.50).

## AGIA ROUMELI Αγία Ρούμελη
**postcode 730 11 • pop 36**
Agia Roumeli is a shadeless, rather bleak village of houses that are too new and streets that are too neatly laid out to make an interesting stroll. The village has little going for it but a wide pebbly beach that looks pretty good if you've just trekked 18km over pointed rocks. After the afternoon crush of gorge-trekkers has left there's

not much to do here except hang-out in one of the tavernas in the village.

### Orientation & Information
Most travellers just pass through Agia Roumeli waiting to catch the boat to Hora Sfakion. The boat ticket office is a small concrete structure near the beach. There's no post office or OTE and no travel agencies.

### Places to Stay & Eat
*Oasis (☎ 2825 091 391, Agia Roumeli)* Doubles €23.50. The friendly and homey Oasis has simple rooms all with private bath and air-con.

*Rooms to Rent Farangi (☎ 2825 091 225, fax 2825 091 325, Agia Roumeli)* Doubles/triples €26.50/32.50. Also on the beach is Hotel Farangi with its attached restaurant. The taverna is open from 11am to 11pm, April till November. Mains €2.70-5.

*Hotel-Restaurant Kri-Kri (☎ 2825 091 089, fax 2825 091 489, Agia Roumeli)* Doubles €29.50. All rooms have air-con and a fridge and downstairs is a very good restaurant too.

*Hotel Agia Roumeli (☎ 2825 091 240, fax 091 232, Agia Roumeli)* Singles/doubles with private bathroom €25/32. There are many domatia but the best hotel is at the far western end of town on the beach. Many have balconies overlooking the sea.

### Getting There & Away
During the months the gorge is open to walkers, there are frequent boats leaving Agia Roumeli. There are three boats a day to Hora Sfakion (€4.50, one hour) via Loutro (€3, 30 minutes). It connects with the bus back to Hania, leaving you in Hora Sfakion just long enough to spend a few euros. There's also a boat from Agia Roumeli to Paleohora (€6.50) at 4.45pm, calling at Sougia (€3).

## Selino Province

Tucked into the south-western corner of the Hania prefecture, Selino is a pretty agricultural region with spectacular views over the sea and a wealth of little villages notable for their Byzantine churches. The district was named after the 'Kastello Selino' fortress built by the Venetians in Paleohora in the 13th century. The village of Kandanos is the capital of the province and contains two Byzantine churches. Kadros, 9km away, has churches with particularly fine frescoes. Kandanos was a centre of resistance against the Germans in WWII and as a result most of the village was demolished and most of its inhabitants massacred. Most tourists head to the lovely beach resorts of Paleohora and Sougia from where there are many interesting walks and boat trips you can take to explore the region.

## SOUGIA Σούγια
**postcode 730 09 • pop 50**

It's surprising that Sougia hasn't yet been commandeered by the package tour crowd. With a wide curve of sand and pebble beach and a shady tree-lined coastal road, Sougia's tranquillity has been preserved only because it lies at the foot of a narrow, twisting route that deters most tour buses. This is another of the languid south-coast villages that offers the visitor little to do other than relax and recharge depleted batteries for a few days.

The ancient town was on the western side of the existing village. It flourished under the Romans and Byzantines when it was the port for Elyros, an important inland city (now disappeared). A 6th-century basilica that stood at the western end of the village contained a fine mosaic floor that is now in the Hania Archaeological Museum.

## Orientation & Information

If you arrive by boat, walk 150m east along the coast to the village centre. If you arrive by bus, the bus will drop you on the coastal road in front of the Santa Irene hotel. The only other road intersects the coastal road by the Santa Irene Hotel and runs north to the Agia Irini Gorge and Hania. Sougia doesn't have a post office, OTE or bank, but you can change money at several places, including Polyfimos Travel (☎ 2823 051 022), open 9.30am to 12pm and 5pm to 10pm March to

October, and Roxana's Office (☎ 2823 051 362), open 8.30am to 11pm April to October. Both are just off the coastal road on the road to Hania. Check your email at Internet Lotos (☎ 2823 051 191) for €3 per hour at one of its six computers.

### Boat Trips

**Roxana Travel** offers a trip to Lissos by taxi boat for €16.20, to Trypiti for €23.50, and to Pikilassos for €28. All prices are for a one-way trip.

### Places to Stay

There's no camping ground, but the eastern end of the long, pebbled beach is popular with freelance campers. It seems that every second building in Sougia is a domatia or pension.

*Pension Galini (☎/fax 2823 051 488, Sougia)* Singles/doubles with bathroom €20.50/23.50, single/double studios €26.50/32.50. Next door to Aretousa, this pension has beautiful rooms.

*Aretousa Rooms to Rent (☎ 2823 051 178, fax 2823 051 178, Sougia)* Singles/doubles €23.50/29.50. Inland, on the road to Hania, Aretousa has lovely rooms with wood-panelled ceilings and balconies.

*Santa Irene Hotel (☎ 2823 051 342, fax 2823 051 182, ⓔ nanadakis@cha.forthnet .gr, Sougia)* Studio singles/doubles €23.50/35.30. The smartest accommodation is here. Air-conditioning costs €5.90 extra.

*Rooms Maria (☎ 2823 051 337, Sougia)* Doubles/triples with bath €29.50/35.30. This place is a block further east on the coast and has clean, white rooms.

*Rooms Ririka (☎ 2823 051 167, Sougia)* Doubles €29.50. Next door to Rooms Maria is the equally attractive Rooms Ririka, also with rooms overlooking the sea.

### Places to Eat

Restaurants line the waterfront and there are more on the main street.

*Kyma (☎ 2823 051 670, Sougia)* Fish dishes €17.60-41kg. Open 8am-midnight Apr-Nov. On the waterfront as you enter town, Kyma has a good selection of ready-made food as well as fish.

*Taverna Rembetiko (☎ 2823 051 510, Sougia)* Ladera €2.70-€3.50. Open noon-midnight Apr-Oct. On the road to Hania, this taverna has an extensive menu including such Cretan dishes as *boureki* and stuffed zucchini flowers.

## Getting There & Away

There's a daily bus from Hania to Sougia (€4.70, 2½ hours) at 1.30pm. Buses from Sougia to Hania leave at 7am. Sougia is on the Paleohora-Hora Sfakion boat route. Boats leave at 10.15am for Agia Roumeli (€3, one hour), Loutro (€5.50, 1½ hours) and Hora Sfakion (€5.90, two hours). There is a departure for Paleohora (€3.80, one hour) at 5.30pm.

## AROUND SOUGIA

Twelve kilometres north of Sougia is the mouth of the pretty **Agia Irini Gorge**, which may not be as fashionable as the Samaria Gorge walk but is less crowded and less gruelling. The gorge is 7km long and is carpeted with oleander and chestnut trees and is fragrant with rosemary, sage and thyme. You'll see the entrance to the gorge on the right side if you're travelling from Sougia. You'll cross a streambed before coming to olive groves but many trees were destroyed in a fire in 1994. The path follows a dried out riverbed bordered by caves carved into the large rocks. There are a number of rest stops along the way and many tranquil places to sit and admire the scenery.

Paleohora travel agents offer **guided walks** through the gorge for €14.70. It's easy enough to organise independently – just catch the Omalos bus from Paleohora or the Hania bus from Sougia, and get off at Agia Irini.

The ruins of ancient **Lissos** are 1½ hours away on the coastal path to Paleohora (see the boxed text 'Paleohora-Sougia Coastal Walk'). Lissos arose under the Dorians, flourished under the Byzantines and was destroyed by the Saracens in the 9th century. It was part of a league of city-states, led by ancient Gortyn, and minted their own gold coins inscribed with the word 'Lission'. At one time there was a reservoir, a theatre and hot springs but these have not yet been excavated. Most of what you see dates from the 1st through 3rd centuries BC when Lissos was known for its curative springs. The 3rd-century-BC Temple of Asklepion was built next to one of the springs and named after the Greek god of healing Asklipios.

Excavations here uncovered a headless statue of Asclepius along with 20 other statue fragments now in the Hania Archaeological Museum. You can still see the marble altar-base that supported the statue next to the pit in which sacrifices were placed. The other notable feature of Lissos is the mosaic floor of multi-coloured stones intricately arranged in beautiful geometric shapes and images of birds. On the way down to the sea there are traces of Roman

---

## Paleohora-Sougia Coastal Walk

From the town centre of Paleohora, follow signs to the camping grounds to the north-east. Turn right at the intersection with the road to Anydri and soon you'll be following the coastal path marked as the E4 European Footpath. After a couple of kilometres, the path climbs steeply for a beautiful view back to Paleohora. You'll pass **Anydri Beach** and several inviting **coves** where people may be getting an all-over tan. Take a dip because the path soon turns inland to pass over **Cape Flomes**. You'll walk along a plateau carpeted with brush that leads toward the coast and some breathtaking views over the Libyan Sea. Soon you'll reach the Minoan site of **Lissos**. After Lissos the path takes you through a pine forest and then a **gorge** bedecked with oleander and outfitted with some perfect picnic spots. The road ends at Sougia Harbour. Since the walk is nearly shadeless it's important to take several litres of water and sunscreen. If you come June through August, it's best to start at sunrise in order to get to Sougia before the heat of the day clamps down.

**WESTERN CRETE**

ruins and on the western slopes of the valley are unusual barrel-vaulted tombs.

Nearby are the ruins of two early Christian basilicas – **Agios Kirkos** and the **Panagia** – dating from the 13th century.

## PALEOHORA Παλαιοχώρα
### postcode 730 01 • pop 1826

Paleohora (Pal-ee-o-**hor**-a) was discovered by hippies back in the '60s and from then on its days as a tranquil fishing village were numbered. The resort operators have not gone way over the top – yet. The place retains a certain laid-back feel. It is also the only beach resort on Crete which does not go into total hibernation in winter.

The little town lies on a narrow peninsula with a long, curving sandy beach exposed to the wind on one side and a sheltered pebbly beach on the other. On summer evenings the main street is closed to traffic and the tavernas move onto the road. The most picturesque part of Paleohora is the maze of narrow streets around the castle.

## Orientation

Paleohora's main street, El Venizelou, runs north-south. Walking south along El Venizelou from the bus stop, several streets lead off left to the Pebble Beach. There's an attractive seafront promenade which is the centre of activity in the early evening. Boats leave from the old harbour at the southern end of this beach. Kondekaki leads from the old harbour to the tamarisk-shaded Sandy Beach.

## Information

The municipal tourist office (☎ 2823 041 507) is next to the town hall on El Venizelou. It is open 10am to 1pm and 6pm to 9pm Wednesday to Monday May to October. The National Bank of Greece and Agricultural Bank are both on El Venizelou and have ATMs. The post office is on the road that skirts Sandy Beach. The OTE is on the west side of El Venizelou, just north of Kondekaki. Internet access is provided at Notos Rentals & Internet (☎ 2823 042 110, e notos@grecian.net) and at Erato Internet (☎ 2823 083 010, e erato@chania-cci.gr).

Both are on El Venizelou, and both charge €4.50 per hour. There's a laundry next to Notos Rentals that charges €4.50 per wash and €4.50 per dry. Interkreta Tourism and Travel (☎ 2823 041 393, fax 2823 041 050) on Kondekaki sells boat tickets and excursions and is a good source of information. It's open 9am to 1pm and 4pm to 9pm daily.

## Things to See & Do

It's worth clambering up the ruins of the 13th-century **Venetian castle** for the splendid view of the sea and mountains. The castle was built so the Venetians could keep an eye on the south-western coast from this commanding position on the hill-top. There's not much left of the fortress however, as it was destroyed by the Venetians, the Turks, the pirate Barbarossa in the 16th century, and later the Germans during WWII.

From Paleohora, a six-hour walk along a scenic coastal path leads to **Sougia**, passing the ancient site of **Lissos**. (See the boxed text, 'Paleohora-Sougia Coastal Walk'.)

Paleohora is known for its excellent **windsurfing** which is best on the island. The strongest winds blow on the Sandy Beach and usually peak in the late morning and early afternoon.

**Planet Windsurf** (☎ *+44 1273 746 700, fax 746 688,* e *info@planetwindsurf.com,* w *www.westwind.org.uk*) runs all-in packages from the UK to Paleohora and also rents equipment to casual surfers.

Travel agents around town offer **boat excursions** to ancient Lissos (€22) and dolphin-watching trips (€13.20).

## Places to Stay

*Camping Paleohora* (☎ *2823 041 225, Paleohora*) Person/tent €3.20/2. This camping ground is 1.5km north-east of the town, near the Pebble Beach. There is a taverna here but no minimarket.

*Homestay Anonymous* (☎ *2823 041 509, Paleohora*) Singles/doubles with shared bathroom €11.80/17.60. This is a great place for backpackers, with clean, simply furnished rooms set around a small garden. There is a communal kitchen. The owner,

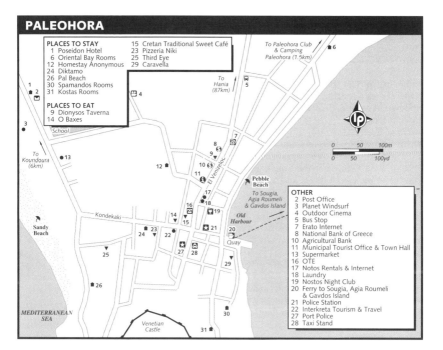

PALEOHORA

PLACES TO STAY
1 Poseidon Hotel
6 Oriental Bay Rooms
12 Homestay Anonymous
24 Diktamo
26 Pal Beach
30 Spamandos Rooms
31 Kostas Rooms

15 Cretan Traditional Sweet Café
23 Pizzeria Niki
25 Third Eye
29 Caravella

PLACES TO EAT
9 Dionysos Taverna
14 O Baxes

OTHER
2 Post Office
3 Planet Windsurf
4 Outdoor Cinema
5 Bus Stop
7 Erato Internet
8 National Bank of Greece
10 Agricultural Bank
11 Municipal Tourist Office & Town Hall
13 Supermarket
16 OTE
17 Notos Rentals & Internet
18 Laundry
19 Nostos Night Club
20 Ferry to Sougia, Agia Roumeli & Gavdos Island
21 Police Station
22 Interkreta Tourism & Travel
27 Port Police
28 Taxi Stand

Manolis speaks good English and is full of useful information for travellers.

**Kostas Rooms** (☎ /fax 2823 041 248, Paleohora) Singles/doubles with private bath €14.70/19. Nearby, Kostas offers attractive rooms with ceiling fans, fridge and sea views.

**Spamandos Rooms** (☎ 2823 041 197, Paleohora) Doubles/triples with bath €23.50/26.50. In the old quarter, Spamandos has spotless, nicely furnished rooms.

**Poseidon Hotel** (☎ 2823 041 374/115, fax 2823 041 115, Paleohora) Singles/double studios €20.50/26.50. The studios here come equipped with fridges, air-con and kitchenettes and all have balconies.

**Oriental Bay Rooms** (☎ 2823 041 076, Paleohora) Singles/doubles with bath & ceiling fans €26.50/29.50. This place occupies the large modern building at the northern end of the pebble beach. The owner, Thalia keeps the rooms immaculate. There's also a shaded terrace-restaurant overlooking the sea that serves decent meals.

**Diktamo** (☎ 2823 041 569, fax 2823 041 581, Paleohora) Singles/doubles €29.50/38.20. This is an attractive two-storey hotel wrapped around a central courtyard with large, nicely furnished rooms.

**Pal Beach** (☎ 2823 041 512, fax 2823 041 578, Paleohora) Singles/doubles €35.30/50. The most expensive Hotel in town is Pal Beach. The occasional bursts of air-con still don't make the rooms worth the price.

## Places to Eat

There are some good eateries in the village.

**O Baxes** (Paleohora) Grills €3.80-5.60. Open noon-midnight. In the street behind the OTE, this is a fine little taverna and does a good job on old favourites like fried aubergine (€2.40), or dakos (€2.40).

**Dionysos Taverna** (☎ 2823 041 243, Paleohora) Cretan dishes €3-5.30. Open 7pm-1am Mar-Oct. The very popular Dionysos is a bit more expensive but serves tasty food

WESTERN CRETE

and a good range of vegetarian dishes from €1.80-4.50. It has a roomy interior and a few tables outside under the trees.

*Pizzeria Niki (☎ 2823 041 534, Paleohora)* Pizzas €3.80-4.70. Open 6.30pm-midnight Apr-Oct. Just off Kondekaki, this place serves superior pizzas cooked in a wood-fired oven and served on a spacious outdoor terrace.

*Third Eye (☎ 2823 041 234, Paleohora)* Meals under €5.90. Open 8am-3pm, 6pm-midnight Mar-Nov. Vegetarians have a treat in store here, near the Sandy Beach. The menu includes curries and a range of Asian dishes.

*Caravella (☎ 2823 041 131, Paleohora)* Fish €22kg. Open 11am-midnight Apr-Nov. Caravella has a prime position overlooking the old harbour and offers fresh and competitively priced seafood.

*Cretan Traditional Sweet Café (Paleohora)* Cakes €1.50-2.40. Open 8am-11pm. Wherever you dine, round your meal off with a delicious dessert from here. It's almost opposite Restaurant Small Garden.

## Entertainment

Most visitors to Paleohora spend at least one evening at the well-signposted *outdoor cinema (Paleohora)*. Entry is €4.50 and screenings start at 9.45pm.

*Paleohora Club (☎ 2823 042 230, Paleohora)* This is another option for a night out. It is next to Camping Paleohora 1.5km east of the village. It kicks in after 11pm.

*Nostos Night Club (☎ 2823 042 145, Paleohora)* Open 6pm-2am. If you've seen the movie and don't fancy the trek to the disco, try this club right in town, between El Venizelou and the Old Harbour.

## Getting There & Away

**Bus** In summer there are three buses a day to Hania (€4.70, two hours); in winter there are two. In summer, this service goes via Omalos at 6.30 am (€4.30, 1½ hours) to cash in on the Samaria Gorge trade. For information call the bus station on ☎ 2823 041 914.

**Boat** In summer there are daily ferries from Paleohora to Hora Sfakion (€8, three hours)

via Sougia (€3.80, one hour), Agia Roumeli (€6.50, two hours) and Loutro (€7.90, 2½ hours). The ferry leaves Paleohora at 9.30am, and returns from Hora Sfakion at 12.30pm.

There's also a boat twice times a week on Monday and Thursday to Gavdos (€8, three hours) that leaves Paleohora at 8.30am. Tickets for all of these boats can be bought at Interkreta Tourism & Travel (☎ 2823 041 393, fax 2823 041 050), Kondekaki 4.

## Getting Around

**Car, Motorcycle & Bicycle** All three can be hired from Notos Rentals (☎ 2823 042 110, e notos@grecian.net) on El Venizelou. Cars rent for around €23.50, a motorbike for €14.70 and bicycle for €3.

**Taxi** Call a taxi (☎ 2823 041 128) or pick one up from the stand on the main street. Fares for various destinations are posted by the stand.

**Ferry** From mid-April M/B *Elafonisos* ferries people to the west coast beach of Elafonisi (€3.80, one hour). The service increases from three times a week to daily in June through September. It departs at 10am and returns at 4pm.

## AROUND PALEOHORA

The village of **Anydri** is 5km north-east of Paleohora and contains the **Church of Agios Georgios** with 14th-century frescoes by the local master, Pagomenos. The founding fathers of the village were two brothers from Hora Sfakion fleeing a murderous vendetta which is why most villagers have the same surname.

The village is accessible by foot from Paleohora. Take the road that goes past the camping ground and follow the paved road that forks off to the left, which is bordered by steep rocks. As you enter the village you'll see a sign directing you to the Anydri Gorge.

After a few hundred metres on a footpath you'll see an overgrown path on the left. Red markers direct you to the gorge. After walking along the dried-out riverbed, signs

Small church near the village of Loutro on the south coast of Crete

Byzantine church, Lefka Ori (White Mountains)

Fishing boats and buildings in the Loutro harbour

The haunted beach and castle at Frangokastello

The steep wooden staircase (at the start of the trek) known as 'the xyloskalo', Samaria Gorge

Frangokastello Fortress

Cape Tigani and the rocky islet of Gramvousa

Interior of a Byzantine church in Lefka Ori

direct you to the wide, deserted Anydri Beach at the end of the gorge. You can take a different path back to Paleohora following the E4 European footpath markers that take you along the coastal cliffs.

## GAVDOS ISLAND Νήσος Γαύδος
### postcode 730 01 • pop 50

Gavdos Island (**Gav**-dos), in the Libyan Sea, 65km from Paleohora, is the most southerly place in Europe. Geographically it is more akin to Africa than Europe and enjoys a very mild climate. Visitors are able to swim in its seas as early as February. The island has 65% vegetation cover and makes for a very enticing alternative destination for serious islands hoppers.

Archaeological excavations indicate habitation as far back as the Neolithic period. In the Greco-Roman era Gavdos Island, then known as Clauda, belonged to the city of Gortyn. There was a Roman settlement on the north-west corner of the island. On his way from Kali Limenes to Rome, St Paul encountered a fierce storm which blew him off course past Gavdos Island and shipwrecked him on Malta, instead of a landing on Phoenix (or Finix). Under the Byzantines Gavdos Island was the seat of bishopric, but when the Arabs conquered Crete in the 9th century the island became a pirates nest.

A severe lack of water limited development of the island. Rain water washes into the sea and the Greek government has had to fund projects drilling for groundwater. Visitors need to be aware that water is scarce; forget about long showers, or any showers at all in some places. Electricity is also limited since it comes from generators that are widespread but often shut down at night because of the noise.

The island's port is Karabe on the east side of the island, while the capital of the island is Kastri in the centre of Gavdos. Here you'll find the only post office, OTE, doctor and police officer. Card phones are available on the island. The best beach is Sarakinikos, in the north-east corner, which has a wide swathe of sand and several tavernas on the side. There's also another excellent beach,

Agios Ioannis, on the northern tip, which has a scraggly summer settlement of campers. There are some wonderful beaches on the north coast such as Potamos and Pyrgos which you can reach by foot from Kastri if you follow the footpath leading north to Ambelos and beyond.

Full and half-day cruises are offered by boat owners on the island ranging in price from €8-15 per person. A trip to the remote, uninhabited island of Gavdopoula costs €15. A good source of information about the island is Interkreta Tourism & Travel in Paleohora.

### Places to Stay & Eat

*Sarakiniko Studios* (☎ *2823 042 182*, e *consolas@netplan.gr*, w *www.gavdos tudios.gr, Gavdos*) Single/double studios €18/23; small villas €89. Perhaps the best place to stay on the island, Sarakiniko Studios are a 20-minute walk north of the port Karabe, on Sarakiniko beach. Prices include breakfast. You can camp for €5 per person nearby under the trees and have access to bathroom facilities.

*Notos Taverna* (☎ *2823 042 182, Gavdos*) Lobster €30kg. Dine on fresh lobster or fish at the beachside taverna belonging to Sarakiniko Studios.

### Getting There & Away

A small post boat operates between Paleohora and Gavdos on Monday and Thursday all year, weather permitting. It leaves Paleohora at 8.30am and takes about four hours (€8).

There's also a boat on Tuesday in summer. The boats turn around from Gavdos almost immediately. There are also four boats a week from Hora Sfakion to Gavdos (€8) and a weekly boat from Sougia (€8).

## ELAFONISI Ελαφονήσι
### postcode 730 12 • pop 12

As one of the loveliest sand beaches in Crete it's easy to understand why people enthuse so much about Elafonisi. At the southern extremity of Crete's west coast, the beach is long, wide and is separated from the Elafonisi Islet by about 50m of knee-deep water. The clear, shallow water and fine white sand create a tropical paradise. There are a few snack bars on the beach near where the road ends and stalls to rent umbrellas and lounge chairs. The islet is marked by low dunes and a string of semi-secluded coves that attract a sprinkling of naturists. The beaches are popular with day-trippers but there are two small hotels and a pension on a bluff overlooking the main beach for those who want to luxuriate in the quiet that descends in late afternoon. There is a minimarket nearby.

### Places to Stay & Eat

**Rooms Elafonissi** (☎ 2825 061 274, fax 2825 097 907, Elafonisi) Singles/doubles with private bath €20.50/26.50. The 21 rooms here have fridges, an outdoor patio and attached restaurant.

**Rooms Elafonissos** (☎ 2825 061 548, Elafonisi) Double/triple studios €23.50/29.50. This place has a taverna overlooking the sea from its commanding position on a bluff.

**Innahorion** (☎ 2825 061 111, Elafonisi) Singles/doubles with bath €23.50/29.50. This is perhaps the least attractive of the three options. The 15 rooms each have a fridge and kitchenette, but are set back a fair way from the beach. Innahorion also has a restaurant.

### Getting There & Away

There are two boats a day from Paleohora (€3.80, one hour) in summer, as well as daily buses from Hania (€7.40, 2½ hours) and Kissamos-Kastelli (€3, 1½ hours). The buses leave Hania at 7.30am and Kissamos-Kastelli at 8.30am. Return buses depart from Elafonisi at 4pm.

### MONI HRYSOSKALITISSAS

Μονή Χρυσοσκαλίτισσας
Moni Hrysoskalitissas (Mo-**nee** Hris-os-ka-**lee**-tiss-as), 5km north of Elafonisi, is inhabited by two nuns. It's a beautiful monastery perched on a rock high above the sea. Hrysoskalitissa means 'golden staircase'. The name comes from a legend that one of the 90 steps leading up from the

sea to the monastery is made of gold but you can only see it if you are pure in spirit.

The church is recent but the monastery is allegedly a thousand years old and may have been built on the site of a Minoan temple. There are tavernas and domatia in the vicinity. Buses to Elafonisi drop passengers here.

### ENNIA HORIA Εννιά Χωριά

Ennia Horia (nine villages) is the name given to the highly scenic mountainous region south of Kissamos-Kastelli, which is renowned for its chestnut trees.

If you have your own transport you can drive through the region en route to Moni Hrysoskalitissas and Elafonisi or, with a little back-tracking, to Paleohora.

Alternatively, you can take a circular route, returning via the coast road.

Heading south from Kissamos you'll pass through some of the lushest and most fertile parts of the island. The scenery is unforgettable and you'll be far away from the tourist track.

You'll first come to the village of **Voulgaro** which has two Byzantine churches. Three kilometres further south is the lovely village of **Topolia** with a cluster of whitewashed houses overhung with plants and vines. There is a post office in the town centre, a couple of kafeneia and just one place to stay.

After Topolia the road skirts the edge of the **Koutsomatados Ravine** bending and twisting and affording dramatic views. Just before a narrow road tunnel there is a **snack bar** on the left which is a good place to stop and take a photo of the ravine. Shortly you will come to a cave, **Agia Sofia,** which contains evidence of settlement from as far back as the Neolithic era. At the top of the rock-cut stairs to the cave there's a taverna with great views over the ravine. It's a spectacular drive to tiny **Koutsomatados** followed by the village of **Vlatos**. After the village you'll see a signposted turn-off on the right for the 'Traditional Village' of **Milia**.

A few years ago, the only two families left in this isolated village managed to persuade the EU to help them reconstruct the village in its original style using traditional materials and furnishing it with Cretan antiques. The rather narrow access road is paved for the first 2km before becoming a driveable 3km dirt road. Park outside the village at the designated parking area. Reach the village along the short Halepa walking track (to the left) through a shady stream gorge, or follow the vehicle access road down to the main complex. If you don't plan to stay here (see Places to Stay & Eat) there's an excellent restaurant for lunch or dinner and some good local walks. See the restaurant owner for details.

Just south of Milia and back on the main highway there is a turnoff for Paleohora via **Strovles** and **Drys**. Most maps don't depict the road as being very good, but it is a good, paved route and affords much quicker access to Paleohora than via the more obvious route via Tavronitis on Hania Bay.

The road south from Elia now passes through extensive stands of chestnut trees which are the major crop of the region. **Elos** is the largest town and the centre of the chestnut trade. It stages a chestnut festival on the third Sunday of October when sweets made from chestnuts are eaten. The plane, eucalyptus and chestnut trees around the main square make Elos a cool and relaxing stop. Behind the taverna on the main square you'll see the remains of the aqueduct that once brought water down from the mountains to power the mill.

Continuing south you'll pass the atmospheric village of **Perivolia** and then come to **Kefali** with its 14th-century frescoed church. From Kefali you can take either the road to **Elafonisi** (see earlier in this chapter), or make a right turn and start the loop back along the picturesque west coast to your starting point. Taking the coastal road from Kefali you will be winding around cliffs with magnificent coastal views unfolding after every bend in the road. Drive carefully, however, because the road changes abruptly from wide and paved to narrow and unpaved. This is one of the most scenic drives in Crete.

You'll first pass the little hamlet of **Pappadiana** driving along the gorge and climbing into the mountains before coming to **Amygdalokefali** which has beautiful sweeping sea

views from a bluff outside town. About 50 minutes from Kefali you'll come to **Kambos** a tiny village on the edge of a gorge. It makes a good overnight stop since you can hike down the gorge to the beach, or alternatively take an alternative hike back to Kissamos via a rough dirt track from Kambos. The trail, touted as an alternative to the better-known **E4 trail** is known as the **F1 trail**. Call in to Hartzoulakis Rent Rooms (see Places to Stay & Eat later in this section) for a rough trail map produced by Dutch hiker John Filos ( **e** afto_odiki @planet.nl) which outlines the F1 trail as well as its southerly extension to **Moni Hrysoskalitissas** and Elafonisi.

Continuing northwards from Kambos road now circles around the other side of the gorge eventually winding down to **Sfinari** after a further 9km. The languid, laid-back agricultural village stretches down to a largish beach which is backed by phalanxes of greenhouses at the northern end but has a gravelly cove, some basic camping grounds and a few tavernas on the southern end.

After Sfinari you'll get more coastal views before the road drops down to **Platanos**, a quiet, tree-lined and rather scattered village of whitewashed houses. From here you can detour left to **Falasarna** or keep to the right for the downhill run back to Kissamos. If you need cash there's a prominently signposted ATM on the right as you leave the village of Platanos.

## Places to Stay & Eat

Accommodation throughout the Ennia Horia is rather scattered and ranges from basic-but-clean to truly excellent. There are no large tourist hotel complexes anywhere in the region.

The village of **Topolia** has just one place to stay.

*Topolia Rooms* (☎ 2822 051 273, Topolia) Singles/doubles €17.60/20.50. These are newish, rather functional domatia with black iron balconies at the southern end of the village.

The little village of **Milia** has some stone cottages and an attached restaurant.

*Milia Settlement* (☎ 2822 051 569, *Milia*) Cottages €41-47. This would have to be the one of the most atmospheric and original places to stay in Crete. The meticulously restored stone cottages have wood heating for winter, thick stone walls for insulation in summer and just one solar-powered light for energy. Using only organic produce from its own extensive gardens the food here is guaranteed genuine. Mains €3.80-6.80. Try their own special *bourekia* or their winter favourite – potatoes, chestnuts and baby onions in red wine sauce (€5).

**Elos** has one option to stay, but at least two places to eat.

*Taverna and Rent Rooms Kokolakis* (☎ 2822 061 258, *Elos*) Doubles €14.70. The only accommodation is here; there's scrumptious food and fresh orange juice in the *Kastanofolia* taverna.

**Kefali** has only one place to stay but a clutch of tavernas along the main road.

*Taverna Polakis* (☎ 2822 061 260, *Kefali*) Rooms €23.50. The only place to stay and eat is here. Rooms have great views.

**Kambos** has two options to stay and eat.

*Sunset Rooms* (☎ 2822 041 128, *Kambos*) Singles/doubles €17.60/20.50. For accommodation there is this new place and the attached *Sunset Taverna* serving up grills for €3.80-4.70 and large salads for around €2.70.

*Hartzoulakis Rent Rooms* (☎ 2822 041 445, *Kambos*) Singles/doubles €11.80/14.70. Rooms are small and basic but very clean. They make a good base for walkers. The *taverna* serves up good Cretan fare and excellent raki.

**Sfinari** has a number of places to stay and at least three beach restaurants.

*Rooms Nerida* (☎ 2822 041 621, *Sfinari*) Singles/doubles €23.50/26.50. For accommodation try this two-storey building with lovely views. Rooms all have kitchenette and fridge.

*Rooms for Rent Georgia* (☎ 2822 041 668, *Sfinari*) Doubles €35.30. Opposite Nerida is this equally reasonable place. There are at least three tavernas plying their trade at the south end of **Sfinari beach**. Three tavernas line up for custom.

*Taverna Dilina* (☎ 2822 041 632, *Paralia Sfinariou*) Fish dishes €8-10. Dilina is about the best of the three. Fish and grills are the main menu items.

*Andonis Theodorakis* (☎ 2822 041 125, *Sfinari*) Ladera €2.40-3.50. Up on the main road to Platanos is Andonis' little taverna. Food is all home-cooked, village style. The oven-baked goat (€5.30) is recommended.

**Platanos** has at least one place to stay and one place to eat. Both are fairly close to each other.

*The Castle* (☎ 2822 041 372, *Platanos*) Double/triple rooms €29.50. On the main through road, the Castle has smallish, but very neat and clean rooms with a fridge. All rooms enjoy a balcony view.

*O Zaharias* (☎ 2822 041 285, *Platanos*). Mayirefta €3-3.50. 'Food like grandma cooked' is the motto at this very pleasant eatery just off the main through highway. All dishes are made according to closely guarded traditional recipes. Ask for *avgokolokytho* (€2.70) – a kind of omelette dish made with zucchini, egg, tomato and olive oil, or boureki with *staka* (€3.20).

# Kissamos Province

## KISSAMOS-KASTELLI

Κίσσαμος–Καστέλλι

**postcode 734 00 • pop 2936**

The Kissamos region in the far west is a wild, rugged land that attracts few tourists. Villages and towns are few and far between and even the spectacular beaches of Elafonisi and Falasarna are surprisingly underdeveloped. The largest town and capital of the province is Kissamos-Kastelli, usually referred to simply as Kissamos. West of Kissamos is the beautiful and deserted Gramvousa Peninsula, most of which is accessible only by boat. East of Kissamos is the Rodopou Peninsula with the small resort of Kolymbari and several interesting villages and churches that are only accessible if you have your own wheels.

If you find yourself in the north coast town of Kissamos-Kastelli, you've probably arrived by ferry from the Peloponnese or Kythira. The most remarkable part of Kissamos-Kastelli is its unremarkableness. It's simply a quiet town of mostly elderly residents that neither expects nor attracts much tourism.

## History

In antiquity, its name was Kissamos, the main town of the province of the same name. When the Venetians came along and built a castle here, the place became known as Kastelli. The name persisted until 1966 when authorities decided that too many people were confusing this Kastelli with Crete's other Kastelli, 40km south-east of Iraklio. The official name reverted to Kissamos, and that's what appears on bus and shipping schedules. Local people still prefer Kastelli, and many books and maps agree with them. An alternative that is emerging is to combine the two into Kissamos-Kastelli, which leaves no room for misunderstanding.

Ancient Kissamos was a harbour for the important city-state of Polyrrinia 7km inland. Vestiges of Roman buildings have been unearthed but most of the ancient city lies under the modern town of Kissamos and cannot be excavated. Kissamos achieved independence in the third century AD and then became the seat of a bishopric under the Byzantines. It was occupied by the Saracens in the 9th century and flourished under the Venetians.

## Orientation & Information

The port is 3km west of town. In summer a bus meets the boats, otherwise a taxi costs around €3. The bus station is just below Plateia Kissamou, and the main street, Skalidi, runs east from Plateia Kissamou. The post office is on the main road. Signs from the bus station direct you through an alley on the right of Skalidi which takes you to the post office. Turn right at the post office and you'll come to the National Bank of Greece which is on the central square. Turn left at the post office and the OTE office is opposite you about 50m along the main road. There is also a string of pensions and tavernas along the sea below the bus station. Kissamos-Kastelli has no tourist office but

Horeftakis Tours (☎ 2822 023 250) on Skalidi is a good source of information.

## Places to Stay

**Camping** *Camping Kissamos (☎ 2822 023 444/322, Kissamos)* Person/tent €4.10/2.40. Close to the town centre, this place is convenient for the huge supermarket next door and for the bus station, but not much else. It's got great views of the olive-processing plant next door. Signs direct you there from the town centre.

*Camping Mithymna (☎ 2822 031 444, fax 2822 031 000; Paralia Drapania)* Person/tent €4.50/2.40. A much better choice is Camping Mithymna, 6km east of town. It's an excellent shady site near the best stretch of beach. Facilities include a restaurant, bar and shop. It also has rooms to rent nearby. Getting there involves either a 4km walk along the beach, or a bus trip to the village of Drapanias – from where it's a pleasant 15-minute walk through olive groves to the site.

*Camping Nopigia (☎ 2822 031 111, fax 2822 031 700, e info@campingnopigia.gr, w www.campingnopigia.gr, Nopigia)* Person/tent €3.90/2.50. This is another good, shaded site, 2km east of Camping Mithymna. The only drawback is that the beach is not good for swimming, but it makes up for that with a swimming pool. Laundry facilities (€4.50 per wash) are available.

**Domatia** *Koutsounakis Rooms (☎ 2822 023 753, Kissamos)* Singles/doubles with bathroom €13/19. One of the best deals in town is adjacent to the bus station. The rooms are spotless.

*Argo Rooms for Rent (☎/fax 2822 023 563, Plateia Teloniou)* Singles/doubles with private bathroom €20.50/29.50. Opposite, the C-class Argo has spacious rooms. From the central square, walk down to the seafront, turn left, and you will come to the rooms on the left.

*Mandy's Suites (☎ 2822 022 825, fax 2822 022 830, Plateia Teloniou)* Studios €35.30. On the beach, this is a white stucco house of studios with balconies and views of the sea.

WESTERN CRETE

*Thalassa* (☎ *2822 031 231,* e *skoulakis @ otenet.gr,* w *www.thalassa-apts.gr, Paralia Drapania)* Double studios €35.30. If you have your own transport, this is an ideal spot to retreat to. All studios (from 2–5 persons) are immaculate, enjoy a garden setting, have Internet connectivity and are 50m from the beach. Thalassa is 6km east of Kissamos near Camping Mythimna.

**Hotels** *Hotel Kissamos* (☎ *2822 022 086, Kissamos)* Singles/doubles with bath €23.50/ 28, including breakfast. The C-class Kissamos, west of the bus station on the north side of the main road.

*Hotel Hermes* (☎ *2822 024 109, fax 2822 022 093, Kissamos)* Singles/doubles €26.50/33. Situated 100m from the beach, Hermes is a B-class hotel with 35 rooms with private bathroom, telephone and large verandas.

*Hotel Holiday Bay* (☎ *2822 023 488, Telonio Beach)* Doubles €44. This two-story C-class hotel is also right on the sea with nine, kitchenette-equipped double rooms.

## Places to Eat

*Restaurant Makedonas* (☎ *2822 022 844, Kissamos)* Ladera €2-2.70. For local colour go to the no-frills place just west of Plateia Kissamou, where you can dine on home-cooked food. The beef patties in tomato sauce *biftekia stifado* (€3.50) are recommended by the owner.

*Papadakis Taverna* (☎ *2822 022 340, Paralia Kissamou)* Fish €29.50kg. Open 11am-midnight. Opposite the Argo Rooms for Rent, this taverna has a good setting overlooking the beach. Some of the well-prepared dishes include oven-baked fish (€5) or fish soup (€5).

*Taverna Petra* (☎ *2822 024 387, Plateia Kissamou)* Grills €4. Right on the main square Petra is a good place for tasty gyros and souvlakia. The Cypriot-style kondo-souvli (€4.10) is also good. Take away a souvlaki (€0.90) if you are in a hurry.

## Shopping

Once of the few places you can still buy hand made wicker chairs in Crete is right here in Kissamos. **Andonis Zouridakis** (☎ *2822 022 690)* just off Plateia Kissamou makes sturdy wood and wicker chairs like they use to have in Greek tavernas, for around €20.50-26.50 each. Drop by his shop and watch him and his off-sider make them.

## Getting There & Away

**Bus** There are 14 buses a day to Hania (€3, one hour), where you can change for Rethymno and Iraklio; and two buses a day for Falasarna (€1.90) at 10am and 5.30pm.

**Ferry** ANEN Ferries operates the F/B *Myrtidiotissa* on a route that takes in Antikythira (€6.50, two hours), Kythira (€12.90, four hours), Gythio (€15.60, seven hours), Kalamata (€17.60, 10 hours) and Piraeus (€17.60, 19 hours). It leaves Kissamos-Kastelli five times a week between 8 and 11 am. Both Horeftakis Tours (☎ 2822 023 250), and the ANEN Office (☎ 2822 022 009 or 24 030) are on the right side of Skalidi, east of Plateia Kissamou.

## Getting Around

Motorcycles can be hired from Motor Fun (☎ 2822 023 400) on Plateia Kissamou and cars can be hired from Hermes (☎ 2822 022 980) on Skalidi.

## AROUND KISSAMOS-KASTELLI

The ancient city ruins of **Polyrrinia** (Pol-ee-ren-**ee**-a) lie about 7km south of Kissamos-Kastelli, above the village of Ano Paleokastro (sometimes called Polyrrinia). It's a steep climb to the ruins but the views are stunning and the region is blanketed with wildflowers in spring. The city was founded by the Dorians in the 6th century BC and was constantly at war with the Kydonians from Hania. Coins from the period depict the warrior-goddess Athena who was evidently revered by the war-like Polyrrinians.

Unlike their rivals the Kydonians, the Polyrrinians did not resist the Roman invasion and thus the city was spared destruction. It was the best fortified town in Crete and the administrative centre of western Crete from the Roman through to the Byzantine period.

It was reoccupied by the Venetians who used it as a fortress. Many of the ruined structures, including an aqueduct built by Hadrian, date from the Roman period.

The most impressive feature of the site is the **acropolis** built by the Byzantines and Venetians. There's also a church built on the foundations of a **Hellenistic temple** from the 4th century BC. Notice also, near the **aqueduct**, a **cave** dedicated to the Nymphs that still contains the niches for Nymph statuettes.

### Getting There & Away
It's a scenic walk from Kissamos-Kastelli to Polyrrinia. To reach the Polyrrinia road, walk east along Kissamos-Kastelli main road, and turn right after the OTE. There are two buses daily in winter and a bus Monday, Wednesday, and Friday in summer (€1.50, 25 minutes).

## FALASARNA Φαλάσαρνα
**postcode 734 00 • pop 24**
Falasarna, 16km west of Kissamos-Kastelli, is a small, scattered agricultural settlement that attracts a mixed bunch of travellers, from seekers of stress relief, to lovers of big beaches, to the just plain curious.

This is as far west in Crete as you can get; beyond Falasarna the next landfall is Malta. There is no settlement as such, just a scattering of widely spaced places to stay and eat and, of course, an enormous, wide sandy beach split up into several coves by rocky spits.

There is no organised 'beach scene' – comfort is provided by the omnipresent beach umbrellas and loungers at scattered locations. If you like solitude but with a rush of controlled activity from mid July to mid August, Falasarna is your kind of place.

### History
Falasarna has been occupied at least since the 6th century BC but reached the height of its power in the 4th century BC. Although it was built next to the sea you will see that the town's ruins are about 400m away from the water because the western coast of Crete has risen over the centuries. The town owed

its wealth to the agricultural produce from the fertile valley to the south. It was the west coast harbour for Polyrrinia but later became Polyrrinia's chief rival for dominance over western Crete. By the time of the Roman invasion of Crete in 67 BC, Falasarna had become a haven for pirates. Stone blocks excavated around the entrance to the old harbour indicate that the Romans may have tried to block off the harbour to prevent it from being used by pirates.

### Orientation & Information
Approaching Falasarna, the main road from Platanos forks to the north and to the south. The northern road takes you to the beaches that continue on for several kilometres. Most of the hotels and domatia are at this end of the settlement. The southern road takes you past a long strip of greenhouses and some goat pastures. You will also see signs to ancient Falasarna. There is no post office, bank, OTE, tourist office or travel agency, but your mobile phone will work and there are cardphones.

### Things to See
The remains of the ancient city of Falasarna are the area's main attraction, although not much is visible. Signs direct you to the ancient city from the main road, following a dirt road at the end of the asphalt.

First you'll come to a large stone throne purpose of which is unknown. Further on there are the remains of the wall that once fortified the town and a small harbour. Notice the holes carved into the wall which were used to tie up boats. At the top of the hill there are the remains of the acropolis wall and a temple as well as four clay baths.

### Places to Stay & Eat
There are numerous places for wild camping on Falasarna's beaches, though like elsewhere in Crete it is officially frowned upon. Accommodation is aimed at the independent traveller and there is a good choice.

***Rooms for Rent Panorama*** (☎ 2822 041 *336, fax 2822 041 777,* **e** *panorama@cha nia-cci.gr, Falasarna)* Singles/doubles €29.50/35.30. This is one of the first places you will come across, signposted to the left along a gravel track. The rooms are spotless and comfortable and have a fridge. Downstairs, the well-run and friendly restaurant with a great view of the beach serves up good Cretan cooking. Order Cretan chicken and rice special the day before (€23.50 for two persons). Mains €3.50-6.50.

*Rooms Anastasia-Stathis (☎ 2822 041 480, fax 2822 041 069, Falasarna).* Double/triple rooms €29.50; 4-5 person apartments €58.70. Owner Anastasia makes her home the friendliest place to stay. The airy, beautifully furnished rooms with fridges and large balconies are perfect for stress relief, as Anastasia puts it. Her enormous breakfasts (€4.50) are open to all-comers and are a sight to be savoured. Look for the prominent sign.

*Petalida Rooms (☎ 2822 041 449, Falasarna)* Doubles/triples €26.50/29.50. Consisting of some older-style and new rooms in two separate blocks Petalida is another very good option, just off the main through road. The attached restaurant is friendly and honest, serving up fish and other Cretan dishes. Fish €29.50kg.

### Getting There & Away
In summer there are two buses a day from Kissamos-Kastelli to Falasarna (€1.80) as well as two buses a day from Hania (€4.70).

## GRAMVOUSA PENINSULA
Χερσόνησος Γραμβούσα
North of Falasarna is the wild and remote Gramvousa Peninsula. A good base for touring this region is the village of **Kalyviani**, 8km west of Kissamos where there are a couple of places to stay and eat. The dirt road to the sandy beach of **Balos** on **Cape Tigani** begins at the far end of the main street of Kalyviani and follows the eastern slope of Mt Geroskinos. From here, the views over the shoreline and the Rodopou Peninsula are spectacular. About 2km before the beach the dirt road becomes a path. One fork takes you to the beach while the other fork runs along the side of the mountain and eventually joins the beach path. The shadeless walk takes around three

hours – wear a hat and take plenty of water. Offshore are two deserted islands, Agria (wild) and Imeri (tame) Gramvousa.

### History
The offshore island of Imeri Gramvousa was an important vantage point for the Venetians who built a fortress here to protect ships passing in front of the island on the way to and from Venice. It was considered an impregnable fort with a large cache of armaments. The Turks did not conquer Imeri Gramvousa along with the rest of Crete in 1645; the fort remained in Venetian hands along with their other forts, Souda and Spinalonga. Eventually the Venetians left and the fort fell into disuse until it was taken over in 1821 by Cretan revolutionaries who needed a base of operations in their war for independence. It later became a notorious base for piracy before the Turks took it again and used it to blockade the coast during the War of Independence. Local legend has it that the pirates amassed a fabulous fortune which they reportedly hid in caves around the island. Who knows? It could still be there today.

### Things to See
On 10 January 1981 a Lebanese-registered ship was on its way from Libya when it struck engine trouble on the way towards Crete. It managed to reach the Bay of Kissamos but foundered in a storm and beached itself on the shore near Kalyviani. No lives were lost. It is now the infamous **Kalyviani shipwreck** and can be spotted lying rotting and rusty on the west side of Kalyviani beach.

### Places to Stay & Eat
There is one exceptionally good place to stay and eat in the village of Kalyviani.

*Kalyviani (☎/fax 2822 023 204, Kalyviani)* Double/triples €29.50/35.30. Tastefully furnished rooms with balconies characterise this ecotourism-oriented hostelry. Downstairs the excellent restaurant serves up the genuine article wherever possible using organic produce. Cretan dishes €2.40-3.50. The *bourekia* (€3) are recommended as is the *gramvousiano yiahni* – a tasty local stew (€5.30). Their home-made wine is tops.

## Excursions
The **Gramvousa-Ballos Maritime Company** (☎ 2822 024 344, *Limani Kissamou; open from 9.30am Mon-Sat Apr-Oct*), in Kissamos-Kastelli, runs a tour that takes in the Gramvousa Peninsula, which is inaccessible by car, and Imeri Gramvousa. White sand beaches, a climb to the top of the Venetian castle and the cove where Prince Charles and Diana honeymooned are also on the itinerary. The tour costs €14.70.

## Getting There & Away
To reach Kalyviani, take a west-bound bus from Kissamos-Kastelli and ask to be let off at the turn-off to the village of Kalyviani (5km from Kissamos-Kastelli). Kalyviani is a 2km walk from the main road.

## RODOPOU PENINSULA
The barren, rocky Rodopou Peninsula has a few small villages clustered at the base of the peninsula but the rest is uninhabited. A paved road goes as far as Afrata but then becomes a dirt track that meanders through the peninsula. If you are travelling by foot, jeep or motorcycle you can reach the **Diktynna Sanctuary** at the end of the peninsula, but make sure you are well-supplied since there is not a drop of gasoline or water, or a morsel of food beyond Afrata. From Afrata a road winds down to the small, gravelly-pebbly **Afrata Beach** which also supports a small seasonal snack bar.

## KOLYMBARI Κολυμπάρι
**postcode 730 06 • pop 151**
Kolymbari, 23km west of Hania, is at the base of the Rodopou Peninsula, and appeals to those seeking a quiet, relaxing holiday. Development is in its embryonic stage, but that is changing fast as hotels and domatia arise to take advantage of the long pebbly beach. In addition to beach activities, Kolymbari is a good base for a walk to Moni Gonias.

## Orientation & Information
The bus from Hania drops you off on the main road from which it is a 500m walk down to the beach settlement. At the bottom of the road you'll see a post office on the left; turn left and the OTE is about 100m further. There is no bank in Kolymbari but there is a post office in the centre of the village. See the wacky Web page at **W** www .inkmonitor.com for an expatriate view of life in the Rodhopou Peninsula.

## Places to Stay & Eat
***Rooms Lefka*** (☎ 2824 022 211, *fax 2824 022 211, Kolymbari*) Singles/doubles €17.60/26.50. On the way into town from the bus stop you will see this place on the right. Rooms are very comfortable. The taverna downstairs serves up good, honest Cretan food. The owner suggests the lamb with garlic (€5.30).

***Hotel Minerva*** (☎ 2824 022 485, *Kolymbari*) Rooms €35.30, 2-bedroom apartments €58.70. This is the best choice along the beach for larger groups or families; it has large rooms with kitchenettes and balconies.

Kolymbari is a good place to sample local fish. In the centre of town are a couple of places.

***Diktina*** (☎ 2824 022 611, *Kolymbari*) Fish €29.50kg. Diktina has sea views and a range of dishes as well as the predictable and usually good fish dishes.

***Argentina*** (☎ 2824 022 243, *Kolymbari*) Fish €29.50kg. Argentina has a street view and a similar range of menu items as its opposite neighbour Diktina.

***Taverna Lefka*** (☎ 2824 022 211, *Kolymbari*) Mains €3-5.30. Recommended by locals and travellers alike.

***Palio Arhondiko*** (☎ 2824 022 124, *Kolymbari*) Mezedes €1.50-5.60. Along the beach, try here for Cretan taverna specialities and a wide range of mezedes.

There's also a minimarket near the bus stop for self-catering.

## Getting There & Away
Buses from Hania to Kissamos-Kastelli stop at Kolymbari (€1.80, 40 minutes).

WESTERN CRETE

## Tops or Bottoms?

Cretans have a long tradition of welcoming foreigners, which has made them tolerant of different customs. Although Greek women are unlikely to go topless, in most places topless sunbathing is allowed. The few south coast beaches where it is frowned upon post signs to that effect. Although naturism is not widely practised and officially is not allowed, you'll find a sprinkling of naturists on the far ends of remote beaches or in secluded coves. Nude beaches change from year to year. Sometimes a taverna suddenly springs up on a popular naturist beach and the naturists disappear only to turn up on another distant cove. Beaches that are currently popular with naturists include Kommos near Matala, Sweet Water Beach, the south end of the sandy beach in Paleohora and the east end of the pebbly beach at Sougia. Glyka Nera, close to Loutro is an old standby as is Orthi Ammos 1km east of Frangokastello. Diktikos west of Lendas is the most reliable of Crete's nude beaches.

## Moni Gonias

Moni Gonias (*Kolymbari; admission free; open 8am-12.30pm & 4pm-8pm Mon-Fri, 4pm-8pm Sat*) was founded in 1618. Although the monastery church was damaged by the Turks in 1645, it was rebuilt in 1662 and extended in the 19th century. The monastery houses a unique collection of icons dating from the 17th and 18th centuries. Some are in the church while others are in the monastery museum. The most valuable icon is that of *Agios Nikolaos*, painted in 1637 by Palaiokapas. It perfectly exemplifies the Cretan school of icon painting that flourished in the 17th century under Venetian rule. The monastery is easy to reach from Kolymbari. Take the beach road north from the town centre for about 500m.

## Diktynna

Right on the tip of the Rodopou Peninsula is the remains of a temple to the Cretan goddess Diktynna, the most important religious sanctuary in the region under the Romans. Diktynna was the goddess of hunting and she was worshipped fervently in western Crete.

According to legend her name derives from the word *diktyon* which means 'net'. Supposedly it was a fisherman's net that saved her when she leapt into the sea to avoid the amorous desires of King Minos. The temple dates to the 2nd century AD but it was probably built on the site of an earlier temple.

After the collapse of the Roman Empire the temple was desecrated but you can see the temple's foundations and a sacrificial altar as well as Roman cisterns. If you're 'templed out' you can relax on a lovely sandy beach. Diktynna is only accessible by dirt road from Kolymbari but many travel agencies in Hania offer boat excursions to Diktynna for €19.

# Eastern Crete

Crete's easternmost prefecture, Lasithi receives far fewer visitors than the rest of the island. The southern coast extends from the village of Myrtos in the west to the commercial centre of Ierapetra and beyond to the lovely and untouched beaches of Xerokambos and Kato Zakros. The centre of the north coast is Sitia with the lovely palm-lined beach of Vai in the far east. The fertile region of the Lasithi Plateau in the west provides excellent cycling opportunities through quiet villages to the Dikteon Cave where Zeus was born. Archaeology buffs will enjoy the Palace of Zakros, an evocative Minoan site in the east next to Kato Zakros Beach.

## North Coast

### AGIOS NIKOLAOS Άγιος Νικόλαος
**postcode 721 00 • pop 8093**

Agios Nikolaos (**ah**-yee-os nih-**ko**-laos) is an undeniably pretty former fishing village. Today it is the home of one of Crete's more attractive resort destinations. Boasting a fetching combination of port, lake, narrow streets, boutiques, cafes and aquamarine seas, 'Agios' attracts a lot of people. Already by the early 1960s, it had become a chic hideaway for the likes of Jules Dassin and Walt Disney. By the end of the decade package tourists were arriving in force. While there is superficially little to attract the independent traveller, there is reasonable accommodation, prices are not too horrendous and there is quite a bit of activity to keep all tastes catered for.

### History

Agios Nikolaos emerged as a port for the city-state of Lato (see Ancient Lato later in this chapter) in the early Hellenic years when it was known as Lato-by-Kamara. The harbour assumed importance in the Greco-Roman period after the Romans put an end to the piracy that had plagued the northern coast.

### Highlights

- Cycling around the Lasithi Plateau
- Wandering among the fascinating ruins on Spinalonga Island
- Exploring the Minoan palace on the beach at Kato Zakros
- Hanging out in Myrtos, an unspoiled seaside village on the south coast
- Relaxing on Vai, Crete's only palm-lined beach

SEA OF CRETE

Agios Nikolaos p223

Sitia p235

Zakros Palace p241

IRAKLIO

Ierapetra p244

LIBYAN SEA

The town continued to flourish in the early Christian years and in the 8th or 9th century the small Byzantine Church of Agio Nikolaos was built.

When the Venetians bought Crete in the 13th century, the Castel Mirabello was built on a hill overlooking the sea and a settlement arose below. The Castel was damaged in the earthquake of 1303 and was burned by pirates in 1537, before being rebuilt according to plans from the military architect Sammicheli. When the Venetians were forced to abandon the castle to the Turks in 1645 they blew it up, leaving it in ruins. There's no trace of the Venetian occupation except the name they gave to the surrounding gulf – Mirabello or 'beautiful view'.

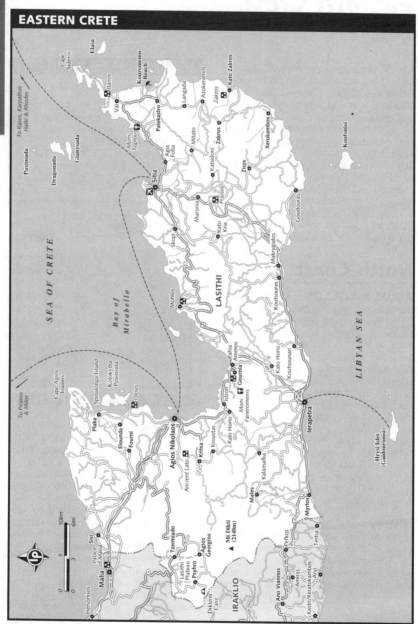

The town was resettled in the mid-19th century by fleeing rebels from Sfakia and it was later named capital of the Lasithi region.

## Orientation

The town centre is Plateia Venizelou, 150m up Sofias Venizelou from the bus station. The most interesting part of town is around the picturesque Voulismeni Lake, 100m north of Plateia Venizelou. From Plateia Venizelou, walk north-east along Koundourou, turn left at the bottom and you will come to a bridge that separates the lake from the harbour. The tourist office is at the far side of the bridge.

## Information

The municipal tourist office (☎ 2841 022 357, fax 2841 082 354, e detadan@agn .forthnet.gr, w www.forthnet.gr/internet city) is open 8am to 9.30pm daily from the beginning of April to mid-November. The Web site to Lasithi Province is excellent.

The tourist police (☎ 2841 026 900, Kondogianni 34), are open 7.30am to 2.30pm daily. The port police (☎ 2841 022 312) are in the same building as the tourist office.

**Money** The National Bank of Greece on Plastira has a 24-hour automatic exchange machine. The tourist office also changes money.

**Post & Communications** The post office (28 Oktovriou 9), is open 7.30am to 2pm Monday to Friday. The OTE is at K Sfakianaki 10. It is open 7am to 11pm daily. Internet access is available at the pleasant Polyhoros (☎ 2841 024 876, e peripou@ agn.forthnet.gr, 28 Oktovriou 13), open 9am to 2am daily, or at Cafe du Lac (☎ 2841 026 837, 28 Oktovriou 17), open 9.30am to 2am daily. Both charge around €4.40 per hour.

**Bookshop** The English book selection at the Anna Karteri Bookshop (☎ 2841 022 272, Koundourou 5) Open 8am to 10pm Monday to Saturday, this shop concentrates on best sellers and books about Crete and Greece with plenty of glossy photos.

There are also a few Lonely Planet books on sale.

**Emergency** Agios Nikolaos' general hospital (☎ 2841 025 221) is at Knosou 3.

## Things to See

The **folk museum** (☎ 2841 025 093, Paleologou 4; admission €0.90; open 10am-3pm Sun-Fri), next door to the tourist office, has a well-displayed collection of traditional handcrafts and costumes.

The **Archaeological Museum** (☎ 2841 022 943, Paleologou 74; admission €1.50; open 8.30am-3pm Tues-Sun) is a modern building housing a large, well-displayed collection from eastern Crete. The exhibits are arranged in chronological order beginning with Neolithic finds from Mt Tragistalos, north of Kato Zakros and early Minoan finds from Agia Fotia in the first room. Room II contains the museum's highlight, *The Goddess of Myrtos*, a clay jug from 2500 BC found near Myrtos. Notice also gold jewellery, stone vases and stone tables with inscriptions in Linear A. Room III displays finds from the Late Minoan period including pottery from Knossos, a marble chalice from Zakros and clay bathtubs decorated with birds and fish. Notice also a gold pin with an inscription in Linear A on the reverse side. Room IV is devoted to the Late Minoan period with many finds from the Myrsini cemetery and a potter's wheel from Kritsa. Room V has pottery from Sitia and clay animals from Olous near Elounda. Room VI is a continuation of Room V and displays more pottery. The exhibits conclude in Room VII with glass and vases from the Greco-Roman period.

The **Local Aquarium of Agios Nikolaos** (☎ 2841 028 030, Akti Koundourou 30; admission €3.80; open 10am-9pm daily) has interesting displays of fish and information about diving (including PADI courses) and snorkelling throughout Crete.

**Beaches** The popularity of Agios Nikolaos has little to do with its beaches. The town beach, south of the bus station, and Kitroplatia Beach, north of the harbour, have more people than pebbles. Ammoudi Beach, on the road to Elounda, is equally uninspiring. The sandy beach at Almyros about a kilometre south of town is the best of the lot and tends to be less crowded than the others. There's little shade but you can rent umbrellas for €1.70 a day.

**Voulismeni Lake** The lake is the subject of many stories in relation to its depth and origins. The locals have given it various names, including Xepatomeni (bottomless), Voulismeni (sunken) and Vromolimni (smelly). The lake isn't bottomless – it's 64m deep. The 'smelly' tag came about because the lake used to be stagnant and gave off quite a pong in summer. This was rectified in 1867 when a canal was built linking it to the sea. The area around this picturesque lake is ringed with tavernas and cafes.

## Activities

**Diexodos Adventure Unlimited** (☎/fax 2841 028 098, e diexodos@acci.gr, w www .forthnet.gr/internetcity/diexodos) in Havania, north of Agios Nikolaos town, offers cycling tours that take in the Lasithi Plateau for around €61. They also have hikes that include the archaeological site of Lato and country villages. The ascent of the summit of Mt Dikti costs around €73, while week-long all-inclusive programs cost around €345. See also the 'Head to the Hills' special section in the Facts for the Visitor chapter.

There are three diving centres in town: **Happy Divers** (☎ 2841 082 546, in front of the Coral Hotel); **Pelagos** (☎ 2841 024 376, in the Minos Beach Hotel); **Creta Underwater Center** (☎ 2841 022 406, In the Mirabello Hotel). All offer boat dives and PADI certification courses.

The **Roseta II** (☎ 2841 022 156, e oanak@ agn.forthnet.gr) is a fishing boat that takes ardent anglers on group fishing trips or private charters. Contact the owner Lorentzo Petras for details.

At the municipal beach on the south side of Agios Nikolaos there is a children's playground, swimming pool and mini golf.

## Organised Tours

Travel agencies in Agios Nikolaos offer coach outings to all Crete's top attractions. **Nostos Tours** (☎ 2841 022 819, fax 2841 025 336, e nostos@agn.forthnet.gr, Koundourou 30) has boat trips to Spinalonga (€8.80) as well as guided tours of Phaestos and Matala (€30.80), the Samaria Gorge (€36.70) and the Lasithi Plateau (€23.50). It's open 8am to 8pm daily from March to November.

## Special Events

In July and August Agios Nikolaos hosts the **Lato Cultural Festival** at various venues around town. There are concerts by local and international musicians, Cretan music played on traditional instruments, folk dancing, *mandinades* contests, theatre, art exhibits, literary evenings and swimming competitions. Ask at the tourist office for details. Agios Nikolaos also celebrates a **Marine Week**, the last week of June in even-numbered years, with swimming, windsurfing and boat races as well as a fireworks display over the port.

## Places to Stay – Budget

Agios Nikolaos receives few guests in the winter and most hotels close.

*Gournia Moon Camping* (☎/fax 2842 093 243, Gournia) Person/tent €3.50/2.60. The nearest camping ground to Agios Nikolaos is near the Minoan site of Gournia. It has a swimming pool, restaurant, snack bar and minimarket. Buses to Sitia can drop you off outside.

*Cronos Hotel* (☎ 2841 028 761, fax 2841 022 217, Arkadiou 2) Singles/doubles €14.70/20.50 Cronos is in the centre of town in an ugly beige building but it has simple large rooms.

*Afrodite Rooms* (☎ 2841 028 058, Korytsas 27) Singles/doubles €16.20/20.50. There's a tiny communal kitchen here.

*Mariella Hotel* (☎ 2841 028 639, Latous 4) Singles/doubles €17.60/20.50 The lobby isn't much in this small, family-run hotel, but the clean white rooms are cheerful and many have balconies. Front rooms can be noisy during the day.

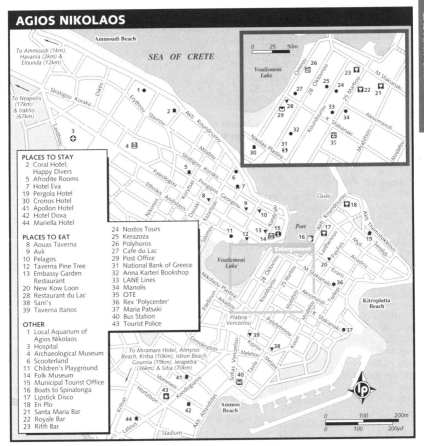

**AGIOS NIKOLAOS**

SEA OF CRETE

To Ammoudi (1km),
Havania (2km) &
Elounda (12km)

Ammoudi Beach

To Neapolis
(17km)
& Iraklio
(67km)

Voulismeni
Lake

Quay

Port

Voulismeni
Lake

Enlargement

Kitroplatia
Beach

To Miramare Hotel, Almyros
Beach, Kritsa (10km), Istron Beach,
Gournia (19km), Ierapetra
(36km) & Sitia (70km)

Ammos
Beach

Stadium

**PLACES TO STAY**
2  Coral Hotel;
   Happy Divers
5  Afrodite Rooms
7  Hotel Eva
19  Pergola Hotel
30  Cronos Hotel
41  Apollon Hotel
42  Hotel Doxa
44  Mariella Hotel

**PLACES TO EAT**
8  Aouas Taverna
9  Avli
10  Pelagos
12  Taverna Pine Tree
13  Embassy Garden
    Restaurant
20  New Kow Loon
28  Restaurant du Lac
38  Sarri's
39  Taverna Itanos

**OTHER**
1  Local Aquarium of
   Agios Nikolaos
3  Hospital
4  Archaeological Museum
6  Scooterland
11  Children's Playground
14  Folk Museum
15  Municipal Tourist Office
16  Boats to Spinalonga
17  Lipstick Disco
18  En Plo
21  Santa Maria Bar
22  Royale Bar
23  Rififi Bar

24  Nostos Tours
25  Kerazoza
26  Polyhoros
27  Cafe du Lac
29  Post Office
31  National Bank of Greece
32  Anna Karteri Bookshop
33  LANE Lines
34  Manolis
35  OTE
36  Rex 'Polycenter'
37  Maria Patsaki
40  Bus Station
43  Tourist Police

***Pergola Hotel*** (☎ 2841 028 152, fax 2841 025 568, Sarolidi 20) Singles/doubles with bath €17.60/23.50. Rooms are comfortable and have a fridge. There is a pleasant outdoor verandah under a pergola to relax on.

***Hotel Doxa*** (☎ 2841 024 214, fax 2841 024 614, Idomeneos 7) Singles/doubles €23.50/29.50 The plant-filled lobby sets a homey tone for this hotel that also boasts an attractive terrace for breakfast or drinks. Rooms are small but inviting and are equipped with telephones and balconies.

***Hotel Eva*** (☎ 2841 022 587, Stratigou Koraka 20) Singles/doubles €23.50/26.50.

This is a neat little place close to the action in the centre of town. Rooms are smallish but quite reasonable.

### Places to Stay – Mid-Range

***Coral Hotel*** (☎ 2841 028 363, fax 2841 028 754, Akti Koundourou 68) Singles/doubles €47/58.70 with buffet breakfast. On the edge of Ammoudi Beach, this hotel is large, modern and offers comfortable rooms with TV and balconies. There's a sauna, outdoor swimming pool and water sports centre.

***Apollon Hotel*** (☎ 2841 023 023, fax 2841 028 939, Kapetanaki 9) Singles/doubles

€47/58.70 including buffet breakfast. Conveniently located near the centre of town and Ammos Beach, this large modern hotel offers rooms with balconies, telephones, fridges and air-con. There's also a small pool and a games room with a pool table.

*Miramare Hotel* (☎ *2841 023 875, fax 2841 024 164, Gargadoros*) Singles/doubles €92/143 including buffet breakfast. Miramare Hotel is about a kilometre south of the town centre. Rooms are outfitted with air-con, satellite TV, fridge, telephone and balcony.

## Places to Eat

Dining can be a hit and miss affair in Agios Nikolaos mainly because restaurants cater to the tourist tastes rather than more discerning Greek palates. The following choices are among the better options.

*Sarri's* (☎ *2841 028 059, Kyprou 15*) Breakfast €3. Open 8am-midnight. Not only is this the best breakfast spot in town but it stays open until the wee hours serving up mouth-watering food to a neighbourhood crowd. Savouring a souvlaki in the shady courtyard is especially pleasant.

*Aouas Taverna* (☎ *2841 023 231, Paleologou 44*) Mezedes €1.80-8. This is the kind of family-run place where your waiter may be a 10-year-old and the cook is her aunt. The interior is plain but the enclosed garden is refreshing and the mezedes are wonderful.

*New Kow Loon* (☎ *2841 023 891, Pasifais 1*) Set menu for two €32.50. Open noon-3pm & 6pm-midnight. The decor blares 'Chinese' with lots of red, gold and multicoloured lights. The menu is large and the food is reasonably authentic. It makes for a pleasant change from traditional Cretan cuisine.

*Embassy Garden Restaurant* (☎ *2841 083 153, Kondylaki 5*) Mains €4.70-7.40. This is a friendly eatery that has a pleasant outdoor terrace and some interesting pasta dishes as well as the standard Cretan fare. Try the 'Greek plate' for €6.75.

*Avli* (☎ *2841 082 479, Pringipos Georgiou 12*) Mezedes €3-5.90. Open 7pm-midnight. Technically an ouzeri, Avli offers an outstanding selection of mezedes that make a meal in itself. Like many ouzeris, it's going upscale and also offers good-value meals in a garden setting. Try chicken and okra (€5.30).

*Taverna Itanos* (☎ *2841 025 340, Kyprou 1*) Ladera €2.50-4. This is a vast place with beamed ceilings and stucco walls. It has a few tables on the sidewalk as well as comfortable banquettes. The food is displayed in a glass case and the house wine is very palatable.

*Taverna Pine Tree* (☎ *2841 023 890 Paleologou 18*) Mezedes €2.80-4.90. Dining along scenic Voulismeni Lake is one of the great pleasures of Agios Nikolaos and this taverna is a good choice. Make your selection from the glass display case inside and then relax in comfortable wicker chairs for a view of the lake.

*Restaurant du Lac* (☎ *2841 022 414, Voulismeni Lake*) Set menus €11.80-20. This place is known for its excellent seafood but there's a full array of Cretan fare on the menu as well as a flashy steak flambe (€13.20). The restaurant offers good-value breakfasts and set-price menus.

*Pelagos* (☎ *2841 025 737, Katehaki 10*) €5.90-12.60. Open 7pm-midnight Mon-Sat Mar-Oct. For an excellent selection of fresh seafood, this place, in a beautifully restored house, is generally considered the best restaurant in Agios Nikolaos.

## Entertainment

You don't need a guide to find the nightlife in Agios Nikolaos – the nightlife will find you. This is a town that slumbers during the day and comes alive at night.

*Lipstick Disco* (*Akti Koundourou 22*) Open 11pm-dawn Apr-Oct. It's loud, crowded and overpriced but this is Agios Nikolaos' premier disco. In fact, it's the only disco. You'll see many foreigners but few locals.

*Royale Bar* (*25 Martiou 20*) Open 6pm-2am. A perennial favourite, Royale is known for its excellent cocktails and relentlessly upbeat mood. It's no place for a quiet conversation but a good place to meet other people.

*Rififi (☎ 2841 023 140, 25 Martiou 2)* Open 10pm-dawn Apr-Oct. Along the lively Agios Nikolaos harbour, Rififi provides a raucous good time to a late-night crowd.

*Santa Maria Bar (☎ 2841 022 984, M Sfakianaki 16)* Open 10pm-2am Apr-Oct. This bar provides more of a local ambience than many of the other bars along the waterfront. There's no live music but the bar has a good selection of contemporary Greek popular music on disc.

*Cafe du Lac (☎ 2841 026 837, 28 Oktovriou 17)* Open 10am-midnight. This cafe is a quiet place to take a breather from the frenzied harbour nightlife with a soothing view over Voulismeni Lake. The decor is modern.

*En Plo (☎ 2841 025 831 Akti Koundourou 4)* Open 10am-midnight Mar-Nov. On a bluff overlooking the harbour, En Plo is a subdued bar/cafe that is usually less crowded than the bars mentioned here. The music is 80s and 90s rock.

*Rex 'Polycenter' (☎ 2841 083 681, M Sfakianaki 35)* This is a 300-seat convention centre that doubles as a cinema, presenting new-release movies.

## Shopping

There are a great many shops in Agios Nikolaos peddling a range of touristy junk to high quality goods.

The offerings run the gamut from cheap Asian imports to luxury watches, but the bulk of the stores offer mid-range ceramics, icons, beach gear, light cotton clothing and postcards.

*Maria Patsaki (☎ 2841 022 001, K Sfakianaki 2)* Open 8am-10pm Mar-Oct. In this eclectic store you'll find embroidery, rugs and antiques that are a cut above the average.

*Kerazoza (☎ 2841 022 562, R Koundourou 42)* Open 10am-10pm Mar-Jan. The name of this place means rainbow in the Cretan dialect and refers to the shop's focus on make-believe and illusion. The unusual items include handmade masks, marionettes and figurines derived from ancient Greek theatre.

## Getting There & Away

**Bus** Destinations of buses from Agios Nikolaos' bus station (☎ 2841 022 234) are:

| destination | duration | fare | frequency |
|---|---|---|---|
| Elounda | 20 mins | €0.90 | 20 daily |
| Kritsa | 15 mins | €0.90 | 12 daily |
| Ierapetra | 1 hour | €2.40 | 8 daily |
| Iraklio | 1½ hours | €4.60 | 19 daily |
| Istron | 30 mins | €0.90 | 11 daily |
| Lasithi Plateau | 3 hours | €5.60 | 1 daily |
| Sitia | 1½ hours | €4.90 | 6 daily |

**Ferry** Agios Nikolaos has the same ferry schedule as Sitia. LANE Lines (☎ 2841 026 465, fax 2841 023 090) K. Sfakianaki 5, has ferries three times per week to Piraeus (€23.20, 12 hours), Karpathos (€13, seven hours) and Rhodes (€19, 10½ hours). Ferry tickets can be bought from LANE, or from travel agents advertising ferry ticket sales.

## Getting Around

You will find many car and motorcycle-hire outlets on the northern waterfront. Scooterland (☎ 2841 026 340) Koundourou 10, has a huge range of scooters and motorcycles. Prices begin at €11.80 a day for a scooter and go to €44 a day for a Kawasaki EN.

You can rent mountain bikes from Manolis (☎ 2841 024 940) Martiou 25, down the street from the OTE office. Prices begin at €7.40 a day.

Local buses run regularly from Almyros Beach to the Candia Park Hotel on the road to Elounda. The buses stop in front of the tourist office or in Plateia Venizelou; the maximum for a journey is €0.80.

## ELOUNDA Ελούντα
**postcode 720 53 • pop 1600**

There are magnificent mountain and sea views along the 11km road north from Agios Nikolaos to Elounda (el-**oon**-da). Although formerly a quiet fishing village, Elounda is now bristling with tourists and is marginally calmer than Agios Nikolaos. The harbour is attractive, however, and there's a sheltered lagoon-like stretch of water formed by the Kolokytha Peninsula, known commonly – but erroneously – as the Spinalonga Peninsula.

Near modern Elounda, about 500m towards Agios Nikolaos, a sign directs you past the remains of Venetian salt pans to the site of the Greco-Roman city-state of Olous (oh-**lous**), which lies on an isthmus that joins the Kolokytha Peninsula to the mainland.

### Orientation & Information

Elounda is a spread-out village, but it's main square abutts the harbour and is identified by a clock prominent clock tower. The bus stop is close to the main square. as is the municipal tourist office (☎ 2841 042 464). It's open 8am to 11pm daily from June to October. They will help you find accommodation and change money. Olous Travel (☎ 2841 041 324, fax 2841 041 132) is in the centre of town and handles air and boat tickets and finds accommodation. It's open 8am to 9pm daily from April to November.

There is no tourist police but the regular police (☎ 2841 041 348) are represented in the village. The Commercial Bank and National Bank of Greece, on the main square both have ATMs. Check your email at Babel Internet Cafe (☎ 2841 042 336, Akti Vritomartidos) on the waterfront, 100m north of the clock tower. The post office is opposite the bus stop. Find used and new English-language books at English-run Eklektos (☎ 2841 042 285). You'll also find maps and some Lonely Planet titles here.

### Organised Tours

Boats from Elounda Harbour offer trips to Spinalonga and all-day swimming and fishing trips, and four-hour cruises that include a visit to Spinalonga Island, swimming and a visit to the sunken city of Olous.

### Places to Stay

There's some good accommodation around, but nothing particularly cheap.

*Katerina Apartments* (☎ 2841 041 484, Elounda) Studios €29.50. These apartments are on the south side of the town and are well equipped.

*Hotel Aristea* (☎ 2841 041 300, fax 2841 041 302, Elounda) Singles/doubles €29.50/44. This hotel is in the town centre and most rooms have a sea view.

*Corali Studios* (☎/fax 041 712, Elounda) Double studios €35.30. On the north side of Elounda, about 800m from the clock tower are these handy self-catering studios, set in lush lawns and a shaded patio.

*Portobello Apartments* (☎/fax 041 712, Elounda) 2-4 bed apartments €47. Next door to Corali and under the same management these spacious apartments are a good option for a group of two or three people.

Most of Elounda's finer hotels are on the beach road south of town on the way to Agios Nikolaos. Local buses to and from Agios Nikolaos stop in front of all the hotels.

*Horizon Hotel* (☎ 2841 041 895, Elounda) Singles/doubles €23.50/29.50. This hotel is about 1km south of town and offers rooms with balconies and sea views.

*Grecotel Elounda Village* (☎ 2841 041 002, fax 2841 041 278, Elounda) Singles/doubles €75/102. This is the first of Elounda's resort hotels on the main road from Agios Nikolaos. It has a splendid outdoor swimming pool, water sports centre, tennis courts and air-conditioned rooms.

### Places to Stay – Top End

If money is no object to your holiday plans, Elounda might just be the place to dispose of it. Long the haunt of Greece's glitterati and euro-flush high flyers, Elounda boasts some of the most ostentatious and expensive hotel accommodation in Greece. Clustered to the south of Elounda a couple of resorts can cater to your every whim.

*Elounda Beach Hotel & Villas* (☎ 2841 041 412, fax 2841 041 373, e elohotel@ eloundabeach.gr, Elounda) This is one of the world's great luxury resorts and is about 1.5km south of Elounda Village. This is the place to go for pampering on a major scale. The rooms run the gamut from 'simple' affairs with fresh flowers, bathrobes, twice-daily maid service, Jacuzzis and TVs in the bathrooms to royal suites with a private indoor swimming pool, personal fitness trainer, butler, secretary and cook. There are also bungalows with a private outdoor swimming pool and platform on the sea. The cost?

A mere €390 for a simple double room or, if your needs are more demanding a cool €1500 for an executive suite with your own swimming pool.

***Elounda Bay Palace*** *(☎ 2841 041 502, fax 2841 041 583, Elounda,* **e** *bay@eloundabay.gr,* **w** *www.eloundabay.gr)* With a similar ticket price this is run by the same management as the Elounda Beach Hotel and is also very swish. You can sleep in a modest garden-view room for €161, or rent a waterfront bungalow for €308. For the seriously cashed-up, the Grand Suite will set you back €2055 a night.

### Places to Eat
***Vritomartis*** *(☎ 2841 041 325, Elounda)* Mixed mezedes for two €29. In the square next to the harbour, Vritomartis bills itself as the oldest fish taverna in the village, and offers an impressive collection of fresh fish. The fish and meat mixed mezes platter is a good option.

***Nikos*** *(☎ 2841 041 439, Elounda)* Grills €3.80-6.20. Another good choice for fish is Nikos, which has outdoor tables under a canopy. Service can be erratic but food is reasonably cheap.

***Kalidon Restaurant*** *(☎ 2841 041 451, Elounda)* Hot mezedes €3.20-12.30. Kalidon offers a good selection of fresh fish and Cretan dishes on a floating pontoon that nearly overlooks the harbour.

***Marilena*** *(☎ 2841 041 322, Elounda)* Mains €7.40-13.20. Marilena is touristy but serves excellent mezedes, fish and lobster.

***The Ferryman Taverna*** *(☎ 2841 041 230, Elounda)* Greek specialities €7.40-9. The Ferryman is *the* place to eat in Elounda. It is expensive, but worth it. Dining is waterside and service is top class. Cretan lamb (€9.10) is a good choice.

### Entertainment
These are currently the most popular nightclubs.

***Katafygio*** *(☎ 2841 042 003, Elounda)* Katafygio is the most scenic place in Elounda, built in a former carob processing plant with tables along the water. It plays live Greek music.

***Lasers Disco*** *(Elounda)* Lasers is south of the town centre next to the ancient city of Olous. It's open nightly in summer from midnight, but weekends only in winter.

***Eden Cafe*** *(☎ 2841 042 242, Elounda)* In town near the church is this spacious comfortable cafe/bar popular with the locals for its eclectic selection of music.

### Getting Around
Elounda Travel (☎ 2841 041 333, fax 2841 041 433) in the town centre rents cars, motorcycles and scooters.

### Getting There & Away
There are 20 buses a day from Agios Nikolaos to Elounda (€0.90, 20 minutes).

### KOLOKYTHA PENINSULA
Χερσόνησος Κολοκύθα
Just before Elounda (coming from Agios Nikolaos), a sign points right to **ancient Olous**, which was the port of Lato. The city stood on and around the narrow isthmus (now a causeway) which joined the southern end of the Kolokytha Peninsula to the mainland. Olous was a Minoan settlement that flourished from 3000 to 900 BC. Around 200 BC Olous entered into a treaty with the island of Rhodos as part of Rhodos Island's desire to control eastern Crete and put an end to the piracy that was ravaging the Aegean. Excavations indicate that Olous was an important trade centre with the eastern islands and minted its own currency. Little is known about Olous during the Greek, Roman and Byzantine eras but it appears that Olous was destroyed by the 9th-century Saracens.

The isthmus sank as a result of the earthquakes that have repeatedly devastated Crete. In 1897 the occupying French army dug a canal across the isthmus connecting Spinalonga Bay to the open sea. Most of the ruins lie beneath the water. The shallow water around here appears to be paradise for sea urchins and the area is known for the many birds that nest here. There is an early Christian mosaic near the causeway that was part of an early Christian basilica.

There is an excellent sandy **beach** 1km along a dirt road (just driveable) on the east side of the peninsula. The beach is sheltered, the water pristine and few visitors use it.

## SPINALONGA ISLAND
Νήσος Σπιναλόγκα

Spinalonga Island lies just north of the Kolokytha Peninsula and was strategically important from antiquity to the Venetian era. The island's massive **fortress** (admission €1.50; open 8am-7pm daily) was built by the Venetians in 1579 to protect the bays of Elounda and Mirabello. It was considered impregnable, withstood Turkish sieges for longer than any other Cretan stronghold but finally surrendered in 1715 some 30 years after the rest of Crete. The Turks used the island as a base for smuggling. Following the reunion of Çrete with Greece, Spinalonga became a leper colony. The last leper died there in 1953 and the island has been uninhabited ever since. Spinalonga is still known among locals as 'the island of the living dead'.

The **cemetery**, with its open graves, is an especially strange place. Dead lepers came in three classes: those who saved money from their government pension for a place in a concrete box; those whose funeral was paid for by relatives and who therefore got a proper grave; and the destitute, whose remains were thrown into a charnel house.

### Getting There & Away
There are regular excursion boats to the island from Agios Nikolaos and a boat every half-hour from the port in Elounda (€6). Alternatively, you can negotiate with the fishermen in Elounda and Plaka (a fishing village 5km further north) to take you across.

The boats from Agios Nikolaos pass Bird Island and Kri-Kri Island, one of the last habitats of the *kri-kri*, Crete's wild goat. Both of these islands are designated wildlife sanctuaries and are uninhabited.

# Lasithi Plateau
## Οροπέδιο Λασιθίου

The first view of the mountain-fringed Lasithi Plateau, laid out like an immense patchwork quilt, is stunning. The plateau, 900m above sea level, is a vast expanse of pear and apple orchards, almond trees and fields of crops, dotted by some 7000 windmills. These are not conventional stone windmills but slender metal constructions with white canvas sails, built by the Venetians to irrigate the land. Unfortunately not many of the original windmills are in use today, but you may see a few examples outside tavernas or shops. There are 20 villages dotted around the periphery of the plateau, the largest of which is Tzermiado.

The plateau's rich soil has been cultivated since Minoan times. The inaccessibility of the region made it a hotbed of insurrection during Venetian and Turkish rule. Following an uprising in the 13th century, the Venetians drove out the inhabitants of Lasithi and destroyed their orchards. The plateau lay abandoned for 200 years.

### Activities
**Cycling** the perimeter of the plateau is a popular activity and on any given day you will be assailed by squadrons of helmet-clad cyclists pedalling their way around the relatively flat plateau landscape. Cycling to the plateau is another matter since the approach roads from either Iraklio or Agios Nikolaos are long and steep and would tax the fitness of all but the most dedicated cyclist. Instead, enterprising cycle tour operators in Iraklio and Agios Nikolaos, ferry bikes and cyclists to the plateau. This way cyclists can tour the 25km perimeter and then cruise *down*hill from the plateau rim on the way home. Instead, cycle tour operators in Iraklio or Agios Nikolaos ferry the bikes and cyclist into the plateau, let them ride the 25km perimeter road and then have them cruise *down*hill from the plateau rim for the ride home.

### TZERMIADO Τζερμιάδο
**postcode 720 52 • pop 1300**
Tzermiado (dzer-mee-**ah**-do) is a sleepy town with dusty little streets lined with houses overgrown with vines and hanging plants. It's the largest and most important

town on the Lasithi Plateau and has a fair amount of tourism from the tour buses going to the Dikteon Cave. There are a fair number of shops selling rugs and embroidered blouses although not of a particularly high quality.

## Orientation & Information

There is only one main road running through town that takes you past the town square.

The post office is on the town's main square and the bank and OTE are on the main street. There is an Agricultural Bank and ATM in the village.

## Places to Stay & Eat

*Hotel Kourites (☎ 2844 022 194, Tzermiado)* Singles/doubles €29.50/35.50 including breakfast. On the left, as you enter town from the east side, you'll see this hotel with additional rooms available in nearby buildings. There is free use of the hotel's bicycles.

*Restaurant Kourites (☎ 2844 022 054, Tzermiado)* Grills €4-5. Part of the hotel of the same name, but 50m further along the street is this large restaurant that often has tour groups stopping by for lunch. Food is filling and wholesome.

*Taverna Kri-Kri (☎ 2844 022 170, Tzermiado)* Mayirefta €3.50-4. On Tzermiado's main street is this little eatery, where you can buy simple, unfussy meals.

## Getting There & Away

From Agios Nikolaos there's an afternoon bus to Tzermiado on Monday, Wednesday and Friday (€5.60, two hours) and a morning bus from Tzermiado to Agios Nikolaos also on Monday, Wednesday and Friday. From Iraklio there are two buses daily (except weekends) to Tzermiado (€4, 1½ hours) and three daily buses (except weekends) returning to Iraklio.

## PSYHRO Ψυχρό

postcode 720 52 • pop 183

Psyhro (psi-**hro**) is the closest village to Dikteon Cave. It has one main street with a few tavernas and rooms, and plenty of souvenir shops selling 'authentic' rugs and mats of non-Cretan origin. It is prettier and less dusty than Tzermiado and makes for a better rest stop. Buses to Psyhro drop you at the end of the town where it's about a kilometre walk uphill to the cave.

## Places to Stay & Eat

There is only one place to stay in Psyhro.

*Zeus Hotel (☎ 2844 031 284, Psyhro)* Singles/doubles with bath €20.50/26.50. This is a modern D-class hotel on the west side of the village near the start of the Dikteon Cave road.

You have two choices of places to eat. They are opposite each other.

*Stavros (☎ 2844 031 453, Psyhro)* Mains €3-4.50. With its neat folksy interior and streetside tables, Stavros serves a good range of traditional Cretan dishes. The meat is all locally produced. Try goat in lemon and rice sauce (€4.40).

*Platanos (☎ 2844 031 668, Psyhro)* Ladera €2.70-3.80. Set under a large plane tree on the opposite side of the road is the other eating option. There's a good range of vegetable-based dishes here, some of which are also cooked with snails (€3).

## Getting There & Away

Public transportation to Psyhro is problematic if you don't have your own wheels. From Agios Nikolaos there's an afternoon bus to Lasithi on Monday, Wednesday and Friday (€5.60, 2½ hours) and a morning bus from Lasithi to Agios Nikolaos also on Monday, Wednesday and Friday. From Iraklio there are two buses daily (except weekends) to Lasithi (€4.60, two hours) and three daily buses (except weekends) returning to Iraklio. All buses go through Tzermiado and Agios Georgios before terminating at Psyhro at the foot of the road leading to the Dikteon Cave.

## DIKTEON CAVE Δίκταιον Αντρον

Lasithi's major sight is the Dikteon Cave (☎ 69-7736 4335, Psyhro; admission €2.40; open 8am-4pm), just outside the village of **Psyhro**. Here, according to mythology, Rhea hid the newborn Zeus from Cronos, his offspring-gobbling father.

The cave, also known as the Psyhro Cave, has both stalactites and stalagmites, and was excavated in 1900 by the British archaeologist David Hogarth. He found numerous votives indicating that the cave was a place of cult worship. These finds are housed in the Archaeological Museum in Iraklio.

The cave began to be used for cult worship in the Middle Minoan period and continued, though less intensely, up to the first century AD. An altar for offerings and sacrifices was in the upper section of the cave. Stone tablets inscribed with Linear A were found here along with religious bronze and clay figurines.

Two deities were worshipped in the cave: one god is of course Zeus, symbolised by the double axe, and the other was a female deity variously referred to as Mother Gaia or Pantheme. Even the stalactites and stalagmites, often taking human or animal form, were worshipped.

There are two sections to the cave; the upper and the lower cave. The upper cave is large and generally devoid of stalactites or stalagmites. A steep downward path brings you to the more interesting lower cave. In the upper cave the ground is strewn with boulders but there is one group of stalagmites. The lower cave is on a north-south axis and is 38m wide, 85m long and five to 14m high. In the back on the left is a smaller chamber where it is alleged that Zeus was born. There is a larger hall on the right which is divided into two sections; the first section has small stone basins filled with water that Zeus allegedly drank from. In the second section there is a spectacular stalagmite which came to be known as the Mantle of Zeus. The entire cave covers 2200 sq metres and is illuminated – though not particularly well, so watch your step in the murky sections.

It is a steep 15-minute walk up to the cave entrance along a fairly rough track, or you can opt to take a rather expensive donkey ride (€8.80) instead. There is a less obvious paved trail to the cave that starts from the left side of the car park, though it's not as shaded as the rougher track. Walk between the two restaurants and you will see people coming down from the paved track.

Drivers pay €1.80 to park their car and motorbike owners €0.30.

## AGIOS GEORGIOS Αγιος Γεώργιος
### postcode 720 52 • pop 781

Agios Georgios (**agh**-ios ye-**or**-gios) is a tiny village on the south side of the Lasithi Plateau. Of all the plateau villages, Agios Georgios would have to be the most pleasant to stay in. There are places to eat and at least one very worthwhile accommodation choice. If you have your own bicycle, base yourself here and explore the plateau at your leisure.

The village also boasts an excellent and worthwhile **folklore museum** (☎ 69-7792 5464, Agios Georgios; admission €2.40; open 10am-4pm Apr-Oct). Housed in the original home belonging to the Katsapakis family, the museum is in several parts and merits a leisurely browse. The entry fee is also valid for the nearby **Eleftherios Museum**, primarily a photo collection dedicated to the former Greek statesman, and the little attached **church** with its Byzantine frescoes. A small snack bar completes the scene.

### Places to Stay & Eat
There are two accommodation options.

*Rent Rooms Maria* (☎ 2844 031 209, Agios Georgios) Singles/doubles €18/20.50. On the northern side of the village, Maria has spacious stucco rooms decorated with weavings. The plant-filled enclosed garden is a pleasant place to relax.

*Hotel Dias* (☎ 2844 031 207, Agios Georgios) Singles/doubles with shared bathroom €12/14.50. On the main street in the village, Hotel Dias has pleasant rooms above the restaurant of the same name.

*Taverna Rea* (☎ 2844 031 209, Agios Georgios) Grills €4.50. Opposite the school on the main street, Taverna Rea rustles up locally produced grilled meats and other staple Cretan fare. The affable owner also owns Rent Rooms Maria.

### Getting There & Away
Agios Georgios has two buses daily from Iraklio (€4.40, two hours) and one daily from Agios Nikolaos (€5.60, three hours).

## The Myth of Zeus

Cronos was the leader of the seven Titans of mythical antiquity. Cronos married his sister Rhea, but wary of his mother Gaia's warning that he would be usurped by one of his own offspring, he swallowed every child Rhea bore him. When Rhea had her sixth child, Zeus, she smuggled him to Crete, and gave Cronos a stone in place of the child, which he duly swallowed. Rhea hid the baby Zeus in the Dikteon Cave in the care of three nymphs.

On reaching manhood, Zeus, determined to avenge his swallowed siblings, became Cronos' cup-bearer and filled his cup with poison. Cronos drank from the cup, then disgorged first the stone and then his children Hestia, Demeter, Hera, Poseidon and Hades, all of whom were none the worse for their ordeal. Zeus, aided by his regurgitated brothers and sisters, deposed Cronos, and went to war against the Titans who refused to acknowledge him as chief god. Gaia, who still hadn't forgotten her imprisoned, beloved offspring, told Zeus he would only be victorious with the help of the Cyclopes and the 100-handed giants, so he released them from Tartarus.

The Cyclopes gave Zeus a thunderbolt, and the three 100-handed giants threw rocks at the Titans, who eventually retreated. Zeus banished Cronos, as well as all of the Titans except Atlas (Cronos' deputy), to a far-off land. Atlas was ordered to hold up the sky.

Mt Olympus became home-sweet-home for Zeus and his family. Zeus soon took a fancy to his sister Hera. He tricked the unsuspecting Hera into holding him to her bosom by turning himself into a dishevelled cuckoo, then violated her. Hera reluctantly agreed to marry him and they had three children: Ares, Hephaestus and Hebe.

## KRITSA Κριτσά
postcode 720 51 • pop 2000

Kritsa (krit-**sah**) village is a charmer from every angle. As you approach from the east, the swathe of whitewashed houses terraced into the mountainside is strikingly photogenic.

From the 600m-high village, there are sweeping views over the valley on one side and steep mountains on the other. The village is a carnival of colour with Kritsa's renowned weavings and embroidery draped and hung on every available surface. Even the bus loads of tourists that swarm through the streets all summer haven't managed to dim Kritsa's allure.

As in many Cretan villages, the men are in kafeneia while the women run the shops. When not hawking their merchandise, the women sit on stools with fingers flying over their fabric. Although the designs are not necessarily authentic, it's still possible to search out the traditional geometric designs of Crete. Kritsa is also within easy reach of two other sights: the Church of Panagia Kera and the archaeological site of Lato.

## Orientation & Information

One narrow street runs through Kritsa. There are no parking spaces, but there are car parks at the bottom and top of the village. The post office is near the bottom car park. There is no bank but there is a Commercial Bank ATM half-way up the hill on the left.

## Places to Stay & Eat

There's very little accommodation in Kritsa.

**Rooms Argyro** (☎ 2841 051 174, Kritsa) Singles/doubles €17.60/29.50. This is the best place to stay. The 12 rooms are immaculate and there is a little shaded restaurant downstairs for breakfast and light meals. The signposted rooms are on the northern side of the village.

**Rooms Kera** (☎ 2841 051 045, Kritsa) Singles/doubles €14.70/16.20. Kera is in the village centre, 100m uphill from the bus stop and offers basic rooms.

**O Kastellos** (☎ 2841 051 254, Kritsa) Mains €5.60-7.40. This is a cool, restful place in the centre of Kritsa to grab a pizza or a hearty meal to eat under a plane tree.

Oven-cooked veal and pasta in a pot (€5.30) is recommended.

## Getting There & Away
There are 12 buses a day from Agios Nikolaos to Kritsa (€0.90, 15 minutes).

## AROUND KRITSA
The tiny triple-aisled **Church of Panagia Kera** *(Kritsa; admission €2.30; open 8.30am-3pm Mon, 8.30am-2pm Fri & Sat; year-round)* is on the right 1km before Kritsa on the Agios Nikolaos road and contains the most outstanding Byzantine frescoes on Crete. The oldest part of the church is the central nave which is from the 13th century, but most of the frescoes date from the early to mid-14th century. The dome and nave are decorated with four gospel scenes: the Presentation, the Baptism, the Raising of Lazarus and the Entry into Jerusalem. On the west wall there's a portrayal of the Crucifixion and grimly realistic depictions of the Punishment of the Damned. The vault of the south aisle recounts the life of the Virgin and the north aisle is an elaborately worked out fresco of the Second Coming. Nearby is an enticing depiction of Paradise next to the Virgin, the Patriarchs, Abraham, Isaac and Jacob. Judgement Day is portrayed on the west end with the Archangel Michael trumpeting the Second Coming.

## ANCIENT LATO Λατώ
The ancient city of Lato (la-**to**) *(admission €1.50; open 8.30am-3pm Tues-Sun)*, 4km north of Kritsa, is one of Crete's few non-Minoan ancient sites. Lato was founded in the 7th century BC by the Dorians and at its height was one of the most powerful cities on Crete until it was destroyed in 200 BC. It sprawls over the slopes of two acropolises in a lonely mountain setting, commanding stunning views down to the Bay of Mirabello.

The city's name derived from the goddess Leto whose union with Zeus produced Artemis and Apollo, both of whom were worshipped here. Lato is far less visited than Crete's Minoan sites.

## Exploring the Site
The **city gate** is the entrance to the site and leads to a long, stepped street. The wall on the left contains two towers which were also residences. Follow the street to reach the **agora**, built around the 4th century BC, that contained a cistern and a small rectangular sanctuary. Excavations of the temple revealed a number of 6th-century BC figurines. The circle of stones behind the cistern was a threshing floor. The western side of the agora contains a **stoa** with stone benches. There are remains of a pebble mosaic nearby. A terrace above the south-east corner of the agora contains the remains of a **rectangular temple** probably built in the late 4th or early 3rd century BC. There is an inscription at the base of the temple statue but it is too damaged to be read. Between the two towers on the northern end of the agora there are steps which lead to the **prytaneion**, the administrative centre of the city-state. The centre of the prytaneion contained a hearth with a fire that burned day and night. On the east side of the prytaneion is a colonnaded court. Below the prytaneion is a semi-circular **theatre** which could seat about 350 people next to an **exedra** (stage platform) with a bench around the walls.

## Getting There & Away
There are no buses to Lato. The road to the site is signposted to the right on the approach to Kritsa. But if you don't have your own transport, it's a pleasant 30-minute walk through olive groves along this road.

## MONI FANEROMENIS
Μονή Φανερωμένης
Just 2km before Gournia, on the Agios Nikolaos-Sitia road, a 5km road leads off right to the late-Byzantine Moni Faneromenis. If you have your own transport, a visit to the monastery is worthwhile for the stunning views down to the coast and to see its 15th-century fresco of the Panagia.

## GOURNIA Γουρνιά
The important Minoan site of Gournia (*gournya*) (☎ 2841 024 943, Gournia; admission €1.50; open 8.30am-3pm Tues-Sun) lies just

off the coast road, 19km south-east of Agios Nikolaos. The ruins, which date from 1550 to 1450 BC, consist of a town overlooked by a small palace. Gournia's palace was far less ostentatious than the ones at Knossos and Phaestos; it was the residence of an overlord rather than a king. The town is a network of streets and stairways flanked by houses with walls up to 2m in height. Domestic, agricultural and trade implements found on the site indicate that Gournia was a thriving little community.

South of the palace is a large rectangular **court** which was connected to a network of paved stone streets. South of the palace is a large **stone slab** used for sacrificing bulls. The room to the west has a stone **kernos** (large earthen dish) ringed with 32 depressions and probably used for cult activity. North of the palace was a **Shrine of the Minoan Snake Goddess,** which proved to be a rich trove of objects from the Postpalatial Period. Notice the storage rooms, workrooms, and dwellings to the north and east of the site. The buildings were two-storey structures with the storage and workrooms in the basement and the living quarters on the first floors.

Gournia is on the Sitia and Ierapetra bus routes from Agios Nikolaos. Buses, from the main bus station in town, can drop you at the site.

## MOHLOS Μόχλος
**postcode 720 57 • pop 80**

Mohlos (**moh**-los) is a pretty fishing community reached by a 6km winding road from the main Sitia-Agios Nikolaos highway. It was joined in antiquity to the homonymous island that now sits 200m offshore and was once a thriving Minoan community dating back to the early Minoan period (3000–2000 BC). Archaeological excavations still continue sporadically on both Mohlos Island and at Mohlos village. A short description of the archaeology of the area is presented on an information board overlooking the tiny harbour.

Mohlos is an atmospheric village bedecked in hibiscus, bougainvillea and bitter laurel. It sees mainly French and German independent travellers seeking peace and quiet. There is a small pebble-and-greysand beach where swimming is reasonable. Beware of strong currents further out in the small straight between the island and the village. There is a good selection of accommodation and places to eat. Mohlos is an ideal traveller rest stop with a high chill-out factor.

## Orientation & Information
Mohlos is all contained within two or three blocks, all walkable within 10 minutes. There is no bank, or post office and few tourist facilities other than a couple of gift shops. There are two minimarkets.

## Activities
**Off Road Motorbike Tours** (*☎/fax 2843 094 725,* **e** *motoff@otenet.gr)* offers guided motorbike or jeep **tours** of Crete. A one-week fully-inclusive bike tour of some out-of-the-way places in Crete costs €763.

**La Chlorophylle** (*☎/fax 2843 094 725,* **e** *annelebrun@caramail.com)* is run by Belgian Ann Lebrun. She takes hikers on **nature walks** around Mohlos ranging in length from 1½ hours to five hours. The longer walks include visits to a church, a pottery atelier and provide a picnic lunch. Tours range in price from €7.50-17.50.

## Places to Stay & Eat
Try these two places to stay.

*Hotel Sofia* (*☎/fax 2843 094 554, Mohlos)* Double/triple rooms €29.50/32.30; double/triple studios €35.30/44. The comfortable rooms are above the Sofia restaurant while the fully equipped 2-3 person studios are 200m east of the harbour.

*Spyros Rooms* (*☎/fax 2843 094 204, Mohlos)* Double rooms €29.50. The very pleasant and modern rooms all have a fridge and air-con and are a little way outside the village. See Spyros at the Kavouria restaurant to check in.

The restaurants abutting the harbour are all good. Pick a new one each day. Start with these two.

*To Bogazi* (*☎ 2843 094 200, Mohlos)* Mezedes €1.50-4.50. With a sea view on two sides, To Bogazi is nearest the island and serves over 30 inventive mezedes, many of which are vegetarian friendly. For a main course the cuttlefish and pan tossed greens is suggested (€5.30).

*Sofia* (☎ *2843 094 554, Mohlos*) Mayirefta €2.50-3.50. Mama's home cooking is the key ingredient on the menu at Sofia. Owner George Petrakis (and his mother) serve up simple home-cooked food as well as fish and grills. Vegetarians will love artichokes with peas (€2.70) or cauliflower in wine sauce (€2.50).

### Getting There & Away
There is no public transport directly to Mohlos. Buses between Sitia and Agios Nikolaos will drop you off at the Mohlos turnoff. From there you'll need to hitch or walk the 6km to Mohlos village. You are better off with your own wheels.

### SITIA Σητεία
**postcode 723 00 • pop 7028**
Sitia (si-**tee**-a) is the perfect escape from the tourist frenzy that grips most of the north coast in summer. You won't see shop after shop of cookie-cutter ceramics, waiters won't try to drag you into their restaurants and the menus aren't translated into four languages. What you will see are ordinary Cretans going about their business in an attractive mid-sized coastal town. The harbourside promenade is clear of taverna tables making it a lovely for an evening stroll.

The bustling streets of the old town wind their way uphill from the harbour and the town's southern end is on a long, narrow stretch of sandy beach. Even at the height of the season, the town has a laid-back feel that is a refreshing antidote to the commercialism of towns further west.

### History
Archaeological excavations indicate that there were Neolithic settlements around Sitia and an important Minoan settlement at Petras, a kilometre east of the current town centre. The original settlement was destroyed and eventually abandoned after an earthquake in 1700 BC.

In the Greco-Roman era there was a town called Iteia in or around modern Sitia although its exact site has not yet been located. In Byzantine times Sitia became a bishopric which was eliminated by the Saracen conquest of Crete in the 9th century. Under the Venetians, Sitia became the most important port in eastern Crete. Sitia was racked by a disastrous earthquake in 1508, a blow from which it never really recovered. Crete's most famous poet, Vitsentzos Kornaros was born in Sitia in 1614, while the Turkish blockade of Sitia in 1648 was the death knell for the town.

The remaining inhabitants fled and the walls and buildings of the town were destroyed. It was not until the late 19th century when the Turks decided to make Sitia an administrative centre that the town gradually came back to life.

### Orientation & Information
The bus station is at the southern end of Karamanli, which runs behind the bay. The town's main square, Plateia El Venizelou is at the northern end of Karamanli. The harbour near the square is for small boats. Ferries use the large quay, about 500m from Plateia Agnostou. There's a Municipal Tourist Information Office and Tzortzakis Travel (☎ 2843 025 080), Kornarou 150, is also a good source of information.

There are plenty of places to change money and lots of ATMs. The National Bank of Greece on the main square has a 24-hour automatic exchange machine.

The post office is at Dimokritou 10; the OTE is at Kapetan Sifi 22 – both close to Plateia Agnostou.

The police and tourist police (☎ 2843 022 266) are housed in the same building at Therisou 31.

### Things to See & Do
The **Archaeological Museum** (☎ *2843 023 917, Pisokefalou; admission €1.50; open 8.30am-3pm Tues-Sun*) in Sitia houses a well-displayed collection of local finds spanning from Neolithic to Roman times, with emphasis on the Minoan civilisation. One of the more interesting exhibits is the

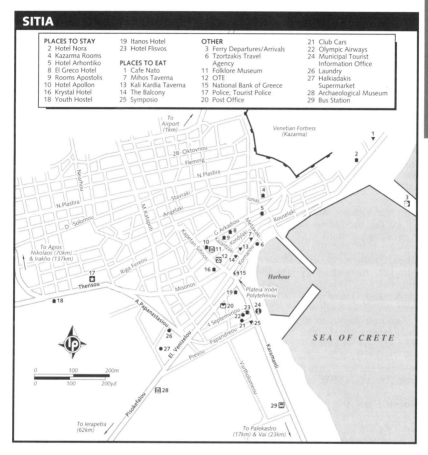

# SITIA

**PLACES TO STAY**
2 Hotel Nora
4 Kazarma Rooms
5 Hotel Arhontiko
8 El Greco Hotel
9 Rooms Apostolis
10 Hotel Apollon
16 Krystal Hotel
18 Youth Hostel
19 Itanos Hotel
23 Hotel Flisvos

**PLACES TO EAT**
1 Cafe Nato
7 Mihos Taverna
13 Kali Kardia Taverna
14 The Balcony
25 Symposio

**OTHER**
3 Ferry Departures/Arrivals
6 Tzortzakis Travel
   Agency
11 Folklore Museum
12 OTE
15 National Bank of Greece
17 Police; Tourist Police
20 Post Office
21 Club Cars
22 Olympic Airways
24 Municipal Tourist
   Information Office
26 Laundry
27 Halkiadakis
   Supermarket
28 Archaeological Museum
29 Bus Station

*Paleokastro Kouros* – a figure pieced together from fragments, composed of hippopotamus tusks and adorned with gold. The finds from the palace at Zakros are also interesting and include a wine press, bronze saw, jars, cult objects and pots that are clearly scorched from the great fire that destroyed the palace. The most valuable objects in the museum are the Linear A tablets which reflect the palace's administrative function. The museum is on the left side of the road from Sitia to Ierapetra.

Towering over the town is the fort or **kazarma** which was a garrison under the Venetians. They are the only remains of the wall that once protected the town. It is now used as an open-air theatre.

There is also a **folklore museum** (☎ 2843 022 861, Kapetan Sifi 28; admission €1.50; open 9.30am-1.30pm and 5-8pm Mon; 9.30am-2.30pm and 5-9pm Tue-Fri; 9.30am-2.30pm Sat) that displays a fine collection of local weavings.

## Special Events

Sitia produces superior sultanas and the town holds a **Sultana Festival** in the last week of August, during which wine flows

Phone numbers listed incorporate changes due in Oct 2002; see p61

freely and Cretan dances are performed. Admission is €7.50, including local wine.

There is also the **Kornaria Festival** that runs from mid-July to the end of August in which concerts, folk dancing and theatre productions are staged in the kazarma and other venues. Posters around town announce the events, some of which are free. For paying events look for a ticket kiosk in the main square.

## Places to Stay

**Hostels** *Sitia Youth Hostel (☎ 2843 028 062, Therisou 4)* Dorm beds €5, doubles with shared bathroom €11.80. Sitia's youth hostel is on the road to Iraklio. It's a well-run place with hot showers and a communal kitchen and dining room, with artistic graffiti-covered walls.

**Domatia** *Rooms to Let Apostolis (☎ 2843 028 172, Kazantzaki 27)* Doubles with fridge €23.50. This is an up-market domatia. Kazantzaki runs uphill from the waterfront, one street north of the OTE.

*Kazarma Rooms to Rent (☎ 2843 023 211, Ionias 10)* Doubles with bathroom €26.50. Another attractive place is Kazarma. There is a communal lounge and a well-equipped kitchen. The rooms are signposted from Patriarhou Metaxaki.

**Hotels** *Hotel Arhontiko (☎ 2843 028 172, Kondylaki 16)* Singles/doubles with bathroom €17.70/20.50. The D-class Arhontiko is beautifully maintained and spotless. On summer evenings, the friendly owner enjoys sharing a bottle of raki with guests on the communal terrace.

*El Greco Hotel (☎ 2843 023 133, fax 2843 026 391, Arkadiou 13)* Singles/doubles with bath €28/38. The well-signposted El Greco has more character than the town's other C-class places.

*Hotel Nora (☎ 2843 023 017, Rouselaki 31)* Singles/doubles €17.60/26.50. Hotel Nora is uphill from the town centre and has rooms with telephone, TV and balconies.

*Hotel Apollon (☎ 2843 028 155, fax 2843 022 733, Kapetan Sifi 28)* Singles/doubles €40/44. The Hotel Apollon has extremely comfortable rooms with air-con on demand, TV, telephone and fridge.

*Krystal Hotel (☎ 2843 022 284, fax 2843 028 644, Kapetan Sifi 17)* Singles/doubles with air-con €40/50. This is a four-storey building with wrap-around balconies in the town centre that has modern rooms.

*Hotel Flisvos (☎ 2843 027 135, fax 2843 027 136, Karamanli 4)* Singles/doubles €26.50/44. On the southern waterfront, Flisvos is a very pretty, new hotel with excellent facilities. Rooms are spotless and have air-con, TV, fridge and phone. There is ample guest parking.

*Itanos Hotel (☎ 2843 022 900, fax 2843 022 915, e itanoshotel@yahoo.com, Karamanli 4)* Singles/doubles €28/47. The B-class Itanos has a conspicuous location on the waterfront and a popular terrace restaurant. The comfortable rooms are outfitted with air-con, satellite TV, balconies and sound-proofing.

## Places to Eat

A string of tavernas along the quay side on El Venizelou offer an array of mezedes and speciality fish dishes at comparable prices.

*Mihos Taverna (Kornarou 117)* Grills €4-5.50. On the waterfront this taverna has excellent charcoal-grilled souvlaki. This is one of the few decent waterfront eateries.

*Kali Kardia Taverna (☎ 2843 022 249, Foundalidou 22)* Mains €4-5.50. Open 10am-midnight. This place is excellent value and popular with locals. Walk up Kazantzaki from the waterfront, take the second right and the taverna is on the right.

*Cafe Nato (☎ 69-7282 8503, Mastropavlou 43)* Mezedes €1.50-2.50. Open noon-midnight. Cafe Nato, 20m further up from Hotel Nora, is a laid-back little taverna with outdoor tables that serves a variety of grilled meat, locally produced gourmet cheeses and good raki.

*Symposio (☎ 2843 025 856, Karamanli 12)* Mains €5.30-6.80. Symposio utilises all-Cretan, natural products such as organic olive oil from the Toplou monastery. The food is top-class. Rabbit in rosemary and wine sauce (€5.30) is recommended.

*The Balcony* (☎ *2843 025 084, Foundalidou 18*) Mains €8.50-10.50. Open noon-3pm & 6.30pm-midnight. The Balcony provides the finest dining in Sitia with an extraordinarily creative menu that combines Greek, Italian and Mexican food.

## Getting There & Away
**Air** The Olympic Airways office (☎ 2843 022 270) is at 4 Septemvriou 3. Sitia's tiny airport has flights to Athens twice a week for €75.40.

**Bus** From Sitia's bus station (☎ 2843 022 272) there are six buses a day to Ierapetra (€3.80, 1½ hours); five buses a day to Iraklio (€8.80, 3½ hours) via Agios Nikolaos (€4.90, 1½ hours); five to Vai (€1.90, one hour); and two to Kato Zakros (one hour) via Palekastro and Zakros (€3.40, one hour). The buses to Vai and Kato Zakros run only between May and October; during the rest of the year, the Vai service terminates at Palekastro and the Kato Zakros service at Zakros.

**Ferry** The F/B *Vitsentzos Kornaros* and F/B *Ierapetra* of LANE Lines link Sitia with Piraeus (€24, 14½ hours), Kasos (€8.50, four hours), Karpathos (€11, six hours) and Rhodes (€20, 10 hours) three times weekly. Departure times change annually, so check locally for latest information.

Buy ferry tickets at Tzortzakis Travel Agency (☎ 2843 022 631, 28 900, Kornarou 150).

## Getting Around
**To/From the Airport** The airport (signposted) is 1km out of town. There is no airport bus; a taxi costs about €3.80.

**Car & Motorcycle** Car and motorcycle hire outlets are mostly on Papandreou and Itanou. Try Club Cars (☎ 2843 025 104, Papandreou 8).

## MONI TOPLOU Μονή Τοπλού
East of Sitia, the imposing Moni Toplou (☎ *2843 061 226, Lasithi; admission €2.40; open 9am-1pm & 2pm-6pm*) looks more like a fortress than a monastery – a necessity imposed by the dangers it faced at the time of its construction. The middle of the 15th century was marked by piracy, banditry and constant rebellions. The monks defended themselves with all the means at their disposal including a heavy gate, cannons (the name Toplou is Turkish for 'with a cannon'), and small holes for pouring boiling oil onto the heads of their attackers. Nevertheless, it was sacked by pirates in 1498, looted by the Knights of Malta in 1530, pillaged by the Turks in 1646 and captured by the Turks in 1821.

With the wealth and treasure that the monastery had accumulated, it's not surprising that it was a tempting target for looters and sackers. The star attraction is undoubtedly the icon *Lord Thou Art Great* by Ioannis Kornaros. Each of the 61 small scenes painted on the icon is beautifully worked out and each is inspired by a phrase from the Orthodox prayer that begins 'Lord, Thou Art Great'. The icon is in the north aisle of the church along with 14th-century frescoes and an antique icon stand from 1770.

Moni Toplou had always been active in the cause for Cretan independence and paid a price for it. Under the Turkish occupation, its reputation for hiding rebels led to severe reprisals. During WWII many resistance leaders were sheltered in the monastery and operated an underground radio transmitter that led to the execution of Abbot Silingakis. It's a 3km walk from the Sitia-Palekastro road. Buses can drop you off at the junction.

## VAI & ITANOS Βάι & Ιτανος
The beach at Vai, on Crete's east coast 24km from Sitia, is famous for its palm forest. There are many stories about the origin of these palms including the theory that they sprouted from date pits spread by Roman legionaries relaxing on their way back from conquering Egypt. While these palms are closely related to the date, they are a separate species found only on Crete.

You'll need to arrive early to appreciate the setting, because the place is packed in July and August. It's possible to escape the worst of the ballyhoo – jet skis and all – by clambering over a rocky outcrop southwards to a small secluded beach. Alternatively, there's a quiet beach over the hill to the north that is frequented by nudists.

**Vai Watersports & Scuba Centre** (☎ 2843 061 070) is on the left side of the beach. You can dive for €30 including equipment or take a certification course for €320.

Eat at the church-run ***Restaurant-Cafeteria Vai*** (☎ 2843 061 129, Vai) Mains €4-5. The restaurant is at the southern end of the beach and while it offers no great culinary treats, is dependable and welcome after a hard day on the beach.

If you're after more secluded beaches, head north for another 3km to the ancient Minoan site of **Itanos**. Although inhabited from about 1500 BC Itanos was clearly prosperous by the 7th century BC since it was an important trading post for exports to the Near East and Middle East. Its archrival was Praisos, near Ierapetra, and in 260 BC Itanos hosted a garrison of Egyptians to fortify its position against Praisos.

When Ierapetra destroyed Praisos in 155 BC Itanos fought with Ierapetra as well and again received foreign help from Magnesia, a Roman city. The town was destroyed somewhere toward the end of the Byzantine era and may have been re-inhabited by the Venetians. It's difficult to discern any recognisable building in Itanos but there are remains of two early Christian basilicas and a Hellenistic wall. The site is well-marked and next to swimming coves shaded by pine trees.

### Getting There & Away

There are five buses a day to Vai from Sitia that stop at Palekastro (€1.80, one hour). Car owners will pay €3 to park their car in the Vai car park. Free parking can be found 500m before Vai itself, on the roadside.

# East Coast

## PALEKASTRO Παλαίκαστρο
**postcode 72 300 • pop 2000**
Palekastro (pah-**leh**-kas-tro) is a modern, rather bland town that is useful more as a

base for exploring eastern Crete than as a destination in itself. It's situated in the midst of a rocky barren landscape but is within easy reach of the lovely Kouremenos Beach, Vai Beach and Moni Toplou. It's best to have your own transport.

### Orientation & Information

The main street of Karamanli, runs through the town and forks to the right and left in the town centre. There's no post office but there is a tourist office (☎ 2843 061 546) combined with the OTE, that changes money and is also a good source of information. It's open 9am to 10pm Monday to Saturday from May to October. The bus stop is in the centre of town.

### Places to Stay & Eat

***Itanos Rooms*** (☎ 2843 061 205, Palekastro) Singles/doubles €16/19. Nearby is Itanos Rooms which has basic but good rooms.

***Hotel Hellas*** (☎ 2843 061 240, fax 2843 061 340, e hellas_h@otenet.gr, Palekastro) Singles/doubles €23.50/32.50. The best accommodation in town is here; rooms have air-con, TV and telephone and double-glazed windows. It's on the right fork from the town centre.

***Rooms and Apartments Nikos*** (☎/fax 2843 061 480, Palekastro) 5-bed apartments with kitchens €50, double rooms €23.50. Near the Hotel Hellas, this place is on the left fork.

***Castri Village Hotel Bungalows*** (☎ 2843 061 100, fax 2843 061 249, Palekastro) Singles/doubles €23.50/30. Two kilometres east of Palekastro on the road to Vai is an attractively designed establishment on the slope of a hill overlooking Kouremenos Beach. Rooms are fresh and modern and there's a swimming pool.

There is a cluster of restaurants and tavernas, all open for lunch and dinner.

***Restaurant Elena*** (☎ 2843 061 234, Palekastro) Mains €3.50-4. Next to the tourist office, this restaurant serves good Cretan cuisine including dishes such as rabbit in wine sauce (€5).

***To Filistrini*** (☎ 2843 061 117, Palekastro) Mezedes €2-4. About 200m along the

Vai road, this neat little ouzeri-cum-meze-dopolio dishes up tasty mezedes that go down well with a shot or 10 of raki.

The Hotel Hellas and Itanos Rooms also have good restaurants.

### Getting There & Away
There are two buses a day from Sitia that stop at Palekastro (€1.90, 30 minutes) before continuing on to Kato Zakros and three buses a day from Sitia that stop at Palekastro on their way to Vai.

## AROUND PALEKASTRO
The closest beach to Palekastro is **Kouremenos**, a nearly deserted pebble beach with good shallow water swimming and excellent windsurfing. You can rent boards from **Kouremenos Windsurfing** (☎ 69-3751 7444).

Hiona Beach, 2km from Palekastro is another quieter choice. There are three beach tavernas to choose from, but no accommodation on the beach.

There's also a Minoan **archaeological site** about a kilometre from Palekastro town. The site is still being excavated and most of it is closed to visitors but it's a pleasant walk getting there and you can still see the layout of the streets. Excavations have produced important finds such as Kamares pottery, amphorae, soapstone lamps and pithoi.

### Places to Stay & Eat
*I Hiona* (☎ 2843 061 228, Hiona Beach) Fish €35.30kg. Hiona is one of the three tavernas on Hiona Beach and preferred by many locals for its super-fresh fish.

*Glaros Apartments* (☎ 2843 061 282, Kouremenos) Double/quad studios €47/ 58.70. One of two places to stay close to Kouremenos Beach is this neat set of self-contained studios. There is also an attached restaurant.

*Apartments Grandes* (☎ 2843 061 496, e grandes_gr@yahoo.com, Kouremenos) Double studios €47. Also on the beach is this pretty place surrounded by a flower garden and trees. It's similarly equipped to Glaros Apartments and has a restaurant.

## ZAKROS Ζάκρος
**postcode 723 00 • pop 765**
The village of Zakros (**zah**-kros), 45km south-east of Sitia, is the nearest permanent settlement to the east-coast Minoan site of Zakros, which is 7km away. The village is an important agricultural centre for the cultivation of olives, oranges, figs and a wide range of vegetables. While there is little incentive to linger in the village (there is only one hotel), it's a lively place where the kafencia and ouzeris are always animated and busy with the locals and there is rarely a tourist in sight. Zakros is also the starting point for the trail through the Zakros Gorge. See the 'Head to the Hills' special section in the Facts for the Visitor chapter.

### Places to Stay & Eat
*Hotel Zakros* (☎ 2843 093 379, Zakros) Doubles with bath €17.60. Zakros has this one rather bleak C-class hotel. Rooms in the back have decent views over the gorge. Kato Zakros is a much better place to stay.

*Restaurant Pizzeria Napoleon* (☎ 2843 093 152, Zakros) Pizzas €4. Try this little place on the Kato Zakros road for pizza and pasta.

### Getting There & Away
There are two buses a day to Zakros (via Palekastro) from Sitia (€3, one hour). They leave Sitia at 11am and 2.30pm and return at 12.30pm and 4pm. In summer, the buses continue to Kato Zakros. The Hotel Zakros offers guests free transport to Kato Zakros.

## ZAKROS PALACE
A visit to Zakros Palace and Kato Zakros (☎ 2843 026 987, Kato Zakros; admission €1.50; open 8am-7pm daily) combines two of the best things about Crete – an intriguing archaeological site and a long stretch of under-populated beach. Although Zakros Palace was the last Minoan palace to have been discovered (1962), the excavations proved remarkably fruitful.

The exquisite rock crystal vase and stone bull's head now in Iraklio's Archaeological Museum were found at Zakros Palace along with a treasure-trove of Minoan antiquities.

## Walking the Valley of the Dead

The spectacular Zakros Gorge – touted locally as the 'Valley of the Dead' – makes for a thoroughly enjoyable two-hour walk from Zakros village to Kato Zakros, or if time is pressing, for a one-hour walk from the half way point to either end.

The signposted walk starts from just below Zakros village and winds it way through an, at times, soaring, narrow canyon. The base of the canyon is a riverbed (dry in summer) and a riot of vegetation and wild herbs such as bitter laurel, oregano, sage and savoury.

About 3km from Zakros is an alternative starting point, indicated by a wooden sign and (usually) parked cars. The approach track dips steeply into the gorge before meeting the main trail after 10 minutes. Turn left for Zakros, or right for Kato Zakros. While not physically taxing, the trail is better tackled in stout footwear and in the early morning or late afternoon to avoid the heat. Take food and drink and make a relaxed picnic of the walk.

The canyon takes its moniker from the fact that ancient burial sites are located in the numerous caves dotting the canyon walls, rather than from hapless trekkers who failed to make it. At the eastern end the trail emerges close to the Zakros Palace site, while the azure sea beckons walkers for a refreshing swim.

Ancient Zakros, the smallest of Crete's four palatial complexes, was a major port in Minoan times, trading with Egypt, Syria, Anatolia and Cyprus. The palace consisted of royal apartments, storerooms and workshops flanking a central courtyard but the ruins are not well-preserved and water levels have risen over the years so that some parts of the palace complex are submerged.

### Exploring the site

If you enter the palace complex on the southern side you will first come to **workshops** for the palace. The **King's apartment** and **Queen's apartment** are to the right of the entrance. Next to the King's apartment is the **Cistern Hall** which once had a cistern in the centre surrounded by a colonnaded balustrade. Seven steps descended to the floor of the cistern which may have been a swimming pool, an aquarium or a pool for a sacred boat. To the left of the cistern room is the **Light Well** and then the **Central Court** which was the focal point of the whole palace. Notice the altar base in the north-west corner of the court; there was a **well** in the south-east corner of the court at the bottom of eight steps. When the site was excavated the well contained the preserved remains of olives that had been offered to the deities.

Adjacent to the central court is the **Hall of Ceremonies** in which two rhytons were found. The room to the south is the **Banquet Hall** so named for the quantity of wine vases found there. To the north of the central court is the **kitchen**. The column bases probably supported the dining room above. To the west of the central court is another **light well** and to the left of the banquet hall is the **Lustral Basin** which once contained a magnificent marble amphora. The Lustral Basin served as a washroom for those entering the nearby **Central Shrine**. You can still see a ledge and a niche in the south wall for the ceremonial idols.

Below the Lustral Basin is the **Treasury** that yielded nearly a hundred jars and rhytons. Next to the treasury is the **Archive Room** that once contained Linear A record tablets. Although there were hundreds of tablets, only the ones baked by the fire that destroyed the palace were preserved. Northeast of the archives room is the **bathroom** with a cesspit.

### KATO ZAKROS Κάτω Ζάκρος
**postcode 723 00 • pop 16**

Little more than a long stretch of pebbly beach shaded by pine trees and bordered by a string of tavernas, Kato Zakros (kah-to zah-kros) is about the most tranquil place to

NEIL SETCHFIELD

Curly horned mountain goat, Lasithi Province

NEIL SETCHFIELD

Flowers in doorway, Mochlos

VITO VAMPATELLA

Three elderly Greek friends, Lasithi Plateau

NEIL SETCHFIELD

Escape the tourist frenzy in Sitia, Lasithi Province

Beachfront at the Hotel Petra Mare, Ierapetra

Outdoor cafe, Lasithi Plateau

Pottery found at the ancient Malia site, Lasithi

Boats moored on Lake Voulismeni, Agios Nikolaos

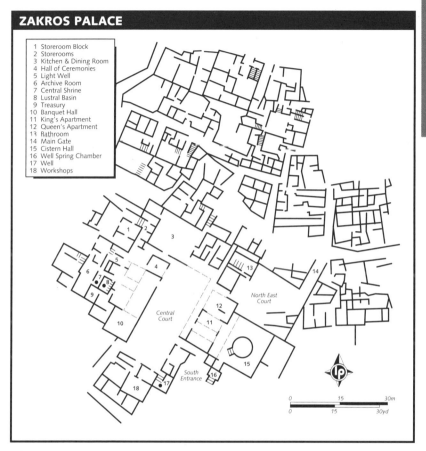

**ZAKROS PALACE**

1 Storeroom Block
2 Storerooms
3 Kitchen & Dining Room
4 Hall of Ceremonies
5 Light Well
6 Archive Room
7 Central Shrine
8 Lustral Basin
9 Treasury
10 Banquet Hall
11 King's Apartment
12 Queen's Apartment
13 Bathroom
14 Main Gate
15 Cistern Hall
16 Well Spring Chamber
17 Well
18 Workshops

North East Court

Central Court

South Entrance

0   15   30m
0   15   30yd

stay on Crete's south-east coast. Many people who come here have been doing so for many years. The settlement is unlikely ever to expand thanks to restrictions imposed by the Ministry of Archaeology and Antiquities. There is little to do here but relax on the beach, snorkel, fish, sleep, eat, poke around the archaeological site or walk the Zakros Gorge.

There is no bank, shops, post office or OTE, but you can change money at the tavernas and make phone calls from a cardphone. Mobile phone users will only pick up Cosmote here.

## Places to Stay

The several domatia in Kato Zakros fill up fast. If there are no rooms available you can camp at the southern end of the beach.

*Poseidon Rooms* (☎ 2843 026 893, fax 2843 026 894, e akrogiali@sit.forthnet.gr, Kato Zakros) Doubles €17.60, with bath €26.50. At the southern end of the waterfront Poseidon Rooms are small but neat and clean and make for a good budget choice.

*Athena Rooms* (☎ 2843 026 893, fax 2843 026 894, e akrogiali@sit.forthnet.gr, Kato Zakros) Doubles with bath €26.50. A better quality choice. These rooms are very pleasant with heavy stone walls and views of the beach from the balcony.

**Rooms Coral** (*☎/fax 027 064, Kato Zakros* **e** *katozakrosgr@yahoo.com*) Doubles €35.50. Excellent small, but clean rooms equipped with Internet connections. All enjoy superb sea views from the communal balcony. There's a kitchen and fridge for guests' use.

**George's Villas** (*☎/fax 026 833, Kato Zakros*) Singles/doubles with bath €26.50/ 32.30. George's has spotless, beautifully furnished rooms with terraces. The villas are in a verdant, pine-tinged setting 800m along the old road to Zakros.

### Places to Eat
**Taverna Akrogiali** (*☎ 2843 026 893, Kato Zakros*) Mains €4.40. Soothing seaside dining and excellent service from owner Nikos Perakis. The speciality is grilled swordfish steak (€7.40).

**Georgios Taverna Anesis** (*☎ 2843 026 890, Kato Zakros*) Ladera €1.50-3.30. The owner specialises in home-cooked food and ladera dishes. Dining is under trees overlooking the beach.

**Restaurant Nikos Platanakis** (*☎ 2843 026 887, Kato Zakros*) Ladera €3-3.80. A wide range of Greek staples is available such as rabbit, and other rarities including pheasant and partridge. Dining is also waterside.

### Getting There & Away
There are two buses a day to Zakros (via Palekastro) from Sitia (€3, one hour). In summer, the buses continue to Kato Zakros.

## XEROKAMBOS Ξερόκαμπος
**postcode 720 59 • pop 25**
Xerokambos (Kse-**ro**-kam-bos) is a quiet unassuming agricultural village on the far south-eastern flank of Crete. Its isolation has so far meant that tourism is pretty much low-key and most certainly of the unpackaged kind. Its attraction lies in its isolation, a couple of splendid beaches, a few scattered tavernas and a scattering of studio accommodation that is ideal for people with peace and quiet in mind.

Ambelos Beach, on the northern side of the rocky headland that splits Xerokambos in two, is the smaller and more intimate beach and enjoys some shade. Mazidas Beach, on the south side is larger, but has no shade whatsoever. Most accommodation and tavernas are on the more populated Ambelos side of Xerokambos. There is a well-stocked mini market on the north side of Mazidas beach.

Travellers usually approach Xerokambos from a long and winding road via Ziros, though there is an 8km dirt road linking Zakros with Xerokambos. This latter road is a bit rough in parts, but quite driveable with a conventional vehicle.

### Places to Stay & Eat
**Ambelos Beach Studios** (*☎/fax 2842 026 759, Xerokambos*) Double/triple studios €29.50/32.50. The six studios are smallish but very cosy, with kitchenette and small sitting area. Air-conditioning (€4.40) is optional. There is a barbecue and outdoor wood oven for guests and a tree-shaded courtyard. The studios are close to Ambelos Beach.

**Apartments Eolos** (*☎/fax 2842 026 197, Xerokambos*) Studios €29.50. These very neat and pleasant two-person apartments have a fridge and kitchenette and optional air-conditioning (€4.40). They overlook Mazidas Beach.

**Taverna Kastri** (*☎ 2842 026 745, Xerokambos*) Fish €29.50kg. A very well-provided for restaurant on Mazidas Beach, Kastri serves up its own fish caught from its own caique. Try their enormous lobster-sized Cretan crayfish.

**Akrogiali Taverna** (*☎ 2842 026 777, Xerokambos*) Mains €3. The only beachside taverna in Xerokambos, Akrogiali is 50m from Ambelos Beach. Food is standard Cretan fare – from grills to fish, to home-cooked mayirefta. The best choice for beach-goers.

### Getting There & Away
There is no public transport to Xerokambos. Approach is made by car or motorbike from Ziros or Zakros, 8km to the north.

# South Coast

## IERAPETRA Ιεράπετρα
postcode 722 00 • pop 11,000

Ierapetra (ee-yer-**ap**-et-rah) attracts few packaged tourists – after the tourist hype of Agios Nikolaos, the unpretentiousness of Ierapetra is refreshing. It is a very pleasant place to base yourself for a week or so. The beach is good, the nightlife busy enough to keep you entertained and the scene is still Cretan enough to make other towns pale into insignificance. From Ierapetra you can visit the offshore, low-lying, sandy island of Gaïdouronisi (also known as Hrysi) where Europe's only stand of cedars of Lebanon can be found.

### History

Ierapetra is Crete's most southerly major town. It was an important city for the Dorians and the last city to fall to the Romans, who made it a major port of call in their conquest of Egypt. Despite its antiquity, virtually nothing survives from the classical period.

The city languished under the Venetians, but they did build a small fortress at the western end of the harbour. In recent years agriculture has made the town wealthy enough to finance the restoration of the old town and the harbourside.

### Orientation & Information

The bus station is on Lasthenous, a five-minute walk from the beachfront north of the town centre. From the ticket office, turn right and after about 50m you'll come to a six-road intersection. There are signposts to the beach, via Patriarhou Metaxaki, and to the city centre, via the pedestrian mall section of Lasthenous.

The mall emerges after about 150m on to the central square of Plateia Eleftherias. To the north of the square is the National Bank of Greece and on the south side is Eurobank. Both banks have ATMs.

The OTE is one block inland at Koraka 25. South of Plateia Eleftherias is Plateia Georgiou Kounoupaki, where you'll find the post office at Vitsentzou Kornarou 7. You can check email at the Polycafe Orpheas

(☎ 842 080 462, Koundouriotou 25) or The Net Internet Cafe (☎ 2842 025 900, e the_net_ier@yahoo.com, Koundourou 16). Both charge around €3 per hour.

South Crete Tours (☎ 2842 022 892, Lasthenous 36), diagonally opposite the bus station is a good source of travel information. It's open 8am to 6pm Monday to Friday.

There's a bookstore with English language books and decent maps of Crete at Markopoulou 71.

### Things to See

Ierapetra's one-room **archaeological museum** (*☎ 2842 028 721, Adrianou 2; admission €1.50; open 8.30am-3pm Tues-Sun*) is perfect for those with a short concentration span. It does have a good collection of headless classical statuary and a superb statue of the goddess of Demeter that dates from the 2nd century AD. Also notable is a *larnax* or clay coffin dating from around 1300 BC. The chest is decorated with 12 painted panels showing hunting scenes, an octopus and a chariot procession among others. It's at the intersection of Adrianou and Keraka.

If you walk south along the waterfront from the central square you will come to the **medieval fortress** (*Kato Meran; admission free; 8.30am-3pm Tues-Sun*), which was built in the early years of Venetian rule and strengthened by Francesco Morosini in 1626. It's in a pretty fragile state but you can visit it.

Inland from here is the labyrinthine old quarter, a delightful place to lose yourself for a while. Notice the **Turkish fountain**, the restored **Turkish mosque** with its minaret, and the old churches of **Agios Ioannis** and **Agios Georgios**

**Beaches** Ierapetra has two beaches. The main town beach is near the harbour and the other one stretches east from the bottom of Patriarhou Metaxaki. Both have coarse, grey sand but the main town beach offers better shade and is closer to restaurants.

### Special Events

Ierapetra's Kyrvia Festival runs from July through August and includes concerts,

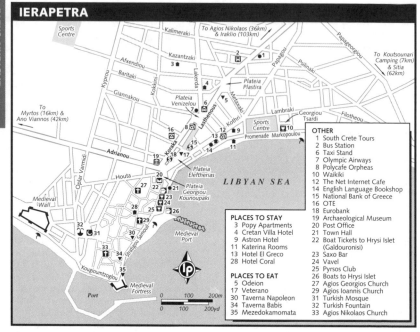

**IERAPETRA**

*LIBYAN SEA*

**OTHER**
1  South Crete Tours
2  Bus Station
6  Taxi Stand
7  Olympic Airways
8  Polycafe Orpheas
10  Waikiki
12  The Net Internet Cafe
14  English Language Bookshop
15  National Bank of Greece
16  OTE
18  Eurobank
19  Archaeological Museum
20  Post Office
21  Town Hall
22  Boat Tickets to Hrysi Islet (Gaïdouronisi)
23  Saxo Bar
24  Vavel
25  Pyrsos Club
26  Boats to Hrysi Islet
27  Agios Georgios Church
29  Agios Ioannis Church
31  Turkish Mosque
32  Turkish Fountain
33  Agios Nikolaos Church

**PLACES TO STAY**
3  Popy Apartments
4  Cretan Villa Hotel
9  Astron Hotel
11  Katerina Rooms
13  Hotel El Greco
28  Hotel Coral

**PLACES TO EAT**
5  Odeion
17  Veterano
30  Taverna Napoleon
34  Taverna Babis
35  Mezedokamomata

plays and art exhibits. Brochures are available in hotels and at the town hall. Some of the bands are free but tickets to top name concerts cost €4.50 to €15. An all inclusive ticket costs about €30.

## Places to Stay

**Camping** *Koutsounari Camping* (☎ 2842 061 213, fax 2842 061 186, Koutsounari) Adult/tent €3.50/2.60. The nearest camping ground to Ierapetra is 7km east at Koutsounari. It has a restaurant, snack bar and minimarket. Ierapetra-Sitia buses pass the site.

**Hotels-Budget** Most of the places to stay are near the bus station or in the old quarter.

*Hotel Coral* (☎ 2842 022 846, Katzonovatsi 12) Singles/doubles €15/18, with bath €17.60/23.50. Rooms here are well-kept and apartments are comfortable. The hotel is signposted just south of the port police building on the waterfront.

*Popy Apartments* (☎ 2842 024 289, fax 2842 027 772, Parodos Kazantzaki 27) Double apartments €30. Hidden away just behind the former Four Seasons Hotel is this pleasant apartment block. All apartments are well-equipped and spacious.

*Cretan Villa Hotel* (☎/fax 2842 028 522, Lakerda 16 ⓔ cretan-villa@cretan-villa .com, Ⓦ www.cretan-villa.com) Singles/doubles with bath €26.50/35.50. This hotel is a lovely, well-maintained 18th-century house with traditionally furnished rooms and a peaceful courtyard.

**Hotels – Mid-Range** *Katerina Rooms* (☎ 2842 028 345, fax 2842 028 591, Markopoulou 95) Doubles with bath €32.50. On the seafront this place has pleasant rooms. To reach the hotel from the bus station, follow Patriarhou Metaxaki to the waterfront, turn right and the hotel is on the right.

*Hotel El Greco* (☎ 2842 028 471, fax 2842 024 515, Kothri 42) Singles/doubles

€35/48.50. El Greco is a pleasant hotel located near the beach and some of its rooms have sea views.

*Astron Hotel* (☎ *2842 025 114, fax 2842 025 91, Kothri 56)* Singles/doubles €41/73.50 including breakfast. The best hotel in town is the B-class Astron at the beach end of Patriarhou Metaxaki. The rooms here are comfortably furnished with satellite TV, telephone and air-conditioning.

## Places to Eat
Most of the souvlaki outlets are on Kyrva (a street running south from Plateia Georgiou Kounoupaki) and there is a swathe of restaurants all along the promenade.

*Taverna Babis* (☎ *2842 024 048, Stratigou Samouil 68)* Mains €3.50-5.50. Open noon-midnight. In the old quarter, this is one of the better tavernas along the waterfront. It has an enormous range of mezes dishes. Ask for *kakavia* (fish soup) or *staka* – a cream cheese made from curds.

*Mezedokamomata* (☎ *2842 028 286, Stratigou Samouil 74)* Mezedes €1.70-3.80. Similar to Babis and only 50m further along is this imaginative restaurant serving up more mezedes. If you like offal, ask for *splinandero*, or *omaties* rice and offal sausages.

*Taverna Napoleon* (*Stratigou Samouil 60)* Mains €4-5. Open noon-midnight. Nearby, this is the oldest taverna in Ierapetra and still manages to serve up a delicious array of Cretan specialties. Try the stuffed cabbage and the local white wine.

*Odeion* (*Lasthenous 18)* Snacks €3-4. For light snacks, this is a converted music school that serves mezedes in the basement while the first floor is a music bar.

*Veterano* (☎ *2842 023 175, Plateia Eleftherias)* Breakfast €3.50. This is a popular hang out for breakfast and light meals during the day.

## Entertainment
Kyrva is Ierapetra's nightlife street with a number of choices for a casual drink. The popularity of the bars waxes and wanes yearly, but the following were popular hang outs when visited.

*Saxo Bar* (*Kyrva 14)* This is a good spot for Greek music.

*Vavel* (*Kyrva 16)* Vavel is small and intimate and more suited to conversations over cocktails.

*Pyrsos Club* (*Kyrva 22)* Big and brassy, Pyrsos is the flashiest nightspot on 'bar street'.

*Waikiki* (☎ *2842 027 731, Georgiou Tzardi 2)* Waikiki would have to be the classiest bar in town. Right on the beach at the eastern end of the promenade it is open all day, is big and breezy and caters to all tastes.

## Getting There & Away
In summer, there are six buses a day to Iraklio (€6.75, 2½ hours) via Agios Nikolaos (€2.40, one hour), Gournia and Istron; eight to Makrygialos (€1.90, 30 minutes); six to Sitia (€4.10, 1½ hours) via Koutsounari (for camp sites); six to Myrtos (€1.20, 30 minutes) and two a week to Ano Viannos (€2.50, one hour). Contact the bus station (☎ 2842 028 237) for further information.

Taxis (☎ 2842 025 512) in town will take you to any number of destinations for fixed fares. The taxi stand on Plateia Venizelou posts all the destinations and their fares. Some of them are: Iraklio (€50), Agios Nikolaos (€20.50) Sitia (€29.50) or Myrtos (€8.80).

The Olympic Airways office (☎ 2842 022 444) is on Plateia Venizelou. The nearest airport is at Iraklio.

## AROUND IERAPETRA
The beaches to the east of Ierapetra tend to be crowded. For greater tranquillity, head for **Gaïdouronisi** (donkey island) – universally marketed in Ierapetra as **Hrysi** or **Hrissi** (golden island) – where there are good, sandy beaches, three tavernas and a stand of cedars of Lebanon, the only one in Europe. It can get a bit crowded when the tour boats are in but you can always find a quiet spot of your own.

In summer a number of excursion boats (€16) leaves from the quay near the town centre for the islet every morning and return in the afternoon. Excursions are very popular and tickets are sold everywhere.

## MYRTOS Μύρτος
**postcode 722 00 • pop 600**

Myrtos (**Myr**-tos), on the coast 17km west of Ierapetra, is a sparkling village of white-washed houses with flower-filled balconies. It is a magnet for independent travellers, many of whom only come for a day or so, yet find themselves inextricably staying on for a couple of weeks. The village has a cosy, lived-in ambience where everyone seems to know each other. Myrtos is one of those few places left in Crete that retains an element of authenticity yet provides the necessary creature comforts.

### Orientation & Information
Myrtos is easily navigable as it is built on a grid system. To get to the waterfront from the bus stop, head south and take the road to the right. There is no post office, bank or OTE, but Aris Travel Agency (☎ 2842 051 017) on the main street has a currency exchange. Internet is available upstairs at Edem Cafe (☎ 2842 051 551), two blocks back from the waterfront.

### Places to Stay
There is a good selection of properties aimed at the independent travellers.

*Hotel Myrtos* (☎ 2842 051 227, fax 2842 051 215, Myrtos; W www.myrtoshotel.com) Singles/doubles with bath €17.50/23.50. This superior C-class place has large, well-kept rooms.

*Big Blue* (☎ 2842 051 094, fax 2842 051 121, Myrtos; e big-blue@ier.forthnet.gr) Singles/doubles with bath €23.50, 2-room apartments with two bathrooms & kitchenette €59. Signposted from the village centre, Big Blue on the western edge of town, is a popular place and is handy for the beach.

*Cretan Rooms* (☎ 2842 051 427, Myrtos) Double €26.50. These excellent traditional-styled rooms with balconies, fridges and shared kitchens are popular with independent travellers. Owner Maria Daskalaki keeps them neat and clean. They are prominently signposted from the village centre.

*Nikos House* (☎ 2842 051 116, Myrtos) Double/quad apartments €35-40. Two blocks back from the waterfront are these large and comfortable apartments. They accommodate up to four people but can usually be rented for just two persons.

*Hotel Panorama* (☎/fax 2842 051 362, Myrtos) Double apartments €30. Uphill from the village centre the Panorama has studios with bathrooms, kitchenettes and spectacular views.

### Places to Eat
The seafront, not suprisingly, has the lion's shares of restaurants and tavernas, but the back streets turn up one or two pleasant choices.

*Myrtos Taverna* (☎ 2842 051 227, Myrtos) Mains €3-6. Myrtos is popular with both locals and tourists for its wide range of mezedes as well as vegetarian dishes. Rabbit in red wine sauce (€4.70) is recommended by the owner.

*O Manos* (☎ 2842 051 548, Myrtos) Mezedes €2.40-5.30. Manos dishes up a good range of mezedes – the aubergine dip (€2.40) is excellent, as is their smooth raki and very palatable draft wine.

*Taverna Akti* (☎ 2842 051 584, Myrtos) Grills €4.40-6. Pleasant seafood dining and good food are Akti's attraction. Look for the 'daily specials' board to see what's on. Order octopus in red wine sauce (€6.50) if you see it.

### Getting There & Away
There are six buses a day from Ierapetra to Myrtos (€1.20, 30 minutes). The twice-weekly Ano Viannos-Ierapetra bus also passes through Myrtos.

# Language

The Greek language is probably the oldest European language, with an oral tradition of 4000 years and a written tradition of approximately 3000 years. Its evolution over the four millennia was characterised by its strength during the golden age of Athens and the Democracy (mid-5th century BC); its use as a lingua franca throughout the Middle Eastern world, spread by Alexander the Great and his successors as far as India during the Hellenistic period (330 BC to AD 100); its adaptation as the language of the new religion, Christianity; its use as the official language of the Eastern Roman Empire; and its eventual proclamation as the language of the Byzantine Empire (380–1453).

Greek maintained its status and prestige during the rise of the European Renaissance and was employed as the linguistic perspective for all contemporary sciences and terminologies during the period of Enlightenment. Today, Greek constitutes a large part of the vocabulary of any Indo-European language, and much of the lexicon of any scientific repertoire.

The modern Greek language is a southern Greek dialect, now used by most Greek speakers in Greece and abroad. It is the result of an intralinguistic influence and synthesis of the ancient vocabulary combined with words from Greek regional dialects, namely Cretan, Cypriot and Macedonian.

Greek spoken in Crete is distinguished in the main by its particular accent, noticeable by the soft palatalisation of the letter 'k' (ie, 'tch'). The spoken vernacular contains many words never heard outside Crete and are often incomprehensible to mainlanders. The amateur linguist will have no problems making themselves understood with the use of standard Greek.

## Pronunciation

All Greek words of two or more syllables have an acute accent which indicates where the stress falls. For instance, άγαλμα (statue) is pronounced *aghalma*, and αγάπη (love) is

pronounced *aghapi*. In the following transliterations, bold lettering indicates where stress falls. Note also that **dh** is pronounced as 'th' in 'then'; **gh** is a softer, slightly guttural version of 'g'.

## Greetings & Civilities

Hello.
  *yasas*      Γειά σας.
  *yasu* (informal)   Γειά σου.
Goodbye.
  *andio*      Αντίο.
Good morning.
  *kalimera*      Καλημέρα.
Good afternoon.
  *herete*      Χαίρετε.
Good evening.
  *kalispera*      Καλησπέρα.
Good night.
  *kalinihta*      Καληνύχτα.
Please.
  *parakalo*      Παρακαλώ.
Thank you.
  *efharisto*      Ευχαριστώ.
Yes.
  *ne*      Ναι.
No.
  *ohi*      Οχι.
Sorry. (excuse me, forgive me)
  *sighnomi*      Συγγνώμη.
How are you?
  *ti kanete?*      Τι κάνετε;
  *ti kanis?*      Τι κάνεις;
  (informal)
I'm well, thanks.
  *kala efharisto*    Καλά ευχαριστώ.

## Essentials

Do you speak English?
  *milate anglika?*   Μιλάτε Αγγλικά;
I understand.
  *katalaveno*      Καταλαβαίνω.
I don't understand.
  *dhen katalaveno*   Δεν καταλαβαίνω.
Where is ...?
  *pou ine ...?*      Πού είναι ...;

LANGUAGE

## The Greek Alphabet & Pronunciation

| Greek | Pronunciation Guide | | Example | | |
|-------|------|------|------|------|------|
| A α | a | as in 'father' | αγάπη | *agha*pi | love |
| B β | v | as in 'vine' | βήμα | *vi*ma | step |
| Γ γ | gh | like a rough 'g' | γάτα | *gha*ta | cat |
| | y | as in 'yes' | για | *ya* | for |
| Δ δ | dh | as in 'there' | δέμα | *dhe*ma | parcel |
| E ε | e | as in 'egg' | ένας | *e*nas | one (m) |
| Z ζ | z | as in 'zoo' | ζώο | *zoo* | animal |
| H η | i | as in 'feet' | ήταν | *i*tan | was |
| Θ θ | th | as in 'throw' | θέμα | *the*ma | theme |
| I ι | i | as in 'feet' | ίδιος | *i*dhyos | same |
| K κ | k | as in 'kite' | καλά | ka*la* | well |
| Λ λ | l | as in 'leg' | λάθος | *la*thos | mistake |
| M μ | m | as in 'man' | μαμά | ma*ma* | mother |
| N ν | n | as in 'net' | νερό | ne*ro* | water |
| Ξ ξ | x | as in 'ox' | ξύδι | *ksi*dhi | vinegar |
| O o | o | as in 'hot' | όλα | *o*la | all |
| Π π | p | as in 'pup' | πάω | *pao* | I go |
| P ρ | r | as in 'road' | ρέμα | *re*ma | stream |
| | | a slightly trilled r | ρόδα | *ro*dha | tyre |
| Σ σ, ς | s | as in 'sand' | σημάδι | si*ma*dhi | mark |
| T τ | t | as in 'tap' | τόπι | *to*pi | ball |
| Υ υ | i | as in 'feet' | ύστερα | *i*stera | after |
| Φ φ | f | as in 'find' | φύλλο | *fi*lo | leaf |
| X χ | h | as the *ch* in Scottish *loch*, or like a rough h | χάνω | *ha*no | I lose |
| | | | χέρι | *he*ri | hand |
| Ψ ψ | ps | as in 'lapse' | ψωμί | pso*mi* | bread |
| Ω ω | o | as in 'hot' | ώρα | *o*ra | time |

### Combinations of Letters

The combinations of letters shown here are pronounced as follows:

| Greek | Pronunciation Guide | | Example | | |
|-------|------|------|------|------|------|
| ει | i | as in 'feet' | είδα | *i*dha | I saw |
| οι | i | as in 'feet' | οικόπεδο | i*ko*pedho | land |
| αι | e | as in 'bet' | αίμα | *e*ma | blood |
| ου | u | as in 'mood' | πού | *pou* | who/what |
| μπ | b | as in 'beer' | μπάλα | *ba*la | ball |
| | mb | as in 'amber' | κάμπος | *kam*bos | forest |
| ντ | d | as in 'dot' | ντουλάπα | dou*la*pa | wardrobe |
| | nd | as in 'bend' | πέντε | *pen*de | five |
| γκ | g | as in 'God' | γκάζι | *ga*zi | gas |
| γγ | ng | as in 'angle' | αγγελία | an*ge*lia | classified |
| γξ | ks | as in 'minks' | σφιγξ | *sfinks* | sphynx |
| τζ | dz | as in 'hands' | τζάκι | *dza*ki | fireplace |

The pairs of vowels shown above are pronounced separately if the first has an acute accent, or the second a dieresis, as in the examples below:

| γαϊδουράκι | *gaidhoura*ki | little donkey |
|------|------|------|
| Κάιρο | *kai*ro | Cairo |

Some Greek consonant sounds have no English equivalent. The υ of the groups αυ, ευ and ηυ is generally pronounced 'v'. The Greek question mark is represented with the English equivalent of a semicolon ';'.

How much?
*poso kani?* Πόσο κάνει;
When?
*pote?* Πότε;

## Small Talk

What's your name?
*pos sas lene?* Πώς σας λένε;
My name is ...
*me lene ...* Με λένε ...
Where are you from?
*apo pou iste?* Από πού είστε;

I'm from ...
*ime apo ...* Είμαι από ...
America
*tin ameriki* την Αμερική
Australia
*tin afstralia* την Αυστραλία
England
*tin anglia* την Αγγλία
Ireland
*tin irlandhia* την Ιρλανδία
New Zealand
*ti nea zilandhia* τη Νέα Ζηλανδία
Scotland
*ti skotia* τη Σκωτία

How old are you?
*poson hronon* Πόσων χρονών
*iste?* είστε;
I'm ... years old.
*ime ... hronon* Είμαι ... χρονών.

## Getting Around

What time does
the ... leave/arrive?
*ti ora fevyi/* Τι ώρα φεύγει/
*ftani to ...?* φτάνει το ...;

plane *aeroplano* αεροπλάνο
boat *karavi* καράβι
bus *astiko* αστικό

I'd like ...
*tha ithela ...* Θα ήθελα ...
a return ticket
*isitirio me* εισιτήριο με
*epistrofi* επιστροφή
two tickets
*dhio isitiria* δυο εισιτήρια

### Signs

| ΕΙΣΟΔΟΣ | Entry |
|---|---|
| ΕΞΟΔΟΣ | Exit |
| ΩΘΗΣΑΤΕ | Push |
| ΣΥΡΑΤΕ | Pull |
| ΓΥΝΑΙΚΩΝ | Women (toilets) |
| ΑΝΔΡΩΝ | Men (toilets) |
| ΝΟΣΟΚΟΜΕΙΟ | Hospital |
| ΑΣΤΥΝΟΜΙΑ | Police |
| ΑΠΑΓΟΡΕΥΕΤΑΙ | Prohibited |
| ΕΙΣΙΤΗΡΙΑ | Tickets |

a student's fare
*fititiko isitirio* φοιτητικό εισιτήριο
first class
*proti thesi* πρώτη θέση
economy
*touristiki thesi* τουριστική θέση

timetable
*dhromologio* δρομολόγιο
taxi
*taxi* ταξί

Where can I hire a car?
*pou boro na nikyaso ena aftokinito?*
Πού μπορώ να νοικιάσω ένα
αυτοκίνητο;

## Directions

How do I get to ...?
*pos tha pao sto/* Πώς θα πάω στο/
*sti ...?* στη ...;
Where is ...?
*pou ine ...?* Πού είναι...;
Is it near?
*ine konda?* Είναι κοντά;
Is it far?
*ine makria?* Είναι μακριά;

straight ahead *efthia* ευθεία
left *aristera* αριστερά
right *dexia* δεξιά
behind *piso* πίσω
far *makria* μακριά
near *konda* κοντά
opposite *apenandi* απέναντι

Can you show me on the map?
*borite na mou to **dhixete** sto **harti?***
Μπορείτε να μου το δείξετε
στο χάρτη;

## Around Town

I'm looking for (the) ...
***psah**no ya ...*
Ψάχνω για ...

| | | |
|---|---|---|
| bank | *tra**peza*** | τράπεζα |
| beach | *para**lia*** | παραλία |
| castle | ***ka**stro* | κάστρο |
| church | *ekkli**sia*** | εκκλησία |
| ... embassy | *tin ... pres**via*** | την ... |
| | | πρεσβεία |
| market | *agho**ra*** | αγορά |
| museum | *mu**sio*** | μουσείο |
| police | *astyno**mia*** | αστυνομία |
| post office | *tahydhro**mio*** | ταχυδρομείο |
| ruins | *ar**hea*** | αρχαία |

I want to exchange some money.
***the**lo na exaryi**ro**so le**fta***
Θέλω να εξαργυρώσω λεφτά.

## Accommodation

Where is ...?
*pou **ine** ...?*    Πού είναι ...;
I'd like ...
***the**lo e**na** ...*    Θέλω ένα ...

a cheap hotel
   *fti**no** xenodo**hio***   φτηνό ξενοδοχείο
a clean room
   *katha**ro** dho-*   καθαρό δωμάτιο
   ***matio***
a good hotel
   *ka**lo** xenodo**hio***   καλό ξενοδοχείο
a camp site
   ***kamping***    κάμπιγκ

| | | |
|---|---|---|
| single | *mo**no*** | μονό |
| double | *dhi**plo*** | διπλό |
| room | *dho**matio*** | δωμάτιο |
| with bathroom | *me **ba**nio* | με μπάνιο |
| key | *kli**dhi*** | κλειδί |

How much is it ...?
***po**so **ka**ni ...?*    Πόσο κάνει ...;
per night
   *ti vradh**ya***    τη βραδυά

### Emergencies

| | |
|---|---|
| Help! | |
|    *voithya!* | Βοήθεια! |
| Police! | |
|    *astynomia!* | Αστυνομία! |
| There's been an accident. | |
|    *eyine atihima* | Εγινε ατύχημα. |
| Call a doctor! | |
|    *fonaxte ena yatro!* | Φωνάξτε ένα ιατρό! |
| Call an ambulance! | |
|    *tilefoniste ya asthenoforo!* | Τηλεφωνήστε για ασθενοφόρο! |
| I'm ill. | |
|    *ime arostos* (m) | Είμαι άρρωστος |
|    *ime arosti* (f) | Είμαι άρρωστη |
| I'm lost. | |
|    *eho hathi* | Εχω χαθεί |
| Thief! | |
|    *klefti!* | Κλέφτη! |
| Go away! | |
|    *fiye!* | Φύγε! |
| I've been raped. | |
|    *me viase kapyos* | Με βίασε κάποιος. |
| I've been robbed. | |
|    *meklepse kapyos* | Μ'έκλεψε κάποιος. |
| Where are the toilets? | |
|    *pou ine i toualetez?* | Πού είναι οι τουαλέτες; |

for ... nights
   *ya ... vradh**yez***   για ... βραδυές
Is breakfast included?
   *symberilam**vani***   Συμπεριλαμβάνει
   *ke pro-**ino?***   και πρωϊνό;
May I see it?
   *boro na to dho?*   Μπορώ να το δω;
Where is the bathroom?
   *pou **ine** to**banio?***   Πού είναι το μπάνιο;
It's expensive.
   *ine akrivo*   Είναι ακριβό.
I'm leaving today.
   ***fe**vgho **si**mera*   Φεύγω σήμερα.

## Food

| | | |
|---|---|---|
| breakfast | *pro-ino* | πρωϊνό |
| lunch | *mesimvrino* | μεσημβρινό |
| dinner | *vradhyno* | βραδυνό |
| beef | *vodhino* | βοδινό |
| bread | *psomi* | ψωμί |
| beer | *byra* | μπύρα |
| cheese | *tyri* | τυρί |
| chicken | *kotopoulo* | κοτόπουλο |
| Greek coffee | *ellinikos kafes* | ελληνικός καφές |
| iced coffee | *frappe* | φραππέ |
| lamb | *arni* | αρνί |
| milk | *ghala* | γάλα |
| mineral | *metalliko* | μεταλλικό |
| water | *nero* | νερό |
| tea | *tsai* | τσάι |
| wine | *krasi* | κρασί |

I'm a vegetarian.
*ime hortofaghos*   Είμαι χορτοφάγος.

## Shopping

How much is it?
*poso kani?*
Πόσο κάνει;
I'm just looking.
*aplos kitazo*
Απλώς κοιτάζω.
I'd like to buy ...
*thelo n'aghoraso ...*
Θέλω ν΄αγοράσω ...
Do you accept credit cards?
*pernete pistotikez kartez?*
Παίρνετε πιστωτικές κάρτες;
Could you lower the price?
*borite na mou kanete mya kaliteri timi?*
Μπορείτε να μου κάνετε μια καλύτερη τιμή;

## Time & Dates

What time is it?
*ti ora ine?*   Τι ώρα είναι;

| | | |
|---|---|---|
| It's ... | *ine ...* | είναι ... |
| 1 o'clock | *mia i ora* | μία η ώρα |
| 2 o'clock | *dhio i ora* | δύο η ώρα |
| 7.30 | *efta ke misi* | εφτά και μισή |
| am | *to pro-i* | το πρωί |
| pm | *to apoyevma* | το απόγευμα |
| today | *simera* | σήμερα |

| | | |
|---|---|---|
| tonight | *apopse* | απόψε |
| now | *tora* | τώρα |
| yesterday | *hthes* | χθες |
| tomorrow | *avrio* | αύριο |

| | | |
|---|---|---|
| Sunday | *kyriaki* | Κυριακή |
| Monday | *dheftera* | Δευτέρα |
| Tuesday | *triti* | Τρίτη |
| Wednesday | *tetarti* | Τετάρτη |
| Thursday | *pempti* | Πέμπτη |
| Friday | *paraskevi* | Παρασκευή |
| Saturday | *savato* | Σάββατο |

| | | |
|---|---|---|
| January | *ianouarios* | Ιανουάριος |
| February | *fevrouarios* | Φεβρουάριος |
| March | *martios* | Μάρτιος |
| April | *aprilios* | Απρίλιος |
| May | *maios* | Μάιος |
| June | *iounios* | Ιούνιος |
| July | *ioulios* | Ιούλιος |
| August | *avghoustos* | Αύγουστος |
| September | *septemvrios* | Σεπτέμβριος |
| October | *oktovrios* | Οκτώβριος |
| November | *noemvrios* | Νοέμβριος |
| December | *dhekemvrios* | Δεκέμβριος |

## Health

I need a doctor.
*hriazome yatro*   Χρειάζομαι ιατρό.
Can you take me
to hospital?
*borite na me pate*   Μπορείτε να με πάτε
*sto nosokomio?*   στο νοσοκομείο;
I want something for ...
*thelo kati ya ...*   Θέλω κάτι για ...
diarrhoea
*dhiaria*   διάρροια
insect bites
*tsimbimata apo*   τσιμπήματα από
*endoma*   έντομα
travel sickness
*naftia taxidhiou*   ναυτία ταξιδιού

| | | |
|---|---|---|
| aspirin | | |
| | *aspirini* | ασπιρίνη |
| condoms | | |
| | *profylaktika* | προφυλακτικά |
| | *(kapotez)* | (καπότες) |
| contact lenses | | |
| | *faki epafis* | φακοί επαφής |
| medical insurance | | |
| | *yatriki asfalya* | ιατρική ασφάλεια |

# Numbers

| | | |
|---|---|---|
| 0 | *midhen* | μηδέν |
| 1 | *enas* | ένας (m) |
| | *mia* | μία (f) |
| | *ena* | ένα (n) |
| 2 | *dhio* | δύο |
| 3 | *tris* | τρεις (m & f) |
| | *tria* | τρία (n) |
| 4 | *teseris* | τέσσερεις (m & f) |
| | *tesera* | τέσσερα (n) |
| 5 | *pende* | πέντε |
| 6 | *exi* | έξη |
| 7 | *epta* | επτά |
| 8 | *ohto* | οχτώ |
| 9 | *enea* | εννέα |
| 10 | *dheka* | δέκα |

| | | |
|---|---|---|
| 20 | *ikosi* | είκοσι |
| 30 | *trianda* | τριάντα |
| 40 | *saranda* | σαράντα |
| 50 | *peninda* | πενήντα |
| 60 | *exinda* | εξήντα |
| 70 | *evdhominda* | εβδομήντα |
| 80 | *oghdhonda* | ογδόντα |
| 90 | *eneninda* | ενενήντα |
| 100 | *ekato* | εκατό |
| 1000 | *hilii* | χίλιοι (m) |
| | *hiliez* | χίλιες (f) |
| | *hilia* | χίλια (n) |

one million
    *ena ekatomyrio*   ένα εκατομμύριο

## Say it in Cretan

To all intents and purposes your everyday Greek will serve you perfectly well in Crete, but the Cretans have their own way of saying things. Influenced by Turkish, Italian and Ancient Greek, the Cretan vocabulary has developed words that on the surface bear little resemblance to their standard counterparts.

Here is a list of words that you may not come across often, but are still used by people speaking the colourful Cretan dialect.

| Cretan | Standard Greek | English |
|---|---|---|
| Αναθιβάλλω *(anathivalo)* | θυμάμαι *(thimame)* | remember |
| Αντέτι *(ahdeti)* | συνήθεια *(sineethya)* | custom, habit |
| Απόις *(apois)* | μετά *(meta)* | afterwards |
| Αφτω *(afto)* | ανάβω *(anavo)* | light (v) |
| Γροικώ *(ghriko)* | ακούω *(akoooh)* | hear, listen |
| Εχταγή *(ehtaghee)* | πόθος *(pothos)* | yearning |
| Θέτω *(theto)* | ξαπλώνω *(ksaplono)* | lie down |
| Μπαλιόστρα *(baleeostra)* | αρένα *(ahrena)* | ring, arena |
| Οβγορο *(ovghoro)* | ξέφωτο *(ksefoto)* | clearing, glade |
| Παινάδι *(penadhi)* | έπαινος *(epenos)* | praise |
| Προβαίνω *(proveno)* | εμφανίζομαι *(emfanizome)* | appear, emerge |
| Σέλι *(seli)* | λόφος *(lofos)* | hill |
| Σινάφι *(sinafi)* | κέφι *(kefi)* | feeling of happiness |
| Σφάκα *(sfaka)* | πικροδάφνη *(pikrodhafni)* | oleander |
| Τάβλα *(tavla)* | τραπέζι *(trapezi)* | table |
| Τσιτώνω *(tsitono)* | τσιμπώ *(tsimbo)* | prick (v) |
| Χαλίσκιος *(haliskios)* | γνήσιος *(gnisios)* | genuine, authentic |
| Χαρά *(hara)* | γλέντι *(ghlendi)* | Cretan festivities |
| Ωρίο *(orio)* | ωραίο *(oreo)* | beautiful |

# Glossary

**Achaean civilisation** – see *Mycenaean civilisation*

**acropolis** – highest point of an ancient city

**agia (f), agios (m) agii (pl)** – saint(s)

**agora** – commercial area of an ancient city; shopping precinct in modern Greece

**amphora** – large two-handled vase in which wine or oil was kept

**ANEK** – *Anonymi Naftiliaki Eteria Kritis*; one of the main shipping lines to Crete

**anthotyro** – cottage cheese

**Archaic period** (800–480 BC) – also known as the Middle Age; period in which the city-states emerged from the 'dark age' and traded their way to wealth and power; the city-states were unified by a Greek alphabet and common cultural pursuits, engendering a sense of national identity

**architrave** – part of the *entablature* which rests on the columns of a temple

**arhontika** – 17th and 18th century AD mansions which belonged to arhons, the leading citizens of a town

**astakos** – lobster

**avgokolokytho** – a kind of omelette dish made with zucchini, egg, tomato and olive oil

baglamas – miniature *bouzouki* with a tinny sound

**bakaliaros** – cod

**barbounia** – red mullet

**basilica** – early Christian church

**bougatsa** – custard-filled pastry

**bouleuterion** – council house

**bourekaki** – bite-sized meat pie

**bouzouki** – stringed lute-like instrument associated with *rembetika* music

**bouzoukia** – 'bouzoukis'; used to mean any nightclub where the *bouzouki* is played and low-grade blues songs are sung; see *skyladika*

**buttress** – support built against the outside of a wall

**Byzantine Empire** – characterised by the merging of Hellenistic culture and Christianity and named after Byzantium, the city on the Bosphorus which became the capital of the Roman Empire in AD 324; when the Roman Empire was formally divided in AD 395, Rome went into decline and the eastern capital, renamed Constantinople after Emperor Constantine I, flourished; the Byzantine Empire dissolved after the fall of Constantinople to the Turks in 1453

**caïque** – small, sturdy fishing boat

**capital** – top of a column

**cella** – room in a temple where the cult statue stood

**choregos** – wealthy citizen who financed choral and dramatic performances

**city-states** – states comprising a sovereign city and its dependencies; the city-states of Athens and Sparta were famous rivals

**classical Greece** – period in which the Greek city-states reached the height of their wealth and power after the defeat of the Persians in the 5th century BC; ended with the decline of the city-states as a result of the Peloponnesian Wars, and the expansionist aspirations of Philip II, King of Macedon (ruled 359–336 BC and his son, Alexander the Great ruled 336–323 BC)

**Corinthian** – order of Greek architecture recognisable by columns with bell-shaped capitals with sculpted elaborate ornaments based on acanthus leaves

**cornice** – the upper part of the *entablature*, extending beyond the *frieze*

**crypt** – lowest part of a church, often a burial chamber

**Cycladic civilisation** (3000–1100 BC) – civilisation which emerged following the settlement of Phoenician colonists on the Cycladic islands

**cyclopes** – mythical one-eyed giants

**dakos** – Cretan salad made up of a rye rusk topped with olive oil, cottage cheese, finely chopped tomato and oregano

**dark age** (1200–800 BC) – period in which Greece was under Dorian rule

**delfini** – dolphin; common name for hydrofoil

**diglossy** – the existence of two forms of one language within a country; has existed in Greece for most of its modern history
**dimarhio** – town hall
**Dimotiki** – Demotic Greek language; the official spoken language of Greece
**dolmades** – stuffed vine leaves
**domatio (s), domatia (pl)** – room; a cheap accommodation option available in most tourist areas
**Dorians** – Hellenic warriors who invaded Greece around 1200 BC, demolishing the city-states and destroying the Mycenaean civilisation; heralded Greece's 'dark age', when the artistic and cultural advancements of the Mycenaeans and Minoans were abandoned; the Dorians later developed into land-holding aristocrats which encouraged the resurgence of independent city-states led by wealthy aristocrats
**Doric** – order of Greek architecture characterised by a column which has no base, a fluted shaft and a relatively plain capital, when compared with the flourishes evident on Ionic and Corinthian capitals

**ELPA** – Elliniki Leshi Periigiseon & Aftokinitou; Greek motoring and touring club
**ELTA** – Ellinika Tahydromia; Greek post office
**entablature** – part of a temple between the tops of the columns and the roof
**EOS** – Ellinikos Orivatikos Syllogos; Greek alpine club
**EOT** – Ellinikos Organismos Tourismou; national tourism organisation which has offices in most major towns
**Epitaphios** – picture on cloth of Christ on his bier
**estiatorio** – restaurant serving ready-made food as well as a la carte dishes
**ET** – Elliniki Tileorasi; state television company

**fasolia** – white haricot beans
**feta** – soft, white goat cheese
**Filiki Eteria** – friendly society; a group of Greeks in exile; formed during Ottoman rule to organise an uprising against the Turks

**fluted** – of a column having vertical indentations on the shaft
**FPA** – *foros prostithemenis axias*; Value Added Tax, or VAT
**frappe** – iced coffee
**frieze** – part of the *entablature* which is above the *architrave*

**galaktopoleio (s), galaktopoleia (pl)** – a shop which sells dairy products
**garides** – shrimps
**Geometric period** (1200–800 BC) – period characterised by pottery decorated with geometric designs; sometimes referred to as Greece's 'dark age'
**GESEE** – Greek trade union association
**gigantes** – lima beans
**giouvetsi** – casserole of meat and pasta
**glossa** – sole
**glyko** – sweet
**gopes** – similar to sardines

**halva** – made from semolina or sesame seeds
**Hellas, Ellas or Ellada** – the Greek name for Greece
**Hellenistic period** – prosperous, influential period of Greek civilisation ushered in by Alexander the Great's empire-building and lasting until the Roman sacking of Corinth in 146 BC
**hohlii bubouristi** – snails simmered in vinegar or snails with barley
**horiatiki salata** – Greek (lit. 'village') salad of tomatoes, cucumber, olives and feta cheese
**hora** – main town, usually on an island
**horta** – cooked wild greens

**iconostasis** – altar screen embellished with icons
**ikonostasia** – miniature chapels
**Ionic** – order of Greek architecture characterised by a column with truncated flutes and capitals with ornaments resembling scrolls

**kafeneio (s), kafeneia (pl)** – traditionally a male-only coffee house where cards and backgammon are played
**kafeteria** – upmarket *kafeneio*, mainly for younger people

**kakavia** – Cretan fish soup
**kalamari** – squid
**kalderimi** – cobbled footpath
**kalimera** – good morning
**kalispera** – good evening
**kallitsounia** – Cretan cheese pies
**karavida** – crayfish
**karpouzi** – watermelon
**kaseri** – mild, slightly rubbery sheep's-milk cheese
**kastelli** – castle; fortress
**kastro** – walled-in town
**kataïfi** – chopped nuts inside shredded wheat pastry or filo soaked in honey
**katholikon** – principal church of a monastic complex
**kefi** – an undefinable feeling of good spirit, without which no Greek can have a good time
**keftedes** – meatballs
**kerasia** – cherries
**kilimia** – flat-woven rugs that were traditional dowry gifts
**KKE** – Kommounistiko Komma Elladas; Greek communist party
**Koine** – Greek language used in pre-Byzantine times; the language of the church liturgy
**kolokythakia** – deep-fried zucchini
**kore** – female statue of the Archaic period; see *kouros*
**koukouvagia** – rusk with tomato and cheese; see also dakos
**kouros** – male statue of the Archaic period, characterised by a stiff body posture and enigmatic smile
**kri-kri** – endemic Cretan animal similar to a goat
**KTEL** – *Kino Tamio Eispraxeon Leoforion*; national bus cooperative; runs all long-distance bus services

**labrys** – double axe symbol of Minoan civilization
**ladera** – food cooked using olive oil (ladi) as one of its main ingredients
**lammergeier** – bearded vulture
**LANE** – *Lasithiotiki Anonymi Naftiliaki Eteria* (Lasithi Shipping Company); main shipping line serving eastern Crete
**leoforos** – avenue

**libation** – in ancient Greece, wine or food which was offered to the gods
**Linear A** – Minoan script; so far undeciphered
**Linear B** – Mycenaean script; has been deciphered
**loukanika** – little sausages
**loukoumades** – puffs or fritters with honey or syrup
**loukoumi** – Turkish delight
**lyra** – small violin-like instrument, played on the knee; common in Cretan and Pontian music

**maïstros** – light to moderate north-westerly wind which rises in the afternoon
**malakas** – literally 'wanker'; used as a familiar term of address, or as an insult, depending on context
**mangas** – 'wide boy' or 'dude'; originally a person of the underworld, now any streetwise person
**mandinada (sin), mandinades (pl)** – traditional Cretan song/s often with improvised lyrics
**marides** – whitebait sometimes cloaked in onion, pepper and tomato sauce
**mayirefta** – pre-cooked food, served up in large cooking trays
**mayirio** – 'cookhouse'; simple restaurant serving ready-cooked dishes
**megaron** – central room of a Mycenaean palace
**melitzana** – aubergine
**melitzanosalata** – aubergine or eggplant dip
**melitzanes papoutsakia** – baked eggplant stuffed with meat and tomatoes and topped with cheese, which looks, as its Greek name suggests, like a little shoe
**meltemi** – north-easterly wind which blows throughout much of Greece during the summer
**metope** – sculpted section of a Doric *frieze*
**metrio** – medium (coffee)
**mezes (s), mezedes (pl)** – appetiser
**Middle Age** – see Archaic period
**Minoan civilisation** (3000–1100 BC) – Bronze Age culture of Crete named after the mythical king Minos and characterised

by pottery and metalwork of great beauty and artisanship

**mitata** – round stone shepherd's huts

**moni** – monastery or convent

**mousakas** – layers of eggplant or zucchini, minced meat and potatoes topped with cheese sauce and baked pastitsio

**Mycenaean civilisation** (1900–1100 BC) – first great civilisation of the Greek mainland, characterised by powerful independent city-states ruled by kings; also known as the Achaean civilisation

**myzithra** – soft sheep's-milk cheese

**narthex** – porch of a church

**Nea Dimokratia** – New Democracy; conservative political party

**necropolis** – literally 'city of the dead'; ancient cemetery

**neo kyma** – 'new wave'; left-wing music of the boçtes and clubs of 1960s Athens

**nomarhia** – prefecture building

**nomos** – prefectures into which the regions and island groups of Greece are divided

**nymphaeum** – in ancient Greece, building containing a fountain and often dedicated to nymphs

**OA** – Olympiaki Aeroporia or Olympic Airways; Greece's national airline and major domestic air carrier

**octopus saganaki** – octopus fried with tomato and cheese

**odeion** – ancient Greek indoor theatre

**odos** – street

**ohi** – 'no'; what the Greeks said to Mussolini's ultimatum to surrender or be invaded; the Italians were subsequently repelled and the event is celebrated on October 28

**ohtapodi** – octopus

**omaties** – rice and offal sausages

**OSE** – Organismos Sidirodromon Ellados; Greek railways organisation

**OTE** – Organismos Tilepikinonion Ellados; Greece's major telecommunications carrier

**oud** – a bulbous, stringed instrument with a sharply raked-back head

**ouzeri** – place which serves *ouzo* and light snacks

**ouzo** – a distilled spirit made from grapes and flavoured with aniseed

**pagoto** – ice cream

**Panagia** – Mother of God; name frequently used for churches

**Pandokrator** – painting or mosaic of Christ in the centre of the dome of a Byzantine church

**pandopoleio** – general store

**paralia** – waterfront

**PASOK** – Panellinio Sosialistiko Komma; Greek socialist party

**pasta stifado** – meat stewed with onions

**pediment** – triangular section, often filled with sculpture above the columns, found at the front and back of a classical Greek temple

**periptero (s), periptera (pl)** – street kiosk

**peristyle** – columns surrounding a building, usually a temple or courtyard

**pinakothiki** – picture gallery

**pithos (s), pithi (pl)** – large Minoan storage jar

**plateia** – square

**Politiki Anixi** – Political Spring; centrist political party

**PRO-PO** – *Prognostiko Podosferou*; Greek football pools

**propylon** (s), **propylaia** (pl) – elaborately built main entrance to an ancient city or sanctuary; a propylon had one gateway and a propylaia more than one

**psarotaverna** – taverna specialising in seafood

**psistaria** – restaurant serving grilled food

**raki** – distilled spirit made from grapes

**rakopagida** – (lit) 'raki trap'; a group of imbibers of raki, who won't let you go until you have drunk your fill

**rembetika** – blues songs commonly associated with the underworld of the 1920s

**retsina** – resinated white wine

**rhyton** – another name for a libation vessel

**rizitika** – traditional, patriotic songs of western Crete

**rizogalo** – rice pudding

**saganaki** – dishes cooked in a small two-handled frying pan *(sagani)*, such as cheese or mussels

**salingaria** – snails in oil with herbs

**sandouits** – sandwiches
**sandouri** – hammered dulcimer from Asia Minor
**SEO** – *Syllogos Ellinon Orivaton*; Greek mountaineers' association
**sketo** – without sugar (coffee)
**skyladika** – literally 'dog songs'; popular, but not lyrically challenging, blues songs often sung in *bouzoukia* nightclubs
**soutzoukakia** – spicy meatballs in tomato sauce
**spanakopitta** – spinach pie
**spileo** – cave
**splinandero** – spleen sausage
**splinogardoumba** – spicy, lamb spleen sausage
**staka** – a cream cheese made from curds
**stafylia** – grapes
**stele** (s), **stelae** (pl) – grave stone which stands upright
**stifado** – stew
**stoa** – long colonnaded building, usually in an *agora*; used as a meeting place and shelter in ancient Greece
**syka** – figs
**synagrida** – snapper

**tahydromia** – post offices
**taverna** – traditional restaurant which serves food and wine
**temblon** – votive screen

**tholos** – Mycenaean tomb shaped like a beehive
**toumberleki** – small lap drum played with the fingers
**triglyph** – sections of a Doric *frieze* between the *metopes*
**trireme** – ancient Greek galley with three rows of oars on each side
**tsikoudia** – Cretan version of *tsipouro*
**Tsingani** – Gypsies or Roma
**tsipoura** – bream
**tsipouro** – distilled spirit made from grapes
**tyropitta** – cheese pie
**tyrozouli** – hard, tasty cheese produced around Mt Psiloritis
**tzatziki** – yogurt, cucumber and garlic dip

**volta** – promenade; evening stroll
**volute** – spiral decoration on Ionic capitals

**xygala** – soft cheese that thickens without the use of rennet
**xysto** – scratch 'n' win; Greek equivalent of scratch lottery cards
**xythomyzithra** – soft sheep's-milk cheese

**zaharoplasteio (s), zaharoplasteia (pl)** – patisserie; shop which sells cakes, chocolates, sweets and, sometimes, alcoholic drinks
**zouridha** – Cretan polecat

# Lonely Planet Guides by Region

onely Planet is known worldwide for publishing practical, reliable and no-nonsense travel information in our guides and on our Web site. The Lonely Planet list covers just about every accessible part of the world. Currently there are 16 series: Travel guides, Shoestring guides, Condensed guides, Phrasebooks, Read This First, Healthy Travel, Walking guides, Cycling guides, Watching Wildlife guides, Pisces Diving & Snorkeling guides, City Maps, Road Atlases, Out to Eat, World Food, Journeys travel literature and Pictorials.

**AFRICA** Africa on a shoestring • Botswana • Cairo • Cairo City Map • Cape Town • Cape Town City Map • East Africa • Egypt • Egyptian Arabic phrasebook • Ethiopia, Eritrea & Djibouti • Ethiopian Amharic phrasebook • The Gambia & Senegal • Healthy Travel Africa • Kenya • Malawi • Morocco • Moroccan Arabic phrasebook • Mozambique • Namibia • Read This First: Africa • South Africa, Lesotho & Swaziland • Southern Africa • Southern Africa Road Atlas • Swahili phrasebook • Tanzania, Zanzibar & Pemba • Trekking in East Africa • Tunisia • Watching Wildlife East Africa • Watching Wildlife Southern Africa • West Africa • World Food Morocco • Zambia • Zimbabwe, Botswana & Namibia
**Travel Literature:** Mali Blues: Traveling to an African Beat • The Rainbird: A Central African Journey • Songs to an African Sunset: A Zimbabwean Story

**AUSTRALIA & THE PACIFIC** Aboriginal Australia & the Torres Strait Islands •Auckland • Australia • Australian phrasebook • Australia Road Atlas • Cycling Australia • Cycling New Zealand • Fiji • Fijian phrasebook • Healthy Travel Australia, NZ & the Pacific • Islands of Australia's Great Barrier Reef • Melbourne • Melbourne City Map • Micronesia • New Caledonia • New South Wales • New Zealand • Northern Territory • Outback Australia • Out to Eat – Melbourne • Out to Eat – Sydney • Papua New Guinea • Pidgin phrasebook • Queensland • Rarotonga & the Cook Islands • Samoa • Solomon Islands • South Australia • South Pacific • South Pacific phrasebook • Sydney • Sydney City Map • Sydney Condensed • Tahiti & French Polynesia • Tasmania • Tonga • Tramping in New Zealand • Vanuatu • Victoria • Walking in Australia • Watching Wildlife Australia • Western Australia
**Travel Literature:** Islands in the Clouds: Travels in the Highlands of New Guinea • Kiwi Tracks: A New Zealand Journey • Sean & David's Long Drive

**CENTRAL AMERICA & THE CARIBBEAN** Bahamas, Turks & Caicos • Baja California • Belize, Guatemala & Yucatán • Bermuda • Central America on a shoestring • Costa Rica • Costa Rica Spanish phrasebook • Cuba • Cycling Cuba • Dominican Republic & Haiti • Eastern Caribbean • Guatemala • Havana • Healthy Travel Central & South America • Jamaica • Mexico • Mexico City • Panama • Puerto Rico • Read This First: Central & South America • Virgin Islands • World Food Caribbean • World Food Mexico • Yucatán
**Travel Literature:** Green Dreams: Travels in Central America

**EUROPE** Amsterdam • Amsterdam City Map • Amsterdam Condensed • Andalucía • Athens • Austria • Baltic States phrasebook • Barcelona • Barcelona City Map • Belgium & Luxembourg • Berlin • Berlin City Map • Britain • British phrasebook • Brussels, Bruges & Antwerp • Brussels City Map • Budapest • Budapest City Map • Canary Islands • Catalunya & the Costa Brava • Central Europe • Central Europe phrasebook • Copenhagen • Corfu & the Ionians • Corsica • Crete • Crete Condensed • Croatia • Cycling Britain • Cycling France • Cyprus • Czech & Slovak Republics • Czech phrasebook • Denmark • Dublin • Dublin City Map • Dublin Condensed • Eastern Europe • Eastern Europe phrasebook • Edinburgh • Edinburgh City Map • England • Estonia, Latvia & Lithuania • Europe on a shoestring • Europe phrasebook • Finland • Florence • Florence City Map • France • Frankfurt City Map • Frankfurt Condensed • French phrasebook • Georgia, Armenia & Azerbaijan • Germany • German phrasebook • Greece • Greek Islands • Greek phrasebook • Hungary • Iceland, Greenland & the Faroe Islands • Ireland • Italian phrasebook • Italy • Kraków • Lisbon • The Loire • London • London City Map • London Condensed • Madrid • Madrid City Map • Malta • Mediterranean Europe • Milan, Turin & Genoa • Moscow • Munich • Netherlands • Normandy • Norway • Out to Eat – London • Out to Eat – Paris • Paris • Paris City Map • Paris Condensed • Poland • Polish phrasebook • Portugal • Portuguese phrasebook • Prague • Prague City Map • Provence & the Côte d'Azur • Read This First: Europe • Rhodes & the Dodecanese • Romania & Moldova • Rome • Rome City Map • Rome Condensed • Russia, Ukraine & Belarus • Russian phrasebook • Scandinavian & Baltic Europe • Scandinavian phrasebook • Scotland • Sicily • Slovenia • South-West France • Spain • Spanish phrasebook • Stockholm • St Petersburg • St Petersburg City Map • Sweden • Switzerland • Tuscany • Ukrainian phrasebook • Venice • Vienna • Wales • Walking in Britain • Walking in France • Walking in Ireland • Walking in Italy • Walking in Scotland • Walking in Spain • Walking in Switzerland • Western Europe • World Food France • World Food Greece • World Food Ireland • World Food Italy • World Food Spain **Travel Literature:** After Yugoslavia • Love and War in the Apennines • The Olive Grove: Travels in Greece • On the Shores of the Mediterranean • Round Ireland in Low Gear • A Small Place in Italy

# Lonely Planet Mail Order

**L**onely Planet products are distributed worldwide. They are also available by mail order from Lonely Planet, so if you have difficulty finding a title please write to us. North and South American residents should write to 150 Linden St, Oakland, CA 94607, USA; European and African residents should write to 10a Spring Place, London NW5 3BH, UK; and residents of other countries to Locked Bag 1, Footscray, Victoria 3011, Australia.

**INDIAN SUBCONTINENT & THE INDIAN OCEAN** Bangladesh • Bengali phrasebook • Bhutan • Delhi • Goa • Healthy Travel Asia & India • Hindi & Urdu phrasebook • India • India & Bangladesh City Map • Indian Himalaya • Karakoram Highway • Kathmandu City Map • Kerala • Madagascar • Maldives • Mauritius, Réunion & Seychelles • Mumbai (Bombay) • Nepal • Nepali phrasebook • North India • Pakistan • Rajasthan • Read This First: Asia & India • South India • Sri Lanka • Sri Lanka phrasebook • Tibet • Tibetan phrasebook • Trekking in the Indian Himalaya • Trekking in the Karakoram & Hindukush • Trekking in the Nepal Himalaya • World Food India **Travel Literature:** The Age of Kali: Indian Travels and Encounters • Hello Goodnight: A Life of Goa • In Rajasthan • Maverick in Madagascar • A Season in Heaven: True Tales from the Road to Kathmandu • Shopping for Buddhas • A Short Walk in the Hindu Kush • Slowly Down the Ganges

**MIDDLE EAST & CENTRAL ASIA** Bahrain, Kuwait & Qatar • Central Asia • Central Asia phrasebook • Dubai • Farsi (Persian) phrasebook • Hebrew phrasebook • Iran • Israel & the Palestinian Territories • Istanbul • Istanbul City Map • Istanbul to Cairo • Istanbul to Kathmandu • Jerusalem • Jerusalem City Map • Jordan • Lebanon • Middle East • Oman & the United Arab Emirates • Syria • Turkey • Turkish phrasebook • World Food Turkey • Yemen **Travel Literature:** Black on Black: Iran Revisited • Breaking Ranks: Turbulent Travels in the Promised Land • The Gates of Damascus • Kingdom of the Film Stars: Journey into Jordan

**NORTH AMERICA** Alaska • Boston • Boston City Map • Boston Condensed • British Columbia • California & Nevada • California Condensed • Canada • Chicago • Chicago City Map • Chicago Condensed • Florida • Georgia & the Carolinas • Great Lakes • Hawaii • Hiking in Alaska • Hiking in the USA • Honolulu & Oahu City Map • Las Vegas • Los Angeles • Los Angeles City Map • Louisiana & the Deep South • Miami • Miami City Map • Montreal • New England • New Orleans • New Orleans City Map • New York City • New York City City Map • New York City Condensed • New York, New Jersey & Pennsylvania • Oahu • Out to Eat – San Francisco • Pacific Northwest • Rocky Mountains • San Diego & Tijuana • San Francisco • San Francisco City Map • Seattle • Seattle City Map • Southwest • Texas • Toronto • USA • USA phrasebook • Vancouver • Vancouver City Map • Virginia & the Capital Region • Washington, DC • Washington, DC City Map • World Food New Orleans **Travel Literature:** Caught Inside: A Surfer's Year on the California Coast • Drive Thru America

**NORTH-EAST ASIA** Beijing • Beijing City Map • Cantonese phrasebook • China • Hiking in Japan • Hong Kong & Macau • Hong Kong City Map • Hong Kong Condensed • Japan • Japanese phrasebook • Korea • Korean phrasebook • Kyoto • Mandarin phrasebook • Mongolia • Mongolian phrasebook • Seoul • Shanghai • South-West China • Taiwan • Tokyo • Tokyo Condensed • World Food Hong Kong • World Food Japan **Travel Literature:** In Xanadu: A Quest • Lost Japan

**SOUTH AMERICA** Argentina, Uruguay & Paraguay • Bolivia • Brazil • Brazilian phrasebook • Buenos Aires • Buenos Aires City Map • Chile & Easter Island • Colombia • Ecuador & the Galapagos Islands • Healthy Travel Central & South America • Latin American Spanish phrasebook • Peru • Quechua phrasebook • Read This First: Central & South America • Rio de Janeiro • Rio de Janeiro City Map • Santiago de Chile • South America on a shoestring • Trekking in the Patagonian Andes • Venezuela **Travel Literature:** Full Circle: A South American Journey

**SOUTH-EAST ASIA** Bali & Lombok • Bangkok • Bangkok City Map • Burmese phrasebook • Cambodia • Cycling Vietnam, Laos & Cambodia • East Timor phrasebook • Hanoi • Healthy Travel Asia & India • Hill Tribes phrasebook • Ho Chi Minh City (Saigon) • Indonesia • Indonesian phrasebook • Indonesia's Eastern Islands • Java • Lao phrasebook • Laos • Malay phrasebook • Malaysia, Singapore & Brunei • Myanmar (Burma) • Philippines • Pilipino (Tagalog) phrasebook • Read This First: Asia & India • Singapore • Singapore City Map • South-East Asia on a shoestring • South-East Asia phrasebook • Thailand • Thailand's Islands & Beaches • Thailand, Vietnam, Laos & Cambodia Road Atlas • Thai phrasebook • Vietnam • Vietnamese phrasebook • World Food Thailand • World Food Vietnam

**ALSO AVAILABLE:** Antarctica • The Arctic • The Blue Man: Tales of Travel, Love and Coffee • Brief Encounters: Stories of Love, Sex & Travel • Buddhist Stupas in Asia: The Shape of Perfection • Chasing Rickshaws • The Last Grain Race • Lonely Planet ... On the Edge: Adventurous Escapades from Around the World • Lonely Planet Unpacked • Lonely Planet Unpacked Again • Not the Only Planet: Science Fiction Travel Stories • Ports of Call: A Journey by Sea • Sacred India • Travel Photography: A Guide to Taking Better Pictures • Travel with Children • Tuvalu: Portrait of an Island Nation

# Index

## Text

## Boxed Text

# MAP LEGEND

## CITY ROUTES

| | |
|---|---|
| Freeway | === Unsealed Road |
| Primary Road | One Way Street |
| Secondary Road | Pedestrian Street |
| Street | Stepped Street |
| Lane | Tunnel |
| On/Off Ramp | Footbridge |

## AREA FEATURES

| | |
|---|---|
| Building | Beach |
| Park, Gardens | Cemetery |
| Market | Campus |
| Sports Ground | Plaza |

## WATER TRANSPORT

| | |
|---|---|
| Daily Ferry | Hydrofoil |
| Low Frequency Ferry | Excursion Boat |

## REGIONAL ROUTES

| | |
|---|---|
| Tollway, Freeway | |
| Primary Road | |
| Secondary Road | |
| Minor Road | |

## BOUNDARIES

| | |
|---|---|
| International | |
| State | |
| Disputed | |
| Fortified Wall | |

## TRANSPORT ROUTES & STATIONS

| | |
|---|---|
| Train | Walking Trail |
| Underground Train | Walking Tour |
| Metro | Path |
| Tramway | Pier or Jetty |
| Cable Car, Chairlift | |

## HYDROGRAPHY

| | |
|---|---|
| River, Creek | Dry Lake, Salt Lake |
| Canal | Spring, Rapids |
| Lake | Waterfalls |

## POPULATION SYMBOLS

| | | |
|---|---|---|
| ✪ **CAPITAL** National Capital | ● **CITY** City | ● Village Village |
| ◉ **CAPITAL** Regional Capital | ● **Town** Town | Urban Area |

## MAP SYMBOLS

| | | |
|---|---|---|
| ■ Place to Stay | ▼ Place to Eat | ● Point of Interest |

| | | | |
|---|---|---|---|
| ✈ Airport | ⌂ Cave | ⚐ Lighthouse | ✉ Post Office |
| Archaeological Site | Church | Mosque | Shelter |
| Bank | Cinema | ▲ Mountain | Taxi Rank |
| Bar | Fountain | Museum | Telephone |
| Bus Stop, Terminal | Hospital, Clinic | Parking | Theatre |
| Castle, Fortress | Internet Cafe | Police Station | Tourist Information |

*Note: not all symbols displayed above appear in this book*

# LONELY PLANET OFFICES

**Australia**
Locked Bag 1, Footscray, Victoria 3011
☎ 03 8379 8000  fax 03 8379 8111
email: talk2us@lonelyplanet.com.au

**USA**
150 Linden St, Oakland, CA 94607
☎ 510 893 8555  TOLL FREE: 800 275 5555
fax 510 893 8572
email: info@lonelyplanet.com

**UK**
10a Spring Place, London NW5 3BH
☎ 020 7428 4800  fax 020 7428 4828
email: go@lonelyplanet.co.uk

**France**
1 rue du Dahomey, 75011 Paris
☎ 01 55 25 33 00  fax 01 55 25 33 01
email: bip@lonelyplanet.fr
www.lonelyplanet.fr

**World Wide Web: www.lonelyplanet.com or AOL keyword: lp**
**Lonely Planet Images: lpi@lonelyplanet.com.au**